Handbook on the Economics of Discrimination

Handbook on the Economics of Discrimination

Edited by

William M. Rodgers III

Rutgers, The State University of New Jersey, USA

Edward Elgar

Cheltenham, UK • Northampton, MA, USA

Published by
Edward Elgar Publishing Limited
Glensanda House
Montpellier Parade
Cheltenham
Glos GL50 1UA
UK

Edward Elgar Publishing, Inc.
136 West Street
Suite 202
Northampton
Massachusetts 01060
USA

A catalogue record for this book
is available from the British Library

Library of Congress Cataloguing in Publication Data

Handbook on the economics of discrimination / [edited by] William M. Rodgers III.
   p. cm. — (Elgar original reference)
   1. Discrimination in employment—United States. 2. Discrimination—
Economic aspects—United States. 3. Discrimination in employment—Research—
United States. 4. Discrimination—Economic aspects—Research—United States.
I. Rodgers, William M. II. Series.

HD4903.5.U58H36 2006
331.13'3'0973—dc22   2005052321

ISBN-13: 978 1 84064 915 4
ISBN-10: 1 84064 915 1 (cased)

Typeset by Cambrian Typesetters, Camberley, Surrey
Printed and bound in Great Britain by MPG Books Ltd, Bodmin, Cornwall

Contents

v

Contributors

Scott J. Adams is an Assistant Professor of Economics at the University of Wisconsin-Milwaukee. His research interests are in labor and health economics and applied econometrics. He has published his work in *Industrial Relations*, *Labour Economics*, *Contemporary Economic Policy* and the *Journal of Human Resources*. Adams received his PhD from Michigan State University.

Lisa R. Anderson is an Associate Professor of Economics at The College of William and Mary. Professor Anderson studies economic questions using laboratory experiments. Her published articles include experimental investigations of information cascades, agendas and strategic voting, and gender differences in generosity and risk aversion. In addition, she has published a number of papers on the pedagogical use of experiments. Anderson received her PhD in economics from the University of Virginia.

M.V. Lee Badgett is an Associate Professor of Economics and a faculty member of the Center for Public Policy and Administration at the University of Massachusetts, Amherst. Badgett is also the Research Director of the Institute for Gay and Lesbian Strategic Studies, a national think tank. Badgett's primary field is labor economics. Her research focuses on race, gender and sexual orientation discrimination in the workplace and on gay family issues. She received her PhD from the University of California, Berkeley.

Marjorie L. Baldwin is a Professor in the School of Health Management and Policy at the W.P. Carey School of Business, Arizona State University. She is a member of the National Academy of Social Insurance. Baldwin is a health economist whose research interests focus on work disability, disability-related discrimination, and the costs and outcomes of work-related injuries. Professor Baldwin received her PhD from the Maxwell School at Syracuse University.

Gary A. Dymski is the Founding Director of the University of California Center, Sacramento (UCCS). Prior to his current directorship Dymski was Founding Director of the Edward J. Blakely Center for Sustainable Suburban Development and associate dean for Research and Graduate Studies in the University of California, Riverside's College of Humanities, Arts and Social

Sciences. Dymski was the Olin Research Fellow in Economic Studies at the Brookings Institution 1985–6 and received his PhD in economics from the University of Massachusetts, Amherst in 1987. He taught at the University of Southern California before joining the economics faculty at the University of California, Riverside, where he is currently on leave. Dymski has been an invited lecturer in 13 nations, and has been a visiting scholar at Tokyo University, the Bangladesh Institute for Development Studies, the Federal University of Rio de Janeiro and the University of São Paulo.

Roland G. Fryer is a Junior Fellow, Harvard Society of Fellows at Harvard University. He is a Faculty Research Fellow at the National Bureau of Economic Research. His research interests are in the areas of affirmative action, discrimination and social economics. He received his PhD from Pennsylvania State University.

Judith K. Hellerstein is Associate Professor of Economics at the University of Maryland, College Park. She is also a Faculty Associate of the Maryland Population Research Center and a Research Associate of the National Bureau of Economic Research. Her main area of research is labor economics and she also does research in health economics. She received her PhD from Harvard University.

Charles A. Holt is the A. Willis Robertson Professor of Political Economy at the University of Virginia. He is Co-founding Editor of the journal *Experimental Economics* and serves on the board of editors of the *American Economic Review*. To date, Holt has written and edited several books and over one hundred articles in experimental economics and related theory, on topics such as coordination, social dilemmas, rent seeking, public goods and games played only once. Holt received his PhD from Carnegie Mellon University.

Harry J. Holzer is Professor of Public Policy and Associate Dean of the Georgetown Public Policy Institute. He is a Senior Affiliate of the National Poverty Center at the University of Michigan, a National Fellow of the Program on Inequality and Social Policy at Harvard University and a Research Affiliate of the Institute for Research on Poverty at the University of Wisconsin at Madison. Prior to coming to Georgetown, Professor Holzer served as Chief Economist for the US Department of Labor. Professor Holzer's research has focused primarily on the low-wage labor market, and particularly the problems of urban minority workers. In recent years he has focused on employer skill needs and hiring practices, as well as the employment problems of less educated young men. He received his PhD in economics from Harvard University.

William G. Johnson is a Professor in the School of Health Management and Policy and the Department of Economics at the W.P. Carey School of Business, Arizona State University. He is also the Director of the Center for Health Information and Research, located in the L. William Seidman Research Institute. Professor Johnson authored the first empirical studies of labor market discrimination against persons with disabilities and is the author or co-author of nearly every subsequent empirical study of the problem. He is a member of the National Academy of Social Insurance and the North American Spine Society. He serves on numerous boards, including the editorial board of *The Spine Journal* and is co-editor of the *Journal of Disability Income and Work Injury Compensation*. Johnson received his PhD in economics from Rutgers, The State University of New Jersey.

Philip Moss is a Professor of Regional Economics and Social Development at the University of Massachusetts Lowell. Moss works primarily on the impacts of structural change in the economy and within firms on the distribution of economic opportunity. He is particularly interested in opportunities for different race and gender groups, in the fate of low-wage workers and low-wage jobs, and in changing skill needs and skill development strategies of firms. He received his PhD in economics from Massachusetts Institute of Technology.

David Neumark is Professor of Economics at the University of California, Irvine. He is also a Senior Fellow of the Public Policy Institute of California and a Research Associate of the National Bureau of Economic Research. Neumark was previously Professor of Economics at Michigan State University. His areas of expertise include labor market discrimination, the economics of ageing and policy analysis on such issues as minimum and living wages. He received his PhD from Harvard University.

William M. Rodgers III is Professor of Public Policy at the Edward J. Bloustein School of Planning and Public Policy, Rutgers, The State University of New Jersey. He is also Chief Economist at the Heldrich Center for Workforce, also at Rutgers. Rodgers is a Senior Research Affiliate of the National Poverty Center, University of Michigan. Prior to coming to Rutgers, he served as Chief Economist at the US Department of Labor from 2000 to 2001, appointed to that position by Alexis Herman, US Secretary of Labor. His research examines issues in labor economics and the economics of social problems. He received his PhD from Harvard University.

Chris Tilly is Professor of Regional Economic and Social Development at the University of Massachusetts Lowell. He does research on low-wage jobs, inequality and community development, and recently expanded his research agenda to include Mexico as well as the United States. Tilly received a joint PhD in economics and urban studies and planning from the Massachusetts Institute of Technology.

Yana van der Meulen Rodgers is Associate Professor of Women's and Gender Studies, Rutgers University. Her research interests lie in the economics of gender, the economics of children and development economics. Recent work examines the effect of globalization on gender earnings inequality and the impact of protective labor market policies on women's income. Professor Rodgers maintains a regular consulting relationship with the World Bank. She received her PhD from Harvard University.

Introduction
William M. Rodgers III

Although discrimination is not as prevalent and widespread today as it was in the past, there is general consensus on its continued existence. However, no consensus exists with regard to its magnitude, causes, consequences and remedies. Because of this lack of agreement, measuring discrimination, describing its causes and crafting efficient and equitable remedies remain active areas of debate among researchers, practitioners and policymakers.

Current debates will continue and new debates will emerge for several reasons. The US labor force will continue to become more racially and ethnically diverse. The structure of employer–employee relationships will continue to change, fueled by globalization, workplace technological innovations and changes in the ability of institutions such as organized labor to insulate workers from market forces. Collectively, these and other structural changes will shift the incentives for employers, employees and consumers to engage in discrimination.

The economics profession has responded to the changes. The number of discrimination studies on African Americans and women that utilize new data sources, econometric and statistical methods has grown. Members of the profession have also begun to study more intensely the market experiences of people with disabilities, older workers, and gays, lesbians and bisexuals.

There have also been a series of important legal developments that may have altered incentives to discriminate. Under Regulation C, which implements the 1975 Home Mortgage Disclosure Act (HMDA) in 2004, financial institutions were required to provide information about the loan rate and more detailed borrower race/ethnic information. Also in 2004, the Supreme Court ruled that only older workers could use the Age Discrimination in Employment Act (ADEA) to claim maltreatment.

Simply put, discrimination is a dynamic process, depending on changes in the supply, demand and institutional features of the economy. This *Handbook* presents nine chapters divided into three parts on the economics of discrimination. Part I discusses recent innovations in methods and data collection. Part II reviews empirical evidence on discrimination of demographic groups that have received less attention from researchers. Part III presents a discussion of anti-discrimination and affirmative action's impacts.

The chapters are written with the goal of being accessible to academic and professional economists, graduate students, advanced undergraduates, practitioners, policymakers and funders of social science research. The methods and data chapters are particularly designed to encourage researchers to utilize the new approaches and develop new data sources. The policy chapters provide readers with a balanced discussion of the impacts of affirmative action and anti-discrimination laws.

Part I of the *Handbook* starts with Yana van der Meulen Rodgers' description of how researchers continue to modify the original Oaxaca–Blinder decomposition to answer a richer set of empirical questions. The innovations focus on identifying the appropriate weights to use in the decomposition and decomposing residual wage distributions into their quantity and price of unmeasured skills components. Rodgers describes how researchers have also begun to utilize quantile regression to understand the contribution of observed characteristics to wage gaps at different segments of the wage distribution.

In other recent work, researchers have developed decompositions that sort changes in the wage gap over time into a portion due to changes in group-specific characteristics and a portion due to changes in market returns to skills. These methods are extremely useful because they illustrate whether the relative status of workers in a particular demographic group has changed over time with regard to changes in education and experience, the distribution of returns to skills and unmeasured group-specific characteristics.

Although the new decomposition methods offer insights and new empirical information they are still subject to criticism. What are the appropriate weights? Has the researcher controlled for all of the supply, demand and institutional factors that could explain a group's lower relative status? If the decomposition's results are sensitive to the choice of weights and/or there are excluded factors, then the decomposition's results are biased and the ability to claim that discrimination has been correctly identified is substantially weakened.

Researchers have responded to these criticisms in a variety of ways. Judith Hellerstein and David Neumark have been at the forefront of developing data sets that link establishment-level employer data to the data of workers in those establishments. In Chapter 2, Hellerstein and Neumark discuss how linking the characteristics of establishments to the workers in those establishments allows a simultaneous test of whether a particular group's lower relative pay is due to their lower productivity. An additional benefit of using matched data sets, especially those that have a time series aspect to them, is that they can be used to answer questions about the extent to which labor market segregation has an impact on wages. They can also be used to directly test discrimination theory. For example, are discriminatory firms less profitable, a prediction of the Becker models of discrimination?

The central theme of Hellerstein and Neumark's chapter is that matched employer–employee data offer significant benefits. They are a potential source of additional information that is not available in the individual-level data. To support this conclusion, Hellerstein and Neumark first describe the advantages that matched employer–employee data offer. They then provide a 'users' guide to matched employer–employee data sets. Third, they review the key studies that have used matched data. The last section of their chapter discusses new directions in which the construction and analysis of matched employer–employee data sets would have the greatest payoff in advancing the profession's understanding of labor market discrimination.

Another approach to going beyond standard decomposition methods and individual-level micro data has been to analyze qualitative and quantitative data from employer interviews. In Chapter 3, Philip Moss and Chris Tilly review studies that measure the attitudes and preferences of employers toward workers from different demographic groups. They start by briefly describing the main employer surveys that have been utilized to measure discrimination. To date, the surveys have typically focused on describing racial attitudes. Moss and Tilly present six issues to consider when developing an employer survey: sampling strategy, employer access, inquiring about the correct job, who to interview in the establishment, the accuracy of employer responses and the ability to distinguish between supply (human capital) and demand (employer stereotypes). The last two areas present researchers with the greatest challenge to create a useful survey. Despite these hurdles, employer surveys are an extremely valuable tool for analyzing employment discrimination.

Moss and Tilly identify three major contributions from employer surveys. The evidence indicates a consistency in negative attitudes towards minority, particularly black, employees and potential workers. Blacks are consistently ranked lowest across the qualitative surveys on both hard and soft skills. Employers with formal job structures, recruiting methods and screening methods provide greater opportunities for minorities, have less gender-based occupational segregation, and women and African Americans have higher promotion rates.

Experimental methods have been used extensively among psychologists to study discrimination but much less among economists. However, the field of experimental economics has grown, and discrimination has been an active area of research. Experimental methods have the potential to identify not only discrimination's existence but also its underlying causes. In Chapter 4, Lisa Anderson, Roland Fryer and Charles Holt survey laboratory studies of discrimination in psychology and economics. They show that, although heavily influenced by the psychology literature, the vast theoretical and empirical literature on employment discrimination and information economics serves as the primary motivation for experimental studies on discrimination. Experimental methods have been used to test statistical discrimination, asymmetric pair-wise tournaments and price-preference auctions.

Anderson *et al.* conclude that a large number of field experiments clearly document differential treatment of some groups, based on certain demographic characteristics. In addition, laboratory experiments provide credible support for a number of theoretical predictions. Laboratory experiments have generated group identification that is caused by discrimination. The economic consequences of this discrimination include the negative outcomes for members of the group that is discriminated against. Less obvious, but of major importance, are reductions in social welfare. Furthermore, discrimination experiments reveal that affirmative action can increase economic efficiency if subsidies to disadvantaged groups increase the competitiveness of effort-based allocations. Anderson *et al.* conclude with a users' guide for developing and conducting discrimination experiments in economics.

Part II of the *Handbook* goes beyond race and gender, by reviewing discrimination studies on disability, sexual orientation and age. A common thread that runs through these chapters is the importance of developing the appropriate definitions and data, and applying the appropriate methodology.

In Chapter 5, Baldwin and Johnson's review of the literature on disability discrimination first starts with a discussion of the terminology used to define disability status. Unlike empirical research on gender and racial discrimination, definitions are extremely important in the disability literature. In disability studies, productivity can be limited by the same health conditions that make disabled workers eligible for civil rights protection.

Baldwin and Johnson then summarize the approaches used to estimate wage and employment discrimination that workers with disabilities face. One group of studies measures discrimination using a single-equation model that includes binary variables to identify persons with disabilities. The second group of studies uses variations of the Oaxaca–Blinder decomposition to measure wage discrimination. Methods for estimating employment discrimination are less well established. Baldwin and Johnson conclude that the literature to date supports the hypothesis that discrimination against persons with disabilities is rooted in prejudice.

Data availability is also a concern of M.V. Lee Badgett, who in Chapter 6 reviews the literature on discrimination faced by gay, lesbian and bisexual individuals. To date, economists' most significant contribution to the broader social science literature in this area has been the application of regression-based tools to estimate discrimination's existence and its magnitude.

Badgett's review indicates that anti-gay pay discrimination occurs and is strongest for gay men. Gay men earn less than similar heterosexual men. The evidence of wage discrimination against lesbians is less clear. Several studies find that lesbians actually earn more than similar heterosexual women. The higher-than-expected earnings for lesbians does not rule out discrimination. To observe clearer evidence of discrimination, Badgett argues, researchers, practitioners and policymakers must take into account the larger body of research on lesbians' work-related choices, self-reports of discrimination and one well-conceived audit study.

More generally, Badgett argues that economists must work harder to explain why discrimination based on sexual orientation exists. The profession has relied on theories designed to explain racial discrimination, excluding other possible sources of or rationales for discrimination. Persistent evidence of anti-gay attitudes should simply begin the conversation, not end it. The anti-gay ballot initiatives during the 2004 election are the most recent forms of anecdotal evidence.

In the final chapter of Part II, Scott Adams and David Neumark review the literature on age discrimination. Age discrimination's relative importance has increased. The number of age-related EEOC discrimination complaints is on a par with the number of gender and racial discrimination complaints. Similar to the experimental methods and sexual orientation literatures, noneconomists have been studying these issues more vigorously than economists.

Adams and Neumark first summarize studies that examine workplace attitudes toward older individuals and how these attitudes may affect management decisions. Second, they describe the composition of the cases filed with the Equal Employment Opportunity Commission (EEOC) and assess whether we can learn anything about age discrimination's impact on older workers. Third, Adams and Neumark summarize the findings of studies that describe the relative hiring, unemployment duration, re-employment wages and promotion outcomes of older workers. The chapter concludes with a discussion of whether the disadvantages are the result of employer discrimination.

Adams and Neumark draw several conclusions. Attitudes about older workers are used in making promotion decisions. Unresolved ADEA cases suggest that age discrimination is a key feature of the labor market. Older workers have longer unemployment durations, lower probabilities of getting rehired, and higher incidences of displacement. Upon re-employment their earnings are typically lower than the re-employment earnings of young workers. Age discrimination is linked to these adverse outcomes, but alternative nondiscriminatory explanations must not be ruled out.

The *Handbook* concludes with two chapters on policy impacts in credit, housing and labor markets. In Chapter 8, Gary Dymski reviews the literature on racial discrimination in credit and housing markets. When able, attention is given to gender discrimination. Dymski starts by putting credit market and housing market discrimination into a legal context. He then lays out the theoretical behavioral models that have guided most of the empirical work in this area. Dymski's review of the empirical literature covers racial redlining (The illegal identification of geographical areas as inappropriate for the offering of commercial credit services, based on criteria such as the average income or the ethnic composition of the area. For example, there may be a decline in loans made available to an area by a bank because that community has a large minority population) and discrimination in credit markets, the impacts of predatory lending, racial discrimination in housing markets and gender discrimination in housing and credit markets. An important contribution of Dymski's chapter is its discussion of the significance of cultural affinity, networks and wealth in explaining discrimination in housing and credit markets.

Dymski concludes that the literature on credit and housing market discrimination is compelling, incomplete, contradictory and controversial. It is compelling because of their centrality to the American experience and debates over the importance of racial inequality for both social policy and theory. The literature is incomplete because it covers a small segment of the demographic groups protected under the Constitution and the Civil Rights Act. There are virtually no studies on sexual orientation and few on gender discrimination. The literature is also incomplete because existing models generate more questions than they answer.

The literature is contradictory. One interpretation of the literature's empirical studies is the successful documentation of many features of racial inequality in housing and credit markets. Another interpretation of the literature is its inability to demonstrate conclusively that a problem exists, which needs to be addressed through public policy. Empirical tests for credit and housing discrimination are controversial owing primarily to reasonable disagreements between practitioners over the design and interpretation of statistical tests for discrimination.

As a result, this creates a dilemma for the economic profession. Professional interest has focused on finding a 'smoking gun', but Dymski argues that while discrimination clearly worsens racial and gender differences in credit- and housing-market outcomes, existing structural gaps in resources and wealth generate most disadvantages. This professional focus on one aspect of a multidimensional, dynamic process, the portion that is hardest to identify precisely, leads Dymski to issue the following challenge to the profession. Because of the US's historical legacy on racial and gender inequality, discrimination theory should have at its heart the legal context and historical basis of the nation's laws against discrimination.

The purpose of the EEO laws is to address employment discrimination. Affirmative action's purpose is actively to improve the experiences of minorities and women in employment, university admissions and government procurement. In Chapter 9, Harry Holzer and David Neumark provide a critical review of the affirmative action and anti-discrimination literatures. Holzer and Neumark review the laws, court decisions and practices, along with the empirical evidence of their impacts.

Holzer and Neumark find that the balance of the empirical evidence is most consistent with the view that EEO laws helped to improve the relative economic status of blacks during the mid-1960s. Although equal pay laws should raise women's wages, they also tend to reduce their relative employment. Overall, Holzer and Neumark interpret the evidence to say that discrimination persists in some parts of the labor market. It plays a role in the persistence of racial and gender wage/employment gaps.

A portion of these gaps might be lessened with more resources for EEO employment monitoring, a different allocation of resources between hiring and other cases, or a different set of enforcement practices. The use of labor market intermediaries to provide employers with more information in hiring disadvantaged groups might be a useful remedy. But, to the extent that persistent wage and employment gaps reflect skill gaps, family time allocation choices and so on, a menu with multiple approaches is required if the goal is to generate greater parity in labor market outcomes across demographic groups.

On affirmative action, Holzer and Neumark write that the evidence clearly shows that, although not large, these programs tend to shift employment, university admissions and government procurement away from white men towards minorities and women. Replacing race-based affirmative action policies in admissions with race and gender-neutral practices would probably reduce the share of minorities on campuses. On the issue of whether beneficiaries of affirmative action are less qualified than white males, Holzer and Neumark's review of the evidence paints a more complex picture that is difficult to summarize here.

Holzer and Neumark believe that the empirical evidence on the effects of EEO policies and affirmative action should be considered in the formulation of any alternative approaches to address the challenges that minorities and women face. However, the evidence to date still continues to be limited, particularly on the relative performance of affirmative action beneficiaries, and most notably in the debate on government procurement activities. Research on the effects of EEO and affirmative action should continue to be on the radar screens of social scientists.

PART I

NEW METHODS

1 A primer on wage gap decompositions in the analysis of labor market discrimination

Yana van der Meulen Rodgers

I Introduction

Empirical studies of labor market discrimination have a long tradition in terms of the development of new methods, application to numerous groups and countries, and their testing of important labor market theories. Some studies have tested the neoclassical theory that industries with market power are characterized by greater discrimination in pay and employment. Other methods to examine the presence of discrimination include audit and correspondence studies, analysis of help-wanted advertisements and the examination of lawsuits.[1] Straightforward regression analysis of the determinants of employment and wages, with control variables that include observed productivity characteristics as well as a binary variable for race or gender, also provides empirical estimates of discrimination. A negative and statistically significant coefficient on the race or gender variable, after controlling for characteristics such as education and experience, is interpreted as evidence of discrimination in the labor market.

Regression analysis underlies another widely-used method to estimate the extent of wage discrimination: the wage gap decomposition. The traditional decomposition, developed in Oaxaca (1973) and Blinder (1973), accounts for differences across demographic groups in wages and in the determinants of wages. The analysis decomposes the wage gap in a particular year into a portion explained by average group differences in productivity characteristics and a residual portion that is commonly attributed to discrimination. Like the single-equation regression approach, the traditional decomposition can be performed with just a single year of cross-section data and basic information on labor market characteristics. Both regression-based techniques are expected to yield similar conclusions about the extent of discriminatory treatment in the labor market. However, the decomposition procedure imposes less structure compared to a single regression model with a group dummy variable since the productivity characteristics are not constrained to have the same regression coefficients across groups. The low-cost data requirements and the intuitive appeal help to explain the popularity of the traditional decomposition procedure as a starting point for estimating the extent of wage discrimination.

Researchers have subsequently introduced a number of extensions that build more detailed steps into the decomposition in order to provide a richer set of results. This chapter presents several alternative decompositions that extend the Oaxaca and Blinder type of approach with a unique dimension in order to further assess wage gap determinants. Evidence from these decompositions can provide a more detailed picture of the degree to which discrimination serves as an explanation for the presence and persistence of group differences in average wages. For example, subsequent studies have utilized alternative wage structures as the reference for nondiscriminatory wages so that the decomposition is consistent with a more general model of discrimination. Newer work is also examining the residual component of wage distributions more closely with interpretations based on quantities and prices of unmeasured skills. More detailed explanations of wage gaps in particular years also include utilizing quantile regression techniques to understand the contribution of observed characteristics across the wage distribution and not just at the mean. Recent innovations also include adding a family dimension in order to explain the role of discrimination associated with female workers who have children.

In other work, adding a time dimension allows the researcher to examine contributions of changes over time in measured and unmeasured group-specific factors and in market returns to skills to changes in the wage gap. This trend technique provides a more detailed analysis of the wage gap compared to analyses that only perform the traditional decomposition with individual years of cross-section data. Results can show whether workers in a particular demographic group have gained over time relative to their counterparts in education and experience, whether the distribution of returns to skills has narrowed or widened, and whether unmeasured group-specific factors have become more or less important over time. Closely related to this, adding a country dimension allows the researcher to examine differences across countries in wage structures and how the overall wage structure contributes to wage disparities between demographic groups. Another variant utilizes an occupational dimension and examines the extent to which pay inequality within occupation groups and employment across occupations explain the wage gap. The remaining sections discuss these methods in turn, with the exposition using the case of gender differences to derive each framework. However, all techniques are more generally applicable.

II Traditional decomposition
The Oaxaca (1973) and Blinder (1973) decomposition procedure has become a standard tool of the trade for estimating the extent of wage discrimination. The approach is quite intuitive and can be performed with one year of micro data containing worker characteristics. Household survey data, labor force

surveys, and census data have all been used in what amounts to hundreds of previously published works. For a given year, one can decompose the gender wage gap in several ways. The most common approach utilizes log-wage function estimates for men and for women. One estimates the following log-wage equation for male and female workers $(i = m, f)$:

$$w_i = X_i\beta_i + v_i, \qquad (1.1)$$

where w_i is the natural logarithm of hourly wages, X_i denotes a matrix of observed productivity characteristics, β_i denotes the vector of regression coefficients, and v_i is a random error term assumed to be normally distributed with a variance of σ_i^2. Productivity characteristics are best measured with variables that do not reflect discrimination by the employer. These variables commonly include years of education, years of labor market experience, years of job-specific tenure, marital status and geographical location. Numerous studies include occupation and industry variables. However, if men and women obtain jobs in different occupations and industries as a result of employment discrimination, including these variables in the X matrix could lead to misleading conclusions about the extent of wage discrimination. A safe rule of thumb is to avoid including variables that may be endogenous to discrimination.

One can then describe the gender gap as follows:

$$w_m - w_f = (X_m\beta_m - X_f\beta_f) + (v_m - v_f). \qquad (1.2)$$

If one evaluates the regressions at the means of the log-wage distributions, the last term becomes zero. Adding and subtracting $X_f\beta_m$ to obtain worker attributes in terms of 'male prices' gives

$$w_m - w_f = (X_m - X_f)\beta_m + X_f(\beta_m - \beta_f) + (v_m - v_f). \qquad (1.3)$$

The left-hand side of equation (1.3) is the total log-wage differential. On the right-hand side, the first term is the explained gap (the portion of the gap attributed to gender differences in measured productivity characteristics) and the second term is the residual gap (the portion attributed to gender differences in market returns to those characteristics). The remaining term is generally ignored as the decomposition is usually done at the means; otherwise, the sum of the last two terms is considered the residual gap. The convention in the literature is to use the male coefficients, with the implication that male wages better reflect the market payoffs for productivity characteristics than do female wages.[2]

Symptomatic of the 'index number problem', results vary depending on the choice of male or female prices for weighting the decomposition equation.

Alternative procedures have based the decomposition on other reference wage structures, such as female wages or some weighted combination of male and female wages.[3] For example, Neumark (1988) has developed a decomposition that is consistent with a general model of discrimination in which employers have varying preferences for different types of workers. The model incorporates the practice of favoritism, in which men are overpaid, and discrimination, in which women are underpaid. When evaluated at the means, the Neumark procedure can be expressed as

$$w_m - w_f = (X_m - X_f)\beta^* + X_m(\beta_m - \beta^*) + X_f(\beta^* - \beta_f), \quad (1.4)$$

where β^* represents the nondiscriminatory reference wage structure. The first term on the right-hand side shows the portion of the gap explained by differences in observed characteristics. The second term shows the extent to which the male characteristics are overvalued and the final term shows the extent to which the female characteristics are undervalued compared to the nondiscriminatory returns. Together, the second and third terms on the right-hand side would be attributed to discriminatory practices by employers. Note that, if the male wage structure were to prevail in the absence of discrimination, then $\beta^* = \beta_m$ and equation (1.4) would be equivalent to the Oaxaca decomposition in equation (1.3).

The wage returns in β^* are unobserved, and there are various options for estimating β^*. Assuming that employers care only about the relative proportions of males and females they hire rather than the absolute numbers, the nondiscriminatory wage structure can be estimated from a wage equation using the pooled sample of male and female workers. The nondiscriminatory wage structure, β^*, is a weighted average of the wage structures for men and women, as follows:

$$\beta^* = \Phi\beta_m + (1 - \Phi)\beta_f. \quad (1.5)$$

Oaxaca and Ransom (1994) propose using the cross-product matrices of the sample characteristics as weights for the estimated parameters β_m and β_f. They show that Neumark's solution is the same as their own in the case when the weighting matrix, Φ, is defined as follows

$$\Phi = (X'X)^{-1}(X_m'X_m), \quad (1.6)$$

where X and X_m are the matrices of observed productivity characteristics for the pooled sample and for the male sample.

Another issue associated with the traditional decomposition also relates to the choice of reference groups. In particular, Blinder's (1973) method isolates the contribution of the constant term as the unexplained part of discrimination. However, Jones (1983) argues that this method is flawed whenever the regressors include sets of dummy variables, since the estimated coefficient for the constant term will vary with the choice of the reference groups in constructing the dummy variables. Oaxaca and Ransom (1999) extend this critique and argue that the traditional decomposition cannot isolate the separate contribution of sets of dummy variables to the unexplained portion of the wage gap. They argue that the estimated contributions of dummy variables to the unexplained gap will vary with the choice of the reference group in structuring the dummy variables. Given this feature of dummy variables, it is only possible to estimate the relative contribution of a dummy variable to the unexplained portion of the wage gap.

III Extensions of the traditional decomposition

A more recent approach utilizes only the coefficients and standard deviation from the male regression.[4] By standardizing the error term, one can rewrite equation (1.1) as

$$w_i = X_i \beta_i + \sigma_i \in_i, \tag{1.7}$$

where $\in_i$ is the standardized residual (meaning it is distributed with a mean of zero and a variance of one) and σ_i is the residual standard deviation of wages (meaning it is the monetary value per unit difference in the standardized residual). One can then specify the gender gap as

$$w_m - w_f = (X_m - X_f)\beta_m + \sigma_m(\theta_m - \theta_f), \tag{1.8}$$

where

$$\theta_m = (w_m - X_m\beta_m)/\sigma_m = \in_m,$$
$$\theta_f = (w_f - X_f\beta_m)/\sigma_m. \tag{1.9}$$

The standardized residual for males, θ_m, is the same as before ($\in_m$). The standardized residual for females, θ_f is based on the male coefficients and standard deviation (that is, the male prices). One is effectively reweighting the female wage equation using the coefficients and standard deviation from the male wage regression. This reweighting is equivalent to predicting the average wage that women would receive, given their qualifications, if they were paid like men. The X_i matrix contains the same set of observed characteristics as those specified for equation (1.1). As noted in Blau and Kahn (1996), if one uses the actual distribution of male residuals in implementing the decomposition, then this procedure is not imposing normality on the distribution of residuals.

The left-hand side of equation (1.8) is the total wage differential between men and women. On the right-hand side, the first term is the explained gap. The second term is the residual gap, which is a function of just the residual prices and the error terms. When evaluated at the means, the residual gap depends on the amount of male residual wage inequality (σ_m) and the mean female's position in the male residual wage distribution (θ_f). Although equations (1.3) and (1.8) differ in their interpretation of the residual, they produce the same measures for the total, explained and residual gaps.

Wage gap decompositions have often needed to correct for selectivity bias, particularly if the analysis centers on differentials by gender. A sample of workers is censored because of a self-selection rule that determines whether the person works. This censoring overstates female wages and understates the gender wage gap. To avoid potentially misleading results, researchers typically control for selectivity bias using a two-step Heckman correction procedure.[5] An equation is estimated that predicts whether individuals in the working-age population are included in the sample of wage earners, in order to calculate the Inverse Mills Ratio. Independent variables include most of the variables found in the wage equation. In addition, unique identifying variables are included to identify the sample-selection effects. Such variables would predict labor force entry but not wages.

Next, this ratio is included as an explanatory variable in Ordinary Least Squares (OLS) wage regressions. Since the ratio is a decreasing function of the probability of inclusion in the sample, a negative coefficient implies that higher wages are associated with greater probability of participation (Dolton and Makepeace, 1987). A negative sign implies that individuals from the lower end of the wage distribution are more likely to select out of the sample than those from the upper tail. This result is common for women, given their lower labor force participation rates than men. For men, a negative sign could imply that the effect of excluding from the sample some low-wage workers (such as unpaid family workers) outweighs the effect of excluding from the sample some high-wage men (such as the self-employed). The magnitude of the selection effect is usually larger for women, although the selection effect is expected to decline over time as labor force participation increases.

An extension of the traditional decomposition developed in Joshi, Paci and Waldfogel (1999) addresses the selection issues and wage penalties associated with the role of working women as mothers. Rather than decomposing a male–female gap, the method focuses on the wage gap between mothers and women with no children. The procedure corrects for selection that varies not only by motherhood and childlessness but also by non-employment, part-time employment and full employment. After generating selection terms specific to motherhood and employment status, four separate wage equations are estimated for mothers and childless women with full-time and part-time jobs.

Next, for both types of employment (full-time and part-time), the family gap is decomposed in line with the traditional procedure into a portion explained by differences between mothers and childless women in observed characteristics, and a portion comprising differences between mothers and childless women in compensation rates to particular characteristics. The procedure determines whether there is a direct pay penalty for women who have children and how this penalty differs from the penalty to engaging in part-time work.

Thus far the discussion has focused on estimations performed at the mean of the conditional wage distribution. However, recent advances also include performing the traditional decomposition across the full distribution of wages using quantile regression techniques. First introduced in Koenker and Bassett (1978) and further discussed in Buchinsky (1994, 1998), the quantile regression model can be considered a location model and written as

$$w_i = X_i\beta_\theta + u_{\theta_i}, \text{Quant}_\theta(w_i \mid X_i) = X_i\beta_\theta. \qquad (1.10)$$

As before, the notation w_i denotes the natural logarithm of wages for the sample of individuals $i = 1$ to n, X_i is the matrix of characteristics. Now β_θ denotes the vector of quantile regression coefficients and u_{θ_i} denotes the random error term with an unspecified distribution. The expression $\text{Quant}_\theta(w_i \mid X_i)$ denotes the θth conditional quantile of w_i, conditional on the matrix of characteristics X_i, with $0 < \theta < 1$. Equation (1.10) does assume that u_{θ_i} satisfies the restriction that $\text{Quant}_\theta(u_{\theta_i} \mid X_i) = 0$.

For a given quantile θ, the coefficients β_θ can be estimated by solving the following minimization problem:

$$\min_\beta n^{-1} \sum_{i=1}^{n} \rho_\theta(w_i - X_i\beta_\theta), \qquad (1.11)$$

where $\rho_\theta(\lambda)$ is a check function defined as $\rho_\theta(\lambda) = \theta\lambda$ for $\lambda \geq 0$, and $\rho_\theta(\lambda) = (\theta-1)\lambda$ for $\lambda < 0$. One can trace the entire conditional distribution of log wages, conditional on the observed characteristics, by steadily increasing θ from 0 to 1. Of course, given the constraint placed by a limited number of observations, it is practical to estimate a finite number of quantile regressions. Each coefficient in the vector β_θ is then interpreted as the marginal change in the θth conditional quantile of wages due to a marginal change in the regressor of interest. These coefficients can then be incorporated into the traditional wage gap decomposition as expressed in equation (1.3). Note that, because equation (1.3) is no longer being evaluated at the means, the third term can no longer be ignored. Hence the wage gap at each quantile θ in the distribution can be separated into a portion due to differences in observed characteristics, a portion due to differences in the returns to those characteristics and a portion due to differences in residual wages.

IV   Wage structures over time

Results from traditional decompositions frequently indicate that a large share of the aggregate wage gap is not explained by observed productivity differences. Although changes in the residual gap are commonly attributed to changing patterns in wage discrimination, they may encompass changes in the overall wage structure that have little to do with discrimination. A trend decomposition technique, developed by Juhn, Murphy and Pierce (1991), henceforth JMP, provides a richer description of the sources of changes in the wage gap than the traditional decomposition. In adding a time dimension, the technique allows us to better understand the composition of the residual wage gap and hence the behavior of the total wage gap.

The trend decomposition continues from equation (1.8). Letting Δ denote the male–female difference within a year in the variable that follows, and adding a subscript t for observations in year t, one can rewrite equation (1.8) as

$$\Delta w_t = \Delta X_t \beta_{mt} + \sigma_{mt}\Delta\theta_t. \tag{1.12}$$

Next, the rate of change in the gender wage gap between any two periods, t and s, can be described as

$$\Delta w_t - \Delta w_s = (\Delta X_t \beta_{mt} - \Delta X_s \beta_{ms}) + (\sigma_{mt}\Delta\theta_t - \sigma_{ms}\Delta\theta_s). \tag{1.13}$$

In the next step, one chooses year s and male prices as the reference wage structure by adding and subtracting the term $(\Delta X_t \beta_{ms} + \sigma_{ms}\Delta\theta_t)$ from the right-hand side. This manipulation yields the following trend decomposition equation:

$$\Delta w_t - \Delta w_s = (\Delta X_t - \Delta X_s)\beta_{ms} + \Delta X_t(\beta_{mt} - \beta_{ms}) \\ + \sigma_{ms}(\Delta\theta_t - \Delta\theta_s) + (\sigma_{mt} - \sigma_{ms})\Delta\theta_t. \tag{1.14}$$

The first term on the right-hand side of equation (1.14) may be thought of as 'measured quantities'. This term represents changes over time in observed gender-specific characteristics, holding market returns fixed. For example, the gender wage gap may narrow over time as a result of an increase in women's educational attainment relative to that of men. The second term, considered 'measured prices', represents changes in market returns, holding observed characteristics fixed. For example, a decrease over time in returns to experience will cause the overall wage gap to narrow if men on average have higher observed levels of experience.

The third term is labeled 'residual quantities'. This term represents changes in unobserved gender-specific characteristics, which result in changes in the percentile ranking of women in the male residual wage distribution. Such unmeasured characteristics can include gender differences in labor force attachment due to intermittency, differences in unobserved skills and wage discrimination by gender. As an example, reduced gender discrepancies in these characteristics could cause the ranking of the average female residual wage to rise from the 35th percentile to the 40th percentile of the male residual wage distribution, all else equal. The final term, considered the 'residual prices', reflects changes in male residual wage inequality. One can think of this last term as changes in the wage penalty for having a position below the mean in the male residual wage distribution.

The gender-specific terms (first and third) reflect changes in the percentile ranking of women in the male overall wage distribution, while the wage structure terms (second and fourth) reflect changes in the shape of the male overall wage distribution. In the computations, changes in the four components (measured quantities, measured prices, residual quantities and residual prices) must sum to the total change for the period. Because some components work in opposite directions, it is possible for the change in one component to offset and even outweigh the contribution of changes in other components.

The JMP procedure, albeit quite useful, is not without its issues. First, the analysis suffers from the familiar index number problem in the choice of a reference group for the competitive wage returns. Also results vary, depending on the choice of base years. One can derive similar equations using different base years. Alternatively, to avoid possible extremes from any particular year, one can use the average across all years as the base. In using the average across all years, the year *s* terms would represent mean quantity differentials across the sample years.

Another issue is the treatment of residual wages. Suen (1997) argues that separating the male and female residuals into a standardized residual (θ) and the standard deviation (σ) can lead to misleading results because these terms are not independent from each other. In particular, increasing inequality in male residual wages causes the male residual wage dispersion to have thicker tails. This change alone in the shape of the male wage distribution will cause women to have a higher mean percentile ranking in the male distribution without any other changes having taken place. Figure 1.1 illustrates Suen's argument by showing how rising inequality in the distribution of male residual wages affects the gender wage gap.[6] The figure shows a widening in the dispersion of male residual wages from $\sigma_{m1}f(\theta_m)$ in period 1 to $\sigma_{m2}f(\theta_m)$ in period 2. One can see that the rising male residual wage inequality causes an increase in the mean female's position in the male residual wage distribution, from θ_{f1} in period 1 to θ_{f2} in period 2. Together, the growing dispersion in male residual wages with an apparent improvement in women's percentile ranking would lead to an observed stability in the residual wage gap between men and women, with $gap_1 = gap_2$.

Intuitively, more women have wages that rank toward the lower end of the male distribution. So, when male residual wage inequality increases, the average female receives a lower wage for a given position in the male distribution. However, at the same time, the average female's position in the male distribution is rising simply because the male distribution now has thicker tails. The JMP procedure would predict a growing wage gap as a result of more inequality in the returns to unmeasured skills. Any observed stability in the overall gender gap would have to be explained by a narrowing gender gap in unobserved gender-specific factors (residual quantities). Accounting for the increase in women's mean percentile ranking that resulted from the changing shape in the male distribution would also explain the overall stability in the gender gap. Suen's arguments imply that researchers using the JMP procedure exercise caution in interpreting changes in residual wage gaps as changes in unobserved skills and returns to those skills. The use of panel data, more direct

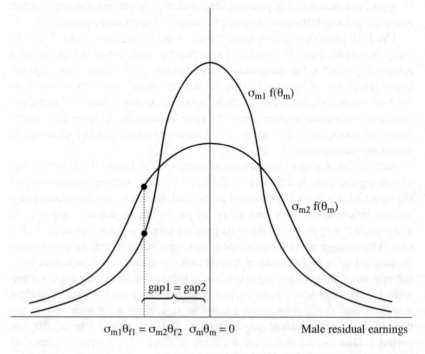

Figure 1.1   Effect of rising male residual wage inequality on gender wage gap

tests on the various impacts of changing wage inequality, or new methods based on quantile regression can each help to clarify the interpretation of wage residuals as unmeasured skills and their returns.[7]

V Wage structures across countries

Researchers can also take advantage of cross-country data on wage determinants to add a country dimension to the traditional decomposition. The procedure is analogous to the JMP method, except that the time differences are replaced by country differences. Blau and Kahn (1996) developed this application in order to assess the importance of a country's overall wage structure relative to other countries in explaining international differences in pay gaps. The new procedure allowed them to address the puzzle of why the gender pay gap in the United States was so high compared to other countries, in the face of relatively favorable job market qualifications for US women and a strong US commitment to anti-discrimination legislation. More broadly, the decomposition along a country dimension allows one to examine the extent to which a country places a wage penalty on individuals with below-average productivity characteristics, compared to other countries.

The procedure continues from the traditional decomposition specified in equation (1.8). Again specifying Δ as the male–female difference in the variable that follows, and adding a subscript c for observations in country c, one can rewrite equation (1.8) as

$$\Delta w_c = \Delta X_c \beta_{mc} + \sigma_{mc} \Delta \theta_c. \qquad (1.15)$$

Equation (1.15) says that a country's wage gap can be divided into gender differences in observed characteristics, ΔX_c, and gender differences in the standardized residual θ (multiplied by the male residual standard deviation in wages). Using equation (1.15), the difference in the gender wage gap between two countries, c and b, becomes

$$\Delta w_c - \Delta w_b = (\Delta X_c \beta_{mc} - \Delta X_b \beta_{mb}) + (\sigma_{mc} \Delta \theta_c - \sigma_{mb} \Delta \theta_b). \qquad (1.16)$$

One can choose country b as the reference point for wage structures by adding and subtracting the term $(\Delta X_c \beta_{mb} + \sigma_{mb} \Delta \theta_c)$ from the right-hand side. This manipulation produces the following cross-country wage gap decomposition:

$$\Delta w_c - \Delta w_b = (\Delta X_c - \Delta X_b)\beta_{mb} + \Delta X_c(\beta_{mc} - \beta_{mb}) \\ + \sigma_{mb}(\Delta \theta_c - \Delta \theta_b) + (\sigma_{mc} - \sigma_{mb})\Delta \theta_c. \qquad (1.17)$$

The first term, 'measured quantities', represents the part of the pay gap that is explained by cross-country differences in the gender gap in observed productivity characteristics. For example, the pay gap in country c may exceed that of country b because for women in country c the gender gap in experience may be relatively larger. The second term, 'measured prices', reflects cross-country differences in returns to labor market characteristics. For example, given a male advantage in years of experience, higher returns to experience in one country will yield a larger overall pay gap. The third term, 'residual quantities', reflects cross-country differences in the position of women in men's residual wage distribution due to international differences in unmeasured gender-specific factors. This term captures the cross-country difference in the gender pay gap that would result if the countries had the same distribution of male residual wages and differed only from each other in the way that women ranked in the male distribution. The fourth term, 'residual prices', measures inter-country differences in residual male wage inequality. It captures the cross-country difference in the gender pay gap that would result if the countries had the same female rankings in the male residual wage distribution, but they differed in the distribution of male residual wage inequality. This final term can be thought of as international differences in the wage penalty for having a position below the mean in the male residual wage distribution.

The first and third terms are gender-specific and together reflect international differences in the percentile ranking of female workers in the male wage distribution. The second and fourth terms are particular to countries' wage structures and together reflect country differences in the shape of the male wage distribution. However, Suen (1997) has argued that this kind of decomposition of the residuals from the male wage regression into quantities and prices of unmeasured skills can generate misleading results. In more recent work, Blau and Kahn (2003) acknowledge that applying the JMP technique to country differences in pay gaps requires important assumptions. In particular, this application assumes that women are influenced by the same wage-setting forces that affect a country's distribution of male wages. Hence both the measured prices for males and the decomposition results for the residual prices for males are assumed to affect men and women in the same way. Blau and Kahn's more recent work provides a more direct test of the proposition that wage-setting institutions have played a major role in determining the gender wage gap in the United States. Results support their earlier findings, and indirectly the JMP procedure, that the United States' relatively high level of wage inequality is the main explanation for the country's relatively high wage gap between men and women.

VI   Occupational decomposition
An alternative decomposition method highlights the role of occupational segregation in explaining the wage gap. The method, first devised in Brown, Moon and Zoloth (1980), henceforth BMZ, decomposes a wage gap into a

component due to differences in employment shares across occupations and a component due to within-occupation pay gaps. Each component is further divided into a 'justifiable' and 'unjustifiable' portion, based on regressions performed with individual years of cross-section data and a few occupation categories. Since its initial application to United States data, this useful technique has been used to analyze labor markets in a wide range of countries.

The procedure begins with a description of overall mean wages as the weighted average of mean wages within occupations. Let W_{mt} and W_{ft} represent overall mean wages for male and female workers at time t, and let w_{mjt} and w_{fjt} represent the corresponding mean wages within occupation j. The gender wage gap can then be written as

$$W_{mt} - W_{ft} = \Sigma_j(\alpha_{mjt}w_{mjt} - \alpha_{fjt}w_{fjt}),$$ (1.18)

where α_{mjt} is the proportion of total men's employment in occupation j and α_{fjt} is the proportion of total women's employment in occupation j.

Next, the term $\Sigma_j\alpha_{fjt}w_{mjt}$ is added and subtracted from the right-hand side of equation (1.18). This term represents the female overall average wage that would be observed if women received the same average wage within each occupation as men. The manipulation produces the following expression for the occupational decomposition:

$$W_{mt} - W_{ft} = \Sigma_j(\alpha_{mjt} - \alpha_{fjt})w_{mjt} + \Sigma_j\alpha_{fjt}(w_{mjt} - w_{fjt}).$$ (1.19)

The first term (the 'across-occupations gap') shows the effect of gender differences in the employment distribution across occupations, given male wages in these occupations. This term represents the portion of the gender wage gap which is explained by women's relative concentration in certain occupations. The second term (the 'within-occupations gap') shows the effect of gender differences in wages within each occupation, given the female occupational structure. The decomposition in equation (1.19) is similar to the traditional decomposition in that it applies to wages, employment and worker characteristics at a given point in time.

The next step in the BMZ procedure is to further decompose the 'across-occupations' gap into a portion attributed to gender differences in qualifications for the occupations ('justifiable'), and a portion attributed to differences between men and women in the structure of occupational attainment ('unjustifiable').[8] Similarly, the 'within-occupations' gap is divided into a portion attributed to productivity differences between men and women ('justifiable') and a portion attributed to gender differences in market returns to those characteristics ('unjustifiable'). This decomposition of the 'within-occupations' gap is analogous to the original Oaxaca procedure, with the caveat that the female occupational distribution is being held constant. The transformation of equation (1.19) is performed by adding and subtracting the term $\sum_j \hat{\alpha}_{fjt} w_{mjt}$ from the right-hand side and by decomposing the within-occupations gap in the usual way. The final BMZ equation becomes

$$W_{mt} - W_{ft} = \sum_j (\alpha_{mjt} - \hat{\alpha}_{fjt}) w_{mjt} + \sum_j (\hat{\alpha}_{fjt} - \alpha_{fjt}) w_{mjt}$$
$$+ \sum_j \alpha_{fjt} (x_{mjt} - x_{fjt}) \beta_{mjt} + \sum_j \alpha_{fjt} x_{fjt} (\beta_{mjt} - \beta_{fjt}). \qquad (1.20)$$

The notation $\hat{\alpha}$ denotes the share of female workers who would be employed in occupation j if females had the same occupational distribution as men. Performing the decomposition in equation (1.20) requires two separate sets of regressions. The first entails constructing the predicted variable $\hat{\alpha}$ since the values for $\hat{\alpha}$ are not actually observed. To estimate $\hat{\alpha}$, one predicts occupational attainment for men using a multinomial logit model of occupational attainment in which the probability that an individual obtains an occupation j depends on a set of labor supply and demand variables. The estimated parameters from the male sample are then combined with the female characteristics in order to predict the female occupational distribution. The second set of regressions required for equation (1.20) entail running within-occupation OLS wage regressions in order to estimate the male coefficients β_{mjt}.

A new decomposition technique developed in Zveglich and Rodgers (2004) extends the BMZ approach by adding a trend analysis that allows the across- and within-occupations gaps to each have a pay dimension and an employment dimension. In contrast, the BMZ across-occupations gap has just an employment dimension and the BMZ within-occupations gap has just a pay dimension. Unlike BMZ, the trend analysis does not formally model the factors affecting women's occupational attainment, so it can say little about the justifiable and unjustifiable distinction for the employment dimension terms. However, in avoiding the high computational costs of making such a distinction, the new procedure can be performed at a much finer level of occupational disaggregation than encountered in the BMZ study and its subsequent applications. The more recent trend analysis can be applied to either the unadjusted wage gap or the residual wage gap. The regression-adjusted approach generates results that reflect changes in occupational wages and employment shares, rather than changes in worker productivity characteristics and their returns.

The procedure follows from the decomposition in equation (1.19) by adding a time dimension in order to explain how changes in the distribution of a large range of occupational wages and shares over time affect trends in the wage gap. This added dimension is gained through mathematical steps that are analogous to the JMP derivation.[9] By differencing equation (1.19) between any two periods, s and t, one can derive an expression for changes in the gender wage gap in terms of changes in the occupational structure and in pay across and within occupations. Again letting Δ denote the gender difference in any variable that follows, the change in the gender wage gap can be expressed as

$$\Delta W_t - \Delta W_s = \sum_j \Delta\alpha_{jt} w_{mjt} - \sum_j \Delta\alpha_{js} w_{mjs} + \sum_j \alpha_{fjt}\Delta w_{jt} - \sum_j \alpha_{fjs}\Delta w_{js}. \quad (1.21)$$

The next step is to choose year s as the base year for prices by adding and subtracting the term $(\sum_j \Delta\alpha_{jt} w_{mjs} + \sum_j \alpha_{fjt}\Delta w_{js})$ from the right-hand side of equation (1.21). This term represents the gender wage gap that would prevail in year t under the base year's occupational wage structure. The manipulation yields the following occupational decomposition of the wage gap:

$$\Delta W_t - \Delta W_s = \sum_j (\Delta\alpha_{jt} - \Delta\alpha_{js})w_{mjs} + \sum_j \Delta\alpha_{jt}(w_{mjt} - w_{mjs})$$
$$+ \sum_j (\alpha_{fjt} - \alpha_{fjs})\Delta w_{js} + \sum_j \alpha_{fjt}(\Delta w_{jt} - \Delta w_{js}). \quad (1.22)$$

Changes in the gender wage gap arise from four sources. The first term shows the contribution of changes in the relative employment distribution between men and women, commonly referred to as occupational segregation ('across-occupations employment effect'). For example, this effect can lead to a widening overall gender wage gap if pay structures within occupations are equitable, but women are becoming more concentrated in lower-paying occupations. The second term shows the contribution of changes in the wage structure across occupations ('across-occupations pay effect'). The degree to which occupational segregation affects the gender wage gap depends on the relative returns to various occupations. If changes in market returns favor female occupations, the gender gap will improve. The third term gives the contribution of changes in the female employment share within each occupation ('within-occupations employment effect'). For example, the overall wage gap will grow if women are becoming more concentrated in occupations that have inequitable pay structures, even if these occupations (such as senior officials and managers) are generally higher-paying occupations. The last term shows the contribution of changes in relative pay between men and women within each occupation ('within-occupations pay effect'). The extent to which wage disparity within occupations affects the overall gap depends on women's occupational distribution. If women are concentrated in occupations that are experiencing more equitable compensation, then the gender gap will improve.

VII Conclusion
This chapter has offered an intuitive exposition on the progression of techniques to decompose the gender wage gap, where all techniques can be generalized to analysis of other demographic groups and types of workers. The

Oaxaca and Blinder technique still constitutes a starting point in many wage gap analyses, with a host of further options available to today's researchers for a more detailed look at the determinants of wage gaps and the potential role of wage discrimination in explaining those gaps. As discussed in this chapter, these options include examining alternative reference wage structures, the importance of unmeasured skills and their returns, wage gap determinants along the full distribution of wages, the role of changing wage structures over time in explaining wage gaps, the role of international differences in wage structures in explaining cross-country differences in wage gaps, and the importance of occupational segregation and pay gaps within occupations in explaining the overall gap. Of course all these decomposition techniques represent just one area in the empirical literature on discrimination, with other innovative techniques explored further in subsequent chapters.

Notes

1. For earlier reviews of these methods and results, see Cain (1986), Darity and Mason (1998) and Altonji and Blank (1999).
2. See Goldin (1990) for a clear exposition on the use of male versus female coefficients.
3. Reimers (1983), Cotton (1988), Neumark (1988) and Oaxaca and Ransom (1994) have all addressed the index number problem using various reference wage structures.
4. This approach is used in Juhn, Murphy and Pierce (1991) and in Blau and Kahn (1996). Also Zveglich, Rodgers and Rodgers (1997) compare this approach with the Oaxaca and Blinder approach.
5. Blau and Beller (1992) criticize the Heckman procedure for the high sensitivity of coefficient estimates to misspecification. Their alternative procedure, while correcting for changes in the self-selection rule, does not correct for the effect of self-selection in the base year or for any bias resulting from their own selection criteria. Newey, Powell and Walker (1990) find that alternative semiparametric techniques to correct for sample selection yield results similar to the two-step procedure.
6. The discussion of the figure draws on Rodgers (1998).
7. For new methods that decompose changes over time in the wage gap using quantile regression techniques, see Machado and Mata (2003) and Albrecht, van Vuuren and Vroman (2004).
8. A similar procedure, with further corrections for index number problems that occur in the choice of the reference wage structure, is found in Appleton, Hoddinott and Krishnan (1999).
9. A related idea is found in Carrington, McCue and Pierce (1996), which uses the time dimension to explain how changes in relative public-sector/private-sector wages and shares over time affect trends in the black–white wage gap.

References

Albrecht, James, Aico van Vuuren and Susan Vroman (2004), 'Decomposing the gender wage gap in the Netherlands with sample selection adjustments', Bonn, Institute for the Study of Labor (IZA) working paper no. 1400.
Altonji, Joseph and Rebecca Blank (1999), 'Race and gender in the labor market', in Orley Ashenfelter and David Card (eds), *Handbook of Labor Economics*, Vol. 3C, Amsterdam: Elsevier Science, pp. 3143–59.
Appleton, Simon, John Hoddinott and Pramila Krishnan (1999), 'The gender wage gap in three African countries', *Economic Development and Cultural Change*, **47**(2), 289–312.
Blau, Francine and Andrea Beller (1992), 'Black–white earnings over the 1970s and 1980s:

gender differences in trends', *Review of Economics and Statistics*, **74**(2), 276–86.

Blau, Francine and Lawrence Kahn (1996), 'Wage structure and gender earnings differentials: an international comparison', *Economica*, **63**(250), S29–S62.

—— (2003), 'Understanding international differences in the gender pay gap', *Journal of Labor Economics*, **21**(1), 106–44.

Blinder, Alan (1973), 'Wage discrimination: reduced form and structural estimates', *Journal of Human Resources*, **8**(4), 436–55.

Brown, Randall, Marilyn Moon and Barbara Zoloth (1980), 'Incorporating occupational attainment in studies of male–female earnings differentials', *Journal of Human Resources*, **15**(1), 3–28.

Buchinsky, Moshe (1994), 'Changes in the U.S. wage structure 1963–1987: an application of quantile regression', *Econometrica*, **62**(2), 405–58.

—— (1998), 'Recent advances in quantile regression models: a practical guide for 23 empirical research', *Journal of Human Resources*, **33**(1), 88–126.

Cain, Glen (1986), 'The economic analysis of labor market discrimination: a survey', in Orley Ashenfelter and Richard Layard (eds), *Handbook of Labor Economics*, vol. 1, Amsterdam: Elsevier Science, pp. 693–785.

Carrington, William, Kristin McCue and Brooks Pierce (1996) 'Black/white wage convergence: the role of public sector wages and employment', *Industrial and Labor Relations Review*, **49**(3), 456–71.

Cotton, Jeremiah (1988), 'On the decomposition of wage differentials', *Review of Economics and Statistics*, **70**(2), 236–43.

Darity, William and Patrick Mason (1998), 'Evidence on discrimination in employment: codes of color, codes of gender', *Journal of Economic Perspectives*, **12**(2), 63–90.

Dolton, Peter and Gerald Makepeace (1987), 'Interpreting sample selection effects', *Economics Letters*, **24**(4), 373–9.

Goldin, Claudia (1990), *Understanding the Gender Gap: An Economic History of American Women*, New York: Oxford University Press.

Jones, F.L. (1983), 'On decomposing the wage gap: a critical comment on Blinder's method', *Journal of Human Resources*, **18**, 126–30.

Joshi, Heather, Pierrella Paci and Jane Waldfogel (1999), 'The wages of motherhood: better or worse?', *Cambridge Journal of Economics*, **23**, 543–64.

Juhn, Chinhui, Kevin Murphy and Brooks Pierce (1991) 'Accounting for the slowdown in black–white wage convergence', in Marvin Kosters (ed.), *Workers and Their Wages: Changing Patterns in the United States*, Washington, DC: The American Enterprise Institute Press, pp. 107–43.

Koenker, Roger and Gilbert Bassett (1978), 'Regression Quantiles', *Econometrica*, **46**(1), 33–50.

Machado, José and José Mata (2003), 'Counterfactual decomposition of changes in wage distributions using quantile regressions', Universidade Nova de Lisboa working paper.

Neumark, David (1988), 'Employers' discriminatory behavior and the estimation of wage discrimination', *Journal of Human Resources*, **23**(3), 279–95.

Newey, Whitney, James Powell and James Walker (1990), 'Semiparametric estimation of selection models: some empirical results', *American Economic Review*, **80**(2), 324–8.

Oaxaca, Ronald (1973), 'Male–female wage differentials in urban labor markets', *International Economic Review*, **14**(3), 693–709.

Oaxaca, Ronald and Michael Ransom (1994) 'On discrimination and the decomposition of wage differentials', *Journal of Econometrics*, **61**(1), 5–21.

—— (1999), 'Identification in detailed wage decompositions', *Review of Economics and Statistics*, **81**(1), 154–7.

Reimers, Cordelia (1983), 'Labor market discrimination against Hispanic and black men', *Review of Economics and Statistics*, **65**(4), 570–9.

Rodgers, Yana (1998), 'A reversal of fortune for Korean women: explaining the 1983 upward turn in relative earnings', *Economic Development and Cultural Change*, **46**(4), 727–48.

Suen, Wing (1997), 'Decomposing wage residuals: unmeasured skill or statistical artifact?' *Journal of Labor Economics*, **15**(3, part 1), 555–66.

Zveglich, Joseph and Yana Rodgers (2004), 'Occupational segregation and the gender wage gap in a dynamic East Asian economy', *Southern Economic Journal*, **70**(4), 850–75.
Zveglich, Joseph, Yana Rodgers and William Rodgers III (1997), 'The persistence of gender earnings inequality in Taiwan, 1978–1992', *Industrial and Labor Relations Review*, **50**(4), 594–609.

2 Using matched employer–employee data to study labor market discrimination

Judith K. Hellerstein and David Neumark*

I Introduction

Wage gaps between individuals of difference races, sexes and ethnicities have been documented and replicated extensively, and have generated a long history in labor economics research of empirical tests for labor market discrimination. The most widely-used approach to test for labor market discrimination is based on wage regressions estimated at the level of individual workers, with the estimate of discrimination inferred from the residual race, sex or ethnic group differential in wages that remains unexplained after including a wide array of proxies for productivity. Such estimates are open to the criticism that the proxies do not adequately capture group-specific differences in productivity, leading to disputes over the interpretation of the estimates that cannot be resolved with the types of data typically used in this approach.

What is absent from the residual wage approach, and in our view leaves the approach vulnerable to being regarded as uninformative regarding discrimination, is any directly observable measure of productivity with which to adjust differentials in wages in trying to infer whether a particular group suffers from discrimination. The ideal solution would be individual-level productivity data that can be compared with wages. Any of the variables that differ across groups and are unobserved in the residual wage regression approach should affect wages and productivity equally, and hence not bias the test. However, such data are extremely rare, in large part because individual productivity is often unobservable and seldom measured.

This chapter focuses on the use of matched employer–employee data sets to carry out a version of this ideal test, but at the establishment level. When these data sets permit the measurement of the demographic characteristics of establishments' workforces, as well as the estimation of production functions, they can be used to infer productivity differentials between workers in different

*   We are grateful to Kimberly Bayard and Kenneth Troske for past collaboration, to Joel Elvery and Gigi Foster for research assistance and to David Levine for helpful comments. Some of the research described in this chapter was supported by the National Science Foundation (grant SBR95-10876) and by the Russell Sage Foundation.

groups. Comparisons of these productivity differentials with wage differentials then provide versions of the ideal test for discrimination at the establishment level.

In addition to providing tests of discrimination, matched employer–employee data sets have proved useful in studying other questions that arise in the economics of discrimination, including measuring labor market segregation and assessing its consequences, and examining hypotheses or predictions that are central to economic models of discrimination.

The unifying theme of this chapter, then, is that matched employer–employee data sets hold out considerable promise for generating empirical evidence regarding labor market discrimination that cannot be gleaned from the individual-level data that have dominated most research on the topic. The chapter proceeds in a few steps. First, it explains some of the advantages that matched employer–employee data offer in studying discrimination. Second, it provides a guide to matched employer–employee data sets, focusing on the United States but also discussing data sets constructed for other countries. Third, it reviews some of the work that has been done using matched employer–employee data, again focusing primarily on the United States. Finally, it discusses new directions in which we think the construction and analysis of matched employer–employee data sets is likely to prove most useful in advancing our understanding of labor market discrimination.

II   The wage residual approach and other methods

Theoretical motivation
The wage residual approach to discrimination can be motivated by Becker's seminal model of employer discrimination (Becker, 1971). This is discussed in some detail because it is also at the core of the test for discrimination based on matched employer–employee data. This model also yields some insights regarding the persistence of discrimination over the longer run; these are discussed later. The assumption in the employer discrimination model is that employers dislike hiring a particular group, such as women. The implication is that, when a woman is hired, an employer considers the cost to be both the wage and the disutility from hiring a woman. Thus, in the simplest case where men and women are perfect substitutes in production, employers can be thought of as maximizing a utility function of the form

$$U_D = U(\pi,F) = \pi - d \times F = f(M + F) - w_M M - w_F F - d \times F,$$

where d is a constant > 0, reflecting discriminatory tastes against women, the D subscript denotes a discriminating employer, w_M and w_F are the wages of male (M) and female (F) labor, and $f(\cdot)$ is the production function, where men and women are equally productive. The price of output is normalized to one. The first-order conditions are

$$MP_L = w_M, \quad MP_L = w_F + d.$$

Since d is positive, the only equilibrium in which men and women are employed is the one in which $w_M = w_F + d$, and if $d = 0$ we must have $w_M = w_F$.

Thinking about the equilibrium requires some care. If d is the same for all employers, then when $w_M = w_F + d$ employers are indifferent between hiring male and female labor, so we expect all employers to hire both men and women. In contrast, if, as seems more likely, d varies across employers (indexed by i), then some equilibrium wage differential between men and women will be generated such that, if $d_i > w_M - w_F$, employer i hires only men, and if $d_i < w_M - w_F$, employer i hires only women. Thus one problem with Becker's employer discrimination model (as an explanation of the wage differential) is that, in the real world, segregation with almost all firms hiring only one sex or the other is generally not observed.

However, this is a result of the specific form of the utility function. If employers care about the relative number of female employees, rather than the absolute number, then the utility function is

$$U_D = f(M + F) - w_M M - w_F F - d \times (F/M),$$

in which case the first-order conditions are

$$MP_L = w_F + d/M, \quad MP_L = w_M - d \times (F/M^2).$$

Clearly w_M will exceed w_F in equilibrium. But now employers can effectively adjust the cost of hiring women by adjusting the relative number of women, so that, for any equilibrium wage ratio, firms should be willing to hire some men and some women. Of course, those with smaller d's will hire relatively more women. So versions of the employer discrimination model can explain the existence of wage differentials without requiring near-complete sex segregation of firms. In general, then, in employer discrimination models of this type, the preferences of employers have an impact on hiring decisions, which in equilibrium generate a market wage differential.

Empirical approach

As the previous first-order conditions suggest, the wage discrimination that results in the employer discrimination model takes the form of unequal wages paid to men and women with the same marginal products. As shown explicitly in Neumark (1988), this model can be used to motivate directly the wage residual approach to discrimination developed by Oaxaca (1973) and Blinder (1973). The simplest approach is to estimate a wage equation of the form

$$\ln(w) = X\beta + F\gamma + \varepsilon,$$

where X is a vector of control variables presumed to capture individual differences in productivity, and F is a dummy variable equal to one for women. The implication of this specification is that the wage differential between men and women is constant (in percentage terms) for all values of the Xs. However, this may be unduly restrictive, failing to capture, for example, variation in the wage gap with the level of education or experience. Thus, the Oaxaca–Blinder procedure is to estimate two wage regressions,

$$\ln(w) = X\beta_F + \varepsilon_F,$$

and

$$\ln(w) = X\beta_M + \varepsilon_M,$$

where X includes the unit vector.

In this case the decomposition of the wage differential varies depending on where it is evaluated, and the residual part of the wage differential now includes, not just the difference between the intercepts, but also the difference between the coefficients on X. Since regression lines go through the means, if $\beta_j, j = F, M$ are the vectors of estimates of β_F and β_M, and $\bar{X}_j$ denotes the mean of X_j, then the difference between the average log wages of men and women can be written in one of two ways:

$$\bar{X}_M\hat{\beta}_M - \bar{X}_F\hat{\beta}_F = \bar{X}_M(\hat{\beta}_M - \hat{\beta}_F) + (\bar{X}_M - \bar{X}_F)\hat{\beta}_F,$$

or

$$\bar{X}_M\hat{\beta}_M - \bar{X}_F\hat{\beta}_F = \bar{X}_F(\hat{\beta}_M - \hat{\beta}_F) + (\bar{X}_M - \bar{X}_F)\hat{\beta}_M.$$

Intuitively, what is the difference between these alternative decompositions? The last term in each equation captures the difference in wages that would remain even if the wage regressions were the same for men and women (that is, $\beta_F = \beta_M$), because there would still be a difference in characteristics between men and women that might lead to a wage differential. Estimating what the contribution of this difference in characteristics would be requires an assumption about what the wage structure would be in the absence of discrimination.

The first decomposition assumes that the wage structure in the absence of discrimination would be β_F, whereas the second assumes it would be β_M. Conversely, using the first decomposition, for example, $\bar{X}_M(\hat{\beta}_M - \hat{\beta}_F)$ measures the share of the wage gap attributable to discrimination. Whether or not this differs from zero is used to establish whether there is any evidence of discrimination.

Criticisms of the wage residual approach

The wage residual approach is subject to numerous criticisms. One important criticism is that it leads to ambiguous empirical answers because of an inherent arbitrariness in deciding the 'base' with which to compare the present wage structure. To see this, note that a more general decomposition is

$$\bar{X}_M\hat{\beta}_M - \bar{X}_F\hat{\beta}_F = [\bar{X}_M(\hat{\beta}_M - \hat{\beta}) - \bar{X}_F(\hat{\beta}_F - \hat{\beta})] + (\bar{X}_M - \bar{X}_F)\hat{\beta},$$

where $\hat{\beta}$ is the 'no discrimination' wage structure. If $\hat{\beta} = \hat{\beta}_F$, then the first decomposition results, while the second results if $\hat{\beta} = \hat{\beta}_M$ (see Neumark, 1988; Cotton, 1988). As evidence that this can be quantitatively important, in a study of pay discrimination in academia, in an admittedly extreme example Ferber and Green (1982) find that using β_M results in an estimate of 2 per cent of the sex wage differential reflecting discrimination, while using β_F results in an estimate of 70 per cent. In addition, as shown in Neumark (1988), there are alternative formulations of the assumption regarding employers' discriminatory tastes that lead to different decompositions. The point of this is not that there is a 'better' decomposition than those proposed by Oaxaca and Blinder, but rather that without some assumption, untested and likely arbitrary, regarding what the wage structure would look like in the absence of discrimination, these decompositions should perhaps not be interpreted as measuring discrimination, even ignoring the additional problems discussed below.[1]

While the foregoing criticism of the residual wage approach is technical, perhaps the most fundamental problem is that the control variables that are included in X may not fully capture marginal productivity differences. In particular, when there are unmeasured productivity differences that are systematically different across groups (such as race or sex), spurious evidence of discrimination can result. Perhaps the best known example of such an argument is Becker's (1985) work on effort allocation, which explicitly posits an unobservable effort that affects wages and is supplied to the labor market with less intensity by women than by men.[2] There are other examples of such arguments in the literature. With respect to sex differences, Mincer and Polachek (1974) criticized early wage residual estimates using potential experience as a control variable because, given the more extensive labor market interruptions of women, potential experience overstates the actual experience, and hence human capital, of women relative to men. More recently, Light and Ureta (1995) documented the implications of different patterns of accumulation of labor market experience for men's and women's wages, suggesting that even with an actual experience measure this issue remains important. With regard to race differences, Neal and Johnson (1996) and O'Neill (1990) argue that pre-market factors (as captured in test scores) account for much of the wage gap between blacks and whites.

The bottom line, in our view, is that, because one can always tell a story about an unobservable that is related to productivity (although Becker's story may be a particularly good one), deciding whether residual wage estimates capture discrimination may be more an act of faith than an act of science. This suggests, in turn, that we should look to other methods.

Audit studies as a response
One response to the absence of convincing evidence from the wage residual approach has been audit studies, which are based on comparisons of outcomes (usually job interviews) for matched job applicants of different races or sexes (see, for example, Turner *et al.*, 1991; Neumark, 1996).[3] In a sense, audit studies can be viewed as an alternative approach to the problem of missing data on productivity. Residual wage discrimination studies attempt to solve this problem by means of regression analysis, starting with men and women or blacks and whites that are on average different across many dimensions, and trying to introduce enough variables such that, after controlling for these variables, the only remaining difference on average is race or sex. Of course, since residual wage discrimination studies use data drawn from a population of individuals in which real differences exist between groups, the need to adjust via regression is unavoidable. The audit study approach, in contrast, creates an artificial pool of labor market participants among whom there are no average differences by race or sex. This is a potentially powerful strategy because, if successful, simple comparisons of means can yield strong evidence regarding discrimination.

This is not the place for a review of audit studies, which have many fans and some detractors. For comprehensive reviews and critiques, see Heckman (1998) and Fix and Struyk (1993). But there are two important criticisms to note here concerning the limited applicability of audit studies to understanding whether wage gaps reflect discrimination. First, audit studies by nature are limited to an examination of the initial interview and hiring process, and are therefore useful only in assessing discrimination in interviewing and hiring in typically low-paid jobs that do not require reference checks, résumé validation, personal recommendations and so on. Second, as has been noted by Heckman (1998), even if audit studies detect some discrimination, this does not imply that the marginal employer discriminates, and it is the marginal employer that, at least in Becker's model of discrimination, determines the wage. Thus the detection of unequal treatment in audit studies does not necessarily generate a 'discriminatory' wage gap.[4,5]

Individual-level productivity data

A more natural response to the problem of unobserved productivity differences is to study data sets with productivity measures for individuals. As noted before, though, such studies are limited because such data are quite rare, and certainly do not exist in a form that permit widely generalizable conclusions to be drawn.

Typifying the idiosyncratic nature of the labor markets for which analysis of individual-level productivity data are available, perhaps the most thorough of such analyses have been done for academia. This is a promising occupation to study, of course, because much of the productivity that is thought to be most relevant to pay setting, namely, publications, is readily observed. Furthermore, although not immune from dispute, evidence on citations or the journals in which articles are published can be used to assess not just quantity of output but also quality. Kahn (1995) summarizes a large number of studies focusing on pay discrimination by sex for economics professors, and there are also studies of academics in other fields as well.

A second source of data on individual productivity arises again idiosyncratically, when workers are paid both time rates and piece rates. Foster and Rosenzweig (1993) consider what one can learn from such data. On the surface, it would seem that, with data on the same worker paid time rates and piece rates for doing the same kind of work, a simple test for taste discrimination would arise, since piece-rate work should capture differences in productivity. Nonetheless, as Foster and Rosenzweig show, one must take great care in attributing wedges between relative wages and relative productivity to any particular form of discrimination. Let w be the time rate wage, F be a dummy variable for the sex of the individual, and μ be actual productivity measured by piece-rate earnings. Then, in the regression

$$w = F\beta + \gamma\mu + \varepsilon,$$

a negative estimated coefficient on the dummy for females would appear to pick up employer taste discrimination.[6]

Foster and Rosenzweig point out, though, that if there are information problems in labor markets, this may not be a good test. They demonstrate this with an example. Suppose there are four types of workers in a population, men with productivity of either two or four, and women with productivity of either one or three. But suppose that employers cannot distinguish the productive from the unproductive men, or the productive from the unproductive women, but only know the average productivity of men and women. In this case, employers pay expected productivity, so men earn three and women earn two. Now suppose we run a regression of pay on actual productivity and on sex. What will the coefficients be? Sex will perfectly explain the observed pay differences, so the coefficient on actual productivity will be zero, and that on sex will be one, even though there is no taste discrimination. So we cannot tell, from a regression like this, whether we are observing taste discrimination or statistical discrimination.

The 'right' way to do the test is to run the regression using expected, rather than actual, productivity, as in

$$w = F\beta + \gamma\mu^* + \varepsilon,$$

where μ^* is expected productivity. Now, in the above example, the coefficients on sex and expected productivity will be zero and one, respectively, indicating (correctly) that there is no taste discrimination. So, if the coefficient on the indicator for females goes to zero in this regression, then we know that we were observing statistical discrimination in the first regression.

We typically do not have information on expected productivity. But, if we assume that employers use all available information in forming this expectation, then we know that

$$\mu = \mu^* + u,$$

where u is a random error that is uncorrelated with μ^*. Thus we can think of the problem of estimating the first equation as a measurement error problem. The true structural equation is for μ^*, but we have an error-ridden proxy μ.[7] Thus we have to instrument for μ with variables that are correlated with μ^*, but uncorrelated with the measurement error $u = \mu - \mu^*$. Otherwise the estimate of γ is biased downward and, if women are on average less productive, the estimated discriminatory sex differential in pay that arises from something other than statistical discrimination is overstated.

As the authors point out, there are three requirements for such instruments. First, they must be correlated with μ^*. Second, they must be known to employers; in this case, they are contained in the information set of employers and are therefore orthogonal to u. Third, they must not themselves appear in the wage equation, implying that they must not be characteristics that are subject to taste discrimination. Satisfying the first two is in fact quite easy, as variables like height, age, education and so on are available. It turns out that in the authors' data (focusing on the results for the Philippines), if we accept these requirements for the validity of the instruments, there is no longer any evidence of taste-based discrimination leading to lower wages for women.[8]

The main contribution of this paper in the context of the present chapter, however, is to point out that, even in the unusual case where we have a measure of actual productivity, care must be exercised in using the simple wage regression approach to test for particular forms of discrimination.[9] If Foster and Rosenzweig's interest in measuring discrimination had been limited to testing for the existence of taste-based wage discrimination, an alternative test using their data would have been available. In particular, one can jointly estimate equations where an observed time-rate wage is regressed on a female dummy in one equation, and the observed piece-rate productivity is regressed on a female dummy in a second equation:

$$w = F\beta + v$$
$$\mu = F\lambda + \eta.$$

The error terms in these equations are correlated with the female dummy since $v = \mu^* + \varepsilon$ and $\eta = \mu^* + u$, and μ^* is correlated with F. As a result, the estimated coefficients on the female dummy in both equations will be biased, but they will be biased by exactly the same amount. Therefore, any estimated difference between β and λ can be interpreted as arising from taste-based discrimination rather than statistical discrimination, and failure to find any difference would be inconsistent with taste discrimination.[10] This approach to using wage and productivity information parallels our technique for testing for wage discrimination using matched employer–employee data.

III Using matched employer–employee data to test for wage discrimination[11]

The test

In order to motivate the approach to testing for wage discrimination that is enabled by matched employer–employee data, we begin with a simple model illustrating the relationship between wages and productivity under perfect competition. Consider an economy consisting of plants that produce output Y with a technology that utilizes two different types of perfectly substitutable labor inputs, L_1 and L_2. The production function of these plants is

$$Y = f(L_1 + \phi L_2),$$

where ϕ is the marginal productivity of L_2 relative to L_1. These plants are assumed to operate in perfectly competitive spot labor markets, and labor supply is assumed to be completely inelastic. The price of output Y is normalized to equal one. Wages of workers of types L_1 and L_2 are w_1 and w_2, respectively. Define the relative wage rate (w_2/w_1) to be λ. Given this set-up, the proportional mix of the two types of labor in each plant will be determined by the relationship between ϕ and λ. If $\phi = \lambda$, then under profit maximization or cost minimization plants will be indifferent to the proportional mix of the two types of labor in the plant. If there is a wedge between the relative marginal product and relative wage so that $\phi \neq \lambda$, then profit-maximizing or cost-minimizing plants will be at a corner solution, hiring either only workers of type L_1 (if $\phi < \lambda$) or only workers of type L_2 (if $\phi > \lambda$). The only equilibrium in this model is when wages adjust so that $\phi = \lambda$, and plants are indifferent between the two types of labor.

Evidence that $\phi \neq \lambda$ is inconsistent with the assumption that we are observing profit-maximizing or cost-minimizing plants in a competitive spot labor market.[12] Our approach can be interpreted as providing empirical tests of this characterization of labor markets. We estimate variants of the plant-level production function simultaneously with plant-level wage equations in order to obtain estimates of parameters corresponding to ϕ and λ for various types of workers. We interpret cases where we cannot reject the equality of ϕ and λ as evidence consistent with competitive spot labor markets. Cases in which we reject the equality of ϕ and λ indicate some deviation from this characterization of labor markets, such as would occur in the presence of taste-based discrimination.[13]

Data
This approach can be implemented using matched data on employers and employees, when the resulting matched data set provides information on demographic characteristics of the employer's workforce, labor costs and the output and input measures needed to estimate standard production functions. The matched employer–employee data set that we originally used for this purpose is the Worker Establishment Characteristics Database (WECD). The WECD, constructed at the US Census Bureau, links information for a subset of individuals responding to the long form of the 1990 Decennial Census of Population to information about their employers in the 1989 Longitudinal Research Database (LRD), with matches based on the physical location and detailed industry of the worker's reported place of work and similar information on establishments.

In particular, the Census Bureau maintains a complete list of all establishments operating in the United States in a given year (the Standard Statistical Establishment List, or SSEL), along with location and industry information for these establishments that is similar to the data available for workers. Thus it is possible to assign all establishments in the United States to an industry-location cell. The WECD is constructed by first selecting all manufacturing establishments in operation in 1990 that are unique in an industry-location cell. Then all workers who are located in the same industry-location cell as a unique establishment are matched to that establishment.

All that the SSEL provides is an establishment list and some cursory information such as total employment and total annual payroll. To obtain the data on a worker's employer needed to estimate production functions, the employer–employee pairs are matched in a second stage to plant-level data in the LRD. The LRD is a compilation of plant responses to the Annual Survey of Manufacturers (ASM) and Census of Manufacturers (CM). Data in the LRD are of the sort typically used in production function estimation, such as output, capital stock, materials expenditures and number of workers. In addition, the LRD contains information on total salaries and wages and total non-salary compensation paid by the plant in a given year (McGuckin and Pascoe, 1988). Since worker earnings and labor force information in the Decennial Census of Population refer to 1989, we match the worker data to the 1989 plant data in the LRD. To increase the representativeness of the sample of workers in each plant, we require plants to have at least 20 employees in 1989 (as reported in the LRD) and at least 5 per cent of their workforce contained in the WECD.

The resulting WECD sample contains data on 3102 plants and 129 606 workers. The average plant has 353 employees, and on average 12 per cent of a plant's workforce is matched to the plant. Further details on the construction of the WECD are given in Hellerstein *et al.* (1999) and Troske (1998). In our view, a major advantage of the WECD relative to idiosyncratic data sets with productivity measures is that it provides a relatively large data set that is at least partially representative of a major sector of the US economy.

However, some limitations are worth noting here, in part because more recent efforts at constructing matched employer–employee data sets address some of these limitations. First, the WECD is restricted to the manufacturing sector, since the production function data come from manufacturing surveys. Second, and most important, because possible matches are restricted to establishments that are unique in their location and industry cell, large manufacturing establishments are overrepresented; this follows because large establishments are more likely to be unique to industry-location cells.[14] As a counter-example that arises when extending the analysis beyond manufacturing, but continuing to use the industry-location cell to match, small retail establishments, which tend to be located in malls, are unlikely to be unique to an industry-location cell, and hence would be badly underrepresented. For similar reasons, nonurban establishments are overrepresented. Third, while a large data set results, the WECD nonetheless covers a small fraction of the workforce (about 5 per cent of manufacturing workers who respond to the Census Long-Form) and a small fraction of manufacturing establishments (about 1 per cent of those in the SSEL). Finally, two general limitations of the WECD, and other related matched employer–employee data sets for the United States described below, are that only a cross-section is currently available, and only a sample of workers from each establishment is matched to the establishment.

Methods

To estimate parameters corresponding to ϕ, we estimate a translog production function in which the value of output Y is a function of capital K, materials M and a quality of labor aggregate QL. In logs, this is

$$\ln(Y) = \ln(A) + \alpha\ln(K) + \beta\ln(M) + \gamma\ln(QL) + g(K, M, QL) + \varepsilon,$$

where $g(K,M,QL)$ represents the second-order terms in the production function.

For each plant in our data set, the WECD provides demographic information on a sample of workers. We assume that, in the quality of labor aggregate QL, workers with different demographic characteristics are perfectly substitutable inputs with potentially different marginal products. For example, if workers are distinguished only by sex, with the relative marginal productivity of women ϕ_F, then QL would be defined as

$$QL = L\left(1 + (\phi_F - 1)\,\frac{F}{L}\right),$$

where L is the total number of workers in the plant and F is the number of women in the plant. Substituting QL into the general production function, we obtain a production function from which we can estimate ϕ_F, using plant-level data on output, capital and materials inputs, and the number of workers and sex composition of the workforce.

We have used these data to estimate expanded versions of the type of production functions outlined above, with the difference that rather than distinguishing between only two types of workers, we distinguish between workers on the basis of sex, race (black and nonblack), marital status (ever married), age (divided into three broad categories, under 35, 35–54, 55 and over), education (distinguishing those with at least some college) and occupation (divided into four groups: (1) operators, fabricators and laborers, that is unskilled production workers, (2) managers and professionals, (3) technical, sales, administrative and service, and (4) precision production, craft and repair). As an example that helps in the ensuing discussion, suppose we use information on sex (male v. female) and race (black v. nonblack). Then the expanded expression for QL is

$$QL = L\left(1 + (\phi_{WF} - 1)\,\frac{WF}{L} + (\phi_{BM} - 1)\,\frac{BM}{L} + (\phi_{BF} - 1)\,\frac{BF}{L}\right),$$

where *WF* is the number of white female workers, *BM* the number of black males and *BF* the number of black females in the establishment, with corresponding subscripts on the ϕs.

Once we incorporate multiple characteristics of the workforce, some complicating issues arise. First, a full categorization of workers by the various characteristics listed above (sex, race, marital status and so on) would require 192 possible combinations of these demographic characteristics. Both the estimation of the share of the workforce in each of these cells, and the estimation of the corresponding parameters, would be impractical.

To reduce the dimensionality of the problem, we often use two types of restrictions on the form of *QL*. First, we restrict the relative marginal products of two types of workers within one demographic group to be equal to the relative marginal products of those same two types of workers within another demographic group. For example, the relative productivity of black women to black men is restricted to equal the relative marginal productivity of white women to white men.[15] Similarly, the race difference in marginal productivity is restricted to be the same across the sexes. Second, we restrict the proportion of workers in an establishment defined by a demographic group to be constant across all other groups; for example, we restrict blacks to be equally represented in all occupations, education levels, marital status groups and so on. Upon imposing these restrictions, the previous equation for *QL* reduces to

$$QL = L\left(1 + (\phi_F - 1)\frac{F}{L}\right)\left(1 + (\phi_B - 1)\frac{B}{L}\right),$$

where *B* is the number of black workers, thus eliminating in this case the parameter ϕ_{BF}. The same restrictions are imposed in estimating the wage equations described below. However, in the empirical work we examine the robustness of the results to relaxing these restrictions along a number of important dimensions identified in previous work (for example, allowing different marriage differentials for men and women, corresponding to differences in estimated marriage-related wage premia). In such a case there are two different implied sex differences, one for married men and women and one for unmarried men and women.

A second issue is that, in the production function based on *QL* above, labor of each type is perfectly substitutable, as each type enters linearly. It is possible, though, that workers of different types are imperfect substitutes. This is most likely to occur, perhaps, along occupational lines. We have therefore also estimated specifications treating workers in production and nonproduction occupations as imperfectly substitutable.

As this discussion indicates, many of the limitations of this framework can be addressed by generalizing the framework, although there are clear trade-offs as we would expect between restrictions imposed and difficulty of estimation, particularly given sample size constraints. But for the purposes of this chapter, the key is that, under many conditions, we can estimate parameters (or sets of parameters) such as ϕ_F, the productivity of women relative to men, and ϕ_B, the productivity of blacks relative to whites.

Because we have information on plant labor costs, we also specify and estimate plant-level earnings equations. These plant-level earnings equations represent the aggregation of individual-level earnings equations over workers employed in a plant, and hence are the plant-level counterparts to the individual-level wage regressions that motivate this research, yielding estimates of parameters λ_F and λ_B (in the example just used), which can be compared to the relative productivity estimates. By simultaneously estimating the production functions and earnings equations at the plant level, we can compare the relative marginal products and relative wages of workers distinguished by various demographic characteristics. While there may be some unobservables in the production function and wage equations, as long as we estimate both of these at the plant level, any biases from these unobservables ought to affect the estimated productivity and wage differentials similarly, at least under the null hypothesis, thus minimizing or eliminating their impact on tests of the equality of relative marginal products and relative wages, and hence isolating the role of discrimination in generating wage differentials.

Evidence

While this framework provides a straightforward and explicit test for wage discrimination, it still leaves open a number of possible variations, including the functional form for the production function, the restrictions imposed on the quality of labor term (QL), whether to instrument for potentially endogenous inputs and so on. The estimates are robust to changes in these three areas.

First, with regard to race, the estimates never provide any statistically significant evidence of wage discrimination. Moreover, the estimates of ϕ_B and λ_B tend to slightly exceed one. With respect to wages, this conflicts with standard wage equation estimates showing that blacks tend to earn less than similar whites. This discrepancy probably arises for two reasons, which are instructive as to some potential pitfalls with matched employer–employee data. First, when we estimate a wage equation for the WECD including fixed plant effects, the estimated wage differential between blacks and whites in the WECD is a bit larger (–0.08) than in the specification without fixed effects (–0.05), indicating that, within plants, blacks earn less than whites, but that blacks work in slightly higher-paying plants.[16] Thus, because the test for

Table 2.1   Results from production function-based tests of wage discrimination by sex

	ϕ_F	λ_F	*p*-value, $\phi_F = \lambda_F$
Translog output production function	0.84	0.55	0.00
Translog value-added production function	0.83	0.56	0.00
Translog output production function, Instrumental Variables (IV) for materials with lagged materials	1.01	0.55	0.00
Translog output production function, dropping dimensionality restrictions on sex and occupation			
Production	0.71	0.49	0.00
Managerial/professional	0.89	0.70	0.33
Technical, sales, administrative and service	1.29	0.70	0.01
Translog output production function, production and nonproduction workers as imperfect substitutes	0.90	0.56	0.00

Note: Estimates are from Hellerstein *et al.* (1999); all estimates are nonlinear least squares, except where otherwise noted.

discrimination we have developed using the WECD relies on variation across plants, the earnings of blacks relative to whites are biased upward. While, as just described, the wage differential associated with race can be estimated within plants, the productivity differential can only be estimated across plants. Second, comparing sample means for the matched sample and manufacturing workers in the Census overall reveals that blacks are underrepresented in the WECD. If this arises as undercounting of blacks relative to whites within plants, then this will tend to bias estimates of ϕ_B and λ_B away from one, as any productivity or wage differential associated with having more black workers is attributed to a smaller share of blacks than are probably in the establishment.

Thus the unusual estimates for blacks may stem from the reliance on across-plant variation for identification, and on non-representativeness of the employees who are matched. There is no obvious solution to the first problem within this framework (although, as discussed later, panel data are potentially helpful), while efforts to construct better, more representative matched employer–employee data sets are described below.

Turning to the results regarding sex discrimination, we begin by noting that the 'problem' to be explained or explored is much more severe with respect to sex than with respect to race. If we simply use the worker data to estimate standard log wage regressions, the estimated race gap is 5 log points, while the estimated sex gap is 35 log points. The production function and wage equation results, many of which are collected in Table 2.1, tell a very consistent story. The baseline estimate of ϕ_F is 0.84, which is significantly less than one, while the estimate of λ_F is 0.55, also significantly less than one, but much smaller than ϕ_F. Moreover, the *p*-value for the test of equality of these two parameters is effectively zero, indicating that the null hypothesis of no discrimination is rejected, in favor of the hypothesis of wage discrimination against women.[17] Across alternative specifications the estimate of λ_F is very robust. The estimate of ϕ_F varies somewhat more, between a range of about 0.71 to 1.01, but the test of the null of no discrimination is rejected in all cases, except for managerial/professional occupations when we relax the dimensionality restrictions by sex and occupation. The estimates suggest that, while in manufacturing in the United States women may be less productive than men, the pay gap is considerably larger, consistent with wage discrimination.

Limitations
There are some inherent limitations to the analysis we have been able to conduct using the WECD. Some of these have been discussed already, including nonrepresentativeness, a relatively small fraction of matched employers and employees, and the cross-sectional nature of the data set and therefore the identification strategy. An issue related to the relatively small fraction of matched workers is measurement error. In particular, our specifications rely on knowing the percentages of workers with various demographic characteristics in each plant, yet these are actually estimated from the sample of workers that are matched to the plant. We have used simulation methods (see Hellerstein *et al.*, 1999, section VIII) to assess the biases caused by this measurement error, generally concluding that the effect of measurement error is to bias our estimates toward finding no discernable productivity or wage differentials across workers, and toward finding no differences between the relative productivity and wage estimates for a given type of worker (since estimates of parameters that are further from one have larger absolute biases toward one). Thus the power of the tests of the equality of wage and productivity differentials is somewhat reduced because of measurement error, strengthening our rejection of this equality. Nonetheless, these simulations do not give a precise answer, and a data set with a much higher fraction of matched workers would be useful.

IV Other uses of matched employer–employee data to learn about labor market discrimination

Exploring the Becker model of discrimination

The Becker model of employer discrimination is often interpreted as ruling out wage discrimination of the type apparently detected by the residual wage gap method, and (more convincingly, we believe) by the production function approach just outlined. Becker shows that under sufficiently competitive conditions discriminatory employers will fail to thrive, and will eventually be competed out of existence. Some have leapt from this theoretical result to the claim that, since the sex-wage differential has persisted, it must reflect unobserved productivity differences rather than discrimination (Fuchs, 1988; O'Neill, 1990).

The argument that competition undermines discrimination is based on two implications of the model. First, there is a static implication that discrimination is likely to exist only where there is product market power, and conversely that product market competition hinders discrimination. Second, there is a dynamic implication that, even if there are firms with product market power that can 'afford' to discriminate in the short run, over the long run market forces eliminate the discrimination. However, whether or not market forces are expected to undermine discrimination depends on the nature of product market competition, barriers to entry, transferability of assets and the form of employers' discriminatory tastes. In particular, if employers' tastes are nepotistic rather than discriminatory, then discrimination will not be eliminated by competition in the market for firms, although product market competition may still suffice.[18] In our view, the conditions for competition to eliminate discrimination have been glossed over by those who interpret the Becker model as implying that discrimination cannot persist. Rather, we think it essential to try to test these implications of Becker's model empirically.

Individual-level wage regression estimates can tell us virtually nothing about the relationship between market forces and discrimination. Matched employer–employee data, in contrast, can be quite informative. In Hellerstein *et al.* (2002) we use the WECD to test both the static and dynamic implications of the Becker model, in both cases exploiting the links to employer-level data that arise from the matching.

We begin with a simple test for sex discrimination. If there is no discrimination against women, then there should be no cross-sectional relationship between profitability and the sex composition of the workforce. Any sex difference in wages must reflect only observed or unobserved productivity differentials between men and women, and firms or plants that employ more women should earn no higher profits. Evidence that plants or firms that employ relatively more women earn higher profits, in contrast, would be consistent with sex discrimination. This test, not surprisingly, parallels the production function-based test described in the previous section.

Then, moving on to the implications of the Becker model for the role of market forces, we first test whether, as the Becker model predicts, there is a positive short-run relationship between profitability and the sex composition of the workforce only among plants with product market power, because only among such plants are there positive economic profits that may be exploited to indulge the discriminatory tastes of some employers. Finally, we use longitudinal data on the plants in our data set to test the dynamic implications of Becker's model, asking whether nondiscriminatory plants, those which, according to the cross-sectional evidence, employ more women and earn higher profits, grow faster or are less likely to undergo a change of ownership, compared with discriminatory plants. The combined static and dynamic evidence provides us with a better understanding of sex discrimination in labor markets, and the role of competitive market forces in reducing or eliminating this discrimination, than can be obtained from conventional wage equation approaches to discrimination, or even from more convincing cross-sectional tests for discrimination (such as audit studies or our production function-based tests), which cannot say anything about the dynamic implications of Becker's model.

The first test relies solely on the WECD, described above. The only new feature is the construction of a measure of performance to use as a proxy for profitability. One measure we use is operating income (sales + inventory accumulation – labor costs – material costs) divided by inventory-adjusted sales (that is, current year sales plus the change in inventories), while a second measure also subtracts out from the numerator purchased business services or overhead costs (such as purchased electricity, legal services, advertising and repairs). These performance measures used as proxies for profitability are essentially price cost-margins (see, for example, Domowitz *et al.*, 1986).

In examining the relationship between profitability and the proportion female, we include as controls other demographic characteristics of the workforce, and plant or firm characteristics that are likely to be associated with profitability, such as age, industry and measures of market power. Estimates of the cross-sectional relationship between profitability and the proportion female indicate that, irrespective of variations in the sample, variable construction, and the use of plants or firms, the proportion female in the workforce is significantly positively related to profitability.

We next consider the implication of the Becker model that product market power can inhibit the influence of competitive forces in eliminating discrimination (although competition in the market for firms may still exert such influence over the long run). This implies that for plants with considerable product market power there will be a positive relationship between employment of women and profitability, whereas, for plants with little market power, the relationship will be nonexistent or at least weaker. The results indicate that for plants with a smaller market share there is a small and statistically insignificant relationship between profitability and the proportion female. But this relationship becomes positive and statistically significant at higher output shares.[19] This positive relationship between the proportion female and profitability among plants with high output share is consistent with the model.[20] In plants that operate in a competitive output market, there is no performance advantage to hiring women; since discriminatory employers are unable to indulge their tastes for discrimination, wages in this sector are quickly bid to equality with marginal products. But in (typically larger) plants where there is market power and where plants can discriminate if they wish, at least in the short run, those that do not discriminate and hire more women, who cost less, achieve better performance.

We interpret our cross-sectional results as suggesting that among the set of plants with product market power, which are typically larger plants, some exploit the supracompetitive profits stemming from their product market power to indulge in discriminatory behavior against women. Given that wages are set by the market, we do not expect the wage gap between men and women to differ between the less-competitive and more-competitive sectors. Rather, a larger gap between relative wages and relative marginal products in the less-competitive sector would have to reflect higher relative productivity of women in the less-competitive sector, possibly because of technological differences (the perfect substitutes case) or because fewer women are employed than would be the case in the absence of discrimination (the imperfect substitutes case) in this sector. The data are consistent with these predictions. In our earlier research, we found no productivity gap between men and women among larger firms, but that in smaller firms women were less productive than men. Moreover, wage regressions using plant-level data indicate that the relative wage of women is not particularly low among plants in the less-competitive sector that employ a high proportion of females.

The cross-sectional results suggest that plants or firms can indulge their discriminatory tastes only when they enjoy product market power. Nonetheless, market forces may reduce or eliminate discrimination as the more profitable plants or firms among those with market power grow relative to the less profitable ones, or as discriminating employers are bought out by non-discriminating employers. We look at evidence regarding this dynamic prediction of the Becker model for plants with relatively high output share (located in the top quartile of the distribution of this market power measure). For these plants, we estimate regressions for growth of both employment and shipments, and probits for ownership change, as functions of, among other things, the proportion of females in a plant's workforce.

When we look at growth, the estimated coefficients on the proportion of females are small and statistically insignificant. There is therefore no evidence that sex discrimination in wages is reduced or eliminated by market forces that cause nondiscriminatory plants to expand relative to discriminatory plants. The estimated effect of higher relative employment of women in the base year on the probability of changing ownership between 1990 and 1995 is negative, consistent with plants employing fewer women being more likely to change ownership, as predicted by Becker's model. However, the relationship is not statistically significant. Overall, then, these results provide little evidence of market forces that bid away the sex discrimination reflected in the cross-sectional relationship between profitability and the proportion of females for plants with product market power. We emphasize, however, that these results on growth and ownership change are derived from five-year changes, and it is possible that this is not a long enough period of time to be able to measure the effect of competitive market forces on discriminatory practices. On the basis of this evidence, though, there is not an empirical case for concluding that market competition alone will suffice to eliminate wage discrimination.

Levine and Leonard (2002) also use matched employer–employee data to examine theories of discrimination. Specifically, they have assembled a large longitudinal data set matching up employees to establishments of a large retail firm, coupled with Census data on the demographics of the population near each establishment. They use these data to examine theories of co-worker and customer discrimination, as well as to try to estimate the effects of workforce diversity on performance (sales).

Sex segregation and the sources of the sex gap in wages
Matched employer–employee data are also critical in providing a full description of segregation in the labor market, and in estimating the contribution of various dimensions of segregation to wage gaps between demographic groups. A prominent example of literature on this topic concerns the wage gap between men and women in US labor markets. Women have consistently earned lower wages than men in US labor markets, although this gap has narrowed in recent decades (Blau, 1998). Previous research has largely focused on the impact on the wage gap of sex segregation by occupation (for example, Macpherson and Hirsch, 1995) and by industry (for example, Fields and Wolff, 1995). However, a smaller literature has focused on the independent contribution of the segregation of men and women into different employers (for example, Blau, 1977) and segregation among occupations or jobs within establishments, or 'job-cell' segregation (Groshen, 1991).

While the latter two dimensions of segregation appear quite important empirically, it is difficult to find systematic evidence on establishment or job-cell segregation. Indeed, there is no empirical work on this issue in the earlier literature using large data sets representative of a wide array of industries, because of the absence of such data sets containing detailed demographic information for multiple workers in the same establishment. Instead, Blau's and Groshen's studies of the effects of establishment and occupation–establishment segregation examined unusual, quite narrow data sets, with Groshen using surveys of wages for a subset of occupations in five specific industries included as part of the Bureau of Labor Statistics (BLS) Industry Wage Surveys, and Blau using the BLS Area Wage Surveys. The focus in these studies on a handful of industries or occupations provides something closer to a set of case studies, with the lack of representativeness limiting their usefulness in assessing the forces at work in generating the sex wage gap in the United States.

In contrast, the methods we have developed to match employer and employee data using the Census data sources can provide much broader and more nationally representative data sets with which to estimate the contributions of sex segregation by industry, occupation and occupation–establishment cell (job cell) to the sex wage gap. Whereas the work described earlier required the estimation of production functions, and hence was restricted to manufacturing establishments, we have constructed an extended version of the WECD in order to study segregation we have constructed an extended version of the WECD. Like the WECD, this data set uses the US Census Bureau's SSEL to identify the employers of individuals who responded to the long form of the 1990 Decennial Census. However, this new data set (the New Worker–Establishment Characteristics Database, or NWECD) includes workers and establishments from all sectors of the economy and all regions; furthermore, because the production function 'ingredients' are not needed, there is no requirement to match to the LRD. As described in Bayard *et al.* (2003), this results in the NWECD containing information on over 600 000 workers in nearly 33 000 establishments, once restrictions similar to those imposed in the construction of the WECD, and other restrictions needed to make the analysis comparable to the existing literature, are imposed. Nonetheless, the constraints imposed by matching employees to employers based on unique industry-location cells remain, leading to overrepresentation of manufacturing establishments and nonurban establishments. Additional work that attempts to address these limitations is described below.

We use the NWECD to provide new estimates of the roles of various dimensions of sex segregation in generating sex differences in wages. Although in some respects our evidence may be viewed as complementary to that in the earlier studies, in our view the NWECD, while having some shortcomings, is clearly better suited to characterizing the effects of sex segregation in US labor markets.[21]

The empirical work proceeds by estimating wage regressions for men and women including a dummy variable for women, and the percentages female in the individual's occupation, industry, establishment and job cell (or establishment–occupation cell). These regressions yield two sets of results. The first is a decomposition of the share of the sex gap in wages attributable to each dimension of segregation, and the second is the unexplained sex gap that remains after controlling for this segregation, or the 'within-job cell' sex gap in wages. Our results indicate that a sizable fraction of the sex gap in wages is accounted for by the segregation of women into lower-paying occupations, industries, establishments and occupations within establishments. For example, using the most-detailed occupational classification, 4 per cent of the gap is attributable to occupational segregation, 11 per cent to industry segregation, 18 per cent to establishment segregation and 24 per cent to segregation across occupations within establishments. However, a substantial part of the sex wage gap remains attributable to the individual's sex, in this example 40 per cent, with other estimates ranging up to around 50 per cent.

These magnitudes are significant because they inform policy. In particular, if within the narrowly defined occupations that we study the jobs performed by men and women require substantially equal skill, effort, responsibility and working conditions, yet wages differ by sex, then enforcement of the Equal Pay Act can play a fundamental role in closing the wage gap between men and women. In contrast, if segregation along various dimensions accounts for most of the sex wage gap, then policies along the lines of comparable worth, equal opportunities in employment and promotion, and affirmative action would be central to any further closing of this gap, and stronger equal pay provisions would not be effective. Our findings suggest that stronger enforcement of equal pay legislation could further reduce the wage gap between men and women, perhaps substantially.[22]

Finally, in a related paper (Bayard *et al.*, 1999) using the same type of wage decomposition analysis, we use the NWECD to determine whether segregation can help explain why racial and ethnic wage gaps are larger for men than for women. In the NWECD, the black–white wage gap for men is –0.23· and the Hispanic–white wage gap is –0.24· for women, the black–white wage gap is –0.16· and the Hispanic–white wage gap is –0.13·. The results indicate that greater segregation between Hispanic men and white men than between Hispanic women and white women accounts for essentially all of the higher Hispanic–white wage gap for men. But the estimates indicate that greater segregation between black and white men than between black and white women accounts for only one-third to one-half of the higher black–white wage gap for men. Another way to interpret these results is to conclude that segregation is an important contributor to the lower wages paid to black and Hispanic men compared to white men with similar individual characteristics, although more so for Hispanic men. And while equal pay laws may offer some scope for reducing the black–white wage differential for men, they offer less scope for reducing the Hispanic–white wage differential for men.

V Other sources of matched employer–employee data

New matched data sets for the United States

We hope that the material presented to this point establishes the value of using matched employer–employee data to study labor market discrimination. But we also noted a few important limitations of the WECD (and the NWECD), including the small fraction of establishments matched and nonrepresentativeness. We have recently made progress on developing matched employer–employee data for the United States that rectify these deficiencies.

In particular, we have developed an alternative method to match workers to employers that does not require establishments and workers to be located in unique industry-location cells. Instead, this method relies on matching the actual employer name and address information provided by respondents to the Decennial Census to name and address information available for employers in the SSEL. We refer to this data set as the Decennial Employer–Employee Dataset, or the DEED. This produces a matched data set that is much larger and more representative than the WECD or the NWECD.[23]

When the NWECD was created, the specific name and address files for Long-Form respondents were unknown and unavailable to researchers. Subsequently, we were able to help track down the name and address files and to participate in their conversion from an internal Census Bureau input/output language to a readable format. Because this name and address file had been used solely for internal processing purposes, it did not have an official name, but was informally known as the 'Write-In' file.

The Write-In file contains the information written on the questionnaires by Long-Form respondents, but not actually captured in the Sample Edited Detail files (SEDF). For example, on the Long Form workers are asked to supply the name and address of their employers, while in the SEDF the only information retained is a set of geographic codes (state, county, place, tract, block). The Write-In file, however, contains the geographic codes as well as the employer's actual business name and address. Because name and address information is also available for virtually all employers in the SSEL, nearly all of the establishments in the SSEL that are classified as 'active' by the Census Bureau are available for matching, allowing us to use employer names and addresses for each worker in the Write-In file to match workers to employers in the SSEL. Additionally, because both the Write-In file and the SEDF contain identical sets of unique individual identifiers, we can use these identifiers to link the Write-In file to the SEDF. This procedure potentially yields a much larger matched data set, and one whose representativeness (as well as size) is not compromised by the need to focus on establishments unique to industry-location cells.

The key complication in implementing this procedure arises because names and addresses are not reported identically (or completely) by workers and their employers. Consequently, it is necessary to utilize 'fuzzy' matching software that constructs matches out of non-identical records. This is a very complex and detailed process, and is described in detail in Hellerstein and Neumark (2003). Suffice it to say that we developed matching algorithms that err very strongly on the side of caution, avoiding matches with a non-negligible probability of being invalid at the risk of eliminating many valid matches. Along the way, we also hand-checked many thousands of matches to detect problems with the matching algorithm and to fine-tune the algorithm to avoid these problems.

The resulting data set is very large. Out of all 12 143 183 workers in the SEDF who met the basic criteria for sample inclusion, 3 291 213 (approximately 27 per cent) are in the DEED, a substantial improvement over the NWECD, which contains only 7 per cent of possible matches. Turning to establishments, there are 5 237 592 establishments in the SSEL; of these, 972 436 (19 per cent) also appear in the DEED, versus 137 735 (slightly more than 2.5 per cent) in the NWECD. In addition, the DEED is far more representative of both workers and establishments. The nonrepresentativeness of the NWECD, stemming from the matching algorithm, was most pronounced with respect to industry, with overrepresentation of workers in manufacturing and underrepresentation of retail workers. This problem is greatly ameliorated in the DEED. Approximately 25 per cent of all workers in the SEDF are employed in the manufacturing sector and, although this number is somewhat greater in the DEED (33 per cent), it is substantially lower than in the NWECD (49 per cent). Retail workers comprise 20 per cent of all workers in the SEDF, and 17 per cent in the DEED, but only 9 per cent of all NWECD workers. Paralleling this, the distributions of establishments across industries in the DEED and NWECD relative to the SSEL are similar to those in the worker sample in the sense that the DEED is much closer to the SSEL. For example, although there are roughly the same shares of services establishments in all three data sets (28 per cent in the SSEL, 26 per cent in the DEED, and 27 per cent in the NWECD), there is a far greater representation of manufacturing establishments in the NWECD (29 per cent) than in the SSEL (6 per cent) or the DEED (13 per cent). Examining the distributions of establishments across geographic areas also reveals that the DEED is more representative of the SSEL than is the NWECD. In both the SSEL and the DEED just over 81 per cent of establishments are in a Metropolitan Statistical Area (MSA), while this is true for only 61 per cent of NWECD establishments.

Thus the DEED offers substantial improvements in providing a matched employer–employee data set for the United States that is larger and more representative of the actual population of workers and establishments. We are confident that the DEED will prove very useful in revisiting some of the questions regarding labor market discrimination that we have studied in the past with the WECD and NWECD. In addition, the massive size of the DEED makes it uniquely suited to studying additional questions regarding labor market discrimination, in particular those that require a very fine disaggregation of workers and/or employers. For example, our first paper using the DEED studies the role of labor market segregation based on Hispanic ethnicity and language proficiency (Hellerstein and Neumark, 2003). We have also used the subset of manufacturing establishments in the DEED to replicate the earlier results in Table 2.1, based on the WECD, regarding sex differences in wages and productivity in this sector (Hellerstein and Neumark, forthcoming). We have found that the results are very similar, although of course the estimates are considerably more precise.

Another national matched employer–employee data set currently under construction at the US Census Bureau is the Longitudinal Employer-Household Dynamics (LEHD) data. The LEHD is very rich in that it contains observations on all workers in covered establishments (not limited to the one-in-six sample of Long-Form respondents) and is longitudinal in nature. However, the LEHD only covers some states (although many of the largest ones). In addition, it is based on firm-level rather than establishment-level data, so that workers can only be accurately matched to establishments when the establishment is not part of a multi-unit firm. However, the LEHD should ultimately permit some of the same analyses described in this chapter, with additional statistical analyses and testing of hypotheses regarding discrimination enabled by the longitudinal nature of the data.[24]

International matched data sets
To this point, the discussion has focused on research using matched data for the United States. As reviewed in Abowd and Kramarz (1999), employer–employee data sets of some variety or other have been assembled for numerous countries. In contrast to the data for the United States, where the main employer–employee data sets have resulted from matches across different surveys, many of the data sets in other countries are based on surveys that set out to cover both establishments and employers, although others are based on matches. For the most part, these data sets have not been used to address questions regarding labor market discrimination. This is probably in part because such questions simply are far more central to labor economics research in the United States. However, some recent work has implemented our production-based tests for wage discrimination for other countries.

Haegeland and Klette (1999) study Norwegian manufacturing plants using data from Statistics Norway including an annual census of establishments, and 'register data files' covering essentially all workers. While there is some noncorrespondence between the employer identification numbers in the two data sources, the authors assert that they match workers to employers for over 70 per cent of the manufacturing establishments they study. The empirical methods they use follow those in Hellerstein *et al.* (1999) closely, but their results are quite different, pointing to wage and productivity shortfalls of women relative to men in the range of about 18–19 per cent, and no significant evidence against the equality of relative wages and marginal products of women and men.

Similarly, Crépon *et al.* (2002) study matched data covering the period 1994–7 for France, based on the Bénéfice Réels Normaux, an employer-level file, and the Déclarations Annuelles des Données Sociales, an exhaustive employee-level file. Again, the available employer identification code does not permit a perfect match, as 9 per cent of establishments do not appear in the employee data file. One downside to this data set is that the worker information is sparse, for example lacking measures of education level and marital status. Crépon *et al.*, also use similar methods to Hellerstein *et al.* (1999), with slight modifications. Paralleling the results for Norway, these authors also find little substantive evidence of discrimination against women. Their estimates imply that women are less productive (by 11 per cent in manufacturing, and 7 per cent in nonmanufacturing) and that the pay differentials, while significantly larger than this (14 per cent and 9 per cent, respectively), are substantively quite close to the productivity differentials.

Finally, as noted earlier, we have also implemented these methods using data on Israeli manufacturing plants (Hellerstein and Neumark, 1999). There, too, we find that there is both a pay gap and a productivity gap favoring men over women, but that the gaps are of roughly equal magnitude, failing to provide evidence of wage discrimination.

Thus, to this point, results from implementing this test based on matched employer–employee data for the United States yield strong evidence of discrimination against women. In contrast, for the handful of other countries for which this method has been used, women appear lower paid *and* less productive, and there is generally little evidence of discrimination. There are a number of possible reasons why the results may vary across countries. First and most obviously, given differences in employment laws and institutions, and given cultural differences about the roles of men and women in the home and at work, one might not expect the answer to be the same across countries. Second, and more subtly, even two economies with the same laws, institutions and cultural norms may yield different equilibria with respect to wage discrimination. Recall that, in the Becker model of taste discrimination, it is the marginal firm that determines the equilibrium wage differential between workers. Differences across countries in the composition of firms (most importantly, perhaps, in the distribution of employers' discriminatory tastes), or differences in the relative supplies of female labor across countries, can yield large differences in the characteristics of the marginal employer, and thus large differences in equilibrium wages across men and women.

For example, in more disaggregated analyses using the data for the United States, we find evidence that the relative wage for women is equal to the relative productivity for women who work in small establishments, but in large establishments women are relatively more productive than in small establishments, but are underpaid. Thus it seems that the market wage differential between men and women is set by small establishments, and large establishments are able to pay that market wage and indulge in a taste for discrimination, presumably because they have market power.

Our full-sample results and those reported for other countries report average estimates across all establishments of relative productivities and relative wages, and it is therefore impossible to tell from these results whether cross-country differences may be due to differences in the identity of the marginal employer, whose tastes determine market wages. Nonetheless, nothing in this argument rules out interpreting the results for the United States as indicating wage discrimination. Rather, the open question is whether the absence of such evidence in a few other countries reflects less discriminatory tastes, differences in the marginal employer or variation in the legal/institutional setting. It remains to future research to probe the cross-country differences more fully, focusing both on questions regarding data and on empirical methods, as well as the economic, legal, institutional or other factors that could underlie these differences.

Two additional points regarding the international data sets are worth noting. First, in contrast to data for the United States, some of the international data sets (including those for Norway and France discussed above) have the advantage of relying on data covering all workers at an establishment, rather than a sample. Second, these two international data sets, as well as others, include repeated observations on employers and their workforces. This feature can in principle be exploited to control for underlying establishment-level heterogeneity, by asking, for example, whether the average wage paid in an establishment actually falls when the proportion of females in the establishment's workforce rises, or whether instead low-wage establishments tend to employ a greater share of women. With cross-sectional data, of course, we cannot distinguish between these two hypotheses.

In the United States, as the matched data are based on the Decennial Census of Population, the best that one can do with respect to constructing panel data is to use observations ten years apart. While this is something we plan to explore using the 2000 Census, the assumption that establishment-level unobservables are constant over such a long time horizon is tenuous. The data used by Haegeland and Klette (1999) consist of a panel of yearly observations over the 1986–93 period, yet they choose to use time averages of the data (the 'between' estimator) to reduce measurement error, rather than to exploit the longitudinal structure of the data set more fully. The French data used by Crépon *et al.* (2002) also have a panel structure, but they, too, rely almost exclusively on the between variation, and only report limited results for the wage equation using differenced estimators. Finally, in other work using the Israeli data, we have attempted to implement versions of our test for wage discrimination using panel data from two years (Hellerstein and Neumark, 1998). We find that increases in the proportion of females are not associated with declines in wages, but are associated with declines in productivity (albeit with imprecise estimates), which we interpret as evidence of lower productivity of female employees, coupled with clustering of women in low-wage plants but some constraints on paying women and men differentially within establishments. However, the extension of these methods to panel data is best characterized as remaining largely unexplored to date.

VI   Summary and conclusions

The recent construction of matched employer–employee data sets has allowed researchers to test in new ways for the presence of market-wide discrimination. Data at the establishment level are used to estimate marginal productivity differentials between workers, which are in turn compared directly to market wage differentials. This is a formal test for the existence of taste-based employer discrimination that, if sufficiently pervasive, generates a wedge between the relative market wages of groups of workers and their relative productivities. Because it directly tests the theoretical prediction of the taste-based model, this kind of analysis is far more convincing than approaches based on residual wage comparisons, and offers advantages over other methods of testing for discrimination as well.

To date, evidence from this analysis that uses matched US employer–employee data provides strong evidence of gender discrimination. In contrast, for the few other countries for which this method has been applied, women are lower paid *and* less productive, indicating little evidence of discrimination. It remains to future research to identify these differences more fully, focusing both on data and empirical methods, along with the legal, institutional, or other economic factors that could underpin these differences.

In addition to enabling this direct test for discrimination, matched employer–employee data sets also hold the potential to provide researchers with more information on the nature of discrimination and labor market differences between groups more generally, and by extension, therefore, to inform debate over possible policy responses. We fully expect that, as the depth and scope of matched employer–employee data sets both in the United States and abroad are expanded, much more will be learned from these data about the existence, extent and nature of labor market discrimination.

Notes

1. However, Oaxaca and Ransom (1994) offer some arguments for preferring Neumark's (1988) decomposition, and provide an integrated discussion of the alternative decompositions.
2. As Darity and Mason (1998) point out, the omitted variables do not necessarily create a bias towards finding evidence of discrimination.
3. Goldin and Rouse (2000) has many features in common with audit studies, although it is actually an unusual case of a natural experiment where the sex of a job applicant was, at times, not revealed to those making hiring decisions. Bertrand and Mullainathan (2004) perform what has been termed a 'correspondence study' in the earlier literature, using résumés rather than actual visits to apply for jobs.
4. As Heckman writes, 'A well-designed audit study could uncover many individual firms that discriminate, while at the same time the marginal effect of discrimination on the wages of employed workers could be zero' (1998, p. 102).
5. On the other hand, Black (1995) shows that, in a search model, discriminatory tastes on the part of some employers can result in a wage gap, even when the discriminatory employers do not hire any minorities.
6. The vector of observable characteristics of individuals can be generalized to include other covariates in addition to a sex dummy.
7. Note that this is a little counterintuitive, since the realization of true productivity is considered the error-ridden variable; in a model in which employers base pay on expected productivity, however, this is the right way to think about things.
8. In an extension, Foster and Rosenzweig (1996) allow for the possibility of comparative advantage that differs across sex and affects the allocation of workers to job tasks. The results are again consistent with statistical discrimination.
9. A similar problem arises when a data set provides a performance rating. See Neumark (1999) for an application with U.S. data. This is potentially relevant to other studies utilizing performance ratings to try to control for productivity differences, such as Holzer (1990) and Medoff and Abraham (1980).
10. In the example considered earlier, if we separately regressed wages on sex, and productivity on sex, we would find a coefficient of -1 in each regression, and correctly conclude that there is no taste discrimination.
11. The framework described here builds on our earlier work in Hellerstein and Neumark (1999) analyzing Israeli manufacturing data, although the data set used in that work is not matched employer–employee data, but is collected from employers only. Cox and Nye (1989) implement a similar approach using employer data from the nineteenth-century French textile industry.
12. Labor supply could be less than completely inelastic; as long as market wages remain above reservation wages, the conclusions are unchanged.
13. This can be couched in the context of section II. If the production function there is $f(M+\phi F)$, then the first order conditions are $MP_L = w_M$ and $\phi MP_L = w_F + d$. Dividing through, we get $MP_F/MP_M = \phi = (w_F + d)/w_M$. So if $d = 0$, $w_F/w_M = \phi$, and if $d > 0$, $w_F/w_M < \phi$.
14. There is also an issue of measurement error in reported industry creating incorrect matches (Bayard, 2001).
15. The analysis is actually done for blacks and nonblacks.
16. See also Carrington and Troske (1998) for similar evidence.
17. Of course, how this result is interpreted depends in part on the source of variation in the share of the plant's workforce that is female. Section II showed how this variation can be driven by differences in discriminatory tastes, in which case all employers adjust gender composition so that their disutility from female workers just matches the wage differential relative to the productivity differential that we estimate. Another possibility we have explored (Hellerstein *et al.*, 1999) is that the percent women is correlated with other variables, such as technological innovation. A separate survey of manufacturing technology for some plants that can be identified in our data (in high-technology industries) suggests that, if anything, the percent women is lower in plants using advanced technologies. This might lead to downward bias in the estimated extent of discrimination, as the apparent higher productivity of men is in part attributable to more advanced technology.

18. See Becker (1971, ch. 3) for a detailed discussion of the conditions under which competition should erode discrimination.
19. Kawaguchi (2003) reports related and similar evidence based on data from a census of Japanese firms meeting minimum thresholds for employment and capital.
20. These results are also consistent with tabulations from the 1940 Census reported by Becker, indicating that, relative to firms operating in competitive industries, firms operating in monopolistic industries appear to engage in discriminatory behavior (1971, Table 2, p. 48); Becker's results, however, refer to hiring of nonwhites.
21. Datta Gupta and Rothstein (2005) replicate this study using matched employer–employee data from Denmark.
22. See Bayard *et al.* (2003) for an analysis of why these findings differ from Groshen's, which concluded that the within-job-cell sex wage gap was very small.
23. Because the WECD contains only manufacturing establishments, while the DEED and the NWECD cover all industries, in the remaining discussion we focus only on comparing the latter two data sets.
24. Yet another source of employer–employee data in prior research is Unemployment Insurance records maintained by states (see Abowd and Kramarz, 1999). But these typically provide very limited information on workers and employers, and hence are unlikely, by themselves, to prove very instructive in studying discrimination.

References

Abowd, John M. and Francis Kramarz (1999), 'The analysis of labor markets using matched employer–employee data', in Orley Ashenfelter and David Card (eds), *Handbook of Labor Economics,* vol. 3B, Amsterdam: Elsevier, pp. 2629–710.
Bayard, Kimberly (2001), 'Measurement error and inter-industry wage differentials', unpublished paper, Board of Governors of the Federal Reserve System.
Bayard, Kimberly, Judith Hellerstein, David Neumark and Kenneth Troske (1999), 'Why are racial and ethnic wage gaps larger for men than for women? Exploring the role of segregation using the new worker–establishment characteristics database', in John Haltiwanger, Julia Lane, James Spletzer, Jules Theeuwes and Kenneth Troske (eds), *The Creation and Analysis of Employer–Employee Matched Data*, Amsterdam: Elsevier Science B.V., pp. 175–203.
Bayard, Kimberly, Judith Hellerstein, David Neumark and Kenneth Troske (2003), 'New evidence on sex segregation and sex differences in wages from matched employee–employer data', *Journal of Labor Economics*, **21**(4), October, 887–922.
Becker, Gary S (1971), *The Economics of Discrimination*, 2nd edn, Chicago: University of Chicago Press.
Becker, Gary S (1985), 'Human capital, effort, and the sexual division of labor', *Journal of Labor Economics*, **3**(1) (pt. 2), January, S33–58.
Bertrand, Marianne and Sendhil Mullainathan (2004), 'Are Emily and Greg more employable than Lakisha and Jamal? A field experiment on labor market discrimination', *American Economic Review*, **94**(4), September, 991–1014.
Black, Dan A. (1995), 'Discrimination in an equilibrium search model', *Journal of Labor Economics*, **13**(2), April, 309–34.
Blau, Francine D. (1977), *Equal Pay in the Office*, Lexington, MA: D.C. Heath and Company.
Blau, Francine D. (1998), 'Trends in the well-being of American women, 1970–1995', *Journal of Economic Literature*, **36**(1), March, 112–65.
Blinder, Alan S. (1973), 'Wage discrimination: reduced form and structural estimates', *Journal of Human Resources*, **8**(4), 436–55.
Carrington, William and Kenneth Troske (1998), 'Interfirm racial segregation', *Journal of Labor Economics*, **16**(2), April, 231–60.
Cotton, Jeremiah (1988), 'On the decomposition of wage differentials', *Review of Economics and Statistics*, **70**, 236–43.
Cox, Donald and John V. Nye (1989), 'Male–female wage discrimination in nineteenth-century France', *Journal of Economic History*, **XLIX**, December, 903–20.
Crépon, Bruno, Nicolas Deniau and Sébastien Pérez-Duarte (2002), 'Wages, productivity, and

worker characteristics: a French perspective', unpublished paper, Centre de Recherche en Économie et Statistique et Institut National de la Statistique et des Études Économiques.

Darity, William A. and Patrick L. Mason (1998), 'Evidence on discrimination in employment: codes of color, codes of gender', *Journal of Economic Perspectives*, **12**(2), Spring, 63–90.

Datta Gupta, Nabanita and Donna S. Rothstein (2001), 'The impact of worker and establishment-level characteristics on male–female wage differentials: evidence from Danish matched employee–employer data', *Review of Labour Economics and Industrial Relations*, **19**(1) (March), 1–35.

Domowitz, Ian, R. Glenn Hubbard and Bruce C. Peterson (1986), 'Business cycles and the relationship between concentration and price–cost margins', *Rand Journal of Economics*, **17**(1), 1–17.

Ferber, Marianne A. and Carole A. Green (1982), 'Traditional or reverse sex discrimination? A case study of a large public university', *Industrial and Labor Relations Review*, **35**(4), 550–64.

Fields, Judith and Edward N. Wolff (1995), 'Interindustry wage differentials and the gender wage gap', *Industrial and Labor Relations Review*, **49**(1), October, 105–20.

Fix, Michael and Raymond J. Struyk (eds) (1993), *Clear and Convincing Evidence: Measurement of Discrimination in America*, Washington, DC: The Urban Institute.

Foster, Andrew D. and Mark R. Rosenzweig (1993), 'Information, learning, and wage rates in low-income rural areas', *Journal of Human Resources*, **28**(4), Fall, 759–90.

Foster, Andrew D. and Mark R. Rosenzweig (1996), 'Comparative advantage, information and the allocation of workers to tasks: evidence from an agricultural labour market', *Review of Economic Studies*, **63**(3), July, 347–74.

Fuchs, Victor R (1988), *Women's Quest for Economic Equality*, Cambridge, MA: Harvard University Press.

Goldin, Claudia and Cecilia Rouse (2000), 'Orchestrating impartiality: the impact of "blind" auditions on female musicians', *American Economic Review*, **90**(4), September, 715–41.

Groshen, Erica L. (1991), 'The structure of the female/male wage differential: is it who you are, what do you do, or where you work?' *Journal of Human Resources*, **26**(3) (Summer), 457–72.

Haegeland, Torbjørn and Tor Jakob Klette (1999), 'Do higher wages reflect higher productivity? Education, gender and experience premia in a matched plant–worker data set', in John Haltiwanger, Julia Lane, James Spletzer, Jules Theeuwes and Kenneth Troske (eds), *The Creation and Analysis of Employer–Employee Matched Data*, Amsterdam: Elsevier Science B.V., pp. 231–60.

Heckman, James J. (1998), 'Detecting discrimination', *Journal of Economic Perspectives*, **12**(2), Spring, 101–16.

Hellerstein, Judith K. and David Neumark (1998), 'Wage discrimination, segregation, and sex differences in wages and productivity within and between plants', *Industrial Relations*, **37**(2), April, 232–60.

Hellerstein, Judith K. and David Neumark (1999), 'Sex, wages, and productivity: an empirical analysis of Israeli firm-level data', *International Economic Review*, **40**(1), February, 95–124.

Hellerstein, Judith K. and David Neumark (2003), 'Ethnicity, language, and workplace segregation: evidence from a new matched employer–employee data set', *Annales D'Économie et de Statistique*, 71–72, July–December, 19–78.

Hellerstein, Judith K. and David Neumark (forthcoming), 'Production function and wage equation estimation with heterogeneous labor: evidence from a new matched employer–employee data set', in Ernst R. Berndt and Charles M. Hulten (eds), *Hard to Measure Goods and Services: Essays in Honor of Zvi Griliches*, Chicago: University of Chicago Press.

Hellerstein, Judith K., David Neumark and Kenneth R. Troske (1999), 'Wages, productivity, and worker characteristics: evidence from plant-level production functions and wage equations', *Journal of Labor Economics*, **17**(3), 409–46.

Hellerstein, Judith K., David Neumark and Kenneth R. Troske (2002), 'Market forces and sex discrimination', *Journal of Human Resources*, **37**(3), Spring, 353–80.

Holzer, Harry J (1990), 'The determinants of employee productivity and earnings', *Industrial Relations*, **29**, Fall, 403–22.

Kahn, Shulamit (1995), 'Women in the economics profession', *Journal of Economic Perspectives*, **9**(4), Fall, 193–206.

Kawaguchi, Daiji (2003), 'A market test for sex discrimination: evidence from Japanese firm-level panel data', unpublished paper, Institute of Policy and Planning Services, University of Tsukuba.

Levine, David and Jonathon Leonard (2002), 'Diversity, discrimination, and performance', unpublished paper, University of California, Berkeley.

Light, Audrey and Manuelita Ureta (1995), 'Early-career work experience and gender wage differentials', *Journal of Labor Economics*, **13**(1), January, 121–54.

Macpherson, David A. and Barry T. Hirsch (1995), 'Wages and gender composition: why do women's jobs pay less?', *Journal of Labor Economics*, **13**(3), July, 426–71.

McGuckin, Robert and Pascoe, George (1988), 'The longitudinal research database (LRD): status and research possibilities', *Survey of Current Business*, November, 30–37.

Medoff, James L. and Katherine G. Abraham (1980), 'Experience, performance, and earnings', *Quarterly Journal of Economics*, **95**(4), December, 703–36.

Mincer, Jacob and Solomon Polachek (1974), 'Family investments in human capital: earnings of women', in T.W. Schultz, (ed.), *Economics of the Family*, Chicago: University of Chicago Press, pp. 397–429.

Neal, Derek A. and William R. Johnson (1996), 'The role of premarket factors in black–white wage differences', *Journal of Political Economy*, **5**(104), October, 869–95.

Neumark, David (1988), 'Employers' discriminatory behavior and the estimation of wage discrimination', *Journal of Human Resources*, **23**(3), Summer, 279–95.

Neumark, David (1996), 'Sex discrimination in restaurant hiring: an audit study', *Quarterly Journal of Economics*, **111**(3), August, 915–41.

Neumark, David (1999), 'Wage differentials by race and sex: the roles of taste discrimination and labor market information', *Industrial Relations*, **38**(3), July, 414–45.

Oaxaca, Ronald L. (1973), 'Male–female differentials in urban labor markets', *International Economic Review*, **14**(3), October, 693–709.

Oaxaca, Ronald L. and Michael R. Ransom (1994), 'On discrimination and the decomposition of wage differentials', *Journal of Econometrics*, **61**(1), March, 5–21.

O'Neill, June (1990), 'Discrimination and income differences', in Susan F. Feiner (ed.), *Race and Gender in the American Economy*, Englewood Cliffs, NJ: Prentice-Hall, pp. 13–7.

Troske, Kenneth R. (1998), 'The worker–establishment characteristics database', in John Haltiwanger, Marilyn Manser and Robert Topel (eds), *Labor Statistics Measurement Issues*, Chicago: University of Chicago Press, pp. 371–404.

Turner, Margery Austin, Michael Fix and Raymond J. Struyk (1991), 'Opportunities denied, opportunities diminished: racial discrimination in hiring', Urban Institute report 91-9, The Urban Institute, Washington, DC.

3 Learning about discrimination by talking to employers

Philip Moss and Chris Tilly

Four main types of studies attempt to measure and analyze employment discrimination: household surveys, employer (establishment) surveys, analyses of administrative data (such as payroll or unemployment insurance data) and behavioral studies such as audits or experiments. Employer surveys offer important advantages over the other three approaches. Unlike household, administrative and audit data, establishment data can measure the goals and attitudes of those in a position to discriminate. In addition, establishment surveys can record details of organizational structure, characteristics and procedures that may affect who gets hired or promoted.

However, six critical problems bedevil establishment surveys. First, researchers must choose a sampling strategy, opting for in-depth study of a small number of job types or a large, broadly representative sample. Second, it is difficult to get busy managers to respond to a survey at all, posing the problem of access. Third, virtually all firms hire for more than one job, so it is necessary to decide what job to inquire about. Fourth, the management of most businesses – all except those owned and managed by a single person – is an organization, not a Euclidean point. Therefore, the question of whom to interview arises. Fifth, many forms of discrimination violate both the law and social norms in the United States (and other countries). This raises the question of honesty: will employers accurately describe their attitudes and behavior? Finally, an establishment survey alone does not make it possible to distinguish between a discriminatory attitude and an accurate assessment of the skills of an individual or the average skills of a group. That is, distinguishing between supply (worker quality) and demand (employer stereotypes) is problematic.

In this chapter, we start by briefly describing the main employer surveys that have attempted to capture discrimination. This set of surveys is small in number and recent in provenance, making a fairly comprehensive listing manageable. The surveys and analyses based on them overwhelmingly address racial, rather than gender discrimination. Then we discuss how these surveys have addressed the six critical issues. The last two problems (honesty and distinguishing between supply and demand) are particularly troublesome, and we accordingly devote more space to them.

The surveys

In assessing how establishment surveys have helped us understand labor market discrimination, it is important to keep in mind the unique contributions of such surveys. These advantages are several:

- We can observe overall hiring, staffing and promotion patterns by race and gender *within individual firms*.
- We can directly observe the reported goals, preferences and perceptions of managers. In quantitative surveys, for instance, this can include responses to questions about a manager's willingness to hire different groups, such as welfare recipients, ex-convicts, inner city residents, or young people who have gone through a government training program – all categories with racial (and in some cases gender) overtones. Qualitative surveys can encompass a broader set of observations about how managers discuss particular groups. In both cases, these measures can both be described and be used as predictors of employment outcomes (hiring, retention, promotion) by race and gender.
- We can measure a variety of organizational variables. These include standard measures such as firm size and industry, which are also available in some household surveys. More importantly, they can include the nature of recruiting and screening, the nature of the job structure (degree of formality, existence of standard job progressions, and so on), pay scales and training practices. Some establishment surveys can even capture the distinction between official employment policies and actual practices. As with employer attitudes, we can use these organizational measures as predictors of race/gender employment outcomes.

Keeping these advantages in mind, we review the most important establishment surveys that address discrimination.

Quantitative surveys

By quantitative surveys, we mean large-scale surveys involving closed-ended (multiple choice or yes/no) questions designed for statistical analysis. The best-known establishment surveys are those conducted by the federal and state governments of the United States. The federal government carries out a quinquennial Census of businesses. State governments collect information for the unemployment insurance system, which the federal government pools into a number of databases, of which *County Business Patterns* (US Department of Commerce, annual) is the most familiar. The Equal Employment Opportunity Commission (EEOC) gathers counts of race and gender categories by occupation. And the Internal Revenue Service collects tax-related information. However, in each of these cases, the information collected is severely limited;

much of the resulting data might better be described as administrative data than as surveys. Moreover, although tabular data from each of these sources are published, micro data are in general not accessible.

There are important exceptions to the inaccessibility of micro data from these government surveys. Sharpe (1993), in a remarkable piece of journalistic research, used the Freedom of Information Act to compile EEOC data on the racial composition of employment at hundreds of large corporations, documenting that, as the US economy slid into recession between 1990 and 1991, black employment in these companies declined while employment of every other racial group increased. The Census Bureau's new Longitudinal Employer-Household Dynamics (LEHD) program links Census-derived household data to establishment data from the states' unemployment insurance record-keeping system; researchers have not yet examined discrimination using these data (Abowd, Haltiwanger and Lane, 2001; Andersson, Holzer and Lane, 2005; Lane, Moss, Salzman and Tilly, 2003). Both the LEHD and the EEOC data offer the possibility of micro data analysis on a very large sample of firms: in the case of the LEHD, for the universe of firms in participating states. However, as with other government data, the amount of information gathered on each firm is fairly thin, foreclosing analysis of employer attitudes or organizational structures and procedures.

Privately undertaken surveys yield smaller samples, but richer information on the firms within the sample. Use of employer surveys to probe managerial attitudes toward African-Americans dates back at least to 1930, when Charles Johnson of Fisk University, in his work *The Negro in American Civilization*, included a chapter entitled 'Employers' Opinions of the Competence of Negro Labor'. But recent years have seen a new proliferation of research based on establishment surveys.

The National Organizations Study (NOS), started in 1991, was a pioneering survey of employing organizations. Although not created to study labor market discrimination, it generated a number of important studies that shed light on issues related to employment discrimination, particularly on gender-related differences in job outcomes (see Marsden, Kalleberg and Knoke, 2000, for a description of the survey and a full review of the studies based upon it). Seven hundred and twenty seven interviews were completed from 688 unique establishments, and the response rate was approximately 65 per cent. Sampling was accomplished by asking respondents to the 1991 General Social Survey (GSS) to name their employer and then interviewing the employers.

The NOS gathered data on three sets of jobs: the 'core job', the one most closely related to the product of the firm; the job of the employee from the GSS that named the firm as his/her employer; and a manager's or administrator's job. The second job, the one held by the GSS respondent, provided a connection to the individual-level data of the GSS respondent and a linked

NOS–GSS data set was constructed. The gender composition of each of the three jobs was gathered. The survey also collected data on a wide variety of characteristics of the organization, including among others the structure of jobs and decision making, and the procedures for recruiting and hiring. Having data on a variety of jobs within the organization distinguishes the NOS from the three other surveys we discuss.

An establishment-based survey such as the NOS provides particularly strong data for studying two important aspects of gender discrimination, occupational segregation by gender and differential promotion opportunities and probabilities by gender. Gender segregation by occupation has been studied primarily with data from individuals. Data from employer surveys have two advantages over household data for studying occupational segregation. Household data can understate occupational segregation precisely because they neglect gender segregation at the occupational level that may occur across firms. Men may dominate an occupation at one firm while women dominate the same occupation at another firm (Bielby and Baron, 1984; Marsden, Kalleberg and Knoke, 2000). Kalleberg *et al.* (1996) used the NOS to study occupational segregation by gender in all three of the occupations on which data were gathered and estimated that as few as 19 per cent of workers held gender-mixed jobs defined as having between 30 and 70 per cent of one gender.

The second advantage of employer surveys for studying occupational segregation is that one can study the organizational factors that are associated with such segregation. Researchers have used the NOS to do just that. Tomaskovic-Devey (1993) and Kalleberg *et al.* (1996) found that sex segregation is lower in larger organizations and those with more formal structure and decision making. Reskin and McBrier (1999) studied the managerial jobs in the NOS and found lower sex segregation among the organizations that had more formalized recruiting procedures. Tomaskovic-Devey and Skaggs (1999) obtained similar results for the GSS jobs in the NOS. The NOS has also provided for comparative work on gender segregation (and gender differences in promotion) between the United States and other countries. Juliane Achatz, Jutta Allmendinger and Thomas Hinz (2000) compared gender segregation in Germany using data from a link of monthly employer reporting to the social insurance system and an annual panel survey of West German establishments. They found a similar extent of gender segregation in the two countries, but with relatively less segregation in managerial jobs in the United States, and less influence in Germany of variables such as formalization and equal employment opportunity programs on the degree of sex segregation in managerial jobs.

The job structure information in the NOS allows research on the opportunities for promotion facing women versus men. Kalleberg *et al.* (1996) discovered that jobs held primarily by men are more likely to be part of job ladders and have higher rates of promotion than jobs held primarily by women. Kalleberg and Reskin (1995) studied differential promotion by gender using the NOS–GSS linked data and a similar establishment survey in Norway. They found that women report fewer promotions than men but that this is in part explained by greater likelihood of full-time work among men and greater representation in the corporate sector compared to greater representation among women in the nonprofit sector.

Baldi and McBrier (1997) used the NOS–GSS linked data to study black–white differences in promotions. Most research on racial differences in hiring and promotion has been cast within the debate on human capital versus overt discrimination, but their use of establishment survey data allowed them to move beyond the terms of this debate to suggest that blacks and whites tend to experience different promotion systems. Blacks tend to operate in what they call a 'contest' system in which objectively measured characteristics such as education govern the likelihood of promotion. Whites, on the other hand, are more likely to function in 'sponsored' systems in which it is the informal ties with managers that differentially influence the chance of promotion. Blacks are less likely to have these ties. The authors found that the black workers in the NOS–GSS data were less likely to receive a promotion in organizations with a higher concentration of black workers, and in establishments with an internal labor market structure. In addition they found the black workers with higher levels of education were more likely to receive a promotion, while education did not have this effect for white workers. Baldi and McBrier suggested that this finding results from blacks and whites tending to occupy separate job ladders within firms with internal labor market structures. The differential impact of education, they argue, is due to their posited distinction between contest and sponsored systems of promotion.

Baldi and McBrier's internal labor market and education findings are good illustrations of the relative advantages to be had by using establishment data. Both results point to the influences on labor market outcomes of social ties and networks *within* firms. These structures and processes are invisible in individual-level data. In addition, if one were to discover, as others have, this differential education result in individual data, one would again be stuck in the debate between meritocracy (human capital) versus pure discrimination, with no obvious way to resolve the dispute. Does the quality of the education blacks receive fall short of that received by whites, or, on the other hand, are the valid qualifications of blacks being discounted by discriminatory managers with a 'taste for discrimination?' The establishment data break this Manichean bind. Education is a more decisive factor in firms with more formal evaluation and promotion processes, and it is less important when social networks, which may be a product of, among other things, discriminatory attitudes and a desire to work and network with one's own kind, are more prevalent. Further, whatever the promotion system, education influences promotion less for whites because they dominate the social networks within firms.

As part of the Multi-City Study of Urban Inequality (MCSUI), Harry Holzer administered a telephone interview of approximately 3200 employers in the Atlanta, Boston, Detroit and Los Angeles metropolitan areas. Holzer wrote about the results of this survey in his important book, *What Employers Want: Job Prospects for Less Educated Workers* (1996). He drew about half of the sample from the employers named by employed individuals in the MCSUI household survey and about half from an organization that develops sampling frames of employers from telephone directories. Joleen Kirschenman, Philip Moss and Chris Tilly supervised the collection of approximately 300 additional interviews of employers named by employed persons in the MCSUI household survey. The results reported below are from analyses we did with the augmented database (Moss and Tilly, 2001). The full set of interviews was divided roughly equally between the four cities, and the response rate was about 69 per cent.

The survey questions addressed the characteristics of the business, of the last person hired and of the job that that person filled. Respondents were directed to consider only jobs that did not require more than high school, and were asked about frequency of performance of certain tasks, recruiting and screening procedures, other hiring requirements, willingness to hire welfare recipients and graduates of government training programs, and the race and gender of the worker hired, as well as of job applicants, employees and customers. Interviewees were also asked about their own attitudes towards different racial groups of workers and their opinion as to whether employees, customers or other employers preferred workers of their own race/ethnic group. This survey broke a lot of new ground for studying how different groups fare in the labor market. The range of information available – about skill and credential demands for jobs, recruiting and hiring methods, characteristics of applicants and customers, employer attitudes, and the latest hires' demography and qualifications – led to a significant set of inquiries on race in the labor market that were not possible using household data alone. Here are some of the results from Holzer's and from our work that most pertain to labor market discrimination.

Both Holzer and we analyzed how certain job demands cut against the likelihood that different groups are hired. Notably, frequent contact with customers cuts against the chances of men being hired, and use of computers and use of arithmetic have a negative effect on the probability that minority (black and Latino) workers are hired (Holzer, 1996, ch. 4, Moss and Tilly, 2001, ch. 3). When formal recruiting methods are used, the fraction of the employers' applicant pool that is black increases. Less formal methods of screening such as use of personal interviews augment hiring of whites, and affirmative action considerations in hiring, as expected, increase the hiring of minorities (Moss and Tilly 2001, ch. 6). The chances of blacks being hired increases when a greater fraction of the firm's customers is black (Holzer 1996, ch. 4). None of these results had been discovered with household surveys. The information on employer attitudes gathered in this survey is discussed below.

In 1998–9, Harry Holzer and Michael Stoll supervised the collection of data from a sample of approximately 750 employers in Chicago, Cleveland, Milwaukee and Los Angeles. The sample was drawn from a sampling frame based upon directories of establishments. The survey utilized a 20-minute questionnaire. The focus of the study was the current and likely hiring of welfare recipients. In addition to establishment characteristics, the survey gathered information on the employer's willingness to hire welfare recipients and, if a welfare recipient had been hired, the race and credentials of the last welfare recipient hired, and the skill demands of the job into which the last welfare recipient had been hired. Although the study was aimed at the labor market opportunities for welfare recipients, it generated interesting findings with regard to race. Holzer and Stoll found that the probability that the organization's last hire was black or Hispanic, conditional on the organization having hired a welfare recipient, was not influenced by the skill demands of the job or the overall demand conditions facing the firm (measured by the firm's vacancy rate). The probability that the last hire was black or Hispanic was diminished, however, if the firm had a suburban (as opposed to central city) location, was smaller in size, and for blacks, if the firm was in the retail sector. Blacks (and Hispanics) had a greater chance of being the firm's last hire when the firm's customers included more blacks (or more Hispanics). For blacks, the same was true for the composition of the firm's applicants. Blacks' chances of being the last hire were also greater at firms that did formal employment tests than at firms that did not.

These results confirm those found in the first Holzer survey, except for the lack of statistically significant impacts of job skills. The authors suggest that this may be due to the possibility that employers hire welfare recipients into the lowest-strata jobs where variation in skill demands is relatively modest.

Nelson Lim (2002) reported results on employer attitudes towards different race/ethnic groups from a survey of organizations conducted in 1997. The survey was launched in the metropolitan areas of Los Angeles, New York, Atlanta, and Philadelphia and the sample was drawn from telephone directories. One thousand sixty-nine employers generated completed responses, fairly evenly distributed across the four areas. The response rate was approximately 70 per cent. Like all of the other surveys we discuss except the NOS, this one focused on entry-level work defined as jobs not requiring college. The survey used the Holzer (1996) survey as a model for the information drawn on the organizations, the jobs and the hiring procedures, but gathered new information on how employers rate different groups of workers. We discuss his results below in the section on honesty of employer responses.

The large sample sizes characterizing these quantitative surveys help identify with confidence (in the statistical sense) the organizational factors that are associated with differential employment outcomes by race and gender. Quantitative surveys also allow us to estimate the magnitudes of the effects of these organizational factors. In quantitative surveys, however, the mechanisms *behind* the associations, for example why larger organizations are more open to applicants of color and to female applicants, what is it about formal testing that opens more doors to minorities and females, and why suburban locations are more hostile to minority applicants, remain unilluminated and cry out for explanation. The explanations come from in-depth qualitative surveys.

Qualitative surveys

Just as privately implemented quantitative establishment surveys offer more information on a smaller sample of employers than do government surveys, *qualitative* establishment surveys embrace still smaller samples, but offer considerably more detailed information. Qualitative surveys are conversational, built around open-ended questions, and are almost invariably conducted in person. They span a spectrum ranging between several types of interviews:

- Semi-structured interviews. In these interviews, there is a prescribed list of questions, but most questions are open-ended. The interviewer typically has discretion to follow up on responses, to alter the order of questions in order to create a more conversational flow, and to restate questions in different words. Most of the qualitative establishment surveys have taken this form.
- Loosely structured interviews. Here the interviewer undertakes a free-flowing conversation with the respondent, seeking to address a set of broad talking points but not necessarily posing questions with a prescribed wording.
- Ethnography. The researcher spends an extended period of time with the subject(s), engaging in conversation on a variety of topics and observing the subject in action. The goal is to learn about the topics of interest within a much broader context. As a practical matter, it is difficult to convince managers to let a researcher 'hang around' for extended periods, and we are not aware of business ethnographies focusing on the issue of discrimination. This end of the methodological spectrum remains only a theoretical possibility at this point.

Given the more informal, intimate, and dense nature of qualitative surveys, they offer windows on two important types of information that are difficult to access in quantitative surveys built around closed-ended questions. First, they can provide a more complete and accurate picture of employer attitudes. Second, they can distinguish between stated policies and actual day-to-day procedures.

British researchers used in-depth interviews to probe negative employer attitudes of racial minorities in their own national context in the early 1980s (Jenkins, 1986; Lee and Loveridge, 1987). In the United States, it was sociologists Joleen Kirschenman and Kathryn Neckerman, interviewing employers in Chicago, who pioneered qualitative employer surveys on racial discrimination (Kirschenman and Neckerman, 1991; Neckerman and Kirschenman, 1991). Speaking to a cross-section of 185 employers in 1988–9, Kirschenman and Neckerman discovered that, in a relaxed, face-to-face conversational setting, many managers were willing to speak relatively openly about their views of different racial categories of workers. They found that many employers rate black workers worse than others and few rate them better. In fact, employers described a racial gradation, placing Anglos above Latinos, and Latinos above blacks. When asked to rank the three groups, 38 per cent of employers rated blacks last (and another 8 per cent rated them tied for last with Latinos); 51 per cent declined to rate the groups. This contrasts sharply with Holzer's experience with his first quantitative telephone survey, in which employers virtually uniformly assigned the same rating to all workers (Holzer, personal communication, 1996). Presumably, the higher frequency with which managers stated negative perceptions of black workers in the face-to-face survey gives a more accurate reading of their actual views. Kirschenman and Neckerman also found that employers' views of racial groups were significantly conditioned by the gender, age, educational level and place of residence of the worker or subgroup under consideration (see, for example, Kirschenman, 1991). Kirschenman and Neckerman's results thus demonstrated the first advantage we have claimed for qualitative approaches, the possibility of gathering more accurate and comprehensive information on employer attitudes.

Kirschenman and Neckerman's findings stirred considerable interest, and motivated other researchers to try similar techniques. One early entry came from two other sociologists, Shirley Harkess and Carol Warren (1994), who analyzed manufacturing manager interviews conducted in 1979–80 in an unnamed southern city. Like Kirschenman and Neckerman, they found that a substantial number of managers expressed negative views of African Americans as employees. Philip Kasinitz and Jan Rosenberg's (1996) study of the Red Hook neighborhood of Brooklyn found that most Red Hook businesses did not hire local black workers, owing to multifaceted discrimination (based on class and location as well as race) and to recruitment through social networks that tended to exclude blacks.

Moss and Tilly (1995, 1996, 2001) undertook two surveys inspired by Kirschenman and Neckerman's work, a smaller sample of 75 managers in 56 Detroit and Los Angeles firms in 1991–2, and a larger sample of 365 managers in 174 firms located across those two metropolitan areas plus Boston and Atlanta in 1994–6. The interview questionnaire used in the latter sample is shown in the Appendix (the instrument for the earlier survey was quite similar). We replicated Kirschenman and Neckerman's findings that managers were in many cases willing openly to voice negative views of African American workers. However, the Moss/Tilly surveys incorporated several distinctive features. We attempted to speak to three managers per firm: a top executive, a human resource official and a frontline supervisor. The surveys questioned employers extensively about skills required for jobs and changes in those skills, making it possible to explore the consequences of changing skill demands for the racial composition of hiring. We also asked about employers' views of inner city areas as a place to do business, and analyzed the results. The smaller, two-city survey in particular focused on four narrowly defined industries (auto part manufacturing, insurance, department stores and the public sector), allowing us to formulate industry-level case studies of hiring needs, processes and outcomes. The four-city survey was subsampled from Holzer's (1996) large quantitative, telephone survey, allowing comparison of results from the two different survey strategies.

The chief finding from the Moss and Tilly surveys is that employers' views of the skills of individuals or groups, and their views of the desirability of various neighborhoods, are entangled with stereotypical perceptions of racial groups. This is particularly the case with 'soft' or social skills, involving motivation and the ability to interact well with customers, co-workers and managers. As with the other qualitative surveys, we encountered complexities in managers' mental maps of the workforce and urban geography that go beyond what quantitative surveys were able to uncover. Direct comparison of the Holzer and Moss/Tilly surveys, the latter conducted on a subsample of the former's sample, provides additional evidence that the face-to-face, qualitative interviews generate more accurate measures of negative employer perceptions. The comparison is sufficiently striking that we present it in some detail in the section on the honesty of respondents, below.

In-depth questioning also revealed gaps between company line and workplace realities. For example, executives and human resource staff, located far from the shop floor, often glorified job skills only to be debunked by the frontline supervisors. At a heavy manufacturing plant in the Detroit area, for instance, the human resource director described the new skills required by computerization of machine controls, whereas the supervisor explained that, although the interface was different, no more skills were required, adding that 'With the computers you need to have a Ph.D – Push Here, Dummy.' On the other hand, it took asking the question a couple of different ways to get the president of a small Atlanta-area manufacturer to describe technology-based changes in skill requirements:

> *Interviewer*:   Have there been any changes in the kind of things you're looking for in a worker? Has that remained kind of constant?
> *Respondent*:   Yeah, we're still doing essentially the same thing we did 31 years ago.
> . . .
> *I*:   Has technology affected the way these people do business, work?
> *R*:   Yeah, it's unbelievable. Technology has changed our business. Technology has changed the way that we deal with our product.
> *I*:   Has it changed the kind of qualities that you're looking for in a worker? Has it affected what you need to look for?
> *R*:   To a degree. Anybody that comes in here, if they were lucky enough at the time, that their school had computers and things of this type, it's just an asset for them to have, and that's technology right there.

We found particularly significant gaps between stated policy and reality when it came to formal recruitment and screening procedures. Nominally formal recruiting approaches often have loopholes that foster hiring through networks (see also Waldinger and Lichter, 2003, on this subject). One uniformed public service agency, for example, advertises in major dailies as well as community newspapers from communities of color, sends notices to community organizations and posts jobs with the state employment agency. Nonetheless, a manager commented that candidates for the dispatcher job are typically found by informal means:

> We'll get calls from somebody who is a [current employee in this job] who'll say, 'Gee, I worked with, I know this kid.' We find that the informal public safety network is quite often the best way to go.

Similarly, at a Boston area hospital, the recruiter for clerical jobs noted that managers often locate candidates on their own and refer them to Human Resources. And, indeed, a supervisor of clericals related:

> If I have a position for an ambulatory practice secretary, then they should send me somebody that they think their qualifications fits that. Doesn't always happen that way, but I also do sort of go through the back door and sort of get résumés on my own and I interview and if I like them then I send them to Human Resources.

She went on to state that her most effective recruiting source is 'a referral from people I know', and that racial diversity is not a high priority. In fact, she made disparaging remarks about the self-presentation and skills of nonwhite secretaries.

At another uniformed public agency, a manager observed: 'The process by which [location] gets its [uniformed public servants] is so convoluted and archaic that we tend to draw from those areas where there are a larger number of people who share the knowledge of how to get that job' – meaning the neighborhoods where incumbent workers live. In this case, complex formal procedures benefit those who learn about the procedures via informal means. The same manager revealed that the agency's cadet program has become an alternate access route to jobs, 'a route that becomes subverted as a way around affirmative action, to be quite honest. Yes, it was done so that, again – this is very confidential – it is a way to have politically connected people get appointed a cadet and bypass the veteran/nonveteran and affirmative action standards'.

In the worst case, the formality of the process is simply subverted. A large Detroit manufacturer has been administering a skills test aimed at 11th grade proficiency in math and language. A supervisor admitted (off the record – when the tape recorder had been shut off) that some time previously, when mostly white men were hired, supervisors would give test answers to people they wanted to hire.

In less blatant cases, some discretion appears to be injected into a formalized screening process. The manager at a public sector university bookstore described the process by which candidates reach him via a very formalized interview and testing process.

> *Respondent:*   Individuals go for a written exam and those that pass the exam go for interviews from a panel. [The supervisor is then given a ranked list of three candidates.]
> *Interviewer:*   Is that a constraint, a problem?
> *R:*   Yes, it is a problem, but it is a solution to a larger problem and therefore I think it is an acceptable problem. If I were a private business and I wanted to hire somebody I would just hire somebody. I can't do that so what I have to do is I have to influence to the best of my ability the oral examinations, and make sure that the panel that's being assembled reflects my values. So it just means that I have to jump through a few more hoops. It does not impede my ability to get a quality staff. It just means I have to play the game a little bit more. I have been able to influence the panels.

Waldinger and Lichter (2003) and Waldinger (1997) used in-depth interviewing to learn about employers' use of immigrant labor in the Los Angeles metropolitan area. During 1992–4, they interviewed hiring managers in 228 establishments spread across six industries: printing, furniture manufacturing, hospitals, departments stores, hotels and restaurants. From these interviews they extracted a very textured analysis of the status of immigrants at the low end of the labor market.

Waldinger and Lichter found that, particularly for less-skilled jobs, employers seek workers with the attitudinal characteristics that Moss and Tilly called 'soft skills'. Since low-level jobs do not justify extensive and expensive screening, employers use categorical generalizations about ethnicity, gender and immigrant status to choose the most 'appropriate' worker for a particular job. They favor immigrants for 'bad' jobs at the bottom of the ladder because recent arrivals bring two important assets. First, newcomers' dual frame of reference leads them to judge jobs in the United States by comparison with opportunities back in their home countries, thus mustering enthusiasm for jobs that natives disdain (see also Piore, 1979). Second, immigrants develop dense social networks to facilitate settlement in a new place. Such networks help employers to recruit and train new employees, and to integrate them smoothly into the social process of work. Once network-linked immigrants have built up a critical mass within a workplace, they often wield the power – whether the employer likes it or not – to gain access to promotion and to exclude other groups such as African-Americans, whether passively (for example, via language) or actively.

Despite newcomers' advantages for managers, Waldinger and Lichter (2003) reported that employers often limit their use of immigrant labor, for a number of reasons. One is the balance of power issue just cited. Another is that in certain kinds of jobs, customers are uncomfortable with a workforce too 'different' from them. Monoethnic hiring can also expose businesses to charges of discrimination. Even so, Waldinger and Lichter described a 'double disadvantage' for African-Americans, who 'shar[e] the liabilities of the native-born American worker – that is, a sense of entitlement greater than the employer thinks appropriate – but few of the advantages that accrue to native whites' (p. 17).

In summary, qualitative surveys paint a much richer picture of managerial attitudes and actions than do quantitative surveys, but at the cost of a much smaller sample size. Quantitative surveys serve to distinguish the statistically significant factors that are associated with particular decisions and attitudes of managers, and to estimate the magnitudes of these effects. The in-depth probing that occurs in qualitative surveys provides reasons why the organization factors have the effects they do, allows the researcher to discover new factors and new explanations she did not know before the survey was begun, and gives policymakers more confidence that they understand the laws of motion of the problem they are trying to address.

The critical issues

In the introduction, we noted six important issues that plague surveys of employers: sampling strategy, access, what job to focus on, whom to interview, honesty, and distinguishing between supply and demand. In this section, we elaborate the nature of these problems and indicate how the major establishment studies have addressed them.

Sampling strategy
Sampling strategy involves at least three important choices: geography, sector and sampling source. Face-to-face interviewing virtually necessitates concentration in a narrow geographic area. Even telephone surveys tend to concentrate on one metropolitan area at a time, for a couple of reasons. Multiple time zones complicate the logistics of making calls during business hours. The commercial business directories that typically form the sampling frame of telephone surveys are available on a geographic basis. Although it is certainly technically possible to use the universe of US businesses as a sampling frame, there are over seven million business establishments in the United States (US Census Bureau, 2005), whereas most telephone employer surveys contact a few thousand employers at most. Buying a nationwide database in order to use only a small fraction of that database is a costly and laborious undertaking. Perhaps most importantly, there are many reasons to expect labor markets to vary significantly by region (Malizia and Feser, 1999). Drawing a nationwide sample compels the investigator either to greatly expand the sample size in order to be able to control for regional variation, or simply to accept variation that may confound results for other variables of interest.

Drawing a sample that is broadly representative of all industrial sectors (Kirschenman and Neckerman, 1991; Holzer, 1996; Holzer and Stoll, 2000; Lim, 2002; Marsden, Kalleberg and Knoke, 2000; Moss and Tilly, 2001) offers the attractive feature of generalizability to the entire population. However, it brings serious drawbacks as well. Firm structures, skill requirements, hiring procedures and patterns of discrimination differ markedly across occupations and industries, and aggregating businesses from many such categories muddies these differences. The result is a broad but shallow understanding of the processes at work. Samples limited to a small number of industries and one or a few occupations per industry (Moss and Tilly, 1996; Waldinger and Lichter, 2003) allow more detailed consideration of the dynamics of discrimination in these particular settings. In our estimation, studies based on both sampling strategies are needed.

Establishment surveys derive their sampling frames from two main sources: business directories (including commercially available directories of which the Dun and Bradstreet database is the best known, but also directories in the public domain such as the Yellow Pages) and household surveys. Qualitative investigators, who use smaller samples and are often less concerned about statistical representativeness, tend to use less complete but readily accessible sources such as the Yellow Pages, and often supplement these samples via key informants or snowball sampling (a framework of surveying an individual, and asking that respondent for contacts. These new contacts are surveyed and once more asked for additional names).

Directories make it possible to draw a large sample with minimum cost and effort. Sampling from household surveys (for instance, by asking respondents for their current employer) is far more costly, but offers the advantage of providing linked supply-side and demand-side data. One issue in the choice of directories versus household links is what universe one wants to generalize to. A sample based on a directory will be a sample of the universe of establishments. A sample based on employers reported in a household survey will be a sample of the universe of jobs germane to the population being sampled for the household survey. A simple probability sample of all *establishments* will contain a very large proportion of quite small firms, while a simple probability sample of all *jobs* will contain many very large firms. The two, of course, can be reconciled by stratified sampling if one has the employment size of the firms in the directory, or by weighting the sample statistics.

Both approaches introduce sources of error. Business directories are notoriously uneven, and inevitably underrepresent new or very small businesses. Household respondents may be unable to give information that makes it possible to identify and locate an employer. They may also define the employment relationship differently than the researcher: for instance, employees of a subcontractor or temporary agency may name the company buying their services rather than the agency that is their legal employer. Moreover, although locating a set of employers through a household survey offers the possibility of obtaining a more current sample, in practice the logistics of conducting multiple surveys introduce significant delays. Kalleberg, Marsden, Aldrich and Cassell (1990), and Kalleberg, Knoke, Marsden and Spaeth (1996) discuss the pros and cons of the various strategies for drawing an establishment survey. They argue that the biases introduced by directories are not insurmountable, although the sample in NOS, with which they were associated, was drawn from household responses.

Access
With the exception of the government surveys mentioned earlier, employers are not obligated to respond to surveys. Given the low response rates of mail surveys (Dillman 2000), successful surveys have been conducted by telephone or in person. To convince employers to take part in their telephone surveys, Holzer (1996) and Holzer and Stoll (2000) (two distinct surveys) and Lim (2002) designed short (roughly 30-minute or less) instruments and devoted considerable effort to completing interrupted interviews via follow-up calls. All three surveys attained a response rate of about 70 per cent. Holzer's comparison of the (limited) information available on respondents and non-respondents in the first of his two surveys showed no evidence of non-response bias

(Holzer, 1996, Appendix A). The questionnaire for the NOS took 42 minutes, on average, and the resulting response rate was slightly lower, at 64.5 per cent.

Convincing managers to take part in the longer qualitative surveys has proved more difficult. Kirschenman and Neckerman (1991) obtained a response rate of 46 per cent. Moss and Tilly (2001), seeking interviews with multiple managers per establishment using an instrument that averaged over one hour per interviewee, devoted additional efforts to persuasion. We sent a letter followed by a phone call, and used experts (doctoral students and ourselves), rather than the survey research organization employees employed in telephone surveys, to explain the importance of the study. In the letters and telephone calls, we stressed that the information we needed depended on employer knowledge and insight, and we pursued unresponsive employers for weeks or in some cases even months to attempt to get an explicit yes or no answer. Like Holzer, we obtained a response rate of about two-thirds. In short, the cost in time and effort of gaining access is quite high. One other tactic that has proved useful in establishment surveys is to promise participants early access to research findings.

In none of the surveys did investigators tell respondents that they were studying discrimination. Instead, they described the surveys as examinations of skill, workforce quality and the like – an accurate but incomplete characterization of the goals of the research.

What job
Variety is the spice of labor economics. Jobs differ along any number of dimensions (see, for example, Jencks, Perman and Rainwater, 1988). In particular, there is evidence that employers see some jobs as better suited to certain racial and gender groups than others (Moss and Tilly, 2001). So it is not adequate to ask an employer about hiring in general; questioning must be directed to a particular job or jobs. Kirschenman and Neckerman (1991) and Holzer (1996) each pioneered a protocol for selecting the *sample job* from among the low-skill jobs they were concerned with. Kirschenman and Neckerman asked about the largest job category requiring no more than a high school education. (Waldinger and Lichter, 2003, similarly, asked about the largest category of 'entry-level' positions.) Holzer inquired, instead, about the high-school-or-less position for which the manager last hired. The sample for our qualitative survey (the Multi-City In-Depth Employer Survey) was drawn from the employers in Holzer's survey that were named in the MCSUI household survey, so we inquired about the same sample job. In our earlier qualitative survey, we instead used Kirschenman and Neckerman's criterion of the largest entry level job that does not require any college. The NOS strategy of getting data on three types of jobs has the advantage that one can learn about race and gender patterns in a wider variety of jobs (along with the disadvan-

tage of a longer survey). In linked household–employer surveys, of course, the goal is to ask about the same job that the household respondent described (Marsden, Kalleberg and Knoke, 2000; Hertz, Tilly and Massagli, 2001). In our earlier study (Moss and Tilly, 1996), we asked some large employers about a variety of jobs, forgoing detailed quantitative data on each job, but gaining a stronger sense of how managers view different jobs and the types of candidates most appropriate for them.

Whom to interview
Most workplaces have multiple gatekeepers and multiple policymakers with regard to hiring. Top managers set company policy. In publicly owned companies, stockholders can also register their approval or displeasure with hiring policy. Human resource officers typically take responsibility for recruiting, conducting testing and initial pre-employment interviews, and monitoring compliance with equal employment opportunity law. Additional interviews, and the final hiring decision, usually fall to the immediate supervisor. Even within a department, several managers and supervisors are often involved in decisions about hiring, promotion and firing.

Collectors of establishment data have adopted two distinct strategies in response to this organizational complexity. The NOS directed their questions to the head of personnel, or to the person in charge of hiring (Marsden, Kalleberg and Knoke, 2000). Holzer (1996) used a pre-screener to identify a manager involved in hiring for the sample job, and interviewed that single manager. The idea is that, with large numbers of interviews, divergences between managers in different roles will average out. Moss and Tilly (2001), on the other hand, set out to obtain interviews with a top executive, a human resource official, and a direct supervisor for the sample job. In small businesses, the roles were often combined, and some businesses refused multiple interviews, but we were able to generate an average of two interviews per firm.

We analyzed differences in views about black, Latino, and Asian workers by managerial position, as shown in Table 3.1. We expect a manager's position to matter for a couple of reasons. Top executives, human resource managers and frontline supervisors differ in their degree and type of contact with entry-level workers. They also differ in their objectives and concerns, with top executives more focused on bottom line profit, human resource managers concerned with the ease of recruiting and retaining workers, and supervisors striving for ease of management (Tilly and Tilly, 1998).

The results in Table 3.1 appear to reflect these differences. Top executives, who have the least contact with entry-level workers, were in general least likely to criticize any of the groups of workers. We attribute this to what we call the 'salience effect'. Racial differences are more salient for those who come directly into contact with workers from a variety of racial groups, and

Table 3.1   Variation by position of respondent: percentage of respondents reporting particular perceptions in Moss/Tilly face-to-face interviews

Comments	Executive or owner	Human resources	Supervisor	Total
About blacks				
Blacks have lagging hard skills	16.0	25.0	20.4	20.3
Blacks have lagging interaction skills	9.6	17.4	17.4	14.6
Blacks have lagging motivation	30.4	30.4	37.9	33.4
Black women are better than black men	4.0	4.3	4.5	4.0
Black men are better than black women	0.8	1.1	1.5	1.1
Blacks are better workers	4.0	1.1	0.0	1.7
About Latinos				
Latinos have lagging hard skills	4.0	6.5	6.1	5.4
Latinos have lagging interaction skills	0.8	0.0	2.3	1.1
Latinos have lagging motivation	7.2	3.3	5.3	5.4
Latinos are better workers	16.0	8.7	14.3	13.4
About Asians				
Asians have lagging hard skills	1.6	2.2	1.5	1.7
Asians have lagging interaction skills	0.0	2.2	0.0	0.6
Asians have lagging motivation	0.0	0.0	0.8	0.3
Asians are better workers	7.2	6.5	8.3	7.4
About immigrants				
Immigrants have a stronger work ethic	12.8	7.6	17.4	13.1
	N=125	N=92	N=132	

Source: Moss and Tilly (2001, Table 4.8, p. 133).

they are thus more likely to express opinions about such differences. But another pattern diverges from the salience effect based on degree of contact: the executives were more likely than other managers to describe blacks and Latinos as better workers. Differing managerial concerns may be at work here. In other analyses of the survey results, we found that employers who rated blacks and Latinos better workers tended to pay below-average wages, suggesting that they are praising the willingness of these workers to settle for less. Executives, with more of an overview of the business's environment than other managers, may be particularly aware of these wage issues. On the other hand, personnel managers and supervisors are likely to worry less about keeping wage costs down, and more about dealing with the rough edges of a low-wage workforce.

Human resource managers were more likely than others to grumble about hard skills and interaction skills. This makes sense, since human resource managers, unlike the other two groups, come directly into contact with the entire applicant pool, and screen applicants primarily using interviews (which assess interaction) and tests (which assess hard skills). Finally, frontline supervisors, who must deal day-to-day with motivation issues such as attendance and tardiness, were more sensitive about motivation than the other groups. They more often complained about black workers' motivation, and more often praised immigrants for a strong work ethic. Waldinger and Lichter (2003) reported a somewhat different finding: owners and general managers were more likely to speak forthrightly about ethnic differences, whereas human resource managers more often resisted generalizing (although they also found that the resistance often broke down over the course of an interview of an hour or more).

In addition to highlighting differences in stated perceptions between different types of managers, interviewing multiple managers permits us to determine in how many workplaces at least one of the interviewed managers expressed a particular view. Thus, though only one-third of employers criticized the motivation of black workers, at least one manager expressed such a view at over half of the businesses surveyed.

Honesty

Race and gender differences are controversial topics, and discrimination on either basis is punishable by law. Consequently, it is not surprising that many interviewees get nervous when the subject comes up. This came across clearly in some of the Moss/Tilly interviews:

> *Interviewer:* A number of the people that we have talked to in the area have commented on the differences between black and white workers. Could you comment on that?

Respondent: [whispers inaudible words]
I: But it's confidential.
R: I know, I know. I guess you hear me hedging a little. It just depends on the individuals. But this has been one of our problems. The . . . a lot of it is the . . . and it's
not true, it's not true, blanket . . . definitely it's not, but unfortunately in the majority of the cases we have problems that tend to be minority. I am going to close my
door in case anyone comes down the hall. *(Clerical supervisor at an Atlanta-area
educational institution)*

Other respondents, rather than expressing anxiety, simply gave a safe, pat
answer. Many managers in the Moss/Tilly study replied to questions about
race and gender differences with some version of 'It all depends on the individual.' While some doubtless sincerely hold this belief, we feel reasonably
confident in supposing that for others it was simply a way of parrying the
question.

The setting in which a question about views of different groups is asked,
and the way in which it is asked, can greatly affect the response elicited.
Comparing the outcomes of a series of questions from the Holzer (1996) and
Moss/Tilly (2001) surveys illuminates this point. Holzer initially tried having
managers rate racial and gender groups as potential workers on a scale of 1 to
10. As early survey results came in, he quickly dropped the question, because
employers almost uniformly gave all groups the same rating. (Holzer, personal
communication, 1995). In the final survey, Holzer did pose three sets of questions about attitudes toward women and people of color as employees.

In Holzer's first such set of questions, he asked managers to score the
performance of the last person hired on a scale of 0 to 100, as well as the
performance of an average employee. Holzer computed the ratio of the two,
and averaged the resulting ratios by race–gender group (Table 3.2A). As a
supplementary analysis, we have calculated what proportion of each group
was rated as being above average in performance (Table 3.2B). Several of the
race and gender differences are statistically significant, and some of the differences in the proportions rated as above average are substantial, indicating that
employers rate blacks lower and Asians higher. However, most differences in
proportions are small, and the size of the differences in average ratings, as
documented in Table 3.2A, is small indeed.

Secondly, Holzer queried whether respondents agreed with statements
about the suitability of race and gender groups (as well as 'inner-city' workers, a term freighted with race and class as well as geographic import) for various jobs (Table 3.3). Substantial minorities of respondents answered 'yes' or
'maybe' to the ideas that some jobs are better suited to one gender than the
other, and that inner city residents are inferior workers. But only a tiny
percentage even ventured 'maybe' to the notion that racial groups fit best into
different types of jobs.

*Table 3.2A   Mean performance rating, by race and gender, of last hire
(1.0 = performance of a typical worker)*

White	Black	Latino	Asian	All racial/ethnic groups
Men and women				
1.06	1.04	1.03**	1.05	1.05
Men only				
1.07	1.04*	1.03**	1.07	1.06
Women only				
1.04††	1.04	1.03	1.03	1.04††

Notes: *Significantly different from whites at the 10 per cent level; **significantly different from whites at the 5 per cent level; ††significantly different from men at the 5 per cent level.

Source: Moss and Tilly (2001, Table 4.1, p. 92).

Third, ethnocentrism questions asked whether the firm's customers or workers, or managers of other businesses in the industry, prefer to deal with their own ethnic group (Table 3.4). Responses to the last question are particularly

*Table 3.2B   Percentage of each race and gender group falling at or above
the stated 'average' performance, for last hire*

White	Black	Latino	Asian	All racial/ethnic groups
Men and women				
72.5	68.5*	68.5	80.6*	71.7
Men only				
71.0	69.5	66.1	81.2	70.2
Women only				
73.6	67.5**	72.1	79.8	62.9††

Notes: *Significantly different from whites at the 10 per cent level; **significantly different from whites at the 5 per cent level; ††significantly different from men at the 5 per cent level.

Source: Calculated by authors using Multi-City Telephone Employer Survey

Table 3.3   Employer generalizations about job performance by race, gender, and inner city residence

Some tasks are performed better by men, others by women	
Yes	18.1%
Maybe	2.0%
No	79.9%

Some tasks are performed better by members of some ethnic or racial groups	
Yes	4.3%
Maybe	0.9%
No	94.8%

On average, inner city residents are weaker job applicants or employees	
Yes	16.1%
Maybe	4.2%
No	79.8%

Note: Within each panel, each column totals to 100%; 'Don't know' and refusal responses omitted.

Source: Moss and Tilly (2001, Table 4.2, p. 93).

noteworthy, since this 'third person' estimate comes in much higher than the proportion who actually agreed that racial differences matter in Table 3.3 (though of course all of these employers could in principle be describing the same 4 per cent who answered affirmatively in Table 3.3).

These results reveal a number of things. Employers are resistant to making general statements about race and gender differences. They are more apt to

Table 3.4   Percentage of employers reporting ethnocentrism by customers, employees, other employers

Customers prefer to deal with employees of their own race or ethnic group	19.7
Employees prefer other employees of their own race or ethnic group	23.2
Other employers in your business prefer employees of their own race or ethnic group	21.4
Any of the types of ethnocentrism	31.6

Source: Moss and Tilly (2001, Table 4.3, p. 94).

express negative views via ratings of individuals from a particular race or gender group, and more apt still to attribute negative perceptions to other employers. This is particularly true with regard to evaluations of people of color: the race question remains radioactive in the United States.

Contrast all of these responses with those from Moss and Tilly's (2001) in-depth interviews, conducted with a representative subset of Holzer's (1996) sample (Table 1; refer to 'Total' column). Clearly the in-depth interview method induces more negative assessments of black workers than any of the telephone survey formulations: assessments that we regard as less guarded and more honest. Twenty per cent of respondents rated blacks' hard skills worse; 15 per cent said they have worse interaction skills, and 33 per cent reported worse motivation on the part of blacks. In total, 46 per cent of respondents stated one of these negative perceptions. Why the big difference? In part, of course, because the longer interview format allows more time to discuss the subject of race. But more important are the face-to-face setting and the semi-structured design that encourages respondents to tell their story in their own words, and permits interviewers to drop unproductive lines of questioning and reapproach them in a different way. These features heighten the rapport between interviewee and interviewer, and bolster the respondent's comfort level.

While qualitative interviewing appears to elicit more complete and accurate statements from employers, sophisticated statistical analysis makes it possible to demonstrate the significance of even small differences in ranking detected by a quantitative survey. In the survey Lim (2002) analyzed, respondents were asked to rate five groups (Whites, Asian Americans, Blacks, Hispanics, Immigrants) on a scale from 1 to 7 (1 is best, 4 is average) on three qualities, (hard workers/not hard workers, good work attitude/bad work attitude, reliable/not reliable). These qualities correspond to the types of 'soft' skills in the Moss and Tilly studies. As with the Holzer survey, the majority of employers rate all groups as average: in this case 60–70 per cent of employers rate all groups in all dimensions as average. Almost 90 per cent of employers rate all groups as average or above average. This is a higher percentage than what we report in Table 3.2B, but is certainly consistent with the pattern that telephone surveys tend not to elicit negative comments on the work qualities of race, ethnic or gender groups. But, as in the Holzer survey, some employers do voice negative views. Lim used a non-parametric test (Wilcoxon signed rank test) on the median responses and found that blacks are consistently (and statistically significantly) ranked below other groups, and Asian Americans are ranked above other groups with statistical significance. The results for other groups were mixed.

Lim then used an innovative statistical model known as the 'exploded logit' to analyze the factors that distinguish the small minority of employers that break rank and rate some groups differently than they rate other groups, and the factors that influence the rankings that those employers give to different groups. Respondents who voiced differential assessments come from larger organizations, organizations with more formal structures and procedures, and organizations with more diverse workforces. The race or ethnicity of the employer is not related to the likelihood of a differential judgment of different groups, however. The analysis of the rankings cements the findings from the non-parametric tests. The only factor consistently related to the way employers rate different groups is the group from which the respondent comes: the rating of a group is higher if the respondent occupies the same group (a finding also reported by Moss and Tilly, 2001). This, presumably, reflects some ethnic loyalty, but may also result from the fact that 80 per cent of the employers are white and whites are rated relatively favorably.

Distinguishing between supply and demand
A critical question is whether negative employer perceptions of the skills of workers of color represent stereotypes or simply reflect true average skill differences. That is, how can we distinguish between supply differences (differences in skill) and demand differences (in particular, discrimination)? Holzer (1996) took some important first steps. To start with, he controlled for the distance from black populations in predicting whether a black person gets hired. And because he gathered information on the demographic composition of those in applicant pools as well as those hired, he was able to calculate the odds that an applicant from a given group gets hired. He found that blacks' odds of getting hired are lower than those of other racial groups. Particularly noteworthy is the fact that black men and women are even less likely to be hired in the suburbs, even though the skill requirements of suburban jobs are lower, a finding that he interprets as evidence for discrimination. Holzer and Stoll (2000) replicated this finding. Still, these findings do not bear directly on evaluating employer attitudes.

One approach would be to gather data from both sides of the labor market by linking data on the workers with the establishment survey data. This approach is not particularly helpful in sizing up the accuracy of statements about the average member of a group, since those statements are usually intended to apply to the general population or to applicants; if a firm's screening processes are effective, group members who have obtained a job will be better than the average member of that group. But linked data can provide a check on employers' ratings of individual workers.

In practice, such links involving quantitative data typically have limited usefulness because of narrow skill measurements on the supply side, and employers' caution (as noted above) about making honest evaluations on the demand side. Consequently, researchers have generally used linked data simply to provide an added control in estimating the determinants of workers' earnings or the likelihood of workers having received a promotion. Braddock and McPartland (1987) surveyed the employers of respondents to the National Longitudinal Survey–Youth. They documented the importance of networks in racial hiring outcomes, and examined the connection between the job's qualifications and the probability of hiring a black worker (though the latter analysis overlooked the distinction between the characteristics of the applicant pool and those of workers who were hired). Hertz, Tilly and Massagli (2001) used linked data from the Multi-City Study of Urban Inequality (including Holzer's employer survey data) to control for supply-side human capital variables as well as organizational characteristics. They found that, after controlling for all of these variables, women of all racial groups, as well as blacks, Latinos and Asians of both genders, started out with a lower wage than their counterparts (men or whites). Wage *growth* over time spent with a single employer was also lower for women and for Latino men and Asian women. Hertz *et al.* also compared employers' stated qualifications for the job with workers' actual qualifications, to determine whether workers of particular groups are more likely to be overqualified or underqualified. The results were mixed, but did indicate that black men and Asians of both genders were disproportionately likely to hold a college degree in jobs where it was not required.

Qualitative establishment surveys rarely provide data on the relevant applicants or workers (the Moss/Tilly study attempted to create such a link, but resulted in too small a number of linked cases for statistical analysis) and, in any case, the relevant comparison is with a broader population of potential workers, so it is not possible to compare directly employer perceptions with reality. We concluded that employer views of blacks as worse workers, immigrants as harder workers, and so on, were a mixture of accurate perceptions, cultural gaps and stereotypes (Moss and Tilly, 2001, ch. 4). The evidence for stereotypes includes the extreme and sweeping nature of some descriptions of racial differences, such as statements describing black men categorically as 'lazy' or 'scary'. Also pointing toward prejudice are commentaries by other managers who described smaller differences, in some cases denying that the differences had a significant impact on job performance, and charged that their peers held stereotypes. One particularly striking instance is the difference in urban and suburban employers' assessments of whether crime poses a problem for employers doing business in the inner city. Suburban employers were twice as likely as their central city counterparts to mention crime as a problem for inner city businesses (Moss and Tilly, 2001, Table 5.4, p. 173). Presumably this reflects an exaggerated view of urban dangers based on media images rather than actual experience. Also striking was the fact that, whereas some suburban businesses stated that they rarely or never received black applicants because of their location, other, nearby, businesses offering similar jobs had substantial black workforces (Moss and Tilly, 2001; Turner, 1997).

We also put forward a proposition that tends to subvert the attempt to distinguish between skills and discrimination: 'soft' or social skills themselves package together skill and discrimination (Moss and Tilly, 1996, 2001). The ability to interact well with customers, coworkers, and supervisors depends on these other people's attitudes and actions toward the worker in question – not just the worker's own, independently formed attitudes. And motivation depends critically on context (pay, treatment, and so on), not just on values inhering to the individual. More broadly, sociologists have argued that defining job requirements in terms of individual knowledge greatly oversimplifies the requisites for successful job performance (Vallas, 1990; Darrah, 1994). In particular, Charles Darrah noted that in most work contexts successful performance depends crucially on a set of relationships with other workers and managers.

One final piece of evidence useful for assessing employers' stated views is the connection between these views and whom the employers actually hire. One might expect that employers criticizing black skills would be less likely to hire blacks, but we found the opposite to be true: negative statements about the African American workforce were positively correlated with black hiring (Moss and Tilly, 1995, 2001). One possible interpretation of this result is that those with African–American employees are more aware of the actual average skill gaps between racial groups. Our reading of the interview data suggests a different interpretation, based on what we call the salience effect (see above). Those who employ significant numbers from a range of racial groups are more apt to think about racial differences concretely; they feel qualified to comment on such differences and are less likely to resort to formulaic responses such as 'It all comes down to the individual', which were relatively common among our respondents.

An alternative to assessing the validity and impact of employers' views directly is to examine group differences in the typical path to hiring and promotion. A number of investigators have generated such indirect evidence, as we have discussed above. Baldi and McBrier (1997) used the linked NOS–GSS data to demonstrate that whites and blacks follow different paths to advancement. Drentea (1998) used the NOS–GSS linked data base to study the relation between the job search methods used by the GSS individual, and the resulting job situation of the individual in the organization, particularly the degree of gender segregation in the resulting job. Similarly, Moss and Tilly (2001), analyzing Holzer's survey data, found that formal recruiting and screening methods generally increased the odds of blacks applying and getting the job. Waldinger and Lichter (2003), and to some extent Moss and Tilly (2001), documented that network hiring for low level jobs most often draws in recent immigrants rather than African-Americans. Thus the difficulties in separating demand from supply do not imply that evidence for discrimination is lacking.

In summary, using employer surveys to understand discrimination confronts a variety of obstacles and tradeoffs. Over the last ten years, researchers have deployed a variety of creative strategies to lessen these problems. While challenges remain, these do not diminish the significant advantages of demand-side surveys as a tool for studying employment discrimination.

Conclusion

Research using employer surveys has significantly advanced our understanding of discrimination in the labor market, beyond what we have learned and can learn from household surveys. Establishment surveys offer a unique and important window on processes of employment discrimination. By shedding light on employer perceptions, policies and actions, they provide information that is not otherwise available. Both quantitative and qualitative surveys have been fruitful: quantitative surveys because they allow statistical analysis, and qualitative ones because they provide more in-depth and in some cases more accurate data. Several contributions from the analyses of qualitative and quantitative employer surveys stand out:

- The extent, nature and consistency of negative attitudes towards minority, particularly black, employees and potential workers. This is most clear in the qualitative surveys, but is also evident in the quantitative surveys done by Holzer and reported upon by Lim.
- The ranking by employers of different groups of workers on both hard and soft skills. Blacks are consistently at the bottom across the qualitative surveys of Kirschenman and Neckerman, both of the Moss and Tilly surveys and the quantitative survey reported on by Lim.
- The important role of formality. Employing organizations with formal job structures, formal recruiting methods and formal screening methods provide more employment opportunity for minorities, have less occupational segregation of women and generate more promotions for women and for blacks.
- The problem is not just race or gender, pure and simple. For example, race matters, but it matters in combination with biased perceptions and attitudes about, as well as the reality of, skill and space. The debate about whether labor market differences are primarily due to market forces acting on differences in skill (educational quality), information (networks) and access (spatial barriers) on the one hand or to racial and gender discrimination on the other probably cannot be resolved with data on households. The employer surveys have shown how attitudes, social and formal systems and procedures with organizations interact with race, skill and spatial location to generate differences in labor market outcomes.

Establishment surveys continue to hold untapped potential for understanding processes of discrimination. One important extension of the technique would be to use in-depth interviewing (which has been employed primarily to understand racial discrimination) to examine *gender* segregation and discrimination. Another direction for future work would be to do longitudinal surveys. Most of what has been inferred from quantitative employer surveys has made implicit dynamic assumptions based on cross-sectional data. It would be very informative to follow a panel of firms with either periodic quantitative or qualitative surveys to see whether changes in size, procedures, regulatory enforcement, attitudes, labor supply or product demand have the kinds of effects that we and others have inferred from the cross-sectional data. While securing acceptance of repeated surveys might prove difficult, the payoffs would be significant. In addition, more employer surveys focused on gender discrimination would help to fill a current gap in discrimination research.

Employer surveys do bump up against a number of difficulties. Perhaps the two least tractable obstacles are those of employer honesty and the question of separating labor supply and demand. The issue of honesty arises most sharply in asking employers to state their views of racial or gender groups, although it also comes up in other contexts such as the discussion of employee skills. Aware both of the social desirability of certain responses and of the illegality of certain other responses, employers tailor their answers. In-depth, qualitative interviewing techniques mitigate this problem, but only to some extent, and at the cost of much smaller sample sizes.

Separating supply (group differences in average worker skills) from demand (discriminatory attitudes and actions toward particular groups) is a challenge in all analyses of discrimination. Steps toward addressing this problem using employer surveys have been helpful, but incremental. Although the evidence from establishments points to stereotyping and discrimination, it does not provide a smoking gun – actual evidence of discrimination. Analyses linking employer with household data in order to measure both supply and demand sides have been informative, but not conclusive. Gathering evidence for differing systems of hiring and advancement for different groups offers one way out of this dilemma.

Despite these difficulties, establishment surveys represent a valuable tool for analyzing employment discrimination. Employer surveys focusing on discrimination are relatively new, and innovation in the survey techniques employed continues to yield dividends of knowledge. Talking to employers holds great promise for revealing more about labor market discrimination.

References

Abowd, John, John Haltiwanger and Julia Lane (2001), 'From workshop floor to workforce clusters', report to the Sloan Foundation, US Census Bureau.
Achatz, Juliane, Jutta Allmendinger and Thomas Hinz (2000), 'Sex segregation in organizations:

a comparison of Germany and the US', paper presented at the American Sociological Association 2000 Meeting in Washington, DC, 12–16 August.

Andersson, Fredrik, Harry J. Holzer and Julia I. Lane (2005), *Moving up or Moving on: Who Advances in the Low-Wage Labor Market?* New York: Russell Sage Foundation.

Baldi, Stéphane and Debra Branch McBrier (1997), 'Do the determinants of promotion differ for blacks and whites?', *Work and Occupations*, **24**, 478–97.

Bielby, William T. and James N. Baron (1984), 'A woman's place is with other women: sex segregation within organizations', in Barbara F. Reskin (ed.), *Sex Segregation in the Workplace: Trends, Explanations, Remedies*, Washington, DC: National Academy Press, pp. 27–55.

Braddock, Jomills Henry and James M. McPartland (1987), 'How minorities continue to be excluded from equal employment opportunities: research on labor market and institutional barriers', *Journal of Social Issues*, **43**(1), 5–39.

Darrah, Charles (1994), 'Skill requirements at work: rhetoric vs. reality', *Work and Occupations*, **21**, 64–84.

Dillman, Don A. (2000), *Mail and Electronic Surveys*, New York: Wiley.

Drentea, Patricia (1998), 'Consequences of women's formal and informal job search methods for employment in female-dominated jobs', *Gender and Society*, **12**, 321–38.

Harkess, Shirley and Carol Warren (1994), 'The good worker: race and gender in a 1970s Southern city', *Sociological Perspectives*, **37**(2), 269–92.

Hertz, Thomas, Chris Tilly and Michael Massagli (2001), 'Linking the Multi-City Study's household and employer surveys to test for race and gender effects in hiring and wage setting', in Alice O'Connor, Chris Tilly and Lawrence Bobo (eds), *Urban Inequality: Evidence from Four Cities*, New York: Russell Sage Foundation, pp. 407–43.

Holzer, Harry J. (1996), *What Employers Want: Job Prospects for Less Educated Workers*, New York: Russell Sage Foundation.

Holzer, Harry J. and Michael A. Stoll (2000), 'Employer demand for welfare recipients by race', JCPR working paper 197, Northwestern University.

Jencks, Christopher, Lauri Perman and Lee Rainwater (1988), 'What is a good job? A new measure of labor-market success', *American Journal of Sociology*, **93**(6), 1322–57.

Jenkins, Richard (1986), *Racism and Recruitment: Managers, Organisations, and Equal Opportunity in the Labor Market*, New York: Cambridge University Press.

Johnson, Charles S (1930), *The Negro in American Civilization*, New York: Holt, Rinehart and Winston.

Kalleberg, Arne L. and Barbara F. Reskin (1995), 'Gender differences in promotion in the United States and Norway', *Research in Social Stratification and Mobility*, **14**, 237–64.

Kalleberg, Arne L., David Knoke, Peter V. Marsden and Joe Spaeth (1996), *Organizations in America: Analyzing their Structures and Human Resource Practices*, Thousand Oaks, CA: Sage Publications.

Kalleberg, Arne L., Peter V. Marsden, Howard E. Aldrich and James W. Cassell (1990), 'Comparing organizational sampling frames', *Administrative Science Quarterly*, **35**, 658–88.

Kasinitz, Philip and Jan Rosenberg (1996), 'Missing the connection: social isolation and employment on the Brooklyn waterfront', *Social Problems*, **43**, 180–96.

Kirschenman, Joleen (1991), 'Gender within race in the labor market', paper presented at the Urban Poverty and Family Life Conference, Chicago, 10–12 October.

Kirschenman, Joleen and Kathryn M. Neckerman (1991), ' "We'd love to hire them, but . . .": the meaning of race for employers', in Christopher Jencks and Paul E. Peterson (eds), *The Urban Underclass*, Washington, DC: Brookings Institution, pp. 203–32.

Lane, Julia, Philip Moss, Hal Salzman and Chris Tilly (2003), 'Too many cooks? Tracking internal labor market dynamics in food service with case studies and quantitative data', in Eileen Appelbaum, Annette Bernhardt and Richard Murnane (eds), *Low-Wage America: How Employers Are Reshaping Opportunity in the Workplace*, New York: Russell Sage Foundation.

Lee, Gloria and Ray Loveridge (eds) (1987) *The Manufacture of Disadvantage: Stigma and Social Closure*, Philadelphia: Open University Press.

Lim, Nelson (2002), 'Who has more soft skills? Employers' subjective ratings of work qualities of racial and ethnic groups', Labor and Population Program working paper series 02-10, RAND Institute, Santa Monica, CA.

Malizia, Emil and Edward Feser (1999), *Understanding Local Economic Development*. New Brunswick, NJ: Rutgers University, Center for Urban Policy Research.

Marsden, Peter V., Arne L. Kalleberg and David Knoke (2000), 'Surveying organizational structures and human resource practices: The National Organizations Study', in Robert T. Golembiewski (ed.), *Handbook of Organizational Behavior*, 2nd edn, New York: Marcel Dekker.

Moss, Philip and Chris Tilly (1995), 'Skills and race in hiring: quantitative findings from face-to-face interviews', *Eastern Economic Journal*, **21**(3), 357–74.

Moss, Philip and Chris Tilly (1996), ' "Soft" skills and race: an investigation of black men's employment problems', *Work and Occupations*, **23**(3), 252–76.

Moss, Philip and Chris Tilly (2001), *Stories Employers Tell. Race, Skill, and Hiring in America*, New York: Russell Sage Foundation.

Neckerman, Kathryn M. and Joleen Kirschenman (1991), 'Hiring strategies, racial bias and inner city workers', *Social Problems*, **38**(4), 801–15.

Piore, Michael (1979), *Birds of Passage*, Cambridge: Cambridge University Press.

Reskin, Barbara F. and Debra Branch McBrier (1999), 'Why not ascription? Organizations' employment of male and female managers', *American Sociological Review*, **65**(2), 210–33.

Sharpe, Rochelle (1993), 'Losing ground: in latest recession, only blacks suffered net employment loss', *Wall Street Journal*, 14 September, A1, A12–13.

Tilly, Chris and Charles Tilly (1998), *Work under Capitalism*, Denver, CO: Westview Press.

Tomaskovic-Devey, Donald (1993), *Gender and Racial Inequality at Work: The Sources and Consequences of Job Segregation*, Ithaca, NY: ILR Press.

Tomaskovic-Devey, Donald and Sheryl Skaggs (1999), 'Organizational processes and gender segregated employment', *Research in Social Stratification and Mobility*, **17**, 139–72.

Turner, Susan (1997), 'Barriers to a better break: employer discrimination and spatial mismatch in metropolitan Detroit', *Journal of Urban Affairs*, **19**(2), 123–41.

US Census Bureau (2005), *County Business Patterns* (web site): http://www.census.gov/epcd/cbp/view/cbpview.html.

US Department of Commerce (annual), *County Business Patterns*, Washington, DC: US Government Printing Office.

Vallas, Stephen (1990), 'The concept of skill: a critical review', *Work and Occupations*, **17**, 379–98.

Waldinger, Roger (1997), 'Black/immigrant competition reassessed: new evidence from Los Angeles', *Sociological Perspectives*, **40**, 365–86.

Waldinger, Roger and Michael I. Lichter (2003), *How the Other Half Works: Immigration and the Social Organization of Labor*, Berkeley, CA: University of California Press.

Appendix
Interview instrument used in the Multi-City Study of Urban Inequality In-depth Qualitative Employer Survey, 1994–6 (Moss and Tilly, 2001)

Greater [Atlanta/Boston/Detroit/Los Angeles] workforce study confidential interview
Principal investigators:
Philip Moss
Chris Tilly
University of Massachusetts Lowell

Cover sheet
Case ID:
Firm name:
Firm address:
Firm phone:
Respondent's name:
Respondent's title:
Interviewer:
Date:
Time began:
Time ended:

Questionnaire
1)   Tell me what you do here, and a little about how you got to this position.
     [ ] Chronology
     [ ] Role in hiring
     [ ] Area of responsibility (how many sites are you responsible for, etc.)
2)   Can you tell me a little about the firm? What kind of firm is it and what
     does it do/produce?
     [ ] Age, history of firm
     [ ] Ownership
     [ ] Public/private/non-profit/government/franchise
     [ ] Minority owned?
          Minority group: _____
     [ ] Female owned?
     [ ] Multi-site or not; what's at this site
     [ ] Product(s)
     [ ] Markets
     [ ] Main customers
     [ ] How has your business been doing recently? (Expanding, contract-
     ing?)

2a)   Can you tell me how many people work here, first a total, and then looking at occupations?

[ ] Number of employees

[ ] Is occupation breakdown as on face sheet? (If not, get)

[ ] Is % unionized as on face sheet? (if any, who?)

[ ] What is the job title for _____? (Find sample job
on face sheet)

[ ] Number employed in _____ sample job.

[ ] What do these workers do? (Link skills/qualities to tasks)

[ ] Entry wage in _____sample job.

[ ] Get health ins.? How much must employees pay?

3)   We'd like to get a picture of who works here. Can you give me a description of the race, gender and age of the workers in the firm (as best you can)?
(Leave worksheet if necessary)

	White	Black	Hispanic	Asian	Other	Total
Men						
Women						
Total						

Total in firm _____

Number/per cent under 25 _____ Average age _____

of Hispanics, main groups _____

of Asians, main groups_____

4)   Could I get the same breakdown for_____ (the sample
job)?

	White	Black	Hispanic	Asian	Other	Total
Men						
Women						
Total						

Total in _____(sample job) _____

Number/per cent under 25 _____ Average age _____

of hispanics, main groups _____

of asians, main groups _____

[ ] How did it turn out this way? (_____sample job only)

What is particular to your firm or hiring practices that produced this
breakdown?

[ ] Compare to other firms (typical for industry – get creative)

[ ] Have there been changes in the composition of _____
(the sample job) over the past 5 to 10 years? What kinds of changes?

5)   Tell me about _____ (city) as a place to do business.

[ ] Workforce issues? (including entry level)

[ ] How easy or difficult is it to get qualified workers? Do you have
sufficient numbers of qualified applicants?

[ ] What area do you mainly recruit workers from? (including entry
level)

[ ] Quality and availability of [_____sample job] specifically

[ ] Advantages and disadvantages of the area (as relevant to location
choice)

[ ] If mentions other areas, ask to compare

[ ] Always been here?
If not:

[ ] Where did you move from? When?

[ ] Why did you move? (Find out push vs. pull)

[ ] Thinking of moving? Where? Why? When?

6)   We've heard some employers say that cities like Boston or
_____ , especially the inner city, are difficult places to do
business. Do you agree? What do you think might be obstacles or problems with running a business in the inner city?

[ ] Let them answer open-ended first . . .

[ ] People/workforce quality in inner city

[ ] Any unwillingness of workers to go to particular locations

[ ] Quality, availability of [sample job] specifically

[ ] What areas do you think of as the 'inner city'?

7)   We've talked to a lot of employers who have problems getting and keeping a satisfactory workforce. What are the main problems you face with
your workforce, thinking specifically about _____(sample
job)?

[ ] Skills

[ ] Work ethic

[ ] Attitude

[ ] Language

[ ] In what way is it a problem?

[ ] Ability to communicate well

[ ] Any problems with workers getting along

[ ] What is turnover?

[ ] What is your single biggest problem?

[ ] How do you deal with that?

8)   Have you seen any changes over the last 5 to 10 years in the quality of the entry level workforce in general?
      [ ] Skills, attitude, work ethic, communication/getting along?
      [ ] Clarify labor supply (Who's out there) v. labor demand (what the firm needs)
9)   What skills and qualities do you look for in a worker for _____ (sample job)?
      [ ] Skills, attitude, work ethic, education
      [ ] What is most important thing you look for?
      [ ] Why are these skills/qualities needed in this job (if not obvious)
10)   Have there been changes in the skills and qualities you look for in a worker? What are those changes?
      [ ] Skills, attitude, work ethic, education, communication/getting along
          Why has there been a change in what you look for?
      Prompt about change in these areas even if say no change in skills or qualities:
      [ ] Technology
      [ ] Organization of work (teams, etc)
      [ ] Competitive pressure
      If say change, prompt for these reasons:
      [ ] Who workers have contact with (customers, co-workers)
      [ ] Less able to take a chance on a worker?
      [ ] Have changes in the types of people applying for jobs led you to change what you look for in a potential worker?
11)   We've talked to quite a few other managers who say there are significant differences between different sorts of workers: blacks, whites, Hispanics and Asians; men and women; natives and immigrants. What do you think? Have you seen any differences along these lines?
      If hesitate, can acknowledge this is difficult. Give examples if needed (skill, work ethic, communication).
      [ ] Differences in turnover?
      Encourage to elaborate on each of these comparisons, e.g. 'Do you see these differences among men as well as women?'
      When elaborate into a story, use:
      [ ] White, black, Hispanic, Asian *men*
      [ ] White, black, Hispanic, Asian *women*
      [ ] White men vs white women (etc.)
      [ ] Women (in general) vs men (in general)
      [ ] Urban vs suburban
      [ ] Younger vs older
      Last ditch: we do know from other research that blacks and other minorities are doing badly in the labor market. Why do you think that is?

[ ] Are these differences you see among your applicants, in your current workforce, or more generally?

[ ] How do these differences play out in the workplace? Examples?

[ ] Have you seen these differences change over time?

[ ] Do other people who hire or supervise in your firm agree with this assessment, or are there differences of opinion?

12) Many employers have told us that the way jobs and skill needs are changing, differences between different groups of workers, such as between white, black and Hispanic workers, actually matter more than they used to. Do you find this to be true?

[ ] Get specifics and examples

[ ] Changes in skill requirements? What kind of skills?

[ ] What about gender differences?

13) Given your skill needs, tell me how you get your workers, especially your _____ (sample job) workers.

[ ] Describe hiring process

[ ] Keep track of who's involved at each step. Who makes each screening/hiring decision?

[ ] Recruiting methods (newspapers, referrals, etc.)

[ ] Which recruiting method do most of the hires come from?

[ ] Interviewing

[ ] Other screening (entry requirements, tests)

[ ] Ask for references from applicants?

[ ] Check references?

[ ] What part of the process is most important in deciding?

[ ] Recent changes in any of this?

14) We've talked about a wide range of workforce issues. Looking into the future, where do you think your company is heading, and what are the workforce issues that are going to be more important?

[ ] Make sure they address workforce issues

[ ] Issues likely to affect (or be affected by) race/gender mix?

15) Is there anything we didn't talk about today that you think we should address?

16) (Ask for company brochures, and so on)

IO. Interviewer observations

[Complete immediately following the interview]

IO.1. Length of the interview.

IO.2. Were there interruptions? Document these.

IO.3. Who else, if anyone, was present during the interview?

IO.4. Where and under what conditions was the interview conducted?

IO.5. What was the respondent's attitude toward the interview?

IO.6.   Give a full description of the respondent.

IO.7.   Describe the office or setting wherein the interview took place.

IO.8.   Describe observations you may have made about the workers and workplace.

IO.9.   Describe the surroundings in which the establishment is located.

IO.10. Relate your sense of the respondent. Was s/he speaking freely, does s/he act autonomously, were some questions difficult, and so on?

IO.11. Are there any peculiarities one should be aware of, or any comments you wish to make?

4 Discrimination: experimental evidence from psychology and economics

Lisa R. Anderson, Roland G. Fryer and Charles A. Holt

I Introduction

Measuring the intensity and impact of overt racism and discrimination has been the subject of much debate over the twentieth century.[1] Few disagree that historical discrimination and other forms of social ostracism partly explain current disparities on a myriad of economic, social and health related outcomes. Disagreement arises in explaining the underlying reasons behind the discriminatory treatment.

Uncovering mechanisms behind discriminatory actions is difficult because attitudes about race, gender and other characteristics that often serve as a basis for differential treatment are not easily observed or measured. Therefore, laboratory experiments have been particularly useful in the study of discrimination under conditions where experience, perceived status and group identity can be partially measured and controlled. For example, cleverly designed experiments allow one to distinguish the effects of underlying biases in preferences for one's in-group from the effects of information-based forms of discrimination (for example, statistical profiling and social categorization) This chapter surveys laboratory studies of discrimination in psychology and economics.

There is a long tradition of experimental studies in psychology that examine the effects of observed characteristics, like status or group identity, on the way subjects treat others. The division into groupings can be based on survey responses or on observed traits like eye color. If deception is permitted, then the groupings can be random, even though people are told that the groupings are determined by some task or questionnaire. The goal of such manipulations is to determine the extent to which people with high status or of one's own group are treated differently in exercises such as a money division task.

Laboratory experiments in economics also reveal that status affects behavior in some market contexts. A number of economics experiments are motivated by formal equilibrium models in which discrimination arises from self-fulfilling expectations. For example, if workers in one group anticipate being discriminated against, they will be less likely to invest in acquiring skills and, as a result, employers will observe systematic differences in investment decisions. Feedback effects can cause discrimination to become entrenched, as noted by Tajfel (1970):

> For example, economic or social competition can lead to discriminatory behavior; that can then in a number of ways create attitudes of prejudice; those attitudes can in turn lead to new forms of discriminatory behavior that create new economic or social disparities, and so the vicious circle is continued.

These discriminatory equilibria may persist even when the two populations are ex ante identical (for example, Arrow, 1973; Coate and Loury, 1993) and this theoretical possibility can be investigated in the laboratory.

Experiments can also be effective in classroom settings, since the relatively neutral context and commonly shared classroom experience may allow for a more objective discussion of otherwise sensitive issues. In fact, some of the earliest discrimination experiments were done in classroom settings. In response to the 1968 assassination of Martin Luther King, a third grade teacher named Jane Elliott devised a simple classroom exercise to facilitate discussion of discrimination.[2] Students were divided into two groups based on eye color, and it was announced that brown-eyed people would be superior to blue-eyed people that day, and that the roles would be reversed the following day. Ms. Elliott further explained: 'What I mean is that brown-eyed people are better than blue-eyed people. They are cleaner than blue-eyed people. They are more civilized than blue-eyed people. And they are smarter than blue-eyed people.' The brown-eyed children got to sit in the front of the room, to go to lunch first, and to have more time at recess. Blue-eyed students slumped in their chairs, as though they accepted their inferior positions. These behavioral differences were reversed when the roles reversed the next day.

II   Psychology experiments

Psychologists have conducted similar experiments in more controlled settings. The focus is often on the effect of group affiliation towards members of one's own group and members of other groups. The group divisions are selected in the laboratory on the basis of a seemingly 'objective' criterion like whether the length of a line was underestimated. In reality, the division is random. Once people are grouped in this manner, they are asked to split money between two other people, only one of whom is in their group. For example, Vaughan, Tajfel and Williams (1981) divided seven- and eleven-year-old children into 'red' and 'blue' groups based on their preferences for a set of paintings. Neither group was described as being superior to the other. The children were then asked to divide 'some pennies' between other people in their class. All they were told about the others was their group identity (red or blue). They were also told that they would get money from other people making similar decisions. In reality, the money promised to the children was later used to have a class party. The kids in both age categories consistently gave more money to members of their own group. This 'in-group bias' persisted even when the participants were told that the group membership was randomly determined (Billig and Tajfel, 1973).

The effect of group affiliation is less clear when additional focal points like self-interest or attitude similarity are incorporated into this design. In particular, Turner (1978) told a group of 14 to 16-year-old boys that their preferences for paintings would be used to determine groupings. The boys were asked to divide money between themselves and an unidentified other person in the class. The other person's group affiliation had no effect in this context, as self-interested behavior dominated. In a similar study, Diehl (1988) had 13 to 15-year-old high school students perform two classification tasks. First, the students had to estimate the lengths of lines drawn on paper and were told that they were separated into groups of overestimators or underestimators. Second, they completed an attitude questionnaire with the understanding that it could be used to compare their attitudes on a variety of issues with those of others in the group. Subjects were told that they were grouped according to their line length estimation and their responses to the attitude questionnaire, but groupings were actually randomly determined. Finally, subjects were asked to divide money between two other people, who were identified by group (over- or underestimator) and by attitude classification relative to the subject making the allocation decision. Group affiliation only had a strong effect when it was consistent with the attitude similarity classification. In-group members who had been designated as having similar attitudes were awarded more than other in-group members, and were awarded more than members from the other group with similar attitude designations. However, the effect of attitude similarity dominated group affiliation when they conflicted; people with similar attitudes in a different group were given more money than people with dissimilar attitudes in a subject's own group.

Psychologists have also studied in-group bias in situations where there is status associated with group affiliation. Turner and Brown (1978) classified undergraduate students as either 'Arts' or 'Sciences' on the basis of their major course of study. They had them meet in groups of three for a 20-minute discussion of the following statement: 'No individual is justified in committing suicide.' At the end of the discussion, one of the three students made a tape-recorded summary of the group's views. They were told that the purpose of the discussion was to evaluate their 'reasoning skills'. Once the tape was recorded, they were asked to comment on how well they did relative to another group. The same 'other group' tape was played for all of the subjects. Arts students were told that the comparison group was from Sciences, and vice versa. In the status treatment of this study, the experimenter singled out one group (Arts or Sciences) as having better reasoning skills than the other group.

The authors concluded that all subjects were biased in favor of their own group, and that groups identified as superior were more biased in favor of their own group.

Klein and Azzi (2001) replicated this finding in a different environment. They had college students take a trivia quiz, which the students were told would be used to divide people into groups. Actually, all participants were put in the same group, which was announced to be the superior group in one treatment and to be the inferior group in the other. Then participants had to rate the creativity of sentences written by fictitious 'other students'. Before making the ratings, they were told that the other students would receive a reward for a high score and that there was no demonstrated relationship between creativity and scores on the trivia quiz. In this treatment, both inferior and superior groups gave higher scores to people in their own group.

In related research, social psychologists employ experimental techniques to measure discrimination that might arise when individuals sort others into groups, rather than having the groups predetermined by the experimenter. Fundamental to their approach is the important notion of 'social categorization'. As the distinguished social psychologist Gordon Allport (1954) noted, 'the human mind must think with the aid of categories. We cannot possibly avoid this process. Orderly living depends upon it'. Most psychologists agree with this idea. More importantly, there is a long tradition in social psychology that treats discrimination, stereotyping and prejudice as inevitable consequences of social categorization.[3]

Devine (1989) conducted a clever experiment to test whether very subtle factors could influence categorizations. One hundred and twenty-nine students enrolled in an introduction psychology course at Ohio State University participated in the experiment for course credit. Participants took the Modern Racism Scale to determine their prejudice level. Participants were then shown subliminal images (appearing on a computer screen for less than 30 milliseconds) of words associated with the social category 'black' (for example, black, poor, ghetto and negroes) using the stimuli priming method developed by Bargh and Pietromonaco (1982). Subjects were told that the experimenter was interested in how people form impressions. They were asked to read the famous 'Donald paragraph', which is a 12-sentence paragraph that has Donald engaging in ambiguously hostile behaviors like withholding rent until an apartment is painted or demanding money back at a retail store. The results were startling; participants who were given the subliminal images rated Donald as significantly more hostile, and this was true for all prejudice levels. This experiment demonstrates the power of implicit associations and how such associations have been measured.

Categorization and stereotyping also manifest themselves in other ways. There is a growing literature in psychology on racial and ethnic differences in facial recognition. The terms 'cross-race recognition deficit', 'cross-race effect' and 'own-race bias' all describe the frequently observed performance deficit of one ethnic group in recognizing faces of another ethnic group compared with faces of one's own group.[4] In other words, 'they all look alike to me' is a reasonable caricature of how members of one group categorize another.

A large body of literature spanning 30 years provides evidence that people recognize members of their own ethnic group better than members of other ethnic groups.[5] Models of categorization predict that individuals with more inter-group contact will be better at distinguishing subtle features about other groups than individuals with less inter-group contact. There is also substantial evidence in this regard. For example, Meissner and Brigham (2001) report: 'Several studies demonstrate that adolescents and children living in integrated neighborhoods are better at recognizing novel other-race faces than those living in segregated neighborhoods.'[6]

An interesting experiment testing the relationship between contact with other groups and facial recognition is reported in Li, Dunning and Malpass (1998). They demonstrated that white 'basketball fans' were superior to white 'basketball novices' in recognizing black faces. The idea is that basketball fans watch the National Basketball Association games on a regular basis, which provides frequent exposure to black faces, given that a sizable majority of the players are black. Participants were black and white men and women. They were presented with black and white faces on a video monitor. The subjects were informed that they would be tested on their ability to recognize the faces viewed. Black and white basketball fans were equally able to recognize black faces, whereas the white subjects who were not basketball fans performed at a significantly worse level. In recognizing white faces, there was no difference between basketball fans and novices.

In summary, early discrimination experiments generally revealed that subjects were biased in favor of groups designated as being superior and/or similar in some dimension. In addition, there is a long tradition in social psychology of quantifying the prevalence and impact of social categorization on prejudice, stereotyping and discrimination. This experimental literature has demonstrated that subtle cues can influence the way people process information and can bias decision making. A common feature of the studies discussed above is that they were based on experiments with hypothetical incentives. This raises the issue of whether such behavioral patterns would persist in market experiments where participants are also concerned with the financial consequences of their actions.

III   Economics experiments

Some economics experiments follow directly from the psychology literature in the sense that status or group identification is induced by laboratory manipulations such as award ceremonies (Ball *et al.*, 2001). Other experimental economics studies on discrimination are motivated by the large literature on employment discrimination and information economics. The main theories that have been tested experimentally include statistical discrimination (Anderson and Haupert, 1999; Davis, 1987; Fryer, Goeree and Holt, 2001, 2005), asymmetric pair-wise tournaments (Schotter and Weigelt, 1992) and price-preference auctions (Corns and Schotter, 1999). In what follows, we provide a description of these theories and a review of the related experimental papers.

Status and group identification

Ball *et al.* (2001) investigated the impact of status on behavior in a market setting using undergraduates. Demand was induced for buyers by giving them a 'redemption value' for a good that could be acquired through trade. Buyers earned the difference between the redemption value and what they paid for the good. Similarly, sellers were told the cost of supplying the good and that they would earn the difference between the cost and price for which the good was sold. The number of buyers' units was equal to the number of sellers' units. Thus there was a vertical overlap of the supply and demand curves, with a range of market-clearing prices between the sellers' costs and the buyers' values. This overlap makes price indeterminate, which leaves more of a chance of observing the effects of non-economic factors like fairness. Trading took place via a double auction, where sellers could call out 'ask' prices and buyers could call out 'bid' prices. The bid prices tended to increase as buyers outbid each other, and ask prices tended to decline as sellers undercut each other. In this sense, there were two auctions at the same time, with prices rising in one and falling in the other. A trade occurred when these two processes met, that is, when a buyer accepted a seller's ask or a seller accepted a buyer's bid.

Two treatments were used to introduce status in this market context. In the 'earned' status treatment, subjects took a trivia quiz and were told that getting a high score on the quiz earned them a gold star. In the random status treatment, subjects observed as people were randomly picked to receive stars. In both cases, stars were actually awarded randomly and were distributed in a ceremony where non-star people were told to applaud the star people, who were moved to a special seating area. People with stars were buyers in some sessions and sellers in others. Those with stars earned significantly more of the available surplus, regardless of whether they were buyers or sellers or whether the status was earned or not. In addition, males earned more than females.

Ball and Eckel (1996, 1998) used the same method to introduce status (both 'earned' and random) into a bargaining situation known as the ultimatum game. After participants were paired, one person in each pair was chosen to propose a split of money or candy, and the other person was given the chance to accept or reject the proposed split. An acceptance finalized the split, and a rejection resulted in zero earnings for both. When college students were asked to split Hershey's Kisses, a small, chocolate candy, with an anonymous partner, both star and non-star proposers offered more Kisses to respondents with stars. When students had to divide a $10 prize, there was no significant difference in offers made to responders with or without stars. Thus we see that the role of incentives is potentially important in mitigating the effects of discrimination.

Fershtman and Gneezy (2001) also used bargaining games to evaluate the effects of non-economic factors. Instead of inducing group membership in the laboratory, they deliberately recruited people from different ethnic backgrounds. All subjects were Jewish Israeli undergraduates with typical ethnic last names, which were revealed in the experiment so subjects could identify other participants as being either of Ashkenazic or of 'Eastern' origin. They used a 'trust game' in which one person has the option to pass all or part of a money endowment to the other. The money passed is increased by a pre-announced proportion. The responder then decides how much (if any) of this augmented sum to keep and how much to return to the original sender. Trust is measured by the proportion of the endowment that is originally sent to the responder. The authors report a systematic mistrust of men of Eastern origin. There are two possible explanations for this behavior: either people have a preference for lower earnings for the members of this group or the senders fear that the men of Eastern origin will not reciprocate by returning some of the money. These two hypotheses were evaluated using a 'dictator' game, where one person simply decides how much of a fixed endowment of money to keep and how much to give to another person (without augmentation or opportunities for reciprocity). Dictated divisions were not systematically affected by the recipient's ethnic background. The authors concluded that behavior in the trust game was driven by the fear that generosity would not be reciprocated by men of Eastern origin.

Slonin (2004) also uses the trust game to study discrimination. Rather than focusing on ethnic origin, this study looked at gender biases in passing and returning money. When the experimenter matched subjects to play the game, there was little evidence of gender discrimination. However, when subjects could choose to play with a male or a female partner, some biases emerged. Male subjects were significantly more likely to select a female partner and men sent more to women than to men. Similarly, female subjects were significantly more likely to select a male partner and women sent more to men than to women. These biases are not supported by experience-based discrimination since men and women were equally trustworthy in the game.

In conclusion, the effect of status on behavior in economics experiments depends on the origin of the status and the nature of the incentives. In the Ball *et al.* (2001) study with a range of equilibrium prices and real financial incentives, price moved in the direction favored by the high status group independent of whether status was perceived to be earned or randomly awarded. In contrast, Ball and Eckel (1996, 1998) reported that assigning status to one group had no effect on bargaining outcomes in ultimatum games with real financial incentives, although some status effects were observed in experiments involving the division of Hershey's Kisses. Fershtman and Gneezy (2001) reported no discrimination based on ethnicity in a dictator game with financial incentives, but they found that lower amounts of money were passed to individuals in a particular ethnic group in a trust game. They concluded that this discrimination was based on mistrust rather than a desire to lower the earnings for those individuals. Finally, Slonin (2004) found significant gender discrimination in the trust game, but only when subjects could choose to be matched with a male or female partner. Contrary to findings from some labor market studies, male subjects chose female partners more often and made higher offers to females. Similarly, female subjects chose male partners more often and made higher offers to males. In both the market experiments and the ultimatum games, the presence of discrimination affects the distribution of earnings but has no effect on overall welfare. However, the lower amount of money passed to particular individuals in the trust game generates a welfare loss, since passed money is multiplied.

Statistical discrimination
The theory of statistical discrimination has become a valuable tool in the study of many labor market phenomena. Kenneth Arrow (1973) and Edmund Phelps (1972) developed the theory independently. The basic framework relies on the fact that employers do not perfectly observe investments in human capital. For simplicity, it is assumed that workers who invest are 'qualified' and those who do not are 'unqualified'. Conditional on the worker's investment decision, employers observe a noisy signal of the worker's qualification level (that is, an interview or a pre-employment test). Finally, employers decide whether or not to hire the worker on the basis of the signal and other characteristics like race or gender.

Within this framework, Phelps (1972) assumes that the signal emitted by minorities is 'noisier' than that of non-minorities. It follows directly from this assumption that minorities who emit low signals are paid a wage above their majority counterparts, and minorities with relatively high signals are paid below their majority counterparts. In Phelps's model, however, there need not be any discrimination 'on average'. The assumption that it is harder to evaluate the qualifications of some ethnic groups has been questioned. Recognizing this, Arrow (1973) provides an alternative model in which some worker characteristics are endogenous, and an employer's a priori beliefs can be self-confirming.

To see this, consider two groups, As and Bs. Now suppose that an employer has a prior belief that Bs are less likely on average to invest in pre-market human capital relative to As. The signaling technology is imperfect, but qualified workers are more likely to emit a higher signal (for example, to pass a test or make a good impression in an interview). These models typically have an equilibrium in which the employer hires workers with signals that exceed a threshold level that can depend on the worker's group. Since the employer is relatively pessimistic about Bs, the threshold for these workers is higher than that for As. This affects the worker's investment decision: B workers (who are held to a more exacting standard) have less incentive to invest relative to A workers (who are held to a more forgiving standard). This behavior by workers confirms the employer's initial asymmetric beliefs that B workers are less likely to invest. The beauty of Arrow's theory is that the employer's biased initial beliefs are confirmed in equilibrium, even though the populations were ex ante identical.

One issue that arises with statistical discrimination experiments is how these biased perceptions are generated in the laboratory. Obviously, different perceptions may arise from learning and past experiences. For example, past discrimination might limit investment opportunities for one group (Davis, 1987). From an experimental perspective, however, it is also interesting to use two populations with identical ability distributions, since the emergence of discrimination under such conditions would be especially noteworthy.

The earliest economics experiment on this topic is Davis (1987), who studied the effects of the relative sizes of 'majority' and 'minority' populations. The intuition behind the experiment is that if more sample observations are drawn from the majority population, this population is more likely to generate a higher *maximum* observation. If employers tend to focus on the maximal draw from each population, this could result in an employer bias in favor of the larger group. It is not implausible that the best candidates would be more likely to be remembered, since many job searches involve narrowing consideration from a large number of applicants to a final short list. In the baseline treatment, subjects saw random realizations drawn from identical normal distributions of monetary prize values, with about 80 per cent of the draws coming from the 'majority population'. In the final period, subjects were free to decide what proportion of draws would come from each population, so that a bias away from equal numbers of draws from each population could be taken as evidence that one population is perceived as being better on average. Even though the two distributions or draws were identical in this baseline treatment, subjects selected about 60 per cent of the draws from the population that was previously sampled more extensively. This effect was characterized as being 'weak', and was only significant at about a 10 per cent level. A somewhat heavy-handed treatment actually provided subjects with a 'tab' sheet listing the maximum draw from each population for each prior period, and this information seemed to have an effect, raising the percentage of final-period majority population draws to about 70 per cent, a significant increase. This study is interesting in that it suggests a mechanism whereby a bias might arise, even when the two populations are identical. As Davis notes, such a bias would be even stronger in the presence of some underlying inequality.

As was the case in the psychology literature on status and group effects, a number of economics experiments were developed to stimulate class discussion. This approach is especially effective, since participants often come to realize that they are discriminating on the basis of prior experience or statistical knowledge rather than on the basis of a personal bias against one type of person. For example, Anderson and Haupert (1999) used colors ('green' and 'yellow') to identify two types of workers in a classroom exercise. Workers were represented by green or yellow index cards, with productivity numbers written on the back of each card. Subjects played the role of employers who were required to hire a specified number of workers, with some incentive to pick workers with the highest productivities. The participants knew the distributions of productivities for each color, but had to pay an 'interview cost' in order to observe the productivity on a specific card. A stack of 20 cards, ten of each color, was shuffled and presented in sequence, with the requirement that eight workers be hired. For each card, the employer decided whether to interview (pay to observe the productivity), but the decision of whether to hire that worker could be delayed until all interview decisions had been made. In markets where the average productivity was lower for one color, employers tended to hire less of that color. The explanation is that, in the absence of an interview, the employer tends to rely on the population average, which is a type of 'statistical discrimination'. Discrimination against the less productive group of workers was somewhat diminished when the interview cost was reduced, since this allowed employers to search for the most productive workers, regardless of color.

The experiments reported in both Davis (1987) and Anderson and Haupert (1999) have the common feature that differences between the two types of workers are exogenous. As noted above, much of the theoretical literature on statistical discrimination pertains to models in which inter-group differences are endogenously determined by workers' investment decisions. Such models are of interest because of the possibility that systematic productivity differences may arise even when the two groups are ex ante identical. These situations may persist in equilibrium if employers come to expect that members of one group are less likely to invest in skills, and hence tend to offer less attractive job assignments to members of that group. The flip side of this story is that workers from the 'disadvantaged' group anticipate reduced job assignment opportunities and hence tend not to invest, which in turn tends to confirm employer expectations.

The experiments reported in Fryer, Goeree and Holt (2001) were conducted in a setting with endogenously determined worker productivities. Half of the workers were randomly designated as being Purple and the other half were Green. Each worker began a round by observing a randomly determined investment cost. Then workers decided whether or not to invest. The employer observed a test outcome (red or blue), with blue being more likely when the worker invested, as in the Coate and Loury (1993) model. Finally, the employer decided whether or not to hire a worker knowing the worker's color and the test score, but not the investment decision.

One of the treatments for this experiment involved having the investment cost draws for the two types of workers come from different distributions for the first ten rounds and then removing this asymmetry for the final 50 periods. This initial asymmetry was not announced, since subjects were only told that the costs would be 'randomly determined' amounts between $0.00 and $1.00. In fact, the Green workers were drawing from a uniform distribution on [$0.00, $0.50], and the Purple workers were drawing from a uniform distribution on [$0.50, $1.00]. After round ten, all draws were from a uniform distribution on [$0.00, $1.00]. Greens invested more and were hired more often than Purples in the first ten periods in all sessions, but what happened next was quite interesting and surprising. The next several investment cost draws tended to look relatively attractive to the Purples and relatively unattractive to the Greens, so the investment rates surged for the initially disadvantaged Purples and fell for the Greens. In one session, this caused a cross-over effect where the Purples invested more often than Greens and were hired more often for the remaining periods. This reversal of the originally induced inequity also occurred in a classroom experiment (Fryer, Goeree and Holt, 2005).

The initial asymmetry did produce a lasting effect for the session, shown in Figure 4.1. The figure reports ten-period average investment and hire rates for Green and Purples. The period is shown on the horizontal axis, and the switch to symmetric costs is indicated by the vertical dashed line at round ten. The surge in investments by Purples is immediate, as indicated by the dashed line in the left panel of the figure. This increase in the tendency for Purples to invest is not reflected in hiring rates until about ten periods later, since employers are not able to observe the investment decisions of workers who are not hired. Even after employers begin to hire Purple workers more often (around round 20), the investment and hiring rates for Greens remain higher. An analysis of the individual decision sequences indicates that four of the six employers used a color-based strategy. Two of the employers in this session tended to hire Greens with bad signals, but not to hire Purples. Two other employers hired Greens but not Purples when the signals were a mix of good and bad elements. The remaining two employers did not appear to use color in making their decisions. While the data patterns do not conform closely to any theoretical prediction, they are qualitatively similar to the predictions of the Coate and Loury model, with biases in employer hiring that have a feedback effect on investment decisions, causing Purples to invest less often than Greens. The differences in investment tendencies have a larger effect on the hiring decisions.

   In summary, statistical discrimination can occur both in situations where workers' types are exogenously determined and in situations where workers make their own productivity investment decisions. In Davis (1987) the exogenous difference was the group size, which afforded employers more draws from the majority population. As a result, the maximum draw tended to be higher for the majority population, which caused subjects to make more draws from the majority population when they were able to decide which workers to hire. In the Anderson and Haupert (1999) classroom experiment, the exogenous difference was the productivity distribution for each population. As expected, students hired more workers from the high productivity group, although this discrimination was mitigated by a reduction in the 'interview cost' of finding out a worker's productivity ex ante. When asymmetries arise

Figure 4.1   Average investment and hire rates for Green (dashed line) or Purple (solid line)

Source: (Fryer, Goeree and Holt, 2005)

endogenously, discrimination can also persist as a result of a self-confirming cycle of low employer expectations and low employee aspirations, which results in low rates of human capital investment for workers in a particular group. The low investment rates for some workers generate a reduction in overall welfare.

Tournament theory and price-preference auctions
Often licenses and government contracts are allocated on the basis of an auction or contest. In such cases, the public officials involved may wish to promote the participation of a particular group (for example, small business or minority owned businesses) that would be underrepresented, perhaps because of size or past discrimination. This raises the issue of how affirmative action policies affect outcomes in auctions and tournaments.

In a simple pair-wise tournament, two people compete for a prize of known value. Every person knows their own private effort cost, which is randomly determined. The agent who exerts the most effort wins the prize. Alternatively, asymmetry can be introduced in the value of the prize, with constant effort costs across participants. Myerson (1981) shows that a seller may maximize revenue by subsidizing some high cost agents, thereby increasing competition. This is in conflict with most economic intuition that any interference with the competitive process must be costly. Similarly, Fryer and Loury (2003) show that providing subsidies for disadvantaged groups can raise the expected effort levels of the winner and the winning rate of disadvantaged groups in a general tournament model. These results illustrate an interesting possibility: that some degree of affirmative action (generally mild) has the dual effect of increasing minority employment and increasing efficiency as the tournament becomes more competitive.

This is the motivation for experiments conducted by Schotter and Weigelt (1992), who used a standard tournament-theoretic framework to show that affirmative action need not yield a cost/efficiency tradeoff. In their experiment, 20 students were each given an envelope when they entered the room. Each envelope contained a card with a random number generated from a uniform distribution. Students were randomly assigned seats and an anonymous partner for the experiment. Once the experiment began, participants were asked to choose a number between 0 and 100, which was referred to as their 'decision number'. Further, they were told that decision numbers had associated costs in the sense that their cost increased with the decision number chosen. After participants recorded their decision number, they opened the envelopes containing their random numbers. This random number was added to their decision number to generate their total amount of effort. The individual with the highest effort in each pair won the prize. Schotter and Weigelt (1992) noted two interesting patterns in the data: there was a slight over-supply of effort, and affirmative action clearly benefited disadvantaged agents. Further, they found that affirmative action worked best when there was a considerable difference between the advantaged and the disadvantaged group.

Corns and Schotter (1999) conducted a similar experiment in an auction setting. Four students were selected to be type B (low-cost) bidders, and two students were selected to be type A (high-cost) bidders. At the beginning of each of 20 rounds, the experimenter walked around the room with two bags marked A and B. Each bag contained chips corresponding to the costs for the two groups. After observing a cost chip, each participant wrote down a bid. The experimenter collected the bids and publicly announced who won, the price paid and the group identity (A or B) of the winner. In some rounds, high cost bidders were offered price subsidies. The authors found that modest (5 per cent) price preferences for disadvantaged groups led to increases in minority representation and cost efficiency. They also found that price preferences that were too high (10 to 15 per cent) were not cost effective, even though they increased minority employment's share.

The experiments reviewed here confirm the theoretical prediction that affirmative action need not entail a cost efficiency/minority representation trade-off. In particular, a subsidy to members of a high-cost group that makes them more competitive can increase total effort from all participants. In this sense, affirmative action has the dual impact of benefiting a disadvantaged group and increasing overall efficiency.

Audit studies and field experiments
In contrast to the relatively small literature on laboratory experiments with discrimination, there is a large literature on field experiments that are designed to detect discrimination in its primal form. Field experiments differ from laboratory experiments in a number of important ways, which are described in Harrison and List (2004). Typically, researchers do not control the group identification or the underlying biases and attitudes of participants in a field study. In many cases, participants in field studies do not even know that they are involved in an experiment. In addition, field experiments are generally conducted with relevant samples from non-student populations such as personnel directors or real estate agents. It is important to note that the added realism of field work brings with it a loss of control. This has prompted some criticism of this form of research.[7] The field experiments reviewed here fall into three broad categories: labor markets, housing markets and product markets.

A small literature using audit studies involving résumés provides some evidence of differential treatment in the initial hiring process.[8] These studies send two résumés of fictitious applicants to potential employers. The main difference between the two résumés is that one applicant has a distinctively black name and the other applicant has a traditionally white name. Such studies have found that résumés with white names are more likely to lead to job interviews than the identical résumés with distinctively black names. Bertrand and Mullainathan (2004) estimate that the response rate is 50 per cent higher for résumés with 'white' names controlling for quality, and there is a greater return to quality of the résumés for white applicants than for black applicants. Interestingly, however, names such as Ebony and Latonya, which are clearly black but not necessarily associated with lower socioeconomic status, received the same number of responses on average as résumés with white names. This raises the possibility that names on résumés confound race and social class as a discriminating factor.

Housing market field experiments typically involve pairs of 'equivalent' buyers who differ only in attributes such as sex, race or ethnic origin. The paired individuals each contact a designated landlord or real estate agent, and the response of that agent is recorded. Specifically, these paired studies measure the extent to which opportunities are denied or diminished for minority applicants (for example, by showing them fewer apartments or by offering them less favorable rental terms). Many of these studies are audits conducted by government organizations and the results are rarely made publicly available. Galster (1990) gained access to a large number of audits conducted in the US and Europe and reported significant discrimination based on race, ethnicity and gender.

Product market field experiments focus on differences in negotiation strategies when dealing with members of specific demographic groups. List (2003) studied dealer behavior in a sports card market. Subjects were recruited to act as either a buyer or a seller of a commonly available sports card with a predetermined redemption value (for buyers) or cost (for sellers). Each participant was instructed to approach a specific dealer and to negotiate a trade. Buyers earned the difference between the purchase price they negotiated and the redemption value given to them previously by the experimenter. Similarly, sellers earned the difference between the negotiated sale price and the predetermined cost of the card. The dealers were not aware that their initial and final price offers were being recorded and the non-dealer buyers and sellers were not aware that the purpose of the experiment was to evaluate possible discrimination. List reported that initial and final offers were less favorable for women, non-whites and older traders. Furthermore, he concluded that this discrimination was statistical in the sense that dealers were responding optimally to differences in the bargaining strategies of minority and majority traders.

These field experiments provide evidence consistent with racial discrimination in a wide range of economic markets, though other explanations such as class-based discrimination are also plausible. In at least some cases, the differential treatment is consistent with a profit-maximizing response to differences in behavior between majority and minority groups. Moreover, List (2003) found that the most experienced sports card dealers fully exploited these differences in bargaining strength. Riach and Rich (2002) survey the studies discussed here and a large number of additional field experiments.

IV   Summary

There are many theories that explain how discrimination might arise and persist in a variety of situations. Since these theories typically rely on specific assumption about beliefs and behavior, they are difficult to test with naturally occurring data. A large number of field experiments clearly document differential treatment of some groups based on certain demographic characteristics. In addition, laboratory experiments provide credible support for a number of theoretical insights. Group identification that results in discrimination can be induced in laboratory experiments. The economic consequences of this discrimination include the obvious negative outcome for members of the group discriminated against and the less obvious, but equally important, potential reductions in social welfare. For example, there is an efficiency loss when lower amounts of money are passed to those from a particular ethnic group in a trust game. In addition, there is a loss in worker productivity caused by experience-based discrimination, which may produce a cycle of low expectations, low aspirations and inferior outcomes. Finally, experiments reveal that affirmative action can increase efficiency if subsidies to disadvantaged groups increase the competitiveness of effort-based allocations.

Notes

1. This research was supported in part by a grant from the National Science Foundation SBR (0094800) and the University of Virginia Bankard Fund.
2. This exercise is described in *A Class Divided* (William Peters, 1971).
3. For example, see Allport (1954), Hamilton (1981), Tajfel (1969) or Fiske (1998) for a recent review. In addition, there are two economic models of categorization (Mullainathan, 2001; Fryer and Jackson, 2003).
4. See Sporer (2001) for a detailed review.
5. Meissner and Brigham (2001) provide a detailed meta-study of the last 30 years of literature investigating the own-race bias in facial recognition. They review 39 articles involving the responses of over 5000 subjects. There are a few studies that fail to find a cross-race effect. The overwhelming consensus among social psychologists, however, is that these effects not only exist, but are quite large (Meissner and Brigham, 2001).
6. For more evidence, see Table 2 in Sporer (2001).
7. Heckman and Seigelman (1993) identify five major threats to the validity of results from audit studies: (1) problems in effective matching; (2) the use of 'overqualified' testers; (3) limited sampling frame for the selection of firms and jobs to be audited; (4) experimenter effects; and (5) the ethics of audit research.
8. See Jowell and Prescott-Clarke (1970), Hubbick and Carter (1980), Brown and Gay (1985) and Bertrand and Mullainathan (2004).

References

Allport, Gordon W. (1954), *The Nature of Prejudice*, Reading, MA: Addison-Wesley.

Anderson, Donna M. and Michael J. Haupert (1999), 'Employment and statistical discrimination: a hands-on experiment', *The Journal of Economics*, **25**(1), 85–102.

Anderson, Lisa R. and Charles Holt (1997), 'Information cascades in the laboratory', *The American Economic Review*, **87**(5), 847–62.

Anderson, Lisa R. and Charles Holt (1999), 'Agendas and strategic voting', *The Southern Economic Journal*, **65**(3), 622–9.

Anderson, Lisa R. and Sarah Stafford (2000), 'Choosing winners and losers in a permit trading game', *The Southern Economic Journal*, **67**(1), 212–19.

Arrow, Kenneth J. (1973), 'The theory of discrimination', in Orley Ashenfelter and Albert Rees (eds), *Discrimination in Labor Markets*, Princeton NJ: Princeton University Press, pp. 3–33.

Ball, Sheryl B. and Catherine C. Eckel (1996), 'Buying status: experimental evidence on status in negotiation', *Psychology and Marketing*, **13**(4), 381–405.

Ball, Sheryl B. and Catherine C. Eckel (1998), 'Stars upon thars: status and discrimination in ultimatum games', working paper, Virginia Tech.

Ball, Sheryl, Catherine Eckel, Philip J. Grossman and William Zame (2001), 'Status in markets', *Quarterly Journal of Economics*, 101–88.

Bargh, John A. and Paula Pietromonaco (1982), 'Automatic information processing and social perception: the influence of trait information presented outside of conscious awareness on impression formation', *Journal of Personality and Social Psychology*, **43**, 437–49.

Bertrand, Marianne and Sendhil Mullainathan (2004), 'Are Emily and Greg more employable than Lakisha and Jamal? A field experiment on labor market discrimination', *American Economic Review*, **94**(4), 991–1013.

Billig, Michael (1985), 'Prejudice, categorization and particularization: from a perceptual to a rhetorical approach', *European Journal of Social Psychology*, **15**, 79–103.

Billig, Michael and Henri Tajfel (1973), 'Social categorization and similarity in intergroup behaviour', *European Journal of Social Psychology*, **3**, 27–52.

Brown, Colin and Pat Gay (1985), *Racial Discrimination: 17 years after the Act*, London: Policy Studies Institute.

Coate, Steven and Glenn Loury (1993), 'Will affirmative action eliminate negative stereotypes?', *American Economic Review*, **83**(5), 1220–40.

Corns, Allan and Andrew Schotter (1999), 'Can affirmative action be cost effective? An experimental examination of price preference auctions', *American Economic Review*, **89**, 291–305.

Davis, Douglas D. (1987), 'Maximal quality selection and discrimination in employment', *Journal of Economic Behavior and Organization*, **8**, 97–112.

Davis, Douglas D. and Charles A. Holt (1993), *Experimental Economics*, Princeton: Princeton University Press.

Devine, Patricia G. (1989), 'Stereotypes and prejudice: their automatic and controlled responses', *Journal of Personality and Social Psychology*, **56**, 5–18.

Diehl, Michael (1988), 'Social identity and minimal groups: the effects of interpersonal and intergroup attitudinal similarity on intergroup discrimination', *British Journal of Social Psychology*, **27**(4), December, 289–300.

Fershtman, Chiam and Uri Gneezy (2001), 'Discrimination in a segmented society: an experimental approach', *Quarterly Journal of Economics*, **116**(1), February, 351–77.

Fiske, Susan Tufts (1998) 'Stereotyping, prejudice and discrimination', in D.T. Gilbert, S.T. Fiske and G. Lindzey (eds), *Handbook of Social Psychology*, vol 2, Oxford: Oxford University Press.

Fryer, Roland G. and Matthew O. Jackson (2003), 'Categorical cognition: a psychological model of categories and identification in decision making', NBER working paper no. 9579.

Fryer, Roland G. and Glenn C. Loury (2003), 'Categorical redistribution in winner-take-all markets', NBER working paper no. 10104.

Fryer, Roland G., Jacob K. Goeree and Charles A. Holt (2001), 'An experimental test of statistical discrimination', discussion paper, University of Virginia.

Fryer, Roland G., Jacob K. Goeree and Charles A. Holt (2005), 'Experienced-based discrimination: classroom games', *Journal of Economic Education*, **36**(2), 160–70.

Galster, George (1990), 'Racial discrimination in housing markets during the 1980s: a review of the audit evidence', *Journal of Planning Education and Research*, **9**, 165–75.

Hamilton, David L. (ed.) (1981), *Cognitive Processes in Stereotyping and Inter-group Behavior*, Hillsdale, NJ: Erlbaum.

Harrison, Glenn and John List (2004), 'Field Experiments', *Journal of Economic Literature*, **52**, 1009–55.

Heckman, James J. and Peter Seigelman (1993), 'The Urban Institute studies: their methods and findings', in Michael Fix and Raymond Struyk (eds), *Clear and Convincing Evidence: Testing for Discrimination in America*, Washington, DC: The Urban Institute Press, pp. 271–5.

Holt, Charles (2005), *Webgames and Strategy: Recipes for Interactive Learning*, Boston, MA: Addison-Wesley.

Holt, Charles and Susan Laury (1997), 'Classroom games: voluntary provision of a public good', *Journal of Economic Perspectives*, **11**(4), 209–15.

Hubbick, J. and S. Carter (1980), *Half a Chance? A Report on Job Discrimination Against Young Black Males in Nottingham*, London: Commission for Racial Equality.

Jowell, Roger and Patricia Prescott-Clarke (1970), 'Racial discrimination and white collar workers in Britain,' *Race*, **11**, 397–417.

Klein, Olivier and Assaad Azzi (2001), 'Do high status groups discriminate more? Differentiation between social identity and equity concerns', *Social Behavior & Personality*, **29**(3), 209–21.

Li, James, David Dunning and Roy Malpass (1998), 'Cross-racial identification among European–Americans: basketball fandom and the contact hypothesis', University of Texas at El Paso working paper.

List, John (2003), 'The nature and extent of discrimination in the marketplace: evidence from the field', working paper, University of Maryland.

Meissner, Christian and John C. Brigham (2001), 'Thirty years of investigating the own-race bias in memory for faces: a meta-analytic review', *Psychology, Public Policy, and Law*, **7**(1), 3–35.

Mullainathan, Sendhil (2001), 'Thinking through categories', mimeo, Harvard University.

Myerson, Roger (1981), 'Utilitarianism, egalitarianism, and the timing effect in social choice problems', *Econometrica*, **49**(4), June, 883–97.

Peters, William (1971), *A Class Divided*, Garden City, NY: Doubleday and Company.

Phelps, Edmund (1972), 'The statistical theory of racism and sexism', *American Economic Review*, **62**, 659–61.

Riach, Peter A. and Judith Rich (2002), 'Field experiments of discrimination in the market place,' *The Economic Journal*, **112** (483), 480–518.

Schotter, Andrew and Keith Weigelt (1992), 'Asymmetric tournaments, equal opportunity laws, and affirmative action: some experimental results', *Quarterly Journal of Economics*, **107**, 511–39.

Slonin, Robert (2004), 'Gender selection discrimination: evidence from a trust game', working paper, Case Western Reserve University.

Sporer, Siegfried Ludwig (2001), 'Recognizing faces of other ethnic groups: an integration of theories', *Psychology, Public Policy, and Law*, **7**(1), 36–97.

Tajfel, Henri (1969), 'Cognitive aspects of prejudice', *Journal of Social Issues*, **25**(4), 79–97.

Tajfel, Henri (1970), 'Experiments in inter-group discrimination', *Scientific American*, November, 96–102.

Turner, John (1978), 'Social categorization and social discrimination in the minimal group paradigm', in Henri Tajfel (ed.), *Differentiation Between Social Groups*, London: Academic Press.

Turner, John and Rupert Brown (1978), 'Social status, cognitive alternatives and intergroup relations', in Henri Tajfel (ed.), *Differentiation Between Social Groups*, London: Academic Press.

Vaughan, Graham M., Henri Tajfel and Jennifer Williams (1981), 'Bias in reward allocation in an intergroup and an interpersonal context', *Social Psychology Quarterly*, **44**(1), 37–42.

Appendix: a guide to conducting discrimination experiments in economics

The most straightforward way to evaluate discrimination in the laboratory is to group people according to actual characteristics (for example, major, home state or astrological sign) and to compare behavior and earnings with baseline experiments where group identification is not available. For example, subjects in a bargaining experiment could be told whether their partner is from the same group or not. Alternatively, market roles (for example, buyer and seller) could be assigned on the basis of some earned status condition (for example, performance on a trivia quiz). Here the issue is whether to make actual group assignment on a random basis, which controls for individual differences, but involves elements of deception that are generally avoided in economics experiments. The alternative is to base the group assignments on preferences that are not likely to be related to decision-making skills in an economic context. For example, psychologists have used preferences for paintings to make group assignments. Once the assignment method has been selected, the instructions for any standard economics experiment can be adapted and used. For example, Holt (2005) contains instructions for 20 experiments covering a wide range of topics. Instructions for other experiments are also widely available (for example, voting, Anderson and Holt, 1999; information cascades, Anderson and Holt, 1997; public goods, Holt and Laury, 1997; a market for pollution permits, Anderson and Stafford, 2000). These experiments can be conducted with a minimal set of props such as cards and dice and a handout with instructions and record sheets. In addition, all of these experiments can be run over the Internet using the software associated with the Holt (2005) book at http://veconlab.econ.virginia.edu/admin.htm This set of programs includes the statistical discrimination game used by Fryer, Goeree and Holt (2005). For a general introduction to the mechanics of conducting a research experiment, see Chapter 1 of Davis and Holt (1993).

PART II

BEYOND RACE AND GENDER

5 A critical review of studies of discrimination against workers with disabilities
Marjorie L. Baldwin and William G. Johnson

1 Introduction

The analysis of wage discrimination against minorities in the context of economic models of labor supply effectively began in the 1970s. Interest in the topic was stimulated by the civil rights movement of the 1960s and facilitated by Becker's (1971) model of discrimination in the labor market. At about the same time, disability activists adopted the concepts and tactics that had been used so successfully by African-Americans in their fight for civil rights. The first study of disability-related wage discrimination that used economic models and methods was published in 1985 (Johnson and Lambrinos, 1985).

The political activism of the 'unexpected minority' of persons with disabilities ultimately led to the passage of the Americans with Disabilities Act (ADA) in 1990. The ADA stimulated interest in documenting the experiences of persons with disabilities in the labor market. Following its passage there has been a proliferation of studies analyzing trends in the wages and employment rates of persons with disabilities in the pre- and post-ADA periods; analyzing the statutory language of the Act and how it is interpreted by the EEOC and the courts; and applying econometric methods to estimate discriminatory wage and employment differentials between disabled and non-disabled workers.

The analysis of disability-related discrimination involves problems, however, that are not found in studies of discrimination against African-Americans, women or other minority groups. The problems are as fundamental as how to define the class of persons with disabilities, an issue that the language of the ADA leaves purposely vague, and as complex as how to control for the fact that health conditions can limit productivity in many jobs. The methods used to estimate disability-related discrimination also face challenges from some disability activists who reject results that control for functional limitations on the grounds that functional limitations are only impediments in the perceptions of non-disabled persons. Controls for health-related limitations on productivity were notably absent from the estimates of employment and wage discrimination presented during the hearings that preceded passage of the ADA.

There is also a serious shortage of data that support empirical analyses of the labor market experiences of persons with disabilities. The data requirements are formidable. The ideal data set includes detailed information on employment, wages, work experience and job characteristics, as well as information on health conditions, functional limitations and disability status. The differences in discrimination against groups with different types of disabilities can only be analyzed if the data provide samples of sufficient size for each group. No current data set meets all these criteria.

The analysis of disability-related discrimination does have a comparative advantage, relative to studies of other minority groups, in providing the opportunity to test directly the widely accepted assumption that discrimination is a reflection of prejudice. A well-established literature on attitudes toward different minority groups includes rankings of attitudes toward persons with different health conditions. Several studies of disability-related discrimination include attitude scales in their models to test the extent to which disability-related discrimination reflects prejudice rather than employer misinformation or economic exploitation of minority workers, the premises of alternate theories of discrimination.

Despite the obstacles, more than a dozen empirical studies of labor market discrimination against workers with disabilities have been published since 1985. This chapter critically reviews the models and methods used by the studies, and compares the results to identify what we know about disability-related discrimination, and where there are gaps in our knowledge.

The plan of the chapter is as follows. The first part sets forth the background for our review: section 2 defines the terminology used to define the minority group in most studies of disability-related discrimination. Section 3 summarizes the best known theoretical models of labor market discrimination, while section 4 presents the econometric methods used in empirical studies. The first part concludes with the authors' conception of the 'gold standard' for an empirical study of disability-related discrimination. This standard is the basis for developing eight criteria, described in section 5, used to evaluate the selected studies.

The second part of the chapter presents a critical review of empirical studies of disability-related discrimination: section 6 explains how the studies were selected for review and presents a brief summary of each. Section 7 applies the evaluation criteria to the selected studies. Section 8 identifies conclusions that emerge as consistent themes in the results, describes inconsistencies in the findings and outlines a direction for future research.

2   Definitions
Any study of disability-related discrimination must first address the problem of defining 'disability'. Unfortunately, there is considerable variation in the

meaning assigned to the term. The assumption that disability can be defined by the nature and severity of a health condition or impairment is the defining characteristic of what has come to be known as the 'medical model' of disability. The medical model was the dominant concept of disability in most research prior to 1974 (Berkowitz and Johnson, 1974). Disability advocates vehemently object to the medical model of disability but have been almost as critical of models that associate disability with functional limitations or non-health-related influences on labor supply. The problem of establishing consistent definitions of disability is further complicated by pressure from advocacy groups to adopt definitions that are politically sensitive, but not practical for empirical studies of discrimination.

An analysis of labor market discrimination against persons with disabilities requires that the researcher distinguish between *impairment, functional limitation* and *disability* so that the effect of a health condition on specific job functions (such as limitations on handling, lifting, walking) can be distinguished from the more global concept of work disability. Work disability can then be treated as an outcome that is influenced by the nature and severity of functional limitations as well as other characteristics, such as the nature of the work environment. The distinction is fundamental to separating the effects of health-related limitations on productivity from the effects of discrimination in the labor market.

Definitions that satisfy these requirements were developed by Nagi (1969) and modified by the World Health Organization (WHO, 1980, 2001). According to Nagi's definitions, an *impairment* is a 'physiological or anatomical loss or other abnormality', a *functional limitation* is a restriction of sensory, mental or physical capacities, and a *disability* is a restriction on the ability to perform normal daily activities, such as working or attending school, that is caused by the functional limitations associated with an impairment.

Consider, for example, a worker with epilepsy. Epilepsy is an impairment that causes a functional limitation, namely, the inability to walk and perform physical tasks during severe seizures. If seizures are not controlled through medication and restrict the worker's ability to perform his or her usual job, the worker is disabled. If seizures are controlled, which is fairly typical, and never interfere appreciably with the worker's job performance, the worker is not disabled.

Most of the economic research on disability uses variants of Nagi's (1969) typology, but compliance with the core concepts of Nagi's definitions has not led to a uniform definition of disability. Part of the problem is that the national surveys that can be used to study discrimination against persons with disabilities use different definitions of disability.[1] The Current Population Survey (CPS) and National Health Interview Disability Survey (NHIS-D), for example, use screener questions asking if individuals are limited in a major life activity, such as work or household responsibilities. Only persons who respond in the affirmative are asked the full set of questions about health and functional limitations. Thus it is difficult or impossible to separate the concepts of functional limitations and disability.

One advantage of the Survey of Income and Program Participation (SIPP), the source data for many empirical studies of disability-related discrimination, is that there is no screener question on work disability. All persons completing the supplementary questionnaire on health and disability status (one of the Topical Modules that accompany the core questionnaire) are asked questions about functional limitations and disability. Unfortunately, only those persons who respond affirmatively to the disability and limitations questions are asked to identify impairments (health conditions). Thus the SIPP data distinguish between the concepts of functional limitations and disability, but cannot identify persons with impairments that do not cause functional limitations.

Subsequent sections compare the definitions of disability across different studies and discuss the implications of those differences for the interpretation of results. The following questions are answered: (1) are the definitions consistent with one another? (2) is disability defined as a limitation on a major life activity? (3) do the definitions yield samples that are representative of the disabled population?

Fortunately, there is much more agreement across studies in defining labor market *discrimination*. Labor market discrimination occurs when groups of workers with equal average productivity are paid different average wages or face different opportunities for employment. Wage discrimination appears as differences between the mean wages of minority and majority workers that cannot be explained by differences between the groups' productivity-related characteristics. Employment discrimination can be expressed as refusals to hire, differentially high rates of job terminations in response to a decrease in the demand for labor, or refusals to rehire workers following absences caused by illnesses or injuries. Competing theories of discrimination, described in the following section, suggest that discrimination results from prejudice (Becker, 1971; Arrow, 1973), informational problems in the labor market (Aigner and Cain, 1977) or firms' economic exploitation of minority workers (Roemer, 1979).

3   Economic theories of discrimination
Economic theories of discrimination are based on a model of labor supply that describes employment as a bargain between employer and worker. The bargain is consummated when the employer offers a job at a wage rate greater than or equal to the wage at which the worker is willing to accept a job. The worker's minimum acceptable wage is termed the 'reservation wage' and the wage an employer is willing to pay is termed the 'offer wage'.

The offer wage is a function of worker productivity (measured by education, experience and health) and the demand for labor in the relevant labor market. The worker's reservation wage is a function of variables that affect the price of time, including non-wage income and personal characteristics (such as age, education and health). In competitive labor markets, the marginal worker (last hired) is hired at a wage rate equal to the value of his or her productivity to the firm.

Deviations between wages and productivity measured across groups of workers reflect discrimination. Competing theories of labor market discrimination are based on assumptions that discrimination occurs because of employer prejudice, poor information or attempts to exploit a minority group that has little bargaining power in the labor market.

Prejudice
Becker (1971) defines discrimination as the willingness of an employer to incur costs to avoid contact with minority workers. Becker's fundamental assumption is that discrimination stems from the desire of prejudiced employers to be physically separated from minority workers. Arrow (1973) extends the concept of physical separation to include social distance as well.

The idea that prejudice is the source of discrimination against persons with disabilities is intuitively appealing because the existence of negative attitudes toward persons with disabilities is documented in numerous studies (Tringo, 1970; Yuker, 1987; Royal and Roberts, 1987; Westbrook *et al.*, 1993). Typically, the studies use social distance scales to rank different health conditions by the degree of prejudice they elicit. The rankings are surprisingly robust over the last 30 years, especially considering the advances in public policy toward persons with disabilities since 1990. Consistently, the strongest prejudice is exhibited toward persons with mental or emotional conditions, or substance abuse problems. Negative attitudes toward persons with these conditions are similar to those exhibited toward ex-convicts.

Becker's theory predicts that prejudiced employers will not hire minority workers unless the workers are willing to work for wages that are lower than the wages paid to equally productive workers against whom the employer is not prejudiced. The reduction in the cost of labor to the employer is conceptualized as the income equivalent of the employer's discomfort from having to work with a minority person. The 'disutility premium' paid by minority workers is the source of discriminatory wage differentials in the labor market.

Becker's model includes some variants, namely situations in which a non-prejudiced employer discriminates against minority workers in response to prejudiced employees or customers. The prejudiced-customer variant is the only one of the three situations in which an employer's discriminatory behavior is profit-maximizing. In other variants of the model, discrimination reduces employer profits and the only monetary benefits resulting from discrimination accrue to majority workers, who are paid higher wages than they would receive in a nondiscriminatory market.[2]

One of the never-realized predictions of Becker's model is that wage discrimination will disappear in the long run in competitive markets, unless all employers are equally prejudiced. The rationale is that non-prejudiced employers can hire minority workers at a wage greater than they would receive from prejudiced employers, but less than the wage paid by prejudiced employers to their majority workforce. Thus non-prejudiced employers can reduce labor costs and earn higher profits than prejudiced employers. Profit-maximizing employers will eventually drive discriminatory firms out of the market.

Information problems
One of the alternatives to a theory of discrimination based on prejudice is a theory based on the premise of asymmetrical information in the labor market, often called 'statistical discrimination'. Models of statistical discrimination assume that employers have greater difficulty evaluating the productivity of members of a minority group, relative to members of a majority group, because of language barriers, cultural differences, lack of experience hiring from the minority group or other reasons. If employers do not have sufficient information to assess the productivity of minority applicants accurately, they may use membership in the minority group as a signal of lower productivity (Phelps, 1972). In this case a discriminatory wage differential arises that can be viewed as a 'risk premium' paid by minority workers to compensate for information problems in the screening process.

There are good reasons to argue that information problems contribute to the low wages and low employment rates of workers with disabilities. Persons with disabilities are a relatively small group (less than 10 per cent of the labor force), so most employers have relatively little experience of evaluating the productivity of workers with disabilities. The group is also extremely hetero-geneous: the functional limitations associated with physical impairments, for example, are vastly different from the limitations associated with mental impairments. Even if an employer has previously hired workers with func-tional limitations, that experience may be difficult to extend to potential employees with different limitations.

The difficulties inherent in evaluating the effects of functional limitations on work capacity are exemplified by the provisions of the Social Security Disability Insurance program (SSDI). SSDI restricts benefits to persons who are permanently and totally disabled and requires extensive clinical documen-tation in support of a claim, but then imposes an earnings restriction on bene-ficiaries. The earning restriction is an acknowledgment of the uncertainty surrounding the effects of impairments on the capacity for work.

The problems in evaluating the productivity of disabled workers are further complicated because experience and skills vary across workers with the same impairment. The extent to which a worker's productivity may be limited by a mental or physical impairment depends not only on the impairment and its associated functional limitations, but also on the mental and physical requirements of the jobs for which the worker is qualified by his or her experience and skills. A functional limitation that is disabling for a worker whose job requires heavy physical labor, for example, may not be disabling for a worker whose job is not physically demanding. Knowing the type of impairment that affects an individual is not, therefore, a clear indicator of the worker's productivity in a particular job.

Information problems in the labor market are an intuitively appealing explanation for discrimination against workers with disabilities but one that is difficult to test empirically. To our knowledge no one has tested the importance of statistical discrimination as an explanation of the low wages and employment rates of persons with disabilities.[3]

Exploitation

The underlying premise of radical, or Marxian, theories of discrimination is that employers or co-workers exploit minority workers to increase profits. Radical models are non-competitive in the sense that they assume some power to control wages in the labor market, through union bargaining rights or the monopsony power of the employer.

Radical models view discriminatory wage differentials as an 'exploitation premium' extracted from members of a minority group who are powerless to demand equal treatment in the labor market. Roemer (1979), for example, proposes a model of discrimination in which employers use minority workers as a divisive tool to weaken the bargaining power of a union. The model is not well suited to explaining discrimination against workers with disabilities because workers with disabilities are such a small part of the workforce that their divisive impact is minimal.

A monopsony model is more appealing because of the limited job mobility of workers with disabilities. Most disabilities occur among older adults who have little opportunity to change occupations or acquire new job skills. A late onset of disability implies that an employer had an opportunity to observe the worker's productivity prior to his becoming disabled and is better informed than other employers regarding the worker's expected productivity. In many cases, the ability of a disabled worker to work is determined by whether or not his pre-disability employer is willing to provide job accommodations that compensate for the effects of the worker's functional limitations (Burkhauser, 1990; Huang *et al.*, 2005).

Typically, empirical studies of labor market discrimination do not provide a direct test of the different theories of discrimination.[4] Some studies of disability-related discrimination have tried to link measures of wage discrimination to negative attitudes expressed toward persons with different impairments in a test of Becker's (1971) prejudice model. The methods used in these and other empirical studies of disability-related discrimination are described in the next section.

4   Methods for estimating discrimination

Single-equation model

The simplest approach to estimating wage discrimination against workers with disabilities is to estimate a single equation, including data for both disabled and non-disabled workers, with a binary variable that identifies workers with disabilities. The dependent variable in the model is a measure of the wage rate; independent variables control for worker productivity and labor market characteristics as well as disability status. A statistically significant negative coefficient for the disability variable is typically interpreted as evidence of wage discrimination against workers with disabilities. The validity of the interpretation rests on the extent to which other variables in the model control adequately for between-group differences in worker productivity.

A variant of the single-equation model replaces the binary for disabled persons with a vector of binary variables identifying persons with different types of impairments. In this specification, the corresponding vector of coefficients estimates productivity-controlled wage differentials between each impairment group and the control group of non-disabled persons. In either version, the implicit assumption of the single-equation model is that discrimination shifts the wage function of the minority group downward, without changing its underlying structure. (The single-equation model is described in further detail in the Appendix.)

Wage decomposition

A more sophisticated approach to estimating wage discrimination, that allows the wage structure to differ between minority and majority workers, is a decomposition technique introduced to the economics literature by Oaxaca (1973). The decomposition is based on wage equations estimated separately for disabled and non-disabled workers. The two-equation specification allows discrimination to affect both the estimated slope coefficients and the intercept of the wage function, in contrast to the single-equation model in which discrimination only affects the intercept. In other words, the single-equation model imposes a constraint (the returns to productivity-related characteristics are equal for disabled and non-disabled workers) that is relaxed in the decomposition model.

The decomposition separates the observed wage differential between non-disabled and disabled workers into two parts. The first, or 'explained' part, is attributed to differences in the average productivity of the two groups of workers, as measured by differences in the means of the explanatory variables in the wage equation. The second, or 'unexplained' part, is attributed to differences in the returns to those productivity-related characteristics, as measured by differences in the estimated coefficients of the wage equation. The unexplained differential can be interpreted as a measure of wage discrimination, but it also includes the effects of unmeasured differences in the productivity of disabled and non-disabled workers. (Further details are provided in the Appendix.)

Employment decomposition
Kidd *et al.* (2000) use a decomposition approach to separate the difference in average employment rates between disabled and non-disabled workers into an explained part attributed to differences in human capital characteristics and an unexplained part that includes the effects of employer discrimination.[5] The method is based on estimated coefficients from a probit employment function. (The method is described in more detail in the Appendix).

Similar to the Oaxaca approach, the decomposition separates the observed difference in probabilities of employment for the average individual in the majority or minority group into explained and unexplained components. The explained part is attributed to differences in the characteristics of the two groups, as measured by differences in the values of the explanatory variables in the probit function. The unexplained component is attributed to differences in the 'returns' to those characteristics, as measured by the estimated coefficients of the employment function. Again, the unexplained differential is interpreted as a measure of discrimination in employment, provided all relevant variables that influence the employment decision are included in the probit model. Kidd *et al.* (2000) adds the caveat that the unexplained component includes the effects of unmeasured differences in tastes and productivity as well as the effects of employer discrimination.

Employment effects of wage discrimination
In theory, wage discrimination also reduces employment because some minority workers who would accept nondiscriminatory wages are not willing to work at the lower, discriminatory offer wage. Ignoring the employment effects implies that the supply curve for minority workers is perfectly inelastic and discrimination has no disincentive effect on minority employment. Baldwin and Johnson (1992a) develop a three-step estimator to calculate the disincentive effects of wage discrimination, and apply the estimator in a study of wage discrimination against African-American men. The estimator has since been

applied in several studies of wage discrimination against disabled men and women (for example, Baldwin and Johnson, 2000; Kidd *et al.*, 2000).

The first step is to estimate the probability of employment for the average minority worker from a probit likelihood function. The dependent variable in the probit function is a binary variable that equals one if the individual is employed. The estimated coefficients of the probit function are used to estimate the difference in the log offer wage and log reservation wage for the average minority worker.

The second step is to estimate probabilities of employment in the absence of discrimination. The estimates are obtained by correcting the log offer wage–log reservation wage differential for the effect of discrimination in offer wages, using weights that represent the wage structure that would be observed in the absence of discrimination. In the third step, the number of jobs lost to the minority group because of wage discrimination is estimated by multiplying the discriminatory differential in the probability of employment by the population of minority workers.

Most studies that have applied the estimator find that the employment effects of wage discrimination are small, relative to the observed differential in employment rates between disabled and non-disabled workers. This suggests that the labor supply curve for minority workers is relatively inelastic.

5   Criteria for review

Table 5.1 lists the eight criteria that define what we believe to be the 'gold standard' for empirical studies of labor market discrimination against workers with disabilities. This section describes the theoretical and empirical foundations for the review criteria, and how each is implemented in evaluating the studies. Some of the criteria are not met by any studies, primarily because of limits on the available data. The unmet criteria define part of the agenda for future research.

Controls for heath-related functional limitations
One of the important differences between disabled workers and other protected classes is the fact that productivity can be limited by the same health conditions that make disabled workers eligible for civil rights protection. The decomposition technique used to estimate discriminatory wage differentials separates observed wage differentials into a part explained by differences in the productivity-related characteristics of the majority and minority groups, and a part that is unexplained and attributed to discrimination. Failure to control for the productivity-limiting effects of health conditions, therefore, introduces an upward bias in the estimates of discrimination against workers with disabilities.

Table 5.1   *Criteria for appraising the methodological quality of empirical studies of disability-related discrimination*

---

1. Do the models control for the functional limitations associated with many health impairments that may influence worker productivity?
2. Do the models control for other confounding variables that may explain some of the differences in labor market outcomes between disabled and non-disabled workers?
    a. human capital (education, job experience)
    b. demand for labor (for example, industry, occupation, union status, region, public sector, part-time)
    c. job demands
    d. interactions between functional limitations and job demands
3. Do the models control for sample selection bias?
4. Does the weighting scheme for the decomposition reflect the proportions of disabled and non-disabled workers in the labor market?
5. Do the results account for an upward-sloping labor supply curve?
6. Do the authors link empirical estimates of discrimination with the theoretical model based on 'tastes' for discrimination?
7. How many different disability groups are considered?
8. Are the estimates based on national survey data?

One example of the problem in the context of disability-related discrimination occurs if the variables measuring disability-related productivity losses omit important functional limitations associated with particular types of impairments. Cognitive limitations are, for example, not included on a number of the surveys used for studies of disability-related discrimination, yet cognitive limitations are generally the most important types of limitations associated with mental illnesses.

There is considerable disagreement in the public policy arena regarding whether it is appropriate to include controls for mental or physical functional limitations in the models used to estimate discrimination against workers with disabilities. Some advocates for persons with disabilities, and some government agencies, maintain that a model associating disabilities with productivity losses is contrary to the premises of the disability movement. They argue that, with appropriate job accommodations, persons with disabilities are as productive as non-disabled persons.[6] Despite the empirical evidence, there are others who argue the other extreme, namely that observed wage and employment differentials between disabled and non-disabled workers are entirely attributed to the effects of health-related limitations on productivity, but this position is much less prevalent today than in the 1970s.

Economists reject estimates of discrimination against workers with disabilities if the models do not include adequate controls for potential limits on productivity, represented by functional limitations. Thus an important point of comparison for the studies reviewed below is the adequacy of the controls for health-related reductions in productivity (that is, functional limitations, both physical and cognitive).

Controls for other confounding variables

Estimates of labor market discrimination are biased if the estimating equations are misspecified because of omitted variables or because variables are measured incorrectly. If, for example, important productivity-related characteristics are not included among the explanatory variables, productivity-related wage differentials will be incorrectly attributed to discrimination, yielding estimates of discrimination that are biased upward. The omitted variables problem is common to all empirical studies of labor market discrimination, not only those focused on workers with disabilities.

The errors-in-variables problem affects any independent variable in a discrimination model that does not capture adequately differences in the productivity of minority and majority workers. Suppose, for example, education is used as a measure of workers' investments in general human capital. If the quality of education differs between majority and minority groups with the same years of schooling, wage differences associated with quality of education would be incorrectly attributed to discrimination. It is well established that children and young adults with disabilities face barriers to access to education and limits on the quality of education that are not faced by non-disabled children. The limits on education may reflect pre-labor market discrimination or simply failures to recognize problems with testing or other requirements that disadvantage children with disabilities. The National Research Council (NRC) report on college admissions tests, for example, identifies the need to alter standard admission testing environments, without changing the substance of the tests, to avoid handicapping students with disabilities (Sherman and Robinson, 1982)

The potential effects of pre-labor market discrimination are, fortunately, limited to a relatively small part of the population of adults with disabilities, namely persons who were disabled as children (Johnson, 1997). The process of maturing in a hostile and restricted environment imposes limitations on opportunities and on an individual's view of the world that are difficult to escape. The process of growing up disabled, with its impact on schooling, socialization and access to employment, parallels the experiences of African-Americans and other minorities in general, even if the specifics differ.

The majority of persons with disabilities, however, have impairments that result from illnesses or injuries occurring during adulthood, most often in middle age. These persons were not segregated in school or limited in their employment opportunities by disability-related discriminatory obstacles at entry into the labor force or during their pre-onset work experiences. The fact that onset of disability occurs most often in middle age limits, but does not eliminate, the possibility that the controls for human capital in the models used to estimate wage discrimination are affected by pre-labor market discrimination.

The second review criterion evaluates whether the independent variables in the discrimination models capture the most important nondiscriminatory determinants of wages. A minimal set of adequate controls includes measures of human capital (for example, education, work experience), job characteristics (such as hours, union membership) and labor demand (occupation, industry, region and so on), in addition to the functional limitations variables noted above. A 'gold standard' model also includes controls for the physical and cognitive demands of jobs, and interactions between those job demands and workers' functional limitations.

Controls for sample selection bias

Estimates of wage discrimination are necessarily limited to samples of employed workers.

It is well known that the estimated coefficients of a human capital wage equation based on employed workers are biased because the researcher is unable to observe the wages that were offered to persons who are not employed. The bias, an example of 'selection bias', can be corrected by including a 'sample selection variable', a measure of the conditional propensity of an individual to be included in the sample of workers, in the wage equation (Heckman, 1980).

The sample selection variable, equal to the inverse of Mill's ratio, is constructed from estimates of an employment function estimated for the full sample of employed and not-employed persons. If the researcher is using the decomposition technique, separate employment functions are estimated for the minority and majority groups. If the researcher is using a single-equation model, one employment function is estimated for the entire sample.

Reimers (1983) was the first to correct for sample selection bias in a discrimination study. It is now standard practice to correct for selection bias, so this criterion is applied to all studies reviewed.

Nondiscriminatory wage structure

Studies of labor market discrimination make an explicit or implicit assumption regarding the wage structure that would prevail in the absence of discrimination. The assumption is explicit in decomposition studies where the researcher selects a set of weights that define the unobservable nondiscriminatory wage structure.

The true nondiscriminatory wage structure, although unobserved, must lie between the observed wage structures for majority and minority workers. The approach adopted by Oaxaca in his first discrimination article (1973) is to provide two sets of estimates, arguing that the actual impact of wage discrimination lies somewhere between the two extremes. An alternative but ad hoc approach, fairly common in studies of gender- or race-related discrimination, is to choose a nondiscriminatory wage structure at the midpoint of the observed wage structures for minority and majority workers.

These weighting schemes characterized discrimination studies until 1988, when two new approaches to weighting were introduced. Cotton (1988) proposes weights equal to the proportions of majority and minority workers in the labor market, so the nondiscriminatory wage structure is a weighted average of the observed wage structures for majority and minority workers. Neumark (1988) proposes weights obtained from a pooled wage regression for majority and minority workers. The estimated coefficients from the pooled regression define the nondiscriminatory wage structure. A comparison of the results of alternative weighting schemes concludes that weights reflecting the proportions of majority and minority workers in the labor market (such as Cotton and Neumark propose) are superior to weights set at extremes or midpoints (Baldwin and Johnson, 1992b). One review criterion, therefore, evaluates whether studies apply proportionate weights in the decomposition formula.

The weights criterion is not applied to single-equation studies. In these studies the authors estimate a pooled regression for disabled and non-disabled groups with binary variables identifying groups with different impairments. The implicit assumption is that the returns to productive characteristics (defined by the estimated coefficients of the wage equation) are identical for persons with and without disabilities, but discrimination shifts the entire wage function downward for the disabled group.

Elasticity of labor supply
Most studies of wage discrimination against African-Americans, women and other minorities assume that labor supply functions are perfectly inelastic, implying that discrimination affects wages but not employment (Cain, 1986). The assumption violates the principles of the labor supply models on which the estimates are based and offends reality by suggesting that variations in the wages offered to potential workers have no influence on workers' willingness to accept employment.

The theory of labor supply predicts that the quantity of labor supplied increases, all else equal, with increases in offer wages. Graphically, labor supply schedules are upward sloping but not vertical (perfectly inelastic). Wage discrimination implies that the mean productivity-adjusted wage offered to disabled workers is lower than the mean nondiscriminatory wage and, there-fore, some workers who would accept employment at a nondiscriminatory wage will not do so in the presence of discrimination. Becker acknowledges the effect of discriminatory wages on employment and predicts that discrimination will both increase employment of majority workers and decrease employment of minority workers. The net effect of discrimination on total employment depends on the relative elasticities of the supply and demand schedules for majority and minority labor (Becker, 1971; Thurow, 1975).

Baldwin and Johnson (1992a) develop a formal estimator of the employment effects of wage discrimination, described above, and apply it to data on discriminatory wage differentials between African-American and white men. The estimator is easily implemented in a discrimination study using the decomposition technique, and has been applied in several studies of wage discrimination against workers with disabilities. One of the review criteria evaluates whether decomposition studies acknowledge the upward-sloping labor supply curve and include estimates of the employment effects of wage discrimination in their results.

Linkage to theoretical model of discrimination
Empirical studies of labor market discrimination against African-Americans, Hispanics and women appeal to Becker's model but rarely test the core assumption that prejudice is the underlying cause of discrimination. The exceptions are audit studies in which actors of different races or ethnic backgrounds are assigned identical credentials and their success in applying for jobs, home purchases and rental accommodations is compared.[7] The possible link between prejudice and discrimination is also tested by several studies of disability-related discrimination.

The hypothesis that prejudice is expressed in terms of physical or social distance can be empirically tested by analyzing the strength of the relationship between negative attitudes (prejudice) and labor market discrimination against persons with disabilities, controlling for differences in productivity. In particular, if prejudice is an important cause of discrimination against disabled persons, then discriminatory wage differentials should vary according to the intensity of prejudice against particular impairments. There are a number of studies ranking the degree of prejudice elicited by different health conditions, making an empirical test of the prejudice hypothesis possible (Tringo, 1970; Albrecht *et al.*, 1982; Royal and Roberts, 1987; Yuker, 1987; Westbrook, *et al.*, 1993).

The research on attitudes shows that the variation in the intensity of prejudice toward different impairments is not necessarily correlated with the extent of functional limitations associated with the impairment (Tringo, 1970; Albrecht *et al.*, 1982; Yuker, 1987). For example, attitudes are extremely negative toward persons with epilepsy, despite the fact that most persons with epilepsy are not restricted in their ability to work because seizures are controlled effectively by medication. Attitudes toward persons with arthritis or cardiovascular disease, which are often associated with greater functional limitations than epilepsy, are quite positive.

One of the review criteria used to evaluate the selected studies is whether or not they capitalize on the availability of prejudice rankings for different impairments to test Becker's theory of discrimination. In general, this is more feasible in studies using the single-equation model, because binary variables can be included for a number of different impairment groups, but some decomposition studies have also structured their models specifically to test for discrimination based on attitudes.

Heterogeneity of the disabled population
An important difference between persons with disabilities and other minority groups is the heterogeneity of the disabled population. Different health conditions impose different types of functional limitations and different degrees of disability. The diversity of the population of persons with disabilities is apparent in policy debates, where persons with different impairments belong to different advocacy groups, often with conflicting interests and objectives. The heterogeneity presents both a challenge (to control for the differences in the estimating equations) and an opportunity (to test Becker's theory that labor market discrimination results from prejudice).

One of the review criteria evaluates the extent to which a study takes into account the different impairment groups that comprise the disabled population. The criterion for comparing studies is a simple count of the number of different impairment groups identified in the models.

National survey data
The strongest evidence of disability-related discrimination would come from studies based on large, nationally representative data sets, with samples of sufficient size to make separate estimates of employment and wage discrimination for each of several types of disabling impairments. In addition to information on impairments, functional limitations and disabilities, the ideal data set also includes comprehensive information on employment, wages, work experience, job characteristics and job demands. Unfortunately, few national data sets exist with even the minimal combination of health and labor market information required to estimate disability-related discrimination.

The national surveys used in the reviewed studies include the 1972 Social Security Survey of Disabled and Non-Disabled Adults (SDNA), the 1984–93 panels of the Survey of Income and Program Participation (SIPP), the 1990 National Consumer Survey of People with Developmental Disabilities and their Families (NCSD) and the 1996 British Labour Force Survey (BLFS). Most of the surveys are not designed to provide representative samples of the disabled population; some are limited because they do not provide adequate measures of impairments and functional limitations (for example, BLFS); others are limited because they do not provide detailed information on employment, job characteristics and work experience (for example, NCSD). Only the SDNA, discontinued in 1976, provides good measures of cognitive limitations.

The Current Population Survey (CPS), National Health Interview Survey of Disability (NHIS-D), and the Panel Study of Income Dynamics (PSID) have also been used to provide descriptive data on the employment experiences of persons with disabilities (for example, Haveman and Wolfe, 1990; Burkhauser and Daly, 1996; Druss *et al.*, 2000). The CPS and PSID have the advantage of long panels, so that changes in the labor market experiences of persons with disabilities can be tracked over time. The data do not, however, provide detailed information on impairments and functional limitations.[8] The NHIS-D collects basic data on disability, health conditions and symptoms, and demographic data. A supplemental questionnaire, administered to those who are currently disabled, collects data on employment, personal assistance needs, household characteristics, participation in social activities and current work status. The data do not provide information on work experience or job characteristics.

One potential new source of national data for studies of disability-related discrimination is the Medical Expenditure Panel Survey (MEPS). The MEPS provides detailed data on demographic characteristics, income, employment, health conditions, health status, health insurance coverage, utilization and costs of medical care, and limited information on job characteristics and work history. The survey design yields relatively large samples of persons with disabilities that can be weighted to represent the US population.

As the above discussion suggests, there is no 'ideal' data set for studies of disability-related discrimination. Our minimal review criterion for the selected studies is that they use national survey data that can be generalized to the disabled population.

6 Selection of studies for review

The articles reviewed are retrieved from a search of *EconLit* and the National Rehabilitation Information Center (NARIC) *Instant Disability Information Center*, using key words that include combinations of disability, discrimination and workplace. An article must satisfy all of the following criteria to be included in the review. (1) The study is an empirical analysis of discrimination against workers with disabilities that includes controls for potential differences between the productivity of disabled and non-disabled workers. (2) The framework of analysis is consistent with economic models used to analyze labor market discrimination against other minority groups. (3) The article focuses on labor market discrimination against groups of workers with disabilities, where the primary outcome measures are wages, employment rates or both.

The criteria exclude descriptive studies of the labor market participation of workers with disabilities; legal and policy studies of the impact of the Americans with Disabilities Act (ADA); studies of attitudes toward persons with different health conditions; and studies that focus on individual perceptions of discrimination.[9] Also excluded are articles published prior to 1985, when Johnson and Lambrinos (1985) first applied the economic methods that had been used to study discrimination against other minority groups to workers with disabilities.

Twelve articles meet the criteria for inclusion. The articles can be broadly classified into two groups. The first group of six studies measure discrimination from a single estimating equation that includes binary variables to identify persons with disabilities. The estimated coefficients of the binary variables are interpreted as measures of wage or employment discrimination against persons with disabilities. The second group of six studies, beginning with Johnson and Lambrinos (1985), use variations of the Oaxaca (1973) decomposition technique to measure wage discrimination against persons with disabilities.

Single-equation studies
Table 5.2 summarizes the studies of disability-related discrimination that use a single equation approach. Four studies are explicitly designed to test the hypothesis that discrimination is related to prejudice. Two of these studies incorporate measures of social distance in a wage equation estimated from data on disabled workers only (Johnson and Lambrinos, 1987; Salkever and Domino, 2000) while two examine correlations between social distance rankings and productivity-adjusted wage differentials using data for both disabled and non-disabled workers (Baldwin and Johnson, 1994b; Hendricks *et al.*, 1997). The remaining studies (Baldwin, 1999, 2000) use the single-equation approach to estimate productivity-adjusted wage and employment differentials for more narrowly defined impairment groups than can be supported in a decomposition analysis.

Johnson and Lambrinos (1987) apply Tringo's disability social distance scale to data from the 1972 Survey of Disabled and Non-Disabled Adults (SDNA). The impairment categories from the SDNA are mapped to the Tringo scale and assigned a ranking equal to the impairment's mean score on the scale.[10] The Tringo score is then included as an independent variable in a semi-log wage equation, corrected for selectivity bias and estimated separately for men and women.

Table 5.2   Studies of disability-related discrimination using a single equation model

Study	Data	Sample	Definition of disability	Authors' conclusions
Johnson & Lambrinos (1987)	1972 SDNA[a]	employed disabled men and women	presence of an impairment ranked on Tringo (1970) social distance scale	Wages are significantly negatively correlated to social distance rankings for males, but not for females.
Baldwin & Johnson (1994b)	1984 SIPP[b]	disabled/ non-disabled men and women	self-reported limitation at work/ home/mobility	There is a weak correlation between wages and social distance rankings, but a stronger correlation with employability rankings.
Hendricks *et al.* (1997)	1999 UI Survey[c]	disabled/ non-disabled college graduates	graduates in rehabilitation division with long-term impairment that causes functional limitations	The adjusted salary differential between disabled and non-disabled workers is 8%. Wages are significantly negatively correlated with social distance rankings.
Salkever & Domino (2000)	1990 NCSD[d]	disabled men and women	persons with developmental disabilities	There is a significant negative correlation between wages and social distance rankings.
Baldwin (1999)	1984, 1990 SIPP[b]	disabled/ non-disabled men and women	self-reported limitation at work/ home/mobility/ communication	Adjusted wage differentials between disabled and non-disabled workers range from insignificant for some impairment groups to 21% for others.
Baldwin (2000)	1990 SIPP[b]	disabled/ non-disabled men and women	self-reported limitation at work/ home/mobility/ communication	Wage losses attributed to discrimination range from 0% to 19%; reductions in the probability of employ-ment range from 0 to 0.25 percentage points, across impairment groups.

Notes:
[a]   Social Security Survey of Disabled and Non-Disabled Adults.
[b]   Survey of Income and Program Participation.
[c]   University of Illinois at Urbana-Champaign, Survey of Graduates of Rehabilitation Education Services.
[d]   National Consumer Survey of People with Developmental Disabilities and their Families.

The results show a statistically significant, negative relationship between intensity of prejudice and the wages of men. On average, a unit change in the social distance score reduces the wages of employed men by 11 per cent. There is no significant relationship, however, between the prejudice measure and the wages of women. Thus the results for men support the hypothesis that wage differences vary with the degree of prejudice against workers' impairments, but the results for women do not. The results must, however, be interpreted as a finding that differences in the degree of prejudice among women with disabilities are not significant. The results do not include an evaluation of the effect of prejudice on wage differences between disabled and non-disabled women.

Baldwin and Johnson (1994b) use data from the 1984 SIPP to test the correlation between empirical estimates of discriminatory wage differentials and rankings of impairments by social distance (Tringo, 1970) and employability (Yuker, 1987). Seven categories of impairments are constructed reflecting progressively more negative attitudes on the social distance scale. The category subject to the weakest prejudice includes arthritis, diabetes and disorders of the stomach. The category subject to the strongest prejudice includes mental illness, senility and nervous or emotional problems. The authors estimate a single equation with binary variables identifying each impairment category, where the reference group includes persons with impairments subject to little or no prejudice (for example, hypertension, back problems) and persons with no reported impairments. The models include controls for seven categories of functional limitations, but are limited because there are no measures of cognitive limitations on the 1984 data.

The results reveal significant unexplained wage differentials for four of the seven impairment categories (arthritis, diabetes, stomach disorders/heart trouble/cancer or stroke/mental conditions). There is no significant correlation between the rank orderings of unexplained wage differentials and the social distance ranking, unless the rankings are restricted to the four impairment categories with significant wage differentials. There is, however, a significant correlation, across all seven categories, between unexplained wage differentials and perceptions of the employability of persons with various health conditions. Overall, the results provide weak support for the prejudice hypothesis.

Hendricks *et al.* (1997) analyze wage discrimination against persons with long-term disabilities using data from a survey of participants in a rehabilitation program at the University of Illinois. Compared to samples of disabled persons drawn from national survey data, the UI sample represents a population that is more severely disabled, has greater functional limitations, was disabled earlier in life, has higher levels of education (all are college graduates) and has a different distribution of impairments (over 50 per cent of the disabled sample uses a wheelchair). The non-disabled comparison group is a sample of UI graduates without disabilities, matched to the disabled group based on year of graduation, gender and field of study.

In general, the results show that these disabled workers fare better in the labor market than disabled workers overall. Employment rates are 78 per cent for the disabled group (compared to 84 per cent for the non-disabled controls) and the observed salary differential is only 15 per cent. Controlling for human capital and demographic variables, the salary gap declines to 8 per cent. Adding controls for functional limitations (limited in amount or kind of work) the gap declines to 2 per cent and becomes insignificant. In other words, there is no significant unexplained wage differential between the two groups.

The authors test the hypothesis that prejudice is a source of discrimination against workers with disabilities by including social distance rankings in the wage model. The coefficient of the social distance score is negative and significant, suggesting that wages decline as negative attitudes become more intense.

Using data from the National Consumer Survey of People with Developmental Disabilities and their Families (NCSD), Salkever and Domino (2000) examine the relationship between attitudes rankings and the employment and wage rates of persons with disabilities. The NCSD is not a representative sample of the disabled population (persons with mental retardation, for example, represent 42 per cent of the sample). The analysis focuses on variations within the group of persons with developmental disabilities.

The study sample includes 6686 persons with disabilities. The authors assign each person a social distance score (Tringo, 1970) and employability ranking (Yuker, 1987) based on his or her primary disabling condition. The scales are included separately in employment and wage functions that also include controls for 12 functional limitations and a count variable indicating the total number of disabling conditions.

The results provide mixed support for the prejudice hypothesis. Both the social distance and employability rankings are significant with a counterintuitive positive sign in the employment function. In other words, persons with impairments that elicit stronger prejudice, or are ranked less employable, are in fact more likely to be employed than persons with developmental disabilities that are subject to less intense prejudice. The social distance ranking has the expected significant negative coefficient in the wage function and the effect is stronger than reported in previous work (Baldwin and Johnson, 1994b). The employability ranking, however, has no significant effect on variations in wages among persons with different types of developmental disabilities. The results do not consider differences between persons with developmental disabilities and non-disabled persons or persons with other types of disabling conditions.

Baldwin (1999, 2000) uses data from the 1984 and 1990 SIPP to estimate the potential benefits of eliminating employment and wage discrimination against workers with disabilities. The impairment groups include persons with cardiovascular conditions, mental conditions, musculoskeletal conditions, respiratory conditions, sensory conditions or other disabling health conditions. The author estimates the extent of employment and wage discrimination against each group, then extrapolates to the disabled population to estimate the losses accruing to persons with disabilities because of discrimination.

The estimates of significant employment differentials attributed to discrimination range from seven to 47 percentage points in 1984, and from five to 25 percentage points in 1990, while the estimates of discriminatory wage differentials range from 10 to 16 per cent of the mean non-disabled wage rate in 1984, and from 8 to 19 per cent in 1990. The results vary considerably across time periods and between men and women, but the groups that typically experience the most discrimination are persons with mental or cardiovascular impairments. Consistent with other research, the results suggest that employment is a more serious problem than wage discrimination for persons with disabilities (Baldwin and Johnson, 2000).

Comments   Most of the single-equation studies define disability in terms of self-reported limitations on a major life activity, consistent with the Nagi (1969) definitions. Salkever and Domino (2000) and Johnson and Lambrinos (1987) further restrict the disabled sample to persons with disabilities that are ranked on a social distance scale. The four studies that compare estimates of discriminatory wage differentials to social distance rankings (Johnson and Lambrinos, 1987; Baldwin and Johnson, 1994b; Hendricks *et al.*, 1997; Salkever and Domino, 2000) generally find weak, but significant, negative correlations, providing some support for Becker's (1971) hypothesis that discrimination is caused by prejudice. The other two studies (Baldwin, 1999, 2000) are not specifically designed to test the relationship between discrimination and prejudice. It is notable, however, that one of the groups that exhibits the largest unexplained wage and employment differentials in these studies is the group with mental impairments, an impairment category subject to relatively intense prejudice on all the attitudes scales.

It is interesting to speculate that the Johnson and Lambrinos (1987) results showing significant linkages between prejudice and discrimination for men but not for women may reflect a problem with the conventional assumptions about attitudes toward women as a minority group in the labor force. Two recent articles suggest that attitudes based on social distance do not represent the preferences that lead to labor market discrimination against women (Baldwin *et al.*, 2001; Goldin, 2002). The articles present models of gender-related discrimination based on assumptions that men derive disutility from working for a female supervisor, or fear a loss of prestige when women enter an occupation. Neither model has been applied to women with disabilities.

Decomposition studies

Table 5.3 summarizes the six studies of disability-related discrimination using the decomposition technique. Johnson and Lambrinos (1985) were the first to apply the decomposition technique to study wage discrimination against workers with disabilities. They use data from the 1972 Social Security Survey of Disabled and Non-Disabled Adults.[11]

The corrected results indicate that, in 1972, disabled men earned 53 cents less per hour than non-disabled men, creating a wage differential of 13 per cent of the average hourly wage of non-disabled men. The discriminatory differential between the offer wages of non-disabled and disabled men is 16 per cent of the non-disabled offer wage. In 1972, disabled women earned 45 cents less per hour than non-disabled women, creating a wage differential of 17 per cent of the average hourly wage of non-disabled women. The discriminatory differential between the offer wages of non-disabled and handicapped women is 61 per cent of the non-disabled wage, an estimate that is considerably larger than that obtained in any of the other discrimination studies.

Baldwin and Johnson (1994a) use a similar approach to estimate wage discrimination against men with disabilities, using data from the 1984 Survey of Income and Program Participation. The authors extend previous research by stratifying the disabled sample into two groups and by estimating the employment effects of wage discrimination. The two groups of men with disabilities are defined according to rankings on the attitudes scales: those with conditions subject to less prejudice (the 'disabled' group) and those with conditions subject to more prejudice (the 'handicapped' group).

The results reveal poorer labor market outcomes for the handicapped group, relative to the disabled group, with respect to both wages and employment. The wage differential between non-disabled men and men in the 'disabled' group is 68 cents per hour, compared to $2.67 for men in the 'handicapped' group. Discrimination reduces the wages of 'disabled' and 'handicapped' men by 12 per cent and 15 per cent of the non-disabled wage, respectively. Productivity-adjusted employment rates are 83 per cent for the 'disabled' group and 68 per cent for the 'handicapped' group, compared to a 96 per cent employment rate for non-disabled men, but the employment effects of wage discrimination account for only a tiny fraction of the employment differential. Eliminating wage discrimination would increase the employment of disabled men by less than 0.5 percentage points, and of handicapped men by less than 1.5 percentage points.

In a companion study, Baldwin and Johnson (1995) use the SIPP data to study wage discrimination against women with disabilities. Here it is not

Table 5.3   Studies of disability-related discrimination using the decomposition technique

Study	Data	Sample	Definition of disability	Results
Johnson & Lambrinos (1985)	1972 SDNA[a]	disabled/ non-disabled men and women	impairments that affect communica-tion/mobility/ appearance	The unexplained wage differential is 16% for males and 61% for females.
Baldwin & Johnson (1994a)	1984 SIPP[b]	disabled/ non-disabled men	self-reported limitation at work/ home/mobility	The unexplained wage differential is 11% to 15%. Wage discrimina-tion reduces the probability of employ-ment by 0.3 to 1.4 percentage points.
Baldwin & Johnson (1995)	1984 SIPP[b]	disabled/ non-disabled women	self-reported limitation at work/ home/mobility	The unexplained wage differential is 7%. Wage discrimination reduces the probability of employment by 0.6 percentage points.
Baldwin & Johnson (2000)	1990 SIPP[b]	disabled/ non-disabled men	self-reported work limitation	The unexplained wage differential is 16% to 24%. Wage discrimina-tion reduces the probability of employ-ment by 1.0–1.6 percentage points.
Kidd *et al.* (2000)	1996 BLFS[c]	disabled/ non-disabled men	persons with long-term health problems that impose work limitations	The unexplained wage differential is 7%. Wage discrimination reduces the probability of employment by 0.06 percentage points.
DeLeire (2001)	1984/ 1993 SIPP[b]	disabled/ non-disabled men	self-reported work and/or functional limitations	The unexplained wage differential is 5% in 1984 and 8% in 1993.

Notes:
[a]   Social Security Survey of Disabled and Non-Disabled Adults.
[b]   Survey of Income and Program Participation.
[c]   British Labor Force Survey.

possible to stratify the disabled group by type of impairment because the sample of employed women with disabilities is so small. Women with disabil-ities are compared to three control groups: non-disabled women, men with disabilities and non-disabled men.

Women with disabilities earn 96 cents less per hour, on average, than non-disabled women. The wage differential attributed to discrimination is 7 per cent of the non-disabled wage. Again, the employment effects of wage discrimination are small, reducing the employment of disabled women, relative to non-disabled women, by less than one percentage point. The estimates of wage discrimination, and its employment effects, increase when disabled women are compared to disabled or non-disabled men, suggesting that disabled women are subject to both disability-related and gender-related discrimination.

In later work, Baldwin and Johnson (2000) update the estimates of discrimination against men with disabilities using data from the 1990 SIPP. Based on the rankings of impairments developed by Tringo (1970), the authors classify men with disabilities into two groups: a group with impairments subject to more prejudice (MP) and a group with impairments subject to less prejudice (LP). Disabled men who report they are unable to work are excluded.

The results show that the MP group is much more seriously disadvantaged in the labor market than the LP group. Employment rates for MP men are 58 per cent, compared to 71 per cent for LP men and 89 per cent for non-disabled men. Mean hourly wages are only $10.90 for MP men, compared to $11.13 for LP men and $13.35 for non-disabled men.

The authors decompose the wage differentials between disabled and non-disabled men into an explained part (attributable to between-group differences in the characteristics that determine wages) and an unexplained part (attributable to discrimination and residual effects.) The part of the wage differential attributed to discrimination is 22 per cent of the non-disabled wage for the MP group and 17 per cent for the LP group, providing some support for the hypothesis that prejudice is the source of discrimination.

Kidd *et al.* (2000) investigate the labor market experiences of British workers with disabilities using data from the 1996 British Labour Force Survey. The data are for a sample of disabled and non-disabled men, where the disabled group includes men who report a health problem that 'has lasted or is expected to last more than 12 months'. The authors estimate separate employment functions for disabled and non-disabled men and decompose the difference in employment rates using the technique introduced by Even and MacPherson (1991). Similarly, earnings equations are estimated for the two groups and the difference in mean earnings is decomposed. Measures of health status or functional limitations are not available for the full sample, so the controls for the effects of disability on worker productivity are limited to three measures of the duration of periods of sickness.

Employment rates for the disabled and non-disabled groups are 34 per cent and 84 per cent, respectively. Approximately half the differential is unexplained by the control variables in the model. The wage differential between disabled and non-disabled men is 14 per cent, and again approximately 50 per cent is unexplained. The authors apply the Baldwin and Johnson (1992a) method to estimate the employment effects of wage discrimination and report a highly inelastic (elasticity = 0.03) response of disabled men to the reduction in wages attributed to discrimination.

DeLeire (2001) estimates discrimination against men with disabilities using data from the 1984 and 1992–3 panels of the SIPP. Exploiting the full range of questions on functional and work limitations on the data, he divides the sample into three groups: (1) men with no functional limitations, (2) men with functional limitations but no reported work limitations, and (3) men with functional limitations that affect their ability to work. DeLeire assumes that unexplained wage differentials between the first two groups are attributed to discrimination (because the workers report no health-related productivity losses), while unexplained differentials between groups (1) and (3) can be attributed to both discrimination and unmeasured productivity differences. Under the assumption that discrimination does not vary between groups (2) and (3), he uses the results for disabled men with no work limitations to identify the discriminatory and nondiscriminatory parts of the unexplained wage differential between non-disabled men and men with work limitations. In this way, DeLeire reduces some of the upward bias in the discrimination estimates associated with omitted variables in the wage equation. However, the assumption that the extent of discrimination against disabled workers who report a work limitation and those who do not is equal, is problematic given the heterogeneity of the disabled population, and the results of several studies reporting different degrees of discrimination against disabled persons with different types of impairments.

DeLeire uses a variant of the decomposition technique based on a Tobit model to correct for sample selection bias, rather than the Heckman (1980) two-stage approach adopted by other authors. The controls for health-related productivity losses are five binary variables constructed from a categorical variable describing self-reported health status (poor, fair, good, average, excellent). In 1993, the predicted wage differential between non-disabled men and men with functional limitations but no work limitations was 18 percentage points, with five percentage points unexplained. The predicted wage differential between non-disabled men and men with work limitations is 67 percentage points, with 50 percentage points unexplained. Adjusting for omitted variables bias under DeLeire's premise, discrimination accounts for only five percentage points of the observed wage differential between non-disabled men and men with work limitations, while the remaining 45 percentage points of the unexplained differential is attributed to unmeasured differences in productivity.

Comments   Four of the decomposition studies analyze discrimination against men with disabilities (Baldwin and Johnson, 1994a; 2000; Kidd, 2000; DeLeire, 2001), one study focuses on women (Baldwin and Johnson, 1995) and the Johnson and Lambrinos (1985) study presents results for both. The decomposition approach requires separate sets of equations for disabled men and women to avoid confusing disability-related discrimination with gender-related discrimination. The small samples of employed women with disabilities greatly limit opportunities to make gender-specific or impairment-specific estimates for women.

With one exception, the decomposition studies define disability as the presence of self-reported limitations in a major life activity (working, household activities, mobility) consistent with Nagi's (1969) concept of disability. The exception is Kidd *et al.* (2000) who define persons with disabilities as those who report long-term health problems that limit the kind of paid work they can do. The authors impose a time dimension to their definition that is consistent with the notion of disability as a limitation associated with a chronic health condition.

The results of five studies (Johnson and Lambrinos, 1985; Baldwin and Johnson, 1994a, 1995, 2000; Kidd *et al.*, 2000) are fairly consistent. Typically, the offer wage differential ranges from 12 to 33 per cent of the non-disabled offer wage and at least half the differential is unexplained. The results of the DeLeire (2001) study are not strictly comparable because his is the only study to use disabled men who report no work limitations as controls to identify the explained and unexplained components of the differential.

7   Review
Table 5.4 summarizes how well the empirical discrimination studies meet our review criteria. The criteria for appraising the methodological quality of the studies are presented in Table 5.1 and described in section 5 above.

Criteria 1,2: control variables
The first two criteria deal with the adequacy of the control variables in the models. One of the most important questions is how well the models control for health-related losses in worker productivity. To provide a complete summary of the health-related productivity controls included in the models, an alphabetic code is assigned to each study corresponding to the appropriate list of functional limitations/health measures appearing in the model (see footnotes to Table 5.4). Nine studies (codes A, B, C, F, H, I) control for disability-related productivity losses by including a number of control variables that measure functional limitations in normal daily activities (such as walking, climbing stairs, participating in conversation, but not work limitations per se) in the models.

Table 5.4   Review of empirical studies of labor market discrimination against workers with disabilities

Decomposition Studies	1[a]	2a	2b	2c	2d	3	4	5	6	7[b]	8
Johnson & Lambrinos (1985)	A	√	√				√			1	√
Baldwin & Johnson (1994a)	B	√	√				√		√	√	2	√
Baldwin & Johnson (1995)	B	√	√				√			√	1	√
Baldwin & Johnson (2000)	C	√	√				√		√	√	2	√
Kidd et al. (2000)	D	√	√				√			√	1	√
DeLeire (2001)	E	√	√				√	√			2	√

Single Equation Studies	1[a]	2a	2b	2c	2d	3	4	5	6	7[b]	8
Johnson & Lambrinos (1987)	A	√	√				√	NA	NA	√	M	√
Baldwin & Johnson (1994b)	F	√	√				√	NA	NA	√	7	√
Hendricks et al. (1997)	G							NA	NA	√	12	
Salkever & Domino (2000)	H	√					√	NA	NA	√	M	√
Baldwin (1999)	I	√	√				√	NA	NA		6	√
Baldwin (2000)	I	√	√				√	NA	NA		6	√

Notes:
[a]   Functional limitations groups for Criterion 1:
A   9 measures of limitations on dexterity, mobility, strength; 16 measures of psychological impairment; 7 measures of clinical conditions;
B   12 measures of limitations: seeing, hearing, speaking, uses an aid to get around, lifting, walking, climbing stairs, getting around inside, getting around outside, getting in and out of bed, preparing meals, doing light housework;
C   14 measures of limitations: seeing, hearing, speaking, lifting, walking, climbing stairs, using the telephone, getting around, getting in and out of bed, bathing, personal care, handling money, preparing meals, doing light housework;
D   3 indicators of duration of sickness/injury;
E   self-reported health status (excellent, good, average, fair, poor);
F   6 measures of limitations: seeing, communicating, walking, lifting, climbing, getting around outside;
G   binary variable indicating health limitations (limited in amount or kind of work);
H   12 measures of 'substantial' or 'a little' limitation in 6 areas: self-care, language, learning, mobility, making decisions, capacity for independent living; continuous measure of the number of health conditions reported;
I: 5 measures of limitations: communication, mobility, strength, daily living, cognitive.
[b]   M indicates continuous variable(s) ranking disability groups by scores on social distance and/or employability scales.

The most glaring weakness in the lists of functional limitations is the lack of measures of cognitive limitations. Only two studies, Johnson and Lambrinos (1985) and Salkever and Domino (1997), use data that include good measures of cognitive limitations. The Survey of Income and Program Participation (SIPP), that is the basis for a number of studies of disability-related discrimination, has good measures of physical limitations along a number of dimensions (mobility, strength, communication, activities of daily living) but only one, admittedly poor, measure of cognitive limitations (ability to handle money and pay bills).

Hendricks *et al.* (1997) uses controls for health-related productivity losses that are direct measures of work limitations (G). Although the work-related variables may be valid indicators of health-related productivity losses, they lack the specificity of the activity-related control variables in the other models. Further, they tend to confuse the concepts of 'limitations' and 'disabilities' as defined above. Recall that a *functional limitation* is defined as a restriction of sensory, mental or physical capacities, whereas a *disability* is defined as a restriction on an individual's ability to perform normal daily activities, such as working. The same work limitations questions that are used to control for health-related productivity losses in the Hendricks *et al.* study are the basis for defining the disabled groups in other studies.

Two studies (Kidd *et al.*, 2000; DeLeire, 2001) use measures of health status to control for health-related productivity losses. These include measures of the duration of sickness or injury (D) and self-reported health status (E). These types of variables are likely to be highly imperfect proxies for health-related productivity losses. An individual may, for example, have numerous functional limitations associated with a chronic condition (such as back pain) but report his health status as good if he has no acute conditions. Similarly, functional limitations are likely to be only weakly correlated with duration of illness.

There is more consistency across studies in the other control variables included in the models. The majority of studies include controls for differences in worker characteristics and human capital (2a) and for factors that influence the demand for labor (2b). None of the studies reviewed include controls for physical and cognitive demands of particular jobs, or interaction effects between job demands and workers' functional limitations.

Criteria 3–5: empirical methods
The next set of review criteria address methodological issues. All the studies we review, except Hendricks *et al.* (1997), control for sample selection bias (criterion 3) in their models. The most common mechanism is to use the Heckman (1980) two-stage approach in which the sample selection variable is constructed from a preliminary probit employment function.

Among the decomposition studies, only DeLeire (2001) uses weights that reflect the proportions of disabled and non-disabled workers in the labor market (criterion 4). He derives the nondiscriminatory wage structure from a pooled regression of disabled and non-disabled workers, as suggested by Neumark (1988). The remaining studies set D equal to one, under the assumption that disabled workers are such a small fraction of the labor force that their presence has little effect on the overall wage structure.

Most of the decomposition studies acknowledge the upward-sloping labor supply curve and use the Baldwin–Johnson (1992a) approach to estimate the labor supply response to disability-related wage discrimination. The exceptions are Johnson and Lambrinos (1985), a study that was completed before the Baldwin–Johnson estimator was introduced, and DeLeire (2001).

Criterion 6,7: links to theoretical model

Six of the studies reviewed attempt to link empirical estimates of disability-related discrimination to attitudes rankings, as a test of Becker's (1971) theory of discrimination based on prejudice. This is more easily accomplished in the single-equation studies where binary variables can be included for different impairment groups. For this reason, the single-equation studies do a better job accounting for the heterogeneity of the disabled population, distinguishing up to 12 different impairment groups in their models. The decomposition studies typically treat the disabled minority as a homogeneous population with at most two subgroups.

Three approaches are used to test the theoretical model. In the decomposition framework, Baldwin and Johnson (1994a, 2000) identify two groups of disabled workers: those subject to stronger prejudice on the attitudes rankings, and those subject to weaker prejudice. Separate estimates of discrimination are computed for each group, compared to the non-disabled population. If Becker's theory is correct, the authors reason, discriminatory wage differentials should be larger for the group subject to more prejudice. The results provide only weak support for the theory. The limitations to this approach are immediately apparent from the authors' published work: they have insufficient samples to perform a similar test for women with disabilities in a 1995 study.

A second approach (Baldwin and Johnson, 1994b; Hendricks *et al.*, 1997) is to include binary variables for each impairment group in a single equation, and compare the magnitudes of the coefficients (an estimate of productivity-adjusted wage differentials) to the attitudes rankings. These studies find stronger support for the theoretical model. A related approach (Johnson and Lambrinos, 1987; Salkever and Domino, 2000), which also shows significant correlations with the attitudes rankings, is to include the attitudes score directly in the wage equation.

Criterion 8: national survey data

Eleven of the 12 studies reviewed use national survey data, from either the US (SSDA, SIPP, NCSD) or Great Britain (BLFS). In most cases, the surveys are not specifically designed to study the disabled population, so the sample sizes are too small to permit estimates of wage discrimination against particular impairment groups (for example, persons with diabetes or epilepsy).

One study uses local survey data from participants in a University of Illinois (UI) rehabilitation program. Typically, only the most severely disabled students apply for services from the program. As the authors note, 'the labor market experiences of these individuals are difficult to generalize to the general population' (Hendricks *et al.*, 1997). Studies using the UI data report both higher employment rates for the disabled samples and smaller wage gaps between disabled and non-disabled workers, than do studies based on national survey data, although the UI samples include a higher proportion of persons with relatively severe disabilities (ibid.; Hallock, *et al.*, 1998; Hendricks *et al.*, 2000). The differences likely reflect the higher average level of education of participants in the UI survey and self-selection of highly motivated individuals into the rehabilitation program.

Salkever and Domino (2000) restrict the disabled sample to persons with developmental disabilities, by nature of the data set. The NCSD sampling strategy is to include 42 per cent persons with mental retardation, 34 per cent persons with physical disabilities, 15 per cent persons with sensory disabilities, and 9 per cent persons with emotional disabilities. The restriction to developmental disabilities limits the generalizability of the results.

8 Discussion

Interpreting results across studies using different models, estimation techniques and definitions of disability demands a cautious approach. We attempt to summarize a set of structural results that appear to be common across most of the studies, but we avoid, as much as possible, inferences based on the magnitude of one or another empirical estimate. Thus, while we conclude that wage discrimination against persons with disabilities is well established, there is little certainty about the size of discriminatory wage differentials.

The results that are consistent across the studies we review can be summarized as follows. First, there are large differences in the average wages of disabled and non-disabled persons in the US. A substantial portion of the wage differential is attributable to differences between disabled and non-disabled workers in their functional capacities and human capital characteristics, such as education and experience. There is still, however, a substantial part of the wage differential that is unexplained and attributed to disability-related discrimination. Results from the UK are limited to one study but are consistent with the findings for the US.

Second, wage discrimination creates disincentive effects that discourage some persons with disabilities from working. The estimates to date suggest that the employment effects of wage discrimination impose large income losses on disabled persons, but the employment effects are only a small part of the large, unexplained, employment differences between disabled and non-disabled persons.

Third, methods for estimating direct employment discrimination against workers with disabilities are less well established than methods for estimating wage discrimination. It is possible that unmeasured forms of employment discrimination may be responsible for much of the unexplained difference in the employment rates of disabled and non-disabled persons.

Fourth, the results support the hypothesis that discrimination against persons with disabilities is rooted in prejudice. The results do not, however, exclude the possibility that statistical discrimination or exploitation also contribute to disability-related discrimination. These possibilities have not been empirically tested.

Finally, the conclusions described above are much less certain for women than for men, because there is substantially less information on disability-related discrimination against women than there is against men. The lack of information on disability-related discrimination against women reflects the limitations of national surveys that are not designed to provide large, representative samples of the different types of impairments that may or may not lead to disability, and the low employment rates among women with disabilities.

Research on disability-related discrimination is the principal source of innovations in the methods used to study discrimination in the last 25 years. With few exceptions, analyses of labor market discrimination against other minority groups have yet to address the employment effects of discrimination (one exception is Baldwin and Johnson, 1992a) or to test the relationship between prejudice and discrimination (an exception is Levitt, 2003).

Future research on disability-related discrimination faces three important obstacles, one of which is political, the second methodological, and the third related to the adequacy of available data. The first obstacle includes political barriers created by the positions taken by disability advocates in their continuing efforts to protect the employment rights guaranteed by the ADA. Some advocates insist that research on disability is only valid if it is conducted by or with the participation of persons with disabilities. Others assert that, with appropriate job accommodations, physical limitations do not affect productivity and should not be included as control variables in the models used to estimate wage discrimination. Finally, the position taken by some advocates, reflected in the recent WHO definitions of disability, is that impairments be viewed as enabling as well as disabling. Advocates of this position argue that some health conditions, most notably deafness, confer special benefits on afflicted persons that outweigh any functional limitations associated with the conditions. The requirement for disabled investigators might or might not affect the objectivity of research on disability-related discrimination. Acceptance of the second or third positions by funding agencies or scholarly journals would, however, effectively eliminate the productivity-standardized models that provide the only objectively verifiable information on wage and employment discrimination against persons with disabilities.

The methodological barriers to disability-related research can be addressed directly by improvements in research methods and more careful specification of the models used to estimate wage discrimination. The failure to include adequate information on employers and profiles of job demands is, in our opinion, the most important omission from current empirical models of disability-related discrimination. The sole characteristic from the employer side in current models is the offer wage, which does not capture adequately all the conditions of the employment bargain. An ideal study would include measures of employer attitudes, including employers' evaluations of the employability and productivity of workers with different types of impairments. Studies of employers' attitudes exist but do not include contemporaneous information on the workers likely to be affected by those attitudes. One can speculate that a useful, more easily measured, proxy for employer attitudes is the nature of firms' disability management programs and return-to-work policies for workers with health-related work absences.

Two other characteristics of interest, omitted from the models in every study we reviewed, are the physical and mental demands associated with workers' customary employment, and the willingness of employers to implement job accommodations that offset workers' functional limitations. One of the weaknesses of the medical model of disability is the failure to compare functional limitations to the functional requirements of a job. A functional limitation (such as the inability to lift 20 pounds) need not result in work disability if the affected function is not part of a worker's job requirements. It is also well established that job accommodations, which are often quite inexpensive, can compensate effectively for the functional limitations associated with many types of impairments (Collignon, 1986).

Omitting employer information from the models used to estimate disability-related discrimination tends to bias the estimates toward the worker or supply side of the model, implicitly ignoring the fact that employment is a bargain requiring agreement by two parties. The next significant methodological improvements in the estimation of disability-related discrimination will be to acquire information on employer actions and attitudes, and to develop profiles of the functional requirements of different jobs. Hirsch and Macpherson (2004) have already linked information on job demands to data on wages and employment in a study of racial composition as an indicator of unmeasured labor productivity differences across different jobs.

The final barrier to disability-related research is the lack of adequate data to support a comprehensive analysis of labor market discrimination against persons with disabilities, recognizing the extreme heterogeneity of the disabled population. There does not exist a large national survey that satisfies all the requirements: detailed information on wages and employment, work history, employer and job characteristics; information on workers' demographic characteristics and human capital; information on impairments and functional limitations for both disabled and non-disabled persons; large, representative samples of persons with different types of impairments. Some of the gaps in the national survey data are supplied by smaller surveys of specific populations, such as the University of Illinois survey, but it is impossible to generalize results from these data to the disabled population.

One of the most serious deficiencies in the data that have been used to study disability-related discrimination to date is the lack of adequate controls for cognitive limitations. The lack of data on cognitive functions limits the applicability of the discrimination models to persons with mental disorders, a group that represents an increasing proportion of the disabled population. The tremendous stigma attached to mental illness suggests that discrimination may account for a significant part of the large wage and employment differentials between persons with mental disorders and non-disabled persons, so the inability to obtain reliable estimates for this group marks a crucial gap in the research on disability-related discrimination.

The body of knowledge on discrimination against persons with disabilities confirms the validity of the significant change in society's view of persons with disabilities from objects of charity to individuals much like members of other minority groups, whose full potential can be realized given adequate protections against discrimination. The types of legal protections most likely to achieve that objective could be better defined, and their effectiveness better understood, if future research on discrimination can improve the methods for distinguishing between the direct effects of functional limitations on productivity and the limitations imposed by discrimination. An equally important direction for future research is the unanswered questions concerning the relative importance of prejudice, information problems and exploitation of workers as the source of disability-related discrimination. Discrimination from different sources should be addressed by different policies; the development of current policy is constrained by simple, untested assumptions that prejudice is the only source of discrimination.

The limitations of research to date on disability-related discrimination should not obscure the importance of the information it has produced documenting the existence of significant productivity-controlled wage and employment differentials between disabled and non-disabled persons. Although often attacked as politically incorrect, the evidence is the strongest objective support for the need for civil rights protections to guarantee labor market opportunities for persons with disabilities.

Notes

1. The United Nations is attempting to gain acceptance for a uniform definition of disability to be used in survey research and the question is being studied by various data collection agencies in the United States (WHO, 2001; Hendershot, 2002).
2. The limits on the employment of minority workers created by discrimination imply that discriminatory employers, at the margin, must hire majority worker substitutes with higher reservation wages, assuming that labor supply is not perfectly inelastic (Thurow, 1975).
3. Levitt (2003) devises a creative test of taste-based vs. information-based models of discrimination using evidence from the television show, *The Weakest Link*. He analyzes discriminatory behavior toward females, blacks, Hispanics, and older players, but not toward players with disabilities.
4. We know of two empirical studies that attempt to identify sources of discrimination. Bodvarsson and Partridge (2001) develop an empirical method to separate the effects of co-worker, employer and customer discrimination and apply the method to evaluate sources of discrimination against non-white basketball players in the NBA. Baldwin (2003) uses rankings of the visibility of health conditions, together with characteristics of the product market, to test the hypothesis that customers are a source of disability-related discrimination.
5. Kidd *et al.* (2000) refer to the method, introduced by Even and MacPherson (1991), as a decomposition of differences in labor force participation rates, but it is in fact a decomposition of differences in employment rates.
6. Yet a third approach is that impairments are both enabling and disabling. Some advocates for persons with hearing impairments, for example, argue that deafness is not a disability but a trait that defines a culture and does not require remediation. At the same time they strongly support the ADA and the rights of deaf persons to accommodations for their impairments (Tucker, 1997).
7. The interested reader is referred to Darity (1994) and the references therein. Hendricks *et al.* (2000) cite a number of audit studies involving workers with disabilities. A more recent example is Gouvier *et al.* (2003) who provided matched résumés with vocational and medical histories of hypothetical job applicants to undergraduate business majors. The students were asked to rate applicants' suitability for two job positions and for doing shift work. The results exhibit distinct patterns of disability-related discrimination.
8. The 1986 PSID includes a Health Supplement that collects information on overall health status and a limited number of functional limitations.
9. The interested reader is referred to the following. For studies describing the labor market experiences of workers with disabilities, refer to the work of Haveman and Wolfe (1990), Kruse (1998), Burkhauser and Daly (1996), Hale *et al.* (1998), Haveman *et al.* (2000) and Charles (2003), for example. For studies focused on the impact of the ADA, Karlan and Rutherglen (1996), Verkerke (1999) and White (2000) are examples of legal studies, and the series of articles by Moss *et al.* (1999a, 1999b, 2001) and DeLeire (2000), Acemoglu and Angrist (2001), Beegle and Stock (2003) and Jolls and Prescott (2004) are examples of policy studies. Also refer to Wehman (1993) and Blanck (2000). For studies of attitudes toward persons with disabilities, see Tringo (1970) and more recent articles by Yuker (1987), Royal and Roberts (1987) and Westbrook *et al.* (1993). Hallock *et al.* (1998) and Hendricks *et al.* (2000) are examples of studies comparing worker perceptions of discrimination with labor market experiences.
10. Values on the Tringo scale range from 0.33 ('would marry') to 4.69 ('would put to death'). The mean impairment-specific scores for the 21 impairment groups common to the Tringo scale and the survey data used in the study range from 0.52 (ulcer) to 1.42 (mental illness). The median score across the impairment groups is approximately equal to the score of 0.64,

for heart disease, somewhere in the interval between 'would accept as close kin by marriage' and 'would have as a next door neighbor'. The scores reflect the fact that the most prevalent impairments are also the most familiar and least threatening to non-disabled persons. Arthritis and heart disease are, for example, familiar to most persons who have one or more older persons in their families.

11. The results summarized here refer to corrected estimates that appeared in Baldwin and Johnson (1994a).

References

Acemoglu, Daron and Joshua D. Angrist (2001), 'Consequences of employment protection? The case of the Americans with Disabilities Act', *Journal of Political Economy*, **109** (October), 915–57.

Aigner, Dennis J. and Glen G. Cain (1977), 'Statistical theories of discrimination in labor markets', *Industrial and Labor Relations Review*, **30** (January), 175–87.

Albrecht, Gary L., Vivian G. Walker and Judith A. Levy (1982), 'Social distance from the stigmatized: a test of two theories', *Social Science and Medicine*, **16** (July), 1319–28.

Arrow, Kenneth J. (1973), 'The theory of discrimination', in Orley Ashenfelter and Albert Rees (eds), *Discrimination in Labor Markets*, Princeton, NJ: Princeton University Press, pp. 3–33.

Baldwin, Marjorie L. (1999), 'The effects of impairments on employment and wages: estimates from the 1984 and 1990 SIPP', *Behavioral Sciences and the Law*, **17** (January/March), 7–27.

Baldwin, Marjorie L. (2000), 'Estimating the potential benefits of the ADA on the wages and employment of persons with disabilities', in Peter David Blanck (ed.), *Employment, Disability Policy and the Americans with Disabilities Act*, Evanston, IL: Northwestern University Press, pp. 258–84.

Baldwin, Marjorie L. (2003), 'New estimates of discrimination against workers with disabilities: the role of customer interaction in the product market', in John S. Heywood and James Peoples (eds), *Product Market Structure and Labor Market Treatment*, Albany, NY: State University of New York Press, pp. 125–54.

Baldwin, Marjorie L. and William G. Johnson (1992a), 'Estimating the employment effects of wage discrimination', *Review of Economics and Statistics*, **74** (August), 446–55.

Baldwin, Marjorie L. and William G. Johnson (1992b), 'A test of the measures of non-discriminatory wages used to study wage discrimination', *Economics Letters*, **39**, 223–7.

Baldwin, Marjorie L. and William G. Johnson (1994a), 'Labor market discrimination against men with disabilities', *Journal of Human Resources*, **29** (Winter), 1–19.

Baldwin, Marjorie L. and William G. Johnson (1994b), 'The sources of employment discrimination: prejudice or poor information', in David Saunders (ed.), *Advances in Employment Issues*, Greenwich, CT: JAI Press, pp. 163–79.

Baldwin, Marjorie L. and William G. Johnson (1995), 'Labor market discrimination against women with disabilities', *Industrial Relations*, **34** (October), 555–77.

Baldwin, Marjorie L. and William G. Johnson (2000), 'Labor market discrimination against men with disabilities in the year of the A.D.A', *Southern Economic Journal*, **66** (January), 548–66.

Baldwin, Marjorie L., Richard J. Butler and William G. Johnson (2001), 'A hierarchical theory of occupational segregation and wage discrimination', *Economic Inquiry*, **29** (January), 94–110.

Becker, Gary (1971), *The Economics of Discrimination*, Chicago: University of Chicago Press.

Beegle, Kathleen and Wendy A. Stock (2003), 'The labor market effects of disability discrimination laws', *Journal of Human Resources*, **38** (Fall), 806–59.

Berkowitz, Monroe and William G. Johnson (1974) 'Health and labor force participation', *Journal of Human Resources*, **9** (Winter), 117–28.

Blanck, Peter David (ed.) (2000), *Employment, Disability, and the Americans With Disabilities Act*, Evanston, IL: Northwestern University Press.

Bodvarsson, Orn B. and Mark D. Partridge (2001), 'A supply and demand model of co-worker, employer and customer discrimination', *Labour Economics*, **8** (June), 389–416.

Burkhauser, Richard V. (1990), 'Morality on the cheap: the Americans with Disabilities Act', *Regulation*, **13** (Summer), 47–56.

Burkhauser, Richard V. and Mary C. Daly (1996), 'Employment and economic well-being following the onset of a disability', in Jerry L. Mashaw, Virginia Reno, Richard V. Burkhauser and

Monroe Berkowitz, *Disability, Work and Cash Benefits*, Kalamazoo, MI: W.E. Upjohn Institute, pp. 59–101.

Cain, Glen G. (1986), 'The economic analysis of labor market discrimination: a survey', in Orley Ashenfelter and Richard Layard (eds), *Handbook of Labor Economics Volume I*, Amsterdam: North-Holland, pp. 693–785.

Charles, Kerwin Kofi (2003), 'The longitudinal structure of earnings losses among work-limited disabled workers', *Journal of Human Resources*, **38** (Summer), 618–46.

Collignon, Frederick C. (1986), 'The role of reasonable accommodation in employing disabled persons in private industry', in Monroe Berkowitz and M. Anne Hill (eds), *Disability and the Labor Market*, Ithaca, NY: Cornell University ILR Press, pp. 196–241.

Cotton, Jeremiah (1988), 'On the decomposition of wage differentials', *Review of Economics and Statistics*, **70** (May), 236–43.

Darity, William (1994), 'Loaded dice in the labor market: racial discrimination and inequality', in Susan F. Feiner (ed.), *Race and Gender in the American Economy*, Englewood Cliffs, NJ: Prentice Hall, pp. 18–21.

DeLeire, Thomas (2000), 'The wage and employment effects of the Americans with Disabilities Act', *Journal of Human Resources*, **35** (Fall), 693–715.

DeLeire, Thomas (2001), 'Changes in wage discrimination against people with disabilities: 1984–1993', *Journal of Human Resources*, **36** (Winter), 144–58.

Druss, Benjamin G., Steven C. Marcus, Robert A. Rosenheck, Mark Olfson, Teri Tanielian and Harold A. Pincus (2000), 'Understanding disability in mental and general medical conditions', *American Journal of Psychiatry*, **157** (September), 1485–91.

Even, William E. and David A. MacPherson (1991), 'Plant size and the decline of unionism', *Economic Letters*, **32** (May), 393–8.

Goldin, Claudia (2002), 'A pollution theory of discrimination: male and female differences in occupations and earnings', NBER working paper no. W8985 (June).

Gouvier, W. Drew, Sara Sytsma-Jordan and Stephen Mayville (2003), 'Patterns of discrimination in hiring job applicants with disabilities: the role of disability type, job complexity, and public contact', *Rehabilitation Psychology*, **48** (August 2003), 175–81.

Hale, Thomas W., Howard V. Hayghe and John M. McNeil (1998), 'Persons with disabilities: labor market activity, 1994', *Monthly Labor Review*, **121** (September), 3–12.

Hallock, Kevin F., Wallace Hendricks and Emer Broadbent (1998), 'Discrimination by gender and disability status: do worker perceptions match statistical measures?', *Southern Economic Journal*, **65** (October), 245–63.

Haveman, Robert and Barbara Wolfe (1990), 'The economic well-being of the disabled', *Journal of Human Resources*, **25** (Winter), 32–54.

Haveman Robert, Karen Holden, Barbara Wolfe, Paul Smith and Kathryn Wilson (2000), 'The changing economic status of disabled women, 1982–1991', in David S. Salkever and Alan Sorkin (eds), *Research in Human Capital and Development*, *Vol. 13*, Stamford, CT: JAI Press, pp. 51–80.

Heckman, James J. (1980), 'Sample selection bias as a specification error with an application to the estimation of labor supply functions', in J.P. Smith (ed.), *Female Labor Supply*, Princeton, NJ: Princeton University Press, pp. 206–48.

Hendershot, Gerry E. (2002) 'Integrating comparable measures of disability in federal surveys: the national center for health statistics', *Vital and Health Statistics*, **4** (32), (July), DHHS Publication No. (PHS) 2002–1469, Hyattsville, MD.

Hendricks, Wallace, Elissa Perry and Emir Broadbent (2000), 'An exploration of access and treatment discrimination and job satisfaction among college graduates with and without physical disabilities', *Human Relations*, **53** (July), 923–55.

Hendricks, Wallace, ChrisAnn Schrio-Geist and Emir Broadbent (1997), 'Labor market outcomes for persons with long-term disabilities and college educations', *Industrial Relations*, **36** (January), 46–60.

Hirsch, Barry T. and David A. Macpherson (2004), 'Wages, sorting on skill, and the racial composition of jobs', *Journal of Labor Economics*, **22** (January), 189–210.

Huang, Ju-Chin, Marjorie L. Baldwin and Karen Smith Conway (2005), 'Post-injury work incentives revisited', working paper.

Johnson, William G. (1997), 'The future of disability policy: benefits payments or civil rights?', *Annals of the American Academy of Political and Social Science*, **549** (January), 160–72.
Johnson, William G. and James Lambrinos (1985), 'Wage discrimination against handicapped men and women', *Journal of Human Resources*, **20** (Spring), 571–90.
Johnson, William G. and James Lambrinos (1987), 'The effect of prejudice on the wages of disabled workers', *Policy Studies Journal*, **15** (March), 571–90.
Jolls, Christine and J.J. Prescott (2004), 'Disaggregating employment protection: the case of disability discrimination', NBER working paper no. 10740.
Karlan, Pamela S. and George Rutherglen (1996), 'Disabilities, discrimination, and reasonable accommodation', *Duke Law Journal*, **46** (October), 1–41.
Kidd, Michael P., Peter J. Sloane and Ivan Ferko (2000), 'Disability and the labour market: an analysis of British males', *Journal of Health Economics*, **19** (November), 961–81.
Kruse, Douglas L. (1998), 'Persons with disabilities: demographic, income, and health care characteristics, 1993', *Monthly Labor Review*, **121** (September), 13–22.
Levitt, Steven D. (2003), 'Testing theories of discrimination: evidence from *Weakest Link*', NBER working paper no. 9449.
Moss, Kathryn, Scott Burris, Michael Ullman, Matthew C. Johnsen and Jeffrey Swanson (2001), 'Unfunded mandate: an empirical study of the implementation of the Americans with Disabilities Act by the Equal Employment Opportunity Commission', *University of Kansas Law Review*, **50** (November), 1–109.
Moss, Kathryn, Michael Ullman, Matthew C. Johnsen, Barbara E. Starrett and Scott Burris (1999a), 'Different paths to justice: the ADA, employment, and administrative enforcement by the EEOC and FEPAs', *Behavioral Sciences and the Law*, **17** (January/March), 29–46.
Moss, Kathryn, Michael Ullman, Barbara E. Starrett, Scott Burris and Matthew C. Johnsen (1999b), 'Outcomes of employment discrimination charges filed under the Americans with Disabilities Act', *Psychiatric Services*, **50** (August), 1028–35.
Nagi, Saad Z. (1969), *Disability and Rehabilitation*, Columbus, OH: Ohio State University.
Neumark, David (1988), 'Employers' discriminatory behavior and the estimation of wage discrimination', *Journal of Human Resources*, **23** (Summer), 279–95.
Oaxaca, Ronald L. (1973), 'Male–female wage differentials in urban labor markets', *International Economic Review*, **14** (October), 693–709.
Phelps, Edmund S. (1972), 'The statistical theory of racism and sexism', *American Economic Review*, **62** (September), 659–61.
Reimers, Cordelia (1983), 'Labor market discrimination against Hispanic and black men', *Review of Economics and Statistics*, **65** (November), 570–79.
Roemer, John E. (1979), 'Divide and conquer: micro foundations of a Marxian theory of wage discrimination', *Bell Journal of Economics*, **10** (Autumn), 695–705.
Royal, George P. and Michael C. Roberts (1987), 'Students' perceptions of and attitudes toward disabilities: a comparison of twenty conditions', *Journal of Clinical Child Psychology*, **16** (June), 122–32.
Salkever, David S. and Marisa E. Domino (2000), 'Within-group "structural" tests of labor-market discrimination: a study of persons with serious disabilities', collective volume article in Alan Sorkin (eds), *The Economics of Disability. Research in Human Capital and Development*, vol. 13, Stamford, CT: JAI Press, pp. 33–50.
Sherman, Susan M. and Nancy M. Robinson (eds) (1982), *Ability Testing of Handicapped People*, Washington: National Academy Press.
Thurow, Lester C. (1975), *Generating Inequality*, New York: Basic Books.
Tringo John L. (1970), 'The hierarchy of preference toward disability groups', *Journal of Special Education*, **4** (Summer/Fall), 295–306.
Tucker, Bonnie Poitras (1997), 'The ADA and deaf culture: contrasting precepts, conflicting results', *Annals of the American Academy of Political and Social Science*, **549** (January), 24–36.
Verkerke, J. Hoult (1999), 'An economic defense of disability discrimination law', University of Virginia School of Law working paper no. 99-14 (June).
Wehman, Paul (1993), 'Employment opportunities and career development', in Paul Wehman (ed.), *The ADA Mandate for Social Change*, Baltimore: Paul H. Brookes Publishing Co., pp. 45–68.

Westbrook, Mary T., Varoe Legge and Mark Pennay (1993), 'Attitudes towards disabilities in a multicultural society', *Social Science and Medicine*, **36** (March), 615–24.

White, Rebecca Hanner. (2000), 'Deference and disability discrimination', *Michigan Law Review*, **99** (December), 532–87.

WHO (1980), *International Classification of Impairments, Disabilities and Handicaps*, Geneva: World Health Organization.

WHO (2001), *International Classification of Functioning, Disability, and Health*, Geneva: World Health Organization.

Yuker, Harold E (1987), 'The disability hierarchies: comparative reactions to various types of physical and mental disabilities', unpublished manuscript, Hofstra University.

Appendix   Methods for estimating discrimination

Single-equation model
When a single equation is used to estimate discriminatory wage differentials, the wage functions are typically estimated in semi-logarithmic form:

$$\ln W_i = \beta \mathbf{X}_i + \gamma Y_i + c\lambda_i + \varepsilon_i. \tag{5A.1}$$

In this specification, the dependent variable is the natural log of the hourly wage rate, $\mathbf{X}$ is a vector of variables representing worker productivity and labor market characteristics, and ε is a mean-zero, random disturbance term. Y represents either a single binary variable identifying persons with disabilities, or a vector identifying persons with different types of impairments. The coefficient (vector) γ defines the relationship between disability and wages (controlling for the productivity-related characteristics in the vector $\mathbf{X}$). The sample selection variable, λ, derived from preliminary probit models of the probability of employment estimated for the full sample of workers and non-workers stratified by disability status, corrects for the selection bias that results because offer wages are not observed for non-workers.

When the equation is estimated with a single binary for disability status (that is, the dependent variable is the natural log of the hourly wage rate), the estimate of γ (after a simple conversion) represents the percentage wage differential between disabled and non-disabled workers, holding constant the productivity differences that are represented by other variables in the model. When Y is a vector of binary variables identifying persons with different types of disabilities, γ is a vector of coefficients that estimates the productivity-controlled wage differentials between each impairment group and the control group of non-disabled persons.

Wage decomposition
The decomposition technique is based on a similar wage equation estimated separately for disabled and non-disabled workers. Typically, the equations have the form,

$$W_{iNP} = \beta_{NP} \mathbf{X}_{iNP} + c_{NP}\lambda_{iNP} + \varepsilon_{iNP} \tag{5A.2a}$$
$$W_{iP} = \beta_{P} \mathbf{X}_{iP} + c_{P}\lambda_{iP} + \varepsilon_{iP} \tag{5A.2b}$$

where the notation has the same interpretation as above, but NP and P represent the non-disabled (no prejudice) and disabled (prejudice) groups, respectively. Because the decomposition is based on separate equations for each group, it allows the slope coefficients of the wage equation to differ between the minority and majority groups, rather than the simpler approach in which only the intercepts may differ (as indicated by the coefficient of Y in equation 5A.1).

Using the means and coefficient estimates of the variables in the wage equation, the difference in mean offer wages between non-disabled (NP) and disabled (P) workers can be decomposed into an 'explained' part generated by differences in average productivity (represented by the variables in the vector $\mathbf{X}$), and an 'unexplained' part generated by differences in the returns to those characteristics, as measured by the regression coefficients:

$$(\bar{W}_{NP} - \bar{W}_P) - (\hat{c}_{NP}\bar{\lambda}_{NP} - \hat{c}_P\bar{\lambda}_P) = (\bar{\mathbf{X}}_{NP} - \bar{\mathbf{X}}_P)(\mathbf{D}\hat{\boldsymbol{\beta}}_{NP} + (1 - \mathbf{D})\hat{\boldsymbol{\beta}}_P)$$
$$+ (\bar{\mathbf{X}}_{NP} (1 - \mathbf{D}) + \bar{\mathbf{X}}_P\mathbf{D})(\hat{\boldsymbol{\beta}}_{NP} - \hat{\boldsymbol{\beta}}_P). \quad (5A.2c)$$

The left side of equation (5A.2c) represents the difference between mean offer wages for majority and minority workers, that is, the difference in observed average wages, corrected for selection bias. The first term on the right represents the difference in offer wages attributable to differences in average productivity, as represented by means of the variables in the wage equation; the second term represents the unexplained part of the wage differential, attributed to discrimination. The second term is a residual (measuring the differential that is not explained by control variables in the model) so it is an unbiased measure of discrimination only if no significant variables are omitted from the wage equations and all variables are accurately measured. The weighting vector $\mathbf{D}$, with elements valued from 0 to 1, represents the assumed relationship of the unobservable nondiscriminatory wage structure to observed wages.

Employment decomposition
The decomposition of differences in employment rates for majority and minority workers is based on estimates of probit likelihood functions for the minority (P) and majority groups (NP):

$$L_P = \prod_{i \in E}[\phi(\boldsymbol{\delta}_P\mathbf{Z}_{iP})]\prod_{i \in \bar{E}}[1 - \phi(\boldsymbol{\delta}_P\mathbf{Z}_{iP})], \quad (5A.3a)$$
$$L_{NP} = \prod_{i \in E}[\phi(\boldsymbol{\delta}_{NP}\mathbf{Z}_{iNP})]\prod_{i \in \bar{E}}[1 - \phi(\boldsymbol{\delta}_{NP}\mathbf{Z}_{iNP})]. \quad (5A.3b)$$

In equations (5A.3a) and (5A.3b), E indicates individuals who are employed, $\bar{E}$ indicates individuals who are not employed, ϕ is the cumulative distribution function of a standard normal random variable, $\mathbf{Z}$ is a vector of individual characteristics that influence the employment decision, and $\boldsymbol{\delta}$ is a corresponding vector of coefficients.

The explained part of the participation gap, *EPG*, is defined as the difference between predicted probabilities of employment for non-disabled and disabled workers that is explained by differences in their average characteristics, holding returns to those characteristics constant. The explained part is measured by

$$EPG = \left[\frac{1}{n_{NP}} \sum_{i=1}^{n_{NP}} \phi(\hat{\delta}_{NP} Z_{iNP}) \right] - \left[\frac{1}{n_P} \sum_{i=1}^{n_P} \phi(\hat{\delta}_{NP} Z_{iP}) \right], \quad (5A.4)$$

the difference between the predicted probability of employment for non-disabled workers, derived from the probit function using individual characteristics and estimated coefficients for the non-disabled sample, and the predicted probability of employment for disabled workers, using individual characteristics for the disabled sample and estimated coefficients for the non-disabled.

The unexplained part of the participation gap, *UPG*, is defined as the difference between predicted probabilities of employment for non-disabled and disabled workers with identical characteristics. Assuming that non-disabled workers have the same characteristics as the disabled group, the unexplained differential is measured by:

$$UPG = \left[\frac{1}{n_P} \sum_{i=1}^{n_P} \phi(\hat{\delta}_{NP} Z_{iP}) \right] - \left[\frac{1}{n_P} \sum_{i=1}^{n_P} \phi(\hat{\delta}_P Z_{iP}) \right], \quad (5A.5)$$

the difference between the predicted probability of employment for non-disabled workers, derived from the probit function using individual characteristics for the disabled group and estimated coefficients for the non-disabled, and the predicted probability of employment for disabled workers, using individual characteristics and estimated coefficients for the disabled sample.

6 Discrimination based on sexual orientation: a review of the literature in economics and beyond

*M.V. Lee Badgett**

Over the last three decades a growing political movement among lesbian, gay and bisexual (LGB) people has led to a heightened public debate about the existence of discrimination against LGB people and about the appropriate government response to actual or perceived discrimination.[1] Academics in general, and economists in particular, have been slower to respond to the need to study discrimination. In the last ten years, however, economists have awakened to some of the interesting intellectual questions implicated by considering discrimination and sexuality. Recently economists have produced a flurry of empirical papers analyzing earnings differences by sexual orientation. Overall, the bulk of the evidence from studies by economists and others fits the hypothesis that lesbian, gay and bisexual people face employment discrimination in the labor market in the United States and in some other countries.

Before reviewing the evidence gleaned from these studies, I will briefly review the historical and policy backgrounds and then outline some of the important methodological issues that shape the design and interpretation of specific studies, including measurement issues and possible endogeneity issues. Even though discrimination can occur in many different market and non-market contexts, almost all empirical research has been conducted with respect to the labor market, which will be the exclusive focus of this chapter.

History and policy context

At one time, asking whether lesbian, gay or bisexual people were treated differently from similarly qualified heterosexual people in the labor market would have seemed a silly question, since many jobs explicitly barred gay people. Since some time after World War I, the United States has forbidden gay people to serve in the military (Eskridge and Hunter, 1997). In the 1950s, government witch-hunts sought out and fired homosexuals in the State Department and in other security-related jobs (Johnson, 1994–5). Openly gay people were (and still are in some places) banned from working with children,

* I thank Jeff Frank and John Blandford for helpful comments on earlier drafts.

and such discrimination has been upheld by the judicial system (Eskridge and Hunter, 1997, pp. 627–9). Licensing requirements for jobs as diverse as barbers or stockbrokers at one time barred individuals who engaged in activities seen as immoral or illegal, such as homosexual behavior (Teal, 1971).

Some of those barriers to the employment of LGB people are now illegal in certain states and cities. Fifteen states (Hawaii, California, Nevada, Wisconsin, Minnesota, Illinois, Massachusetts, Vermont, New Hampshire, New Mexico, New York, Connecticut, New Jersey, Rhode Island and Maryland) outlaw sexual orientation discrimination by private employers, as do 285 cities, counties and government organizations (Human Rights Campaign, 2003). One estimate is that roughly a quarter of the US population is covered by statewide sexual orientation nondiscrimination laws, and another 14 per cent are covered by local laws (van der Meide, 2000). Clinton's 1998 Executive Order 11478 prohibited discrimination based on sexual orientation in civilian federal employment. Most of these new policies were enacted in the latter half of the 1990s, and the intensity of enforcement is not known, so their impact on the existence or degree of discrimination is also unknown.

Despite these legal changes, at least one form of differential compensation of LGB workers is still common and legal. Employers typically offer compensation that includes both wages and other noncash fringe benefits, such as family leave, vacation time, health insurance and pensions. In 2000, for instance, 61 per cent of full-time employees were offered health insurance benefits, and most of those workers can get health insurance coverage for their families (US Bureau of Labor Statistics, 2000). But since LGB employees cannot legally marry their same-sex partners, those partners are not eligible for available health insurance coverage or other marriage-linked benefits. This differential treatment of same-sex partners – even when those partnerships are virtually indistinguishable from marriage in terms of relationship commitment, longevity and economic interdependence – constitutes one obvious form of explicit compensation discrimination against LGB employees.[2] While a growing number of employers are beginning to offer spousal benefits to their employees' same-sex domestic partners, only 14 per cent of firms that offer health insurance are willing to provide benefits to a same-sex domestic partner (Kaiser Family Foundation, 2004), demonstrating that most LGB employees do not have access to partner benefits. This particular compensation discrimination issue has only recently been discussed at a public policy level and has not been the subject of much study by economists (see Badgett, 2001, for a longer discussion of partner benefits).

In the current policy environment, the question of whether LGB people experience labor market-based discrimination has taken center stage in many debates about appropriate civil rights policies. Policymakers who see nondiscrimination laws as a burden to employers will not add protected categories lightly. Legislative hearings and lobbying highlight the issue of the existence of discrimination based on sexual orientation.

Methodological issues

Not all observers agree that pervasive wage or employment discrimination occurs against LGB people, illustrating the need for further study by economists and others. Undertaking systematic studies that compare the workplace experiences of LGB and heterosexual workers for evidence of discrimination runs into several conceptual issues that complicate the development of valid and reliable survey instruments and sampling designs.

The first complication is defining what one means by 'sexual orientation', or being gay, lesbian, bisexual or heterosexual. Sexuality encompasses several potentially distinct dimensions of human behavior, attraction and personal identity, as decades of research on human sexuality have shown. Perhaps the findings from the 1992 National Health and Social Life Survey (NHSLS) reveal the complexity most clearly (Laumann *et al.*, 1994). One group of respondents, 6.2 per cent of men and 4.4 per cent of women, report feeling sexual attraction to people of the same sex. A smaller group, 4.1 per cent of women and 4.9 per cent of men, have engaged in sexual behavior with someone of the same sex since the age of 18. An even smaller group, 2.8 per cent of men and 1.4 per cent of women, reported that they think of themselves as gay (or lesbian, for women) or bisexual. And the potential nesting is not necessarily complete or consistent: some people who have same-sex desires have never acted on them, and even a small number of men who think of themselves as gay or bisexual report no same-sex behavior or attraction, for instance.

For economists and other social scientists interested in survey-based comparisons of economic outcomes by sexual orientation, the different possible measures of sexual orientation obviously pose an empirical challenge. One approach is to choose the definition that best fits the social context being studied. For labor market interactions, self-identity might best capture a characteristic that could cause differential treatment by employers or fellow employees, since identity might influence labor market decisions and openness about one's sexuality in the workplace.[3] For studies of health-related issues or studies of identity development, sexual behavior might be a better measure. Unfortunately, little actual choice exists for researchers since currently only the NHSLS offers a set of questions encompassing more than one dimension of sexuality for adults and including identity.

In practice, relatively few good data sets exist that both are probability samples and ask questions on sexuality. Researchers studying labor market issues who would prefer self-identity measures have used behavioral measures in two major ways. One approach that I have used with data from the General Social Survey (Badgett, 1995, 2001) involves identifying LGB people on the basis of relative lifetime frequency of same-sex sexual behavior. In other words, I classify a person as LGB if he or she has had at least as many same-sex partners as different-sex partners since the age of 18. Other economists (for example, Black, Makar, Sanders and Taylor, 2003; Blandford, 2003) have used GSS data on sexual partners in the last year or last five years to classify sexual orientation, although such definitions have the disadvantage of not being able to classify people without recent sex partners.[4] Blandford (2003) further separates 'open' LGB people who are not currently married from the 'masked' LGB who are currently married.

While both methods are likely to sort individuals whose same-sex orientation is relatively weak into the 'heterosexual' category, the potential for misclassifying individuals is obvious but unavoidable, since the GSS provides no data on the length or nature of relationships. Therefore my measure probably misclassifies someone who had five very brief different-sex relationships while in college, followed by a 20-year same-sex relationship. The second measure probably misclassifies someone who ended a 20-year same-sex relationship and followed it with one brief different-sex relationship over the next five years.

The NHSLS, which did collect data on length of relationships, is too small to make definitive statements about which of these measurement strategies is more prone to misclassification. That survey suggests, however, that the first behavioral measure using behavior since age 18 comes fairly close to a measure of identity, since less than 16 per cent of people with at least as many same-sex as different-sex partners considered themselves 'heterosexual' (Badgett, 2001, p. 30) Another 69 per cent considered themselves gay, lesbian or bisexual, and the rest considered themselves 'something else'. But Blandford shows that supplementing the more recent data on sexual behavior with current marital status to create sexual orientation classifications matches up better with the NHSLS identity variable, especially for women. His variable matches up with the LGB identity variable for 92 per cent of men and 77 per cent of women in this small sample.

Even with appropriate questions on sexuality, a second major methodological complication emerges. Because homosexuality is a stigmatized behavior and identity, respondents may not answer questions truthfully for fear of embarrassment or disclosure beyond the survey takers, even when anonymity or confidentiality is assured. While we do not have a clear idea of how much this problem affects our data, evidence suggests that survey methods influence respondents' answers. A recent extensive review of methodological issues related to studying lesbians by an Institute of Medicine panel indicates that self-administered forms and audio computer-assisted self-interviews (ACASI) appear to elicit more truthful information about sensitive topics (Institute of Medicine, 1999).

However, perhaps the larger question is whether misreporting is correlated with a potential dependent variable, such as income. In that case, the coefficient on an independent variable for being LGB, for instance, will be biased. Only one study of this possibility exists, in which two convenience samples of cohabiting same-sex couples were asked whether they used the 'unmarried partner' option on the 2000 US Census (a data set that will likely be used extensively by economists to study LGB people) (Badgett and Rogers, 2002). Although the unmarried partner category best fit their household situations, 13 per cent of couples in one sample and 19 per cent of a second sample did not use this option. Respondents with higher income levels (in the first sample) and higher education levels (in the second sample) were more likely to call themselves unmarried partners than those with lower income or lower education. If this reporting bias holds in the overall sample of same-sex couples from the Census, we would predict that the income levels of unmarried partners are *higher* than the actual average in Census 2000. We do not know whether such a bias exists in the samples used in the research discussed below, however.

A closely related third methodological issue concerns other sources of endogeneity. Disclosure of homosexuality may be a necessary condition to put individuals at direct risk of discrimination by employers or co-workers.[5] Disclosure may be involuntary if, for example, co-workers guess, assume or discover that an individual is LGB from other sources, but there is no obvious relationship between involuntary disclosure and economic variables. Voluntary disclosure, on the other hand, may well be related to income or occupation. Having a high income might increase what an individual perceives to be at stake in risking discrimination through workplace disclosure. Alternatively, higher incomes and the status that accompanies high incomes may help to insulate individuals from direct discrimination. No probability samples exist to explore the extent of this issue.[6]

Further complicating matters, sexual behavior and sexual identities might also be related in some way to economic outcomes or to an individual's socioeconomic class background.[7] From a rational choice perspective *à la* Richard Posner (1992), the choice of a same-sex partner is an outcome determined by individual preferences and budget constraints. According to Posner, factors like high incomes that reduce search costs for sexual partners will increase homosexual sex for men, especially those with a strong preference for homosexual sex. A more sociological model of behavior that involves sexual scripts and social networks (Laumann *et al.*, 1994) could have a similar implication: a family's economic status might influence the scripts and networks that individuals eventually operate within, and openness to homosexuality might vary by economic class or other norms correlated with family background. The finding, by Laumann *et al.* (1994), that more educated women and men are more likely to have had same-sex partners and to identify as LGB could fit either theory. The opportunity for and costs of engaging in stigmatized behavior are quite likely to vary systematically with some of the regressors that economists typically use. This complication should, at the very least, influence our interpretation of findings in statistical comparisons of income or wages by sexual orientation and should lead us to collect new data that would allow for more direct consideration of these effects.

Overall, these measurement and endogeneity complications challenge economists to construct and interpret econometric tests carefully, since we currently have no direct way of measuring the impact of these theoretical relationships. Such issues are generally not present in studying race and sex discrimination, since those characteristics are more reliably observed or reported.

A final difficulty in studying discrimination based on sexual orientation might be summed up as 'We have big concerns about existing data, but the biggest problem is that we have so little of it.' Very few probability samples ask questions about sexual orientation and other economic variables, and those surveys that exist are typically of small samples. Researchers studying LGB people in the United States have primarily relied on data from the General Social Survey, which has measures of sexual behavior but has a small sample size in any given year, and the 1990 and 2000 US Censuses, which have a large sample size but allow us only to identify individuals who have same-sex 'unmarried partners'.[8] However, researchers in other countries have used more detailed data or developed creative research strategies to gather data, which suggest promising methodological paths for US research.

Evidence of discrimination from sources outside of economics traditions
Some evidence of discrimination against LGB people comes from studies using methods that are not typically used by economists, including data from convenience samples, ethnographic studies and attitude studies. While such findings might be less convincing to economists who tend to look for evidence of discrimination in actual economic outcomes, such as wages, employment status or occupational attainment, this other body of research is helpful in assessing perceptions and in identifying possible sources of discriminatory behavior.

One approach that has been used primarily outside of academia by political groups concerned about sexual orientation discrimination is to ask LGB people directly whether they believe they have experienced discrimination in employment or other economic arenas. These surveys typically address a particular geographic area or occupation and use LGB organization mailing lists, social gathering places or snowball techniques to recruit respondents. The only known national probability sample of this kind, from a 1989 study conducted for the *San Francisco Examiner*, found that 16 per cent of LGB respondents reported an experience of employment discrimination based on sexual orientation at some point in their lives (*San Francisco Examiner*, 1989). This finding fits within the range of estimates from nonrandom samples, which generally range from 16 per cent to 30 per cent of respondents reporting employment discrimination of some kind (Levine, 1980; Levine and Leonard, 1984; Badgett, 1997).

While these surveys clearly suggest that individuals believe they experience discrimination, the self-reporting strategy is less helpful for assessing the incidence of discrimination and its economic effects. Employees might misperceive the motivation of acts, such as failing to receive a job or promotion, either ascribing discriminatory motives where none existed or failing to suspect discrimination where it actually occurred. Also LGB people who believe they have experienced discrimination might be more likely to respond to surveys, skewing the prevalence rate found in a nonrandom sample.

A related empirical strategy is to look at the number of actual complaints in jurisdictions with nondiscrimination laws that include sexual orientation. Complaints are likely to be a function of knowledge about the law and enforcement effort, which may not be substantial in cities or counties but is perhaps greater when statewide laws exist. Rubenstein (2002) collected data on complaints from nine states with such laws and from the District of Columbia. The actual numbers of complaints seemed small, as in Connecticut in 1995, where only 25 people filed complaints alleging sexual orientation discrimination. But Rubenstein argues that the raw numbers are misleading, and he shows that the ratios of sexual orientation complaints to the likely state LGB population were comparable to ratios for sex or race discrimination complaints.

A rarer but also revealing strategy is to survey heterosexuals and ask whether they have witnessed discrimination. One survey of heterosexual political scientists found that 11–14 per cent of them had witnessed anti-gay discrimination in academic employment decisions, including hiring and tenure decisions (Committee on the Status of Lesbians and Gays in the Profession, 1995). Similarly, 24 per cent of female heterosexual lawyers and 17 per cent of male heterosexual lawyers in Los Angeles reported experiencing or witnessing anti-gay discrimination (Los Angeles County Bar Association Committee on Sexual Orientation Bias, 1994).

Finally, some inequality researchers, particularly psychologists and political scientists, have focused on underlying attitudes that might motivate employers or co-workers to act in a discriminatory way. Evidence of anti-gay animus exists, but over time that evidence has grown more complex to interpret. In public opinion polls large majorities of individuals in the United States state that they support equal employment opportunities for LGB people (Yang,

1997). Nevertheless, support for laws prohibiting discrimination based on sexual orientation comes from a bare majority of respondents. Furthermore, measures designed to gauge more subtle attitudes toward LGB people, such as the National Election Studies 'feeling thermometer' or questions about the morality of same-sex sexual behavior, uncover lingering ambivalence and hostility toward LGB people (ibid.). Herek and other social psychologists have found that attitudes towards lesbians and gay men are negatively correlated with being male, less educated and more traditional in gender roles (Herek, 1991). One study suggests that employers appear to share negative attitudes. A survey of Alaskan employers in 1987 found that over a quarter would not hire or promote an employee believed to be gay, and 18 per cent would fire a gay employee (Brause, 1989).

Of course, attitudes are only one influence in individual behavior, so anti-gay attitudes (or even positive attitudes, for that matter) might not significantly influence behavior in the workplace. Economic and psychological models of behavior stress the importance of constraints, whether economic constraints (income and relative prices) or more social constraints (such as social norms) in determining actual behavior. The likelihood of moving from individual anti-gay attitudes to actual discriminatory behavior will depend on the social, cultural and economic context that individuals operate within (for example, MacCoun, 1996).

While the evidence presented in this section may not definitively establish the existence, extent or effects of sexual orientation discrimination, such evidence nevertheless points economists in familiar directions. Negative attitudes evoke a Becker-type model of discrimination, focusing on individual prejudice as a source of differential treatment in the workplace. The potential for conflict between gay workers and those with anti-gay attitudes calls to mind models of productivity-detracting workplace conflict that results in poorer treatment for the less favored group of gay workers. The early evidence of discrimination and discriminatory motives from non-economic studies should – at the very least – make economists curious.

Looking for differences in economic outcomes

A new direction in research on discrimination against LGB people has developed over the last decade as economists have analyzed existing data for differences in economic outcomes that might be related to sexual orientation. Most attention has focused on wages, not surprisingly, since measuring wage differentials dominates the research on race and sex discrimination. The standard econometric test for discrimination is whether wage differences between LGB and heterosexual workers exist after controlling for human capital and other relevant characteristics. Other more direct tests of discrimination, such as the matched-pair audit methodology (also known as 'correspondence testing') used to measure race and sex discrimination (for example, Turner *et al.*, 1991) have only been attempted twice in studying sexual orientation discrimination and will be presented after the wage study discussion.

Twelve studies summarized in Table 6.1 have compared the earnings of LGB and heterosexual people using data from probability samples, primarily from the United States. The two main US data sets used have been the GSS (usually supplemented with data from the National Health and Social Life Survey, which used comparable questions), which collects data on the sex of sex partners, and the 1990 US Census of Population, which allows identification of people with same-sex unmarried partners. The questions on these surveys allow researchers to categorize people's sexual orientation according to their sexual or social behavior. As yet no national probability samples with data on respondents' self-identified sexual orientation have been both publicly available and large enough to study labor market outcomes, although one recent study of California data provides such data and is included in Table 6.1.

As in the traditional approach to assessing discrimination, the 12 studies have controlled for factors that are known to influence earnings (age, experience, geographic location, marital status, race and gender, in general, and sometimes occupation and other variables of interest) and have looked at the coefficient on LGB in an ordinary least squares (OLS) model of earnings. In other words, the issues of endogeneity and disclosure raised earlier have been largely set aside, because the effect of those issues is thought either to be small or simply unmeasurable given current data.[9]

In addition to coming from several different countries, the studies in Table 6.1 differ along several other obvious dimensions, some of which appear to be related to differences in findings. First, the most important factor, as discussed below, appears to be the method for categorizing respondents into sexual orientation categories. Second, the time period varies, and some recent studies use samples pooled from different years of the GSS, which seems to have a particularly important impact on findings for women. Finally, the categorical nature of reported income data in the GSS has led some researchers to use a maximum likelihood model that takes the reported intervals into account, but the findings discussed below do not turn out to be very sensitive to this choice of technique.

Results for men in the United States
The results of these studies for gay/bisexual men have been remarkably consistent across data sets and categorization strategies. As Table 6.1 shows, every study using US data has found that gay/bisexual men earn less than heterosexual men, with a range of 13 to 32 per cent. This finding of a negative wage gap for gay men is robust to a variety of ways of classifying individuals' sexual orientation, which include behavioral classifications based on sexual

Table 6.1   Findings from studies of sexual orientation earnings differences

Study	Data	Sexual orientation definition	Findings: gay/ bisexual men	Findings: lesbian/ bisexual women
Allegretto and Arthur (2001)	1990 Census (men)	Sex of unmarried partner or spouse	Earn 14.4% less than married heterosexual men; earn 2.4% less than unmarried partnered heterosexual men	Not studied
Arabsheibani, Marin and Wadsworth (2005)	UK Labour Force Survey, 1996–2001	Sex of partner	Earn 5.2% less than married and cohabiting men	Earn 10.9% more than married and cohabiting women
Badgett (1995)	GSS (1989–91)	At least as many same-sex partners as different-sex partners since 18	24% lower	18% lower evaluating interaction between GLB and potential experience term at mean (not stat. signif.)
Badgett (2001)	GSS and NHSLS (1989–94)	Same as Badgett (1995)	17% lower	11% higher (not statistically significant)
Berg and Lien (2002)	GSS (1991–6)	At least one same-sex partner in last 5 years	22% lower earnings	30% higher earnings
Black, Makar, Sanders and Taylor (2003)	GSS and NHSLS (1989–96)	More same-sex than opposite-sex partners	19% lower	6% higher earnings (not stat. signif.)
		Same-sex partners in last year	15% lower	22% higher
		Same-sex partners in last 5 years	13% lower	27% higher
Blandford (2003)	GSS and NHSLS (1989–96)	Same-sex partners in last 1 or 5 years, interacted with whether currently married	30–32% lower	17–23% higher

Study	Data	Sexual orientation definition	Findings: gay/ bisexual men	Findings: lesbian/ bisexual women
Carpenter (2005)	2001 California Health Interview Survey; GSS (1988–2000)	Self-report whether gay, lesbian, or bi-sexual (CHIS); same-sex partners in last 5 years (GSS)	California Health Interview Survey (CHIS): gay men earn 2–3% less (not stat. signif.); bi-sexual men earn 10–15% less GSS: gay men earn 10% less (not stat. signif.); bisexual men earn 5% less (not stat. signif.)	CHIS: lesbians earn 3–6% less (not stat. signif.); bisexuals earn 6–10% less (sometimes signif.) GSS: lesbians earn 31% more; bisexual women earn 7% less (not stat. signif.)
Clain and Leppel (2001)	1990 Census (1/1000 sample, (used inter-action terms and main effects selected for inclusion based on statistical significance)	Sex of unmarried partner or spouse for those living with partner or spouse; unknown for those without partners	16% less than married men (if college educated); 22% less than men living without partners or spouses	2.2% less than women without partners or spouses (evaluated at average age assuming no kids and not in Midwest) More than married women in Midwest only
Frank (2002)	Academic and non-academic employees of 6 UK universities	Self-identity	Salary: no stat. signif. Difference Attainment of higher rank: roughly half as likely	Salary: no stat. signif. Difference overall; 12% higher for LGB women in academic positions Attainment of highest rank: no difference
Klawitter and Flatt (1998)	1990 Census	Sex of unmarried partner or spouse	13–31% lower earnings for men in same-sex couples	No stat. signif. Difference in earnings for women working full-time
Plug and Berkhout (2004)	Employed higher education graduates in Netherlands	'Concerning your sexual preference, what do you prefer?' Only men; only women; both men and women	3% lower hourly wages for those employed full-time	3% higher hourly wages for those employed full-time

Note: Findings reflect the range of point estimates from the study in roughly comparable speci-fications.

partners (GSS) and more social classifications based on the sex of an 'unmarried partner' (US Census).

The one partial exception to the pattern for men is the study by Carpenter (2005). He has data on California residents who were asked an identity-related question, 'Are you gay, lesbian or bisexual?' A follow-up question allows distinctions between bisexual and gay or lesbian respondents that Carpenter uses in his models. Carpenter finds a negative but statistically insignificant effect of being gay on men's wages in California, while bisexual men earn significantly less in most of Carpenter's California models. His models using 1988–2000 GSS data on behaviorally gay, lesbian or bisexual people (based on the last five years) find that the earnings of gay and bisexual men are lower but not statistically significantly different from heterosexual men's earnings.[10] Carpenter's findings are not generalizable, though, since they come from one state that is well-known for its large gay communities and has had a nondiscrimination law including sexual orientation since 1992. Furthermore, empirically distinguishing between the earnings differences for gay and bisexual men might make more sense in measures based on self-identity than in definitions using behavioral measures.

An issue that floats throughout the studies of men's incomes is how to account separately for the effect of the well-known male 'marriage premium', which some economists argue is an effect of unmeasured personal characteristics valued by employers (see Ginther and Zavodny, 2001, for a recent perspective), and the strong expected negative correlation between being married and being gay. Some studies simply leave out marital status (Berg and Lien, 2002) or control for both characteristics (Badgett, 1995, 2001; Black, Makar, Sanders and Taylor, 2003).

Allegretto and Arthur (2001), on the other hand, argue that comparisons of men in couples in the US Census data require a more subtle approach with a range of comparisons, since married heterosexual men will have certain desirable characteristics and men with unmarried female partners (and perhaps gay men with partners) will not. If gay men in couples are more like married men, then the wage gap of 14.4 per cent is an appropriate estimate (but is completely accounted for by the 15.1 per cent marriage premium that they find). If gay men are more like men with unmarried female partners, then the 2.4 per cent lower earnings in that comparison is a better measure of a sexual orientation wage gap. Blandford interacts marital status with behaviorally-defined sexual orientation and finds a smaller marital status gap for heterosexual men than in other studies, and a large and significant wage penalty for gay/bisexual men who are unmarried. Given these findings, he argues that the previously measured marriage premium for men mixes a positive employer demand for the job stability implied by marriage and a premium related to heterosexuality. Since his data set includes married and unmarried individuals, he can estimate the general marriage premium and finds that it is only about half the size of the wage penalty for gay men. Carpenter (2005) also experiments with inclusion and exclusion of marital status and same-sex partnership variables. He finds that gay men's earnings are significantly lower than heterosexual men's earnings when marital status is not controlled for, but the earnings effect is reduced with controls for partnership and marital status. Carpenter interprets this pattern as evidence of an earnings advantage for heterosexual married men.

A few other salient points emerge from this literature. First, Klawitter and Flatt (1998) do not find any evidence that the gay wage gap is lower in places that have nondiscrimination laws that forbid sexual orientation discrimination. They suggest that enforcement effort might be low or that policies need more time to take hold.

Second, differences in occupations by sexual orientation do not consistently affect the wage gap. I find that the wage gap increases slightly when controlling for broad occupational categories (Badgett, 1995). But Blandford finds that adding two-digit occupational controls reduces the gay earnings gap slightly, and Black, Makar, Sanders and Taylor (2003) also see a small decrease in the coefficients on being bisexual and gay, suggesting some occupational sorting by gay men into lower earning occupations.[11] Allegretto and Arthur (2001) find that occupational controls reduce the wage gap with married men slightly but increase the wage gap compared with unmarried heterosexual men. Thus there is little consistent evidence that sorting into occupations influences wages, even though such sorting may be a strategy to avoid discrimination (decreasing the wage gap) or a secondary form of discrimination (increasing the wage gap). Further preliminary investigation into the occupational positions of LGB people by Badgett and King (1997) suggests that gay/bisexual men are avoiding occupations that are likely to bring them into contact with co-workers who have negative attitudes toward homosexuality or are going into more heavily female occupations than are heterosexual men (Badgett, 1998).

Third, the observed earnings difference is not likely due to measurement error in respondents' reporting of their own sex, a source of error that is not common but could have a big impact on the measurement of incomes for the small numbers of LGB people. If some heterosexual women mistakenly reported that they were men, then the above studies would classify those women as gay men, which would tend to create a negative but spurious income impact of being gay for men (Black, Gates, Sanders and Taylor, 2000; Black, Makar, Sanders and Taylor, 2003). (The opposite would be true for women.) Black, Makar, Sanders and Taylor (2003) repeat their estimations while reclassifying as LGB people only those who report *both* same-sex and different-sex partners, arguing that having same-sex partners is rare for heterosexuals but having different-sex partners is common for LGB people. Their income results are substantially the same for both men and for women using this classification, suggesting that measurement error is not the cause of the income differences.

Results for women in the United States

In contrast to comparisons of gay and heterosexual men, the findings for women are less consistent and are sensitive to the method of defining sexual orientation and to the time period studied. Because of the differences in wages and hours for part-time and full-time workers, a difference that is especially important for women, all studies offer comparisons of lesbians and heterosexual women who are full-time workers.

Only one study (Badgett, 1995) finds a negative effect of being lesbian/bisexual on earnings, and that effect is statistically insignificant and appears to be limited to the earliest GSS data. Studies pooling GSS data from later years all find that lesbians earn more than heterosexual women, but the size and significance of the coefficient on being lesbian/bisexual is highly sensitive to the behavioral time frame used to classify sexual orientation. Classifying as lesbians all women who have had at least as many same-sex partners as different-sex partners (Badgett, 1995, 2001) or more same-sex partners (Black, Makar, Sanders and Taylor, 2003) since the age of 18 results in a small but statistically insignificant positive wage difference for lesbians. Using measures of more recent experience, having any same-sex partners in the last year, or in the last five years, results in a much larger and statistically significant earnings advantage for lesbians: 22–27 per cent higher earnings (Black, Makar, Sanders and Taylor, 2003). (Considering lesbians separately from the bisexual women shows that bisexuals earn more, too, but that effect is smaller and statistically insignificant.) Blandford classifies women as 'open' lesbians or bisexuals if they have had same-sex partners in the last year (or five years, if no partners in the last year) and are currently unmarried. He finds that lesbian/bisexual women earn 23 per cent more than heterosexual women (holding occupation constant with one-digit level dummy variables), but adding two-digit occupational controls reduces the positive earnings effect to 17 per cent.

In contrast to the GSS results, the two studies using the 1990 Census data (Klawitter and Flatt, 1998; Clain and Leppel, 2001) appear to agree that on average, for full-time workers, women who have female partners do not earn more than women with male partners. Klawitter and Flatt report positive and statistically significant coefficients for women with female partners in their published tables, but they note that the positive coefficient for lesbians was small and statistically insignificant in other regressions limited to full-time, full-year workers (p. 675). Evaluating Clain and Leppel's findings is more difficult, since they used a smaller sample of the Census with few people reporting same-sex partners (only 58 women and 91 men, in contrast to Klawitter and Flatt's 13 500 plus from a larger sample) but more complex specifications involving interaction terms.[12] In their regression results that compare women with male partners to women with female partners, Clain and Leppel do not report coefficients for having a same-sex partner or for any of the sexual orientation–age interaction terms, suggesting that those variables were not statistically significant (Table 5, p. 44). Their reported coefficients for two interaction terms show that only lesbians in the Midwest and lesbians with children earned more than heterosexual women with those characteristics.[13]

One fairly consistent conclusion one could draw from the comparisons of women's earnings is that lesbians do not earn less than heterosexual women, at least not when controlling for our imperfect measures of experience and human capital (a problem discussed further below). But these studies do not lead to a clear conclusion that lesbians earn *more* than heterosexual women. The earnings findings for lesbians are not robust across classification schemes, and no obvious standards for choosing one set of current findings over another are apparent. One strand of work using GSS data from the most recent years suggests that women with female sex partners earn more than women with only male sex partners, but only clearly for those women with female sex partners in the previous one to five years. Black, Makar, Sanders and Taylor, (2003) argue that the measures based on more recent sex partners are better indicators of identity and of a current 'lifestyle' that might be observed by employers. However, lifetime sexual histories might well be relevant for early decisions about investments in training and education, even if later employers observe a bisexual woman in a relationship with a man, for instance. The other strand of research using census data shows that women with female partners earn about the same as women with male partners after controlling for full-time work. This inconsistency is particularly troubling since we might expect a larger lesbian 'advantage' given heterosexual women's traditional household responsibilities (discussed further below). Findings from Carpenter (2005) further demonstrate that variation in findings for lesbians might be related to the methods for classification of sexual orientation: self-identified lesbians and bisexuals earn slightly less than heterosexual women in California, although the difference is not statistically significant other than in some specifications for bisexual women. Perhaps more confidence in the direction of any earnings difference will emerge when better data on sexual identity, workplace disclosure, actual experience and human capital investments appear.

Results from other countries
Three studies find similar gender patterns but different employment effects for

more limited populations studied in other countries. Plug and Berkhout (2004) analyze the earnings of recent graduates of the higher education system in the Netherlands and find a remarkably similar pattern. They argue that examining the experiences of a younger cohort allows for better measures of contemporary discrimination, if discrimination exists. Their measure of sexual orientation comes from a survey question asking, 'Concerning your sexual preference, what do you prefer?' Respondents could answer that they prefer only men, only women, or both men and women.[14] After controlling for type of degree, age, partner status, full-time employment, industry, occupation and region, the gay men earn 3 per cent less and the lesbians 3 per cent more than otherwise similar workers (they pool men and women).[15]

From the United Kingdom, Arabsheibani, Marin and Wadsworth (2005) use data from the Labour Force Survey and identify people with same-sex partners. They find that gay men earn 5.2 per cent less than men with female partners, and lesbians earn 10.9 per cent more than heterosexual women. Frank (2002) analyzes data from 813 responses to a survey at six British universities conducted by the UK Association of University Teachers.[16] Controlling for rank, age, experience, race and London location, as well as the quality of university where the respondents were educated and employed, an OLS model of salaries shows no statistically significant wage gap for LGB men or women, while women in general are paid 12 per cent less. Repeating the procedure on those in academic jobs reveals that LGB women earn 12 per cent more, however, which is significant at the 6.5 per cent level and completely balances out the gender effect. Frank also tests for a 'glass ceiling' effect, using a probit model to see the impact of sexual orientation on attainment of highest ranks in academic and non-academic positions. Here he finds evidence of a statistically significant disadvantage for gay men and for women in general, but no added sexual orientation effect for LGB women.

Interpreting the findings as evidence of discrimination
Authors of these wage studies have interpreted the results in two general ways to reconcile the seemingly different experiences of gay men and lesbians. One interpretation is that the findings of a significant wage gap for gay men are evidence of labor market discrimination (Badgett, 1995, 2001; Blandford, 2003; Klawitter and Flatt, 1998). In this interpretation, the findings of higher or at least similar earnings for lesbians seem inconsistent with a hypothesis that sexual orientation discrimination exists (Klawitter and Flatt, 1998; Clain and Leppel, 2001; Berg and Lien, 2002), but at least some proponents of the discrimination interpretation argue that the two sets of findings may still be consistent with sexual orientation discrimination against both gay men and lesbians.

First, unobserved heterogeneity among women might explain the gender pattern. Lesbians are in a very different economic position vis-à-vis hetero-sexual women in the context of existing gender roles, since lesbians may be less likely to have children and will not marry (higher earning) men. As a result, lesbians might invest in more human capital than do heterosexual women, at the very least accumulating more actual labor market experience (Badgett, 1995, 2001; Blandford, 2003 ; Black, Makar, Sanders and Taylor, 2003). (This prediction also flows from Gary Becker's model of the household division of labor, discussed further in the second interpretation below.) Thus lesbians' decisions create a positive wage effect that could offset the possible anti-gay bias effect seen in gay men's wages.

Some evidence supports this hypothesis. Lesbians work more hours and weeks than heterosexual women (Klawitter and Flatt, 1998), are more likely to work than comparable heterosexual women (Carpenter, 2005) and have higher levels of education than heterosexual women (Klawitter and Flatt, 1998; Black, Makar, Sanders and Taylor, 2003; Carpenter, 2005). Unfortunately, the available data sets do not allow us to measure experience or on-the-job training directly, and the usual proxies for experience (age minus years of education minus five) will be inadequate to pick up this difference, transferring some of the positive effect of human capital investment to the sexual orientation coefficient in an OLS wage equation. If we could measure experience and other human capital measures directly, we might instead see that lesbians earn less than heterosexual women with the same characteristics.

Second, discrimination might be stronger against gay men than lesbians for a couple of reasons. Psychological studies show that heterosexual men, who are also more likely to be bosses, have attitudes toward gay men that are more negative than those toward lesbians (Herek, 1991; Kite and Whitley, 1996). Furthermore, employers might use a man's (but not a woman's) homo-sexual orientation as a proxy for the probability that he has or will contract HIV. Since employers are not allowed to discriminate on the basis of HIV status in the United States according to the Americans with Disabilities Act, employers might instead discriminate against all gay men, which is legal in most states.

Third, some evidence suggests that lesbians are less likely than gay men to disclose their sexual orientation in the workplace, which should reduce the amount of direct discrimination possible (Badgett, 2001). Unfortunately, most of these hypotheses for the gendered pattern of differences cannot be tested directly with existing data (but see an important exception below).

Interpreting the findings as the impact of gender nonconformity
The second general interpretation of the wage study patterns seeks a more symmetric treatment of gay men and lesbians by attributing both sets of econometric findings to gender nonconformity. Gay men earn less than

expected because they act or are viewed as being more like heterosexual women, and lesbians earn more than expected because they act or are viewed as being more like heterosexual men.

The theoretical explanation offered most frequently in this second interpretation is that the wage patterns reflect family-based human capital investments as modeled in Becker's theory of the household division of labor (Black, Makar, Sanders and Taylor, 2003; Plug and Berkhout, 2004; Berg and Lien, 2002). According to Becker (1991), couples will allocate time to household production and to market production in an efficient way to maximize overall output of family goods. Members of the household take on both current tasks and human capital investment based on their comparative advantages in either household or market work.

In heterosexual marriages, biological differences, prior socialization and market wage differentials combine to give men a comparative advantage in market work and women in household labor (especially child-rearing). In anticipation of this pattern of specialization, heterosexual men will accumulate market-related human capital and women will invest in human capital that enhances home production skills. If gay men anticipate that they will partner with another man – and if the gay man assumes that his partner will also work in the labor force – then gay men will have less of an incentive than heterosexual men to invest in labor market human capital. Lesbians, on the other hand, will not expect to partner with a man and will make greater market-oriented human capital investments than will heterosexual women. Since gay men will have less and lesbians more human capital than their heterosexual counterparts, gay men will earn less than heterosexual men and lesbians more than heterosexual women.[17]

On closer examination, however, this explanation for the wage patterns is less than satisfactory, partly because it rests on Becker's uninformed vision of the family lives of same-sex couples (see Badgett, 2001) and partly because the explanation does not appear to fit other empirical patterns. First, the explanation assumes that same-sex couples will not face the same incentives as different-sex couples to specialize, drawing on Becker's claim that gay couples have a less extensive division of labor because they are similar and will not produce children.[18] But gay or lesbian individuals partnering with another of the same sex will likely come to a relationship with differences in productivities that create a comparative advantage, and many couples also have children (although a smaller percentage than heterosexual couples). And strictly speaking, Becker's model implies that couples will create a comparative advantage through human capital investment, even where none exists beforehand. Thus the incentives for specialization are arguably the same as for same-sex and different-sex couples when taking this model at its word.

Blandford also notes two other weaknesses of the Becker-style theoretical argument. First, Becker's theory supports a very different prediction for gay men's allocation of labor, in that two men in a couple might both decide to work and use their higher incomes to purchase substitutes for household production.[19] Second, the fact that gay male couples are less likely to have children, at the very least since legal and practical considerations would make acquiring children costly, means that gay men will have much less demand for household-produced goods like childcare than would married couples with children, further reducing incentives for investing in household-related human capital.

Becker's model has two primary empirical predictions that might give us gender-symmetric explanations of the sexual orientation earnings patterns: gay men will work less and lesbians more in comparison to heterosexual men and women (Berg and Lien's preferred explanation), respectively, and gay men will accumulate less and lesbians more market-related human capital (preferred by Black, Makar, Sanders and Taylor, and Plug and Berkhout). Findings from empirical studies cast grave doubt on both predictions for gay men.

We can evaluate the labor supply prediction from comparative studies of the household division of labor collected from nonrandom samples and from the 1990 Census. Those studies show that lesbians work far more than heterosexual women, as Becker's model predicts, but reveal little evidence of the Becker prediction for gay men. The 1990 US Census shows that the probability of both members of a couple working full-time is highest for same-sex male couples (Klawitter, 1995), followed closely by lesbian couples, a finding consistent with Blumstein and Schwartz's (1983) earlier study comparing couples of different sexual orientations and marital statuses. Gay male couples have the *least* amount of specialization between household and market labor of all couple types. On an individual level in the Census, the 'householder' in male same-sex couples is only 3.2 per cent less likely to work than is a married man, but the male partner is 2.5 times more likely to be employed than a wife, and hours worked are quite similar for all partnered and married men (Allegretto and Arthur, 2001, pp. 643–4, as corrected).[20] Finally, it is also worth noting that the simple labor supply explanation would not take us very far toward explaining the gay male wage gap, anyway, since most of the studies reviewed here consider only men working full-time.

Assessing the human capital prediction is obviously more difficult, given the lack of good data on anything other than educational attainment, as noted earlier in the discussion of lesbians' incentives. But what we can see does not support the Becker hypothesis for gay men. Gay men's average educational attainment is consistently higher than that of heterosexual men in the GSS and US Census. Furthermore, Black, Makar, Sanders and Taylor (2003) show that gay men's fathers' education levels are comparable to those of the heterosexual men's fathers (their Table 10). They interpret this to mean that gay men and heterosexual men have similar family backgrounds but make different educational decisions. And since sexual orientation seems to influence observable choices, they argue, it probably affects unobservable choices as well. However, Black, Makar, Sanders and Taylor do not explain why they believe that gay men would choose higher levels of observable human capital but lower levels of unobservable human capital. It seems more plausible to believe that gay men will also invest in greater unobservable human capital, perhaps to compensate for an expected disadvantage in the labor market. Overall, then, we see only evidence that lesbians have a pattern of labor supply and human capital investment that is gender nonconforming.

Other variants of the gender nonconformity explanations suffer from similar asymmetric empirical work. Clain and Leppel (2001) focus on gender-typed personality traits and speculate that lesbians might have characteristics similar to those of heterosexual men (assertiveness, dominance and so on) that make them attractive to employers. However, they offer no evidence that gay men have nonmasculine personality characteristics. Blandford (2003) bases his argument on socially normative gender roles and argues that being unmarried – a gender nonconforming position for both lesbians and gay men – places gay men at a disadvantage to heterosexual men but lesbians at an advantage as related to heterosexual women. But Blandford's own evidence is not consistent with this story: 'masked' gay/bisexual men who report being married also have lower wages than heterosexual married men (although the effect is not quite statistically significant), contrary to Blandford's prediction. However, the 'masked' lesbian/bisexual women have incomes comparable to married and unmarried heterosexual women, as Blandford would predict. Other anecdotal evidence also calls into question whether gender nonconformity is a helpful strategy for women: for instance, Ann Hopkins was denied a partnership at Price Waterhouse for being too masculine.[21]

Thus in the end we have an explanation for the observed sexual orientation wage patterns that relies at least partly on unobservable processes – the discrimination story – and an explanation that has an elegant symmetry but is contradicted by available evidence: the Becker household division of labor story and variants related to gender nonconformity. Neither seems completely satisfying, unfortunately, suggesting that we need better data and probably different methods for distinguishing the impact of discrimination and household structure on earnings.

In the last decade, economists have turned to other more direct tests for the presence of discrimination in the labor market, and the use of 'correspondence testing' or matched-pair audits has revealed clear evidence of discrimination against women and against racial minorities in the United States (for example, Bertrand and Mullainathan, 2004; Neumark, 1996). In an early example of using this method to study anti-gay discrimination, sociologist Barry Adam mailed two identical résumés for pairs of fictional Canadian law students to employers seeking interns. He labeled one applicant as gay by stating, 'Active in Gay People's Alliance' on the résumé. The gay-labeled applicant received fewer offers of an interview, which Adam interpreted as evidence of discriminatory treatment. Unfortunately, he did not test the success rates for statistical significance, and he may have confounded the sexual orientation effect with a bias against political activists, making this a limited test for discrimination.

More recently, in a carefully constructed correspondence study of the Austrian labor market, Weichselbaumer (2003) tests for discrimination against lesbians. In an attempt to sort out some of the hypotheses discussed earlier related to lesbians' earning patterns, she designed the study to distinguish any negative differential treatment of all lesbians (that is, sexual orientation discrimination) from the effect of positive differential treatment for women who have masculine characteristics that might signal a greater commitment to the workforce to a prospective employer.

Weichselbaumer sent out résumés in response to advertisements for secretaries and accountants in an Austrian newspaper. The résumés were identical except for variations to indicate sexual orientation and gender characteristics. In keeping with local practices, she sent out a picture, school transcript, reference letters and résumé for four different applicants: a feminine heterosexual woman, a masculine heterosexual woman, a feminine lesbian and a masculine lesbian. She coded femininity with long blond hair, flowing clothes and feminine hobbies, while masculine women were indicated with the opposite characteristics. Being a lesbian was indicated with a résumé listing of past managerial experience with a local gay organization.

Weichselbaumer's outcome measure was an invitation to an interview. Overall, lesbian applicants were much less likely to be invited for an interview, regardless of gender characteristics. Masculine lesbians were 13.1 percentages points less likely to be invited and feminine lesbians 12.1 percentage points less likely. These lower invitation rates were not statistically significantly different for the two groups of lesbians.

Weichselbaumer's study controls for many of the factors that are relevant for wages but cannot be directly measured in the wage studies: disclosure, training, experience, productivity and individual firm effects. The main disadvantage of the audit study is the narrowness of jobs covered, and the location of the study prevents direct comparison with the US wage results. But the fact that she finds negative differential treatment of lesbians regardless of gender characteristics casts further doubt on the gender nonconformity explanations and strengthens the case for discrimination as at least one possible influence on lesbians' earnings. She suggests that customer discrimination is an unlikely motive for differential treatment, since people in these positions have little direct customer contact, pointing to co-worker or employer tastes for discrimination as the likely cause.

At the end of the first decade of research on the economics of sexual orientation, therefore, the scorecard clearly favors the existence of discrimination, even though discrimination might not be the only influence on the earnings of lesbian, gay and bisexual people – especially for lesbians and bisexual women. However, the evidence is not supportive of a symmetric application of the gender nonconformity hypothesis principle, since only lesbians reveal labor supply and human capital decisions that are significantly different from their heterosexual counterparts.

Concluding thoughts
Economists are now catching up to the research conducted on sexual orientation discrimination in other disciplines. The most significant contribution by economists has been to use a standard economic test for the existence and size of the potential economic effects of discrimination in the workplace. Such discrimination is harder to detect than the more common differential treatment embedded in employment benefits, in which employees with same-sex partners rarely receive the same compensation as employees with different-sex married partners.

To summarize what economists have found, the evidence that anti-gay discrimination occurs is strongest for gay men when looking only at wage studies. Gay men earn significantly less, both in a statistical sense and in terms of magnitude, than do similarly situated heterosexual men. The economic evidence of discrimination against lesbians is murkier, however, since in at least some studies lesbians earn more than similar heterosexual women. The interpretation of the evidence offered in this chapter is that the higher-than-expected earnings for lesbians mean, not that discrimination does not occur, but that to see clearer evidence of it we must take into account the larger body of research on lesbians' work-related choices, self-reports of discrimination (discussed in an earlier section) and one well-designed audit study. Clearly more research is necessary to disentangle the complex position that lesbians find themselves in, but the balance of evidence weighs against the gender nonconforming hypotheses and in favor of the presence of discrimination.

Discrimination comes in many other forms in the labor market, of course, and economists could productively take on questions related to occupational position (with some early work by Badgett and King, 1997; and unpublished work by Badgett, 1998, and Blandford), unemployment and (the all-too-obvious) benefits compensation with existing data sets. Using experimental methods that carefully control for variables that do not appear in most data sets (such as disclosure) will be essential for sketching out the discrimination faced by LGB people in the labor market in a convincing way, however.

Finally, this chapter ends with a call for economists to think harder and longer about why discrimination based on sexual orientation exists.[22] Economists have been quick to rely on theories designed to explain racial discrimination, such as Becker's taste models, without thinking through other possible sources of or rationales for discrimination. Persistent evidence of anti-gay attitudes should simply begin the conversation, not end it. Why do anti-gay attitudes exist? Do they serve some important psychological or economic purpose? Can policy change behavior? Can policy change attitudes? How does sexual orientation discrimination interact with discrimination against women or people of color or HIV-infected people? In what productive or unproductive ways does sexuality (broadly defined) influence what happens in the workplace? Rather than simply running more wage regressions as new data sets emerge, economists should craft tests to fit new ways of thinking about why sexual orientation discrimination might exist.

Notes

1. Discussions about the existence of discrimination against people who identify as transgender or transsexual has become an important topic, but discrimination based on gender identity has been largely ignored by economists. Lesbian, gay and bisexual people might share experiences of discrimination with transgendered people, and employers or co-workers might not make distinctions between sexual orientation and gender identity. But so far, in the academic realm, economists have focused attention only on the analytical category of sexual orientation, or having a sexual, romantic and/or emotional attraction to people of the same sex. See a longer discussion of measures of sexual orientation below.
2. Some employers have argued that spousal benefits are not sexual orientation discrimination, since employees with a different-sex domestic partner are also ineligible. That argument, however, ignores the fact that same-sex couples are not allowed to marry.
3. Same-sex sexual behavior is likely also to stigmatize individuals, thus leading to possible discriminatory treatment. However, having same-sex partners without a gay or bisexual identity seems likely to be less apparent to bosses or co-workers than would be identity. Political strategizing about disclosure of self-identity, or 'coming out', appears to be tied to identity rather than behavior.
4. The importance of those unclassifiable people is clear from the negative coefficients in wage models for those with no sex partners in Black *et al.*, (2003).
5. In Badgett (1995) I argue that nondisclosure may also put LGB people at an indirect risk of lower incomes because of being unable to advance in careers when using some typical strategies for hiding one's sexual orientation.
6. In Badgett (2001), I find that in one convenience sample there was no statistically significant relationship between disclosure and income.
7. Carpenter (2005) makes a similar point.
8. Black, Gates, Sanders and Taylor (2000) and Carpenter (2004) present evidence that suggests that people in same-sex couples are likely to be LGB.
9. One exception is Berg and Lien (2002), who simultaneously model income and being in an 'autonomous occupation' (very broadly defined but not clearly explained) and find that the choice of such an occupation does not depend on income. However, the test statistic they calculate to assess the independence of occupation and income is 16.17, very close to the 5 per cent threshold of 16.9 that would have implied that occupational choice was a function of income (p. 412).
10. Most of the other GSS studies summarized in Table 6.1 do not distinguish the men with same-sex partners only from those with male and female partners, although Black *et al.* (2003) do so in one table.

11.   Blandford notes that he observes clustering of gay men in detailed three-digit occupational categories, but the small sample size of the GSS makes incorporating these distinctions problematic.

12.   The small sample size apparently led them to adopt a stepwise regression approach to weed out variables that had insignificant coefficients, even some standard wage equation variables.

13.   These results come from their comparisons of women in different kinds of couples. They also estimate models of wages comparing women with female partners to women with no partners. Such a comparison is of dubious usefulness since we cannot classify the sexual orientations of single women in the Census data, but the average effect of interaction terms for being lesbian and age was a small negative effect (roughly 2–4 per cent) for lesbians with no kids and who lived outside the Midwest.

14.   Plug and Berkhout interpret this question as a measure of identity, and it is difficult to assess, given the translation. 'Sexual preference' sometimes refers to identity in English, but the focus on 'preference' and the possible answers that ask for the gender of prospective sexual partners rather than terms used for identity (such as 'gay' or 'heterosexual') seems more closely related to the measures of attraction.

15.   The authors include a separate variable to identify bisexuals but find no statistically significant difference in their earnings. The sample of bisexuals is quite small, however.

16.   A letter recruiting respondents to an online survey was apparently sent to all academic and non-academic staff at the six universities. The author notes that a low response rate (15 per cent), a high proportion of LGB respondents (14 per cent) and differences compared to other academic data sets suggest the possibility of sample selectivity (Frank, 2002).

17.   Note that this explanation for the observed wage patterns must relate to unobserved human capital, since the wage studies control for education and a proxy for experience.

18.   Survey data on same-sex couples find that many are, in fact, raising children. See Badgett (2001) for a review.

19.   See Chauncey (1994) for historical evidence that gay men's ability to purchase meals and shelter were instrumental in the development of a gay community in New York City in the early twentieth century.

20.   The original article reports that 'a gay couple's household head is 43.4% less likely to be employed than is the husband', but the 43.4% was an error (author's personal communication with Sylvia Allegretto, 4 November 2002).

21.   Weichselbaumer (2003) makes a similar point. See also the US Supreme Court decision in *Price Waterhouse* v. *Ann B. Hopkins*.

22.   I offer a longer discussion of this issue in my book.

References

Allegretto, Sylvia A. and Michelle M. Arthur (2001), 'An empirical analysis of homosexual/heterosexual male earnings differentials: unmarried and unequal?', *Industrial and Labor Relations Review*, **54**(3), 631–46.

Arabsheibani, G. Reza, Alan Marin and Jonathan Wadsworth (2005), 'In the pink: homosexual–heterosexual wage differentials in the UK', *International Journal of Manpower*, **25**(3/4), 343–54.

Badgett, M.V. Lee (1995), 'The wage effects of sexual orientation discrimination', *Industrial and Labor Relations Review*, **49**(4), 726–38.

—— (1997), 'Vulnerability in the workplace: evidence of anti-gay discrimination', *Angles: The Policy Journal of the Institute for Gay and Lesbian Strategic Studies*, **2**(1).

—— (1998), 'Tolerance, taboos, and gender identity: the occupational distribution of lesbians and gay men', unpublished manuscript, July.

—— (2001), *Money, Myths, and Change: The Economic Lives of Lesbians and Gay Men*, Chicago: University of Chicago Press.

Badgett, M.V. Lee and Mary C. King (1997), 'Occupational strategies of lesbians and gay men', in Amy Gluckman and Betsy Reed (eds), *Homo Economics: Capitalism, Community, and Lesbian and Gay Life*, London: Routledge Press.

Badgett M.V. Lee and Marc Rogers (2002), 'Left out of the count: missing same-sex couples in Census 2000', Institute for Gay and Lesbian Strategic Studies, Amherst, MA.

Becker, Gary S. (1991), *Treatise on the Family*, Cambridge: Harvard University Press.

Berg, Nathan and Donald Lien (2002), 'Measuring the effect of sexual orientation on income: evidence of discrimination?', *Contemporary Economic Policy*, **20**(4), 394–414.

Bertrand, Marianne and Sendhil Mullainathan (2004), 'Are Emily and Greg more employable than Lakisha and Jamal? A field experiment on labor market discrimination', *American Economic Review*, **94**(4), September, 991–1013.

Black, Dan, Gary Gates, Seth Sanders and Lowell Taylor (2000), 'Demographics of the gay and lesbian population in the United States: evidence from available systematic data sources', *Demography*, **37**, 139–54.

Black, Dan A., Hoda R. Makar, Seth G. Sanders and Lowell J. Taylor (2003), 'The effects of sexual orientation on earnings', *Industrial and Labor Relations Review*, **56**(3), 449–69.

Blandford, John M. 2003. 'The nexus of sexual orientation and gender in the determination of earnings', *Industrial and Labor Relations Review*, **56**(4), 622–42.

Blumstein, Philip and Pepper Schwartz (1983), *American Couples*, New York: William Morrow & Co.

Brause, Jay K. (1989), 'Closed doors: sexual orientation bias in the Anchorage housing and employment markets', in Melissa S. Green and Jay K. Brause (eds), *Identity Reports: Sexual Orientation Bias in Alaska*, Anchorage, AK: Identity Incorporated.

Carpenter, Christopher (2004), 'New evidence on gay and lesbian household incomes', *Contemporary Economic Policy*, **22**(1), January 78–94.

— — (2005), 'Self-reported sexual orientation and earnings: evidence from California', *Industrial and Labor Relations Review*, **58**(2), January 258–73.

Chauncey, George (1994), *Gay New York: Gender, Urban Culture, and the Making of the Gay Male World 1890–1940*, New York: Basic Books.

Clain, Suzanne Heller and Karen Leppel (2001), 'An investigation into sexual orientation discrimination as an explanation for wage differences', *Applied Economics*, **33**, 37–47.

Committee on the Status of Lesbians and Gays in the Profession (1995), 'Report on the status of lesbians and gays in the political science profession', *PS: Political Science and Politics*, **28**.

Eskridge, William N. and Nan D. Hunter (1997), *Sexuality, Gender, and the Law*, New York: Foundation Press.

Frank, Jeff (2002.), 'Gay glass ceilings', unpublished manuscript.

Ginther, Donna and Madeline Zavodny (2001), 'Is the male marriage premium due to selection? The effect of shotgun weddings on the return to marriage', *Journal of Population Economics*, **14**(2), 313–28.

Herek, Gregory M. (1991), 'Stigma, prejudice and violence against lesbians and gay men', in John C. Gonsiorek and James Weinrich (eds.), *Homosexuality: Research Implications for Public Policy*, Newbury Park, CA: Sage Publications.

Human Rights Campaign (2003), 'The State of the Workplace for Gay, Lesbian, Bisexual, and Transgender Americans, 2003', Washington, DC.

Institute of Medicine (1999), *Lesbian Health: Current Assessment and Directions for the Future*. Washington, DC: National Academy Press.

Johnson, David K. (1994–95), 'Homosexual citizens: Washington's gay community confronts the civil service', *Washington History*, **6**(2) (Fall–Winter), 44–63.

Kaiser Family Foundation and Health Research and Education Trust (2004), 'Employer health benefits 2004, annual survey' (http://www.kff.org/insurance/7148/sections/ehbs04-2-8.cfm, accessed 4/21/05).

Kite, Mary E. and Bernard E. Whitley (1996), 'Sex differences in attitudes toward homosexual persons, behaviors, and civil rights: a meta-analysis', *Personality and Social Psychology Bulletin*, **22**, 336–53.

Klawitter, Marieka (1995), 'Did they find or create each other? Labor market linkages between partners in same-sex and different-sex couples', paper presented at the annual meeting of the Population Association of America, San Francisco.

Klawitter, Marieka and Victor Flatt (1998), 'The effects of state and local antidiscrimination policies for sexual discrimination', *Journal of Policy Analysis and Management*. Fall.

Laumann, Edward O., John H. Gagnon, Richard T. Michael and Stuart Michaels (1994), *The Social Organization of Sexuality : Sexual Practices in the United States*, Chicago: University of Chicago Press.

Levine, Martin (1980), 'Employment discrimination against gay men', in Joseph Harry and Man Singh Das (eds), *Homosexuality in International Perspective*, New Delhi: Vikas and New York: Advent Books.

Levine, Martin and Robin Leonard (1984), 'Discrimination against lesbians in the work force', *Signs: Journal of Women and Culture in Society*, **9**(4).

Los Angeles County Bar Association Committee on Sexual Orientation Bias (1994), 'Report', June.

MacCoun, Robert J. (1996), 'Sexual orientation and military cohesion: a critical review of the evidence', in G.M. Herek, J.B. Jobe and R.M. Carney (eds), *Out in Force: Sexual Orientation and the Military*, Chicago: University of Chicago Press, pp. 157–76.

Neumark, David (1996), 'Sex discrimination in restaurant hiring: an audit study', *Quarterly Journal of Economics*, **111**(3), August, 915–41.

Plug, Erik and Peter Berkhout (2004) 'Effects of sexual preferences on earnings in the Netherlands', *Journal of Population Economics*, **17**(1), 117–31.

Posner, Richard (1992), *Sex and Reason*, Cambridge: Harvard University Press.

Rubenstein, William B. (2002), 'Do gay rights laws matter? An empirical assessment', *Southern California Law Review*, 65–120.

Teal, Donn (1971), *The Gay Militants*, New York: Stein & Day.

Turner, Margery Austin, Michael Fix and Raymond J. Struyk (1991) *Opportunities Denied, Opportunities Diminished: Racial Discrimination in Hiring*, Urban Institute report 91-9, Washington, DC: The Urban Institute Press.

US Bureau of Labor Statistics, Dept. of Labor (2000), 'National compensation survey: employee benefits in private industry in the United States, 2000'.

Van der Meide, Wayne (2000), 'Legislating equality: a review of laws affecting gay, lesbian, bisexual, and transgendered people in the United States', Policy Institute of the National Gay and Lesbian Task Force, New York.

Weichselbaumer, Doris (2003), 'Sexual orientation discrimination in hiring', *Labour Economics*, **10**(6), 629–42.

Yang, Alan (1997), 'From rights to wrongs: public opinion on gay and lesbian Americans moves toward equality', *National Gay and Lesbian Task Force*, Washington, DC: NGLTF Policy Institute.

7 Age discrimination in US labor markets: a review of the evidence

Scott J. Adams and David Neumark

I Introduction

Newspapers, magazines and trade publications are filled with anecdotes such as the following that paint a picture of the undervalued older worker:

> I have an M.B.A. from Columbia University and have held senior-level positions at major financial services companies. After returning to the United States at the age of 48 from three years in England, I found it impossible to find a job at anywhere near my previous level. Why? Someone my age is generally considered too old to have the dynamics to manage a group, and younger group heads don't want what they perceive as the headache of dealing with older staff. So I stay home and do all the work on my house and cars that I would otherwise have to pay somebody else to do. There are many others like me who cannot accept the diminution or the rejection of our skills. (Richmond, 1999)

There is a widespread belief that older workers are viewed differently in the workplace than younger workers. They are thought to be set in their ways and therefore less receptive to new approaches and less creative. Some evidence points to declines in acuteness of vision or hearing, ease of memorization and computational speed (see the evidence reviewed in Posner, 1995, ch. 4). Also they may be more prone to injuries and absenteeism (Finkelstein *et al.*, 1995). However, older workers may offset these declines with greater effort, and some faculties may increase with age, as others decrease. As an example, Posner (1995, ch. 7) argues that aging is associated with declines in creativity but increases in leadership ability.

The past several decades have also seen many older workers claiming wrongful treatment by their employer under the provisions of the Age Discrimination in Employment Act (ADEA) of 1967. Claims filed under the ADEA have steadily increased since 1967 and currently rival race and gender discrimination in terms of number of cases. Moreover, while wages for older workers may be high relative to young workers, there are several other areas in which older workers fare poorly. Most notably, older people who have lost their jobs face fewer opportunities for re-employment than younger workers. Also, if re-employed, they often experience greater earnings losses on the new job. Finally, in the past, many firms had explicit policies that forced workers into retirement when they reached a certain age. Even though an amendment to the ADEA in 1986 banned the use of mandatory retirement, many firms still have been successful in inducing workers to retire at certain ages.[1]

It is unclear whether these disadvantages for older people in the labor force, and their reflection in age discrimination claims, result from blatant age discrimination. For example, firms may have a good reason to remove workers at a certain age. Lazear (1979) presents a model of efficient contracting where young workers accept wages below the value of their marginal product because they know that they will be paid a higher wage later on if they continue to perform well at their jobs, although there is a date beyond which the worker's employment will be ended. This delayed payment 'contract' may in fact be an optimal way to reduce shirking among workers, and be acceptable to workers initially. However, workers earning wages above their marginal value of leisure at older ages, as happens in Lazear's model, will not want to leave their firm. Thus what may look like age discrimination is simply the enforcement of the endpoint of the implicit contractual arrangement.

With regard to the refusal to hire older workers, the part that discrimination plays is also complex. Although animus toward older workers may be a factor, a refusal to hire may also be a product of a lack of information, where applicants are assigned the average characteristics of people in their age group. This may result in statistical discrimination against individual older workers if, on average, older workers have characteristics that are less attractive to potential employers. It would be particularly worrisome if these decisions were based on negative stereotypes of older workers, some of which have no empirical evidence to support them.

In this chapter, we review the existing evidence on age discrimination and its effects in US labor markets.[2] First, we look at attempts to describe attitudes in the workplace toward older individuals and how these may affect managerial decision making. Second, we review the types of cases filed with the Equal Employment Opportunity Commission (EEOC) and assess whether this tells us anything about the nature and effect of age discrimination. Third, we document the disadvantageous positions of older individuals in the labor force in terms of central labor market barometers, including hiring, unemployment duration, re-employment wages and promotion. Finally, we look at attempts to assess whether the disadvantageous positions are the result of discrimination on the part of employers.

II   Attitudes toward older workers and managerial decision making

Industrial psychologists and industrial gerontologists have conducted many studies aimed at investigating attitudes about age in the workplace, with attention to the way older workers are viewed, how these views come about, and how they shape managerial decisions. While the conclusions are mixed, some important insights arise.

First, many stereotypes exist about older workers and these appear to be used by co-workers and managers to rate applicants for jobs. Industrial psychologists use the term 'stereotypes' to refer to the association between behaviors/traits and social categories, which include age groups and particular jobs. With age, the use of stereotypes is made easier by the fact that age is not a characteristic easily hidden during the applicant screening process (Perry *et al.*, 1996).

Evidence is mixed as to whether these age-based stereotypes ultimately play a part in rating applicants, and more importantly in the decisions to hire or not to hire applicants. Several studies find no significant effect of age in selection decisions. For example, Connor *et al.* (1978) use 177 students at Loyola Marymount University to evaluate applicants using a transcript from a job interview. The raters were divided into two groups, with one group told that an applicant was young (age 24) and the other group told an applicant was old (age 63). There was almost no difference in the way the students assessed the two applicants. Other studies failing to find a significant effect of age include Locke-Connor and Walsh (1980), Triandis (1963) and Fusilier and Hitt (1983).

Other studies find evidence that younger applicants are treated more favorably than older applicants. For example, Avolio and Barrett (1987) use 156 students at a large midwestern university to listen to audiotapes of an interview of a prospective managerial hire for a temporary position. The raters were asked to evaluate an applicant. The interviews were identical, with only age being manipulated in the tapes. Participants were divided into three groups, with applicant age being identified for only two of the groups (32 and 59, respectively). Higher overall rankings were given to the younger applicant than either the older applicant or the applicant for whom no age was given. Other studies finding an age effect include Haefner (1977), Gordon *et al.* (1988) and Singer and Sewell (1989).[3]

The use of age stereotypes has been found in other areas of managerial decision making. Rosen and Jerdee (1977) conducted a study of employer behavior based on reactions to hypothetical scenarios regarding how managers would respond to various situations involving workers. Specifically, managers were presented with scenarios regarding personnel decisions (covering, as examples, unsatisfactory performance, investment in training, and promotion) and were asked how they would respond. For some survey respondents, the scenarios involved a worker that was described as young (age 32). For others, the worker was described as old (age 61). It was clear that stereotypes were considered, and the researchers concluded that they affected the elicited decisions. Several conclusions emerged. First, managers perceive older workers as less flexible and more resistant to change. Second, managers are less inclined to provide support for career development and training of older workers. Finally, promotion opportunities for older workers are more likely to be limited in jobs requiring flexibility, creativity and high motivation.

Perry *et al.* (1996) provide perhaps the most complete treatment of age discrimination in this literature. They aim to explain the underlying reasons for the use of stereotypes in decision making, and argue that the inconclusive results in previous studies may be due to the lack of appreciation of the complex ways in which other factors interact with age to influence bias. First, the use of stereotypes may be a function of the rater's bias against older workers. Other studies only consider the basic demographic characteristics of the raters. Second, there may be jobs that are perceived to be more suited for younger or older workers. This may play a part in the use of stereotypes. Finally, the preoccupation of decision makers with other aspects of their job or personal life may influence their use of age as an arbitrary decision criterion. The authors call this 'cognitive busyness'.

Using college students as hypothetical decision makers in a business environment, they measured the raters' biases against older workers. They also assigned raters to two groups, one which evaluated applicants for a job that was obviously more suited to an older worker (stamp and coin salesperson) and one that was more suited to a young worker (CD salesperson). In other tests, they assigned some raters another task to increase their 'cognitive busyness'. They find that the three factors mentioned above interact to play a role in selection decisions. However, they find no evidence that those raters who were highly biased to begin with were more likely to use age in their decision making. Although the authors did not explicitly make this point, the latter result suggests that age discrimination may be a product more of statistical discrimination than of animus. That is, raters appear to be influenced by the type of job, along with their inability to obtain more information about individual applicants (if 'cognitively busy'), rather than just preconceived negative notions about older workers.

The evidence to date has established that there exist attitudes that are unfavorable to older workers. Under certain conditions, these opinions may matter and influence firm decisions. In a recent meta-analysis, Gordon and Arvey (2004) show that these laboratory and field studies on age discrimination have revealed that older applicants and workers are evaluated less favorably than younger applicants and workers. They characterize the estimates as significant but modest. There are several important questions that remain, however. First, the studies focus on hiring decisions. As we discuss in the next section, the majority of age discrimination complaints in courts have nothing to do with the screening or treatment of job applicants. Second, most of the research is conducted in a hypothetical context, sometimes using raters with little business experience (college students). Although this evidence may mirror what occurs in actual business climates, it would be better to examine whether discriminatory activity can be observed in micro data drawn from surveys of actual employees or employers. Most important, while some of the researchers engage in conjecture about the ultimate impact of unfavorable attitudes on older workers, there is no evidence that explicitly addresses this question.

III   ADEA enforcement as evidence of age discrimination[4]

Background on the ADEA

One way to gauge the nature and extent of age discrimination in labor markets is simply to review the claims that have been filed with the EEOC. In 1979, the EEOC took over administrative responsibility for the ADEA from the Department of Labor (Stone, 1980). This change was viewed as increasing the power of the ADEA, as it was accompanied by increased enforcement resources. In this section, we first describe what activities the ADEA prohibits. Second, we review recent charges filed under the ADEA and discuss whether these charges accurately reflect the state of discrimination in the US or whether they are more driven by the relative ease of establishing cases for particular types of wrongful treatment.

The roots of the ADEA lie in Title VII of the Civil Rights Act. Like Title VII, the ADEA aims to prohibit the arbitrary use of a personal characteristic in employer decision making. Specifically, age may not be used as a basis for refusal to hire an applicant, discharge an employee or setting the conditions of employment in regard to compensation, terms or privileges of employment. Moreover, the ADEA prohibits using any advertisement related to employment indicating preferences or limitations based on age. The ADEA also regulates the behavior of employment agencies and labor unions (US Code, Section 623).

The ADEA differs from Title VII in several important ways, all of which to some extent reflect the fact that differential treatment based on age may have a nondiscriminatory basis in many instances. First, it allows for seniority systems as long as such systems are not in place to evade the act. The ADEA recognizes, for example, that pension plans and other benefits are related to age and seniority, and the EEOC and the courts have established careful guidelines to clarify what is and what is not permitted. The ADEA also allows employers to use age as an occupational qualification that is 'reasonably necessary to the normal operation of a business' (US Code, Section 623). This arises out of the presumption that there may be some productivity declines stemming from age-related work limitations.[5]

In 2004, the Supreme Court decided that the ADEA could not be used by younger people to claim that they have been unfairly treated in comparison with older people, even if the younger group was within age ranges covered by the ADEA. In *Cline* v. *General Dynamics Land Systems, Inc.,* plaintiffs under age 50 (but at least 40 years old) claimed they were discriminated against because a collective bargaining agreement provided for favorable treatment to workers over 50 regarding retirement benefits. Justice Souter, in the majority opinion, wrote that 'the ADEA was concerned to protect a relatively old worker from discrimination that works to the advantage of the relatively young'. Thus, from a legal perspective, age discrimination can only be claimed by older workers regarding their treatment relative to younger workers.

EEOC claims
On its face, a review of EEOC charge data suggests that age discrimination is prevalent in the US and is on the rise. In 1968, the year following the passage of the ADEA, there were only 1000 claims of age discrimination. This was during a period of limited enforcement, however, as the Department of Labor, entrusted with administering the ADEA, did not have the resources to follow through on claims or, to some extent, the authority to follow through on claims. After the enforcement of the ADEA was switched to the EEOC, claims increased. For example, in 1982, there were 11 000 claims of age discrimination filed with the EEOC. In 2004, there were 17 837 charge receipts filed under the ADEA. This could be compared to the 24 249 charges alleging sex discrimination and the 27 696 charges filed alleging race discrimination filed under Title VII.[6]

How many of these charges have merit? Table 7.1 presents more information about charges that were resolved during the last ten years (1995–2004). The table presents information for charges under the ADEA and Title VII. It also breaks down the Title VII resolutions into those that originated from race-based and sex-based charges, respectively. Of the 166 098 ADEA charges resolved during the last ten years under the ADEA, 9282 were settled, with benefits accrued to the complainant. Another 6726 were withdrawn after the complainant received benefits. In 8149 of the remaining cases, reasonable cause was found, based on the evidence. This totals 24 157 cases reaching a merit resolution (14.54 per cent of total charges filed). The percentage of race-based and sex-based charges with merit were 13.72 per cent and 17.75 per cent, respectively. Thus the vast majority of cases are resolved in a manner that deems the claim to be without merit. Many of these were the result of administrative closures, which were caused by the failure to communicate on the part of the charging party, closure of related litigation that makes the charge futile, a determination of no jurisdiction, or a related reason. In others, no reasonable cause was established to rule that discrimination occurred.

Table 7.1 Claims filed under the ADEA or Title VII that were resolved during the last ten years (1995–2004)

	All statutes	ADEA	Title VII	Race-based	Sex-based
Total Claims	952 883	166 098	569 573	332 827	294 053
Merit resolution	153 395	24 157	90 005	45 676	52 193
Settlements	62 464	9 282	38 115	21 240	20 761
Withdrawal with benefits	38 197	6 726	21 745	10 987	13 268
Reasonable cause	52 734	8 149	30 145	13 449	18 164
Successful conciliation	14 205	1 688	7 569	3 701	4 917
Unsuccessful conciliation	38 529	6 461	22 576	9 748	13 247
Administrative closures	233 842	44 184	134 124	66 780	81 913
No reasonable cause	565 646	97 757	345 444	220 371	159 947

A review of ADEA charges also provides some information about the types of discriminatory activities that occur in firms. The most prevalent type of charge is for wrongful discharge, which comprises over one-quarter of all cases (Neumark, 2003). Not surprisingly, charges alleging pay discrimination are relatively uncommon among older workers establishing claims. Discrimination charges based on pay are more prevalent in Title VII charges. There are more charges of discrimination in benefits provision filed under the ADEA, however. Charges related to promotion or demotion issues are about equally prevalent among those filed under the ADEA and Title VII. Given the large amount of anecdotal evidence that older workers have trouble finding jobs, however, the very low number of charges alleging hiring discrimination, which comprise only about 10 per cent of total charges (Posner, 1999; Neumark, 2003), may be surprising.[7]

This does not necessarily mean that hiring discrimination among older people is not a significant problem, however. Even if hiring discrimination exists, there may be reasons why very few charges come about. First, proving that one has been discriminated against in hiring is difficult. Posner (1999) reports results from a study he conducted that found plaintiffs in hiring cases won an unimpressive 11.6 per cent of their cases. Moreover, damages in hiring cases tend to be smaller because it is difficult to believe that an applicant who truly deserved the job would earn substantially more at the new job for which he was passed over than he earns at his current job or one found subsequently, and if the worker found another job the damages may have been incurred over a short period. In contrast, wrongful termination cases are potentially more lucrative because a discharged worker can claim damages that would include the lost returns to the firm-specific human capital he has accumulated.[8]

Effects of the ADEA
If age discrimination exists, legislation that bans it (assuming it is enforced) should have an effect. There have been several studies that present evidence on the impact of age discrimination legislation. Neumark and Stock (1999) study the effects of age discrimination laws by exploiting the existence of anti-discrimination statutes in some states prior to the ADEA. Specifically, they look at changes in employment rates of older workers (in protected age groups specified by the state legislation) relative to young workers.[9] Using Census data from 1940, 1950, 1960, 1970 and 1980, and treating the federal law as binding or enforced only after the 1979 amendments, Neumark and Stock find that age discrimination laws boost employment rates of protected workers under age 60 by a small amount but boost employment rates of protected workers age 60 and over by a substantially higher amount (about six percentage points).[10]

Adams (2004) repeats this analysis using Current Population Survey (CPS) data from 1964 to 1967, a time period during which a number of states enacted age discrimination legislation. He finds employment effects that are very similar to Neumark and Stock's (1999). Adams extends this analysis to several other outcomes, including hiring and retirement. He finds no significant effects of legislation on the probability of being hired,[11] but finds that legislation significantly reduces the probability of retirement.

Taken together, these studies provide evidence that is consistent with the existence of age discrimination in the periods prior to the passage of age discrimination legislation. However, it is not conclusive. The improvement of labor market outcomes after the passage of legislation may simply be due to firms becoming fearful of litigation. They treat older workers favorably as a result, even though they may not have been discriminating against them before. Also little can be inferred from these studies about the continuing existence of age discrimination subsequent to the ADEA.

On the other hand, the review of charges filed under the ADEA from the previous subsection can establish that age discrimination (at least as defined by the law) continues to exist.[12] The thousands of cases that do reach a merit resolution are evidence of this. The geneses of the charges, however, appear heavily dependent on the likelihood of proving a case and the substantial damages that could be awarded, suggesting that there may be many other examples of age discrimination that go unreported. Moreover, the ADEA does not prohibit all uses of age as a criterion, as it recognizes that age may result in work limitations that make it impossible for a business to continue its normal operations, and that age may play a part in legitimate firm practices. To the extent that these uses of age as a criterion arise from negative stereotypes with no evidentiary basis, however, they may still represent arbitrary age discrimination.

IV Disadvantageous position

Age discrimination is an important issue to the extent that older people experience adverse outcomes in labor markets as a result of it. Here, we review a number of studies that identify an outcome or outcomes for which older workers are not well off when compared with younger workers. Although this is not evidence of age discrimination in itself, it at least points to several problem areas that call out for investigation.

Hiring

Although claims filed with the EEOC tend not to be related to hiring discrimination, the popular press contains much anecdotal evidence suggesting that older applicants are not considered on their merits alone in the job screening process.[13] Moreover, the industrial psychology literature, which we reviewed above, includes several studies that find that older applicants for a job are judged less favorably than are younger applicants.[14] The differential treatment is a problem if it is observed in micro data that older people have greater difficulty in finding work. Indeed, there is some evidence that older workers face reduced opportunities in hiring. First, the unemployment duration of older workers is typically longer. For example, according to Bureau of Labor Statistics (BLS) data on unemployment duration for 2001, workers aged 55–64 had the longest unemployment spells, with the median length being 9.8 weeks (US Bureau of Labor Statistics, 2001). As a comparison, workers aged 25–34 had a median unemployment duration of 6.7 weeks. This is suggestive of the difficulty that older workers have finding work.

Moreover, Hutchens (1988) shows that older workers face a smaller set of job choices when searching for work. In his analysis, he compares the distribution of young and old workers across industries and occupations. He defines recently hired workers as those with fewer than five years of tenure and older workers as those aged 55 years or greater. As a test, he proposes that, if older workers have fewer job opportunities, then recently-hired older workers should be clustered into relatively few industries and occupations when compared with recently hired young workers. Using the January 1983 CPS, Hutchens constructs 'segregation curves' from older and younger worker distributions by industry and occupation.[15] He finds that older workers who have been recently hired are not as equally distributed across industries and occupations as younger workers who have been recently hired or older workers in general. He cautions, however, that this is evidence consistent with fewer job opportunities, not necessarily discrimination. He does not rule out alternative explanations, some of which will be discussed in the next section.

A series of related papers investigates the experiences of workers who have been displaced from their job and have searched for a new one. Farber (1993) focuses on workers who lost or left their job because of a plant closing, a company going out of business, a position or shift being abolished, or another related reason, using the Displaced Worker Supplements (DWS) of the CPS. When linked to tenure supplements and outgoing rotation group files of the CPS, which contain information on earnings, much about the effects of displacement is learned. Using data covering separations from 1982 to 1991, Farber finds that the probability of employment among displaced workers is lower among older workers. Among displaced workers who are re-employed, the probability of full-time employment is significantly lower among those aged 55 and over, as compared with younger workers.

Farber's (1993) evidence is similar to that presented by Gardner (1995) using the 1994 DWS. Gardner reports that among workers displaced from a full-time job in 1991 or 1992 who had at least three years of tenure at that job, 60.1 per cent were re-employed at a full-time job at the time of the 1994 survey. Breaking this down by age, she finds that 70.0 per cent of those aged

25–34 were re-employed, while among those aged 55–64 only 41.3 per cent were re-employed.[16]

Promotion

Another frequently heard claim in the popular press is that older workers are passed over for promotion because of being undervalued by their employers. Herz and Rones (1989) report results of a Gallup survey conducted in 1985, in which 6 per cent of workers aged 40 and over reported that they had experienced age discrimination, mostly in the form of being denied a promotion or chance for advancement based on age. As noted above, Rosen and Jerdee (1977) found evidence of this behavior when they presented hypothetical situations to a sample of *Harvard Business Review* readers. They suggest that this behavior reduces opportunities for older workers, but no evidence is presented that explicitly establishes this. Pergamit and Veum (1999), however, do present evidence that promotions are associated with increased supervisory responsibilities and the receipt of training. Moreover, wage growth often accompanies promotions (McCue, 1996).

Incidence of displacement

While the inability of older workers to find work once displaced is suggestive of bias against hiring older workers, it may be the case that older workers are less likely to be displaced in the first place, thus mitigating the problem. After all, if a plant is downsizing, it might be expected that seniority rules or specific human capital will lead to retention of more senior workers. On the other hand, the previous section highlighted that many of the claims of age discrimination filed with the EEOC have to do with discharge. Here we review what the data show about displacement of older workers.

At one time, it was true that older workers were less likely to be displaced. Gardner (1995) reviews rates of displacement calculated from DWS data for 1984–94. Using displacements in 1981 and 1982 and the overall rate of employment for that period, she calculates that 3.8 per cent of working men aged 55–64 were displaced, while among those aged 25–34 5.0 per cent were displaced.[17] Looking at displacement and employment data for 1991–2, the overall rate of displacement was similar to that of 1981–2. There was a notable shift in the age distribution of the displaced, however. Among those aged 55–64, 4.5 per cent were displaced workers, while among those 25–34 years old the rate of displacement was 3.8 per cent. Additionally, using the 1998 DWS, Bowman and Eisenstadt (2000) find that those aged 45–54 are also beginning to make up a more substantial portion of displaced workers.

A related strain of evidence has focused on involuntary job terminations stemming from corporate restructuring and the layoffs that ensue (for example, Cappelli, 2000). Although much of this research is contentious,[18] one piece of fairly unambiguous evidence finds increased involuntary terminations of more-tenured workers (Polsky, 1999). Although this evidence has not been viewed through the prism of age discrimination, it is potentially consistent with an increased tendency to treat workers differentially according to age.

Consequences of displacement: re-employment earnings
Even though an increasing number of older workers are displaced and these workers face more difficulty getting hired, displaced older workers may be receiving income following displacement through private pensions. This should mitigate the problems associated with their displacement when compared with younger workers. Moreover, it could be the case that older workers have longer spells of unemployment because they are holding out for higher wages. Thus a review of the evidence on re-employment income, both through earnings and through other sources, is needed to determine more accurately whether older workers are hurt by their displacement.

In general, displacement is associated with lower earnings upon re-employment for all workers.[19] Among workers aged 20 or higher and re-employed full-time, Gardner (1995) found earnings to be 8.2 per cent lower on the new job. And in multivariate analyses the percentage reduction in re-employment wages is even greater (see, for example, Carrington and Zaman, 1994). Following workers for four years after displacement, Ruhm (1991b) finds that their earnings have rebounded, but still remain lower than prior to displacement.

A few studies present evidence on whether the earnings losses are greater for older workers. Gardner (1995), for example, reports that, among those aged 45–54, the percentage reduction in earnings following re-employment in a full-time job is 15.0 per cent, while among those aged 55–64 there is a 14.1 per cent reduction. As noted above, she found an 8.2 per cent reduction for all workers, and for young workers aged 25–34 a 2.1 per cent increase in earnings. In multivariate analyses, the difference by age in the estimated effects of displacement on earnings is not conclusive. This may be due to the fact that age is related to tenure and experience, factors that are often controlled for in the existing work. A few studies find disparate impacts for older workers, however. For example, Ong and Mar (1992) study the semiconductor industry and find that workers over age 54 face greater post-displacement earnings losses.

Shapiro and Sandell (1985) provide the most topical study on the re-employment experiences of older workers. They use the National Longitudinal Survey of Older Men (NLSOM), however, which predates the transfer of enforcement authority to the EEOC. They first choose a sample of involuntary job losers, and estimate a wage equation for the pre-displacement job accounting for both age and tenure. They then use this estimated regression to predict the wages on the post-displacement job, in the most relevant case accounting for the loss of tenure resulting from the job loss, and adjusting for age. Finally, they ask whether the gap between the predicted and actual wage on the subsequent job varies with age. The adjustments for age and tenure are important to control for other sources of larger wage losses among older men. Without the adjustment for tenure, the wage loss could be attributable to loss of specific human capital, which might be highest for the older workers. But, with the adjustment for tenure, loss of specific human capital should not play a role. Similarly, adjusting for age should allow for depreciation in general human capital at older ages. The findings indicate that only men aged 65 years and older appear to suffer disproportionate wage losses upon displacement.

Consequences of displacement: re-employment income
With income losses, there are several factors at work. First, many of the existing studies do not account for the lower re-employment rates when studying re-employment earnings. The lower rates of re-employment and the longer spells of unemployment of older workers suggest that earnings losses may be understated. Moreover, older workers who are displaced before their planned retirement age could see their retirement assets decline, owing both to lower contributions toward the stock of retirement assets and to a raiding of their retirement savings. The need to dip into their retirement assets becomes greater the longer their unemployment duration.

Couch (1998) uses the Health and Retirement Study (HRS) to determine how these factors play out, and assesses the ultimate impact of displacement on older workers. His HRS sample contains workers aged 51–61. He finds that, among those displaced during 1990 and 1991, the average loss in earnings was 39 per cent. This is larger than reported in the rest of the literature. Couch argues that this may be due to his inclusion of people that were not re-employed at the time of the 1992 survey, something that the rest of the literature tends not to do. This suggests that the existing estimates of the effects of displacement may be understated. Couch also investigates the extent to which other sources of income may offset earnings losses. Pension income is not an important factor. Income from other family members, however, does cushion the overall effect of the earnings decline on household economic well-being. Still, household income falls by 24 per cent for the families of displaced workers.[20]

Discrimination against younger workers
This section has outlined the disadvantageous position in labor markets faced by older workers. In many ways, however, outcomes for the old compare favorably to those of the young. For example, as discussed in the next section,

older workers earn more. Moreover, while it is true that many older workers are passed over for promotion, it is also true that some young workers lose out on promotions because of their age. It is also true that older workers may be treated better on the job because of their perceived experience and accumulated skills. For example, in certain industries, customers may prefer to deal with older workers rather than younger workers.

Economists have devoted little attention to documenting the extent of discrimination against the young, however. One reason may be that age discrimination legislation does not protect younger workers against favorable treatment given to older workers, as made clear by the recent Supreme Court decision in *Cline* v. *General Dynamics Land Systems, Inc.* Moreover, the lower wages, benefits and privileges provided to younger workers often have explanations grounded in human capital models and delayed payment contract models (for example, Lazear, 1979). Workers will naturally see their wages rise as they receive training and/or progress to later stages of their incentive-based contracts with firms. In short, discrimination against the young is a problem that will correct itself as workers age, a point made in the industrial psychology literature. For example, Garstka *et al.* (2004) show that young adults differ in their responses to discrimination because they perceive their disadvantaged status as temporary. For these reasons, this section and the subsequent section focus on discrimination faced by older workers.

V   Detecting effects of age discrimination
The previous section establishes that there is some evidence that older workers suffer labor market disadvantages compared with younger workers. Moreover, there is a large and growing number of older people claiming discrimination with the EEOC. The link between discrimination and these adverse outcomes, however, remains unclear. In this section, we review the unique difficulties that exist when examining this link. We then review the handful of papers that aim to detect the effects of discrimination.

Methods
Researchers attempting to detect age discrimination have found themselves in uncharted territory. One would expect the vast literature on race and gender discrimination to be a useful guide.[21] There are several reasons why applying the methods from that literature is problematic, however.

Unlike the case of race and sex, the link between age and productivity is likely much more complex. On one hand, workers may become more skilled in their work with experience. On the other hand, older workers may suffer from a diminished capacity to perform their work as age-related physical limitations arise. Researchers trying to measure the effect of age on productivity have produced mixed results. McEvoy and Cascio (1989) present results of a meta-analysis of 22 years of studies and conclude that the research tends not to show a strong link between age and job performance. However, some studies do find that age leads to diminished performance (for example, Salthouse *et al.*, 1996). A recent study of production function estimates for the manufacturing sector finds evidence of lower productivity of workers aged 55 and older (Hellerstein and Neumark, 2004).

The inability to capture the effect that age has on productivity is a major problem that researchers confront when applying the methods from the literature on race and sex discrimination to the question of age discrimination. The standard approach in that literature is to regress the log of wages on a number of individual and job characteristics that are meant to capture underlying productivity differences between individuals, and to interpret the residual as reflecting discrimination.[22] Unlike the case of sex and race discrimination, however, capturing productivity differences through other observables and attributing the remaining differences by age to discrimination is unappealing, precisely because productivity differences by age are inherently plausible (and indeed central to the human capital model).[23]

Another difficulty in using the effect of age on earnings to detect age discrimination is that age (on net) appears to influence earnings positively. In the first quarter of 2002, median usual weekly earnings for full-time workers aged 55–64 years were $671, while median weekly earnings for workers aged 25–34 years were $598. While this may reflect productivity differences, it has also been observed that age–earnings profiles slope upwards and more steeply than age–productivity profiles (for example, Medoff and Abraham, 1980; Kotlikoff and Gokhale, 1992).[24] The positive differentials in pay associated with age do not necessarily mean that age discrimination in pay does not exist; perhaps older workers would earn more absent discrimination. The bottom line, though, is that it is unlikely that one would or could detect age discrimination via wage regressions.

There are other outcomes that may be used as dependent variables in attempts to detect discrimination. As with earnings, however, some of these outcomes indicate that older individuals fare well when compared with younger ones. For example, unemployment rates for older workers tend to be lower.[25] Even in terms of non-labor income (Hurd, 1990), older people are in relatively advantageous positions. Thus, while one problem is the limitations of the standard regression approach to discrimination when applied to age, another is that on some dimensions older workers may in fact be in an advantaged position. While there may be good economic reasons for this apparently advantaged position (rather than 'reverse discrimination'), this suggests that we need to refocus our attention on both outcomes other than pay and methods other than regression analysis.

As an alternative to the regression approach, audit studies are a convincing way to detect race and sex discrimination in employment. These studies involve sending matched pairs of applicants with similar characteristics to employers. Differential treatment is attributed to discrimination. For example, audit studies were used to compare outcomes for Hispanic and Anglo job-seekers (Kenney and Wissoker, 1994), blacks and whites (Bendick *et al.*, 1994) and women and men (Neumark, 1996). Such an approach for older workers is fraught with unique problems, however. First, audit studies are often conducted for entry-level positions, because audit studies are most easily – and perhaps only feasibly – conducted for positions with relatively simple and quick hiring decisions, and for positions that are relatively homogeneous across employers. For older people, studies of hiring into entry-level positions might not be particularly relevant. More important, making older and younger workers look identical on paper is difficult, especially when it comes to relevant experience. As discussed above, a similar problem is encountered in the interpretation of the industrial psychology and industrial gerontology evidence.

A different technique was devised by Johnson and Neumark (1997). They used the NLSOM, which contains the question, 'During the past five years, do you feel that, so far as work is concerned, you were discriminated against because of your age?' Longitudinal information on responses to this question, and on subsequent labor market behavior, is used to study the impact of age discrimination. This approach is not without problems either, however. Specifically, underlying differences in the propensity to report discrimination may be correlated with the outcomes studied. Also workers with poor labor market experiences may be tempted to blame their employers' alleged age discrimination. Finally, some workers may simply be disgruntled with their employer and be willing to report something negative about them regardless of the truth. Since these workers are perhaps more likely to have adverse experiences, correlations between self-reported age discrimination and poor labor market outcomes may be spurious. Johnson and Neumark deal with these problems by focusing on those who switch from reporting no age discrimination to reporting age discrimination, hoping that a lagged measure of perceived discrimination controls for some of these other factors.

Evidence of age discrimination
Perhaps because of the methodological difficulties, there are only a handful of studies that speak directly to the effect of age discrimination on the ultimate labor market experiences of older workers. One study uses the audit method discussed above (Bendick *et al.*, 1996). In that study, 775 large employers and employment agencies were sent résumés for two job candidates. One of the candidates was presented as about 57 years old, and the other as about 32 years old.[26] The résumé of the older applicant received a less favorable response (on

average) than that of the younger applicant. Higher growth companies were less likely to discriminate against older workers.

Attempts were made to get around the problems with using audit studies to detect age discrimination. First, the positions that were applied for were not entry-level. Second, attempts were made to render the applicants as identical as possible, while still adding to the older workers' résumés some explanation for having the same relevant experience as the younger workers. For example, in the résumés that were sent to information technology companies (about one-third of the sample), older workers and younger workers were given ten years of experience in the field. The years on the older workers' résumés between college and the beginning of the experience in the field were accounted for by giving the older applicants experience as high school math teachers. While this is a clever approach, it nevertheless may still suffer from the problem of older workers being penalized for all of the years that they were not gaining experience in the field. A younger applicant may gain favor through the fact that he 'hit the ground running' out of college. Nevertheless, the evidence is consistent with age discrimination reducing hiring opportunities.

The second study on the impact of age discrimination was conducted by Johnson and Neumark (1997), whose approach was discussed above. Their first finding is that only a relatively small percentage of older men reported age discrimination (7 per cent of the sample).[27] However, this refers to men with jobs, and hence might not cover the type of discrimination in hiring posed by age restrictions on new hires (although it could do so partially if they had searched for other jobs). More to the point, Johnson and Neumark find that those workers who report discrimination are more likely to separate from their current employer, and less likely to be employed subsequently. In addition, those who report discrimination and separate from their employer suffer a wage loss on the order of 10 per cent. Thus the evidence points to adverse consequences of differential treatment by age. It is important to note, however, that the study predates the switch in enforcement of the ADEA from the Department of Labor to the EEOC, which means that the study cannot speak directly to the existence and impact of age discrimination in today's labor market.

Adams (2002) conducts a similar analysis to Johnson and Neumark (1997), in that he uses self-reported information provided by workers about employer behavior to estimate the effects of perceived discrimination, with a couple of important differences. First, he uses the 1992 and 1994 waves of the HRS, which allows the study to speak to the question of age discrimination in the post-ADEA period. The question in the HRS that is used to infer discrimination is based on responses to the statement: 'In decisions about promotion, my employer gives younger people preference over older people.' Thus the study only focuses on one particular type of employer discriminatory behavior, albeit one that is highlighted in other evidence (Herz and Rones, 1989; Rosen and Jerdee, 1977). Finally, the study is primarily cross-sectional, which does not allow for Johnson and Neumark's (1997) approach of using multiple reports on discriminatory behavior to control for sources of a spurious relationship.[28] On the other hand, the HRS does contain variables that can be used to control for the worker's general satisfaction with the job and his employer. Adams finds that, among workers reporting that their firm passes over older workers for promotion, there is lower wage growth. In addition, such workers are more likely to separate from their employer and more likely to rate their probability of early retirement higher. These effects persist once basic individual and job satisfaction controls are added. Thus this provides more evidence that perceived discriminatory behaviors do result in poorer outcomes.

Alternative explanations

The three studies that have most directly addressed the correlation between discriminatory behavior and adverse outcomes have found evidence of a relationship. However, there are alternative explanations for this evidence, which leaves one concerned that these correlations may not be truly reflecting the impacts of age discrimination. With regard to hiring effects (as found by Bendick *et al.*, 1996), there are several alternative explanations. First, some firms may rightly conclude that older applicants cannot perform the tasks necessary for the job. This may be especially true if the job requires physical tasks that some older workers might not be able to perform as well. Second, firms may correctly assume that older workers will not remain with the firm as long as younger workers. Such differences in prospective tenure with an employer partially explain why human capital investments are more associated with younger workers, as firms have a greater incentive to invest in training the young (Oi, 1962).

Related to this argument, Lazear and Rosen (1990) conjecture that differences in promotion rates between men and women may arise because firms hold workers to a higher ability standard when deciding on a promotion if non-market abilities and opportunities are assumed to be greater. In their model, women are assumed to be as able as men in labor market activity but more able in activities outside of labor markets. The fact that they may have greater value outside of the labor market increases their chances of separation from the labor force and leads employers to hold them to a higher ability standard when deciding on their promotion. One can also argue that there are more non-market opportunities for the old than there are for the young. At the very least, their marginal disutility of work can be assumed to be greater. The promotion results found by Adams (2002) may reflect this conjecture.

A more all-encompassing alternative explanation for the alleged correlation between firm discriminatory behavior and poor outcomes is the use of delayed payment contracts modeled by Lazear (1979) and discussed in the Introduction. In particular, Hutchens (1986) investigated the relationship between the use of delayed payment contracts and hiring. He first presents a model where delayed payment contracts introduce a fixed cost into the hiring decision. Because firms delay payments to reduce worker shirking, employees fear that firms will renege on long-term arrangements and lay them off before higher wages or pensions are realized.[29] Lazear's model originally assumed that a firm was bound to the wage (and employment) path that it offered by reputation effects. In practice, however, information asymmetries exist. These may arise for a variety of reasons. Just as firms cannot costlessly observe worker output, neither can fellow workers. Thus, when a worker is fired, it is not always the case that workers can determine if the firing was justified. Moreover, firms may have to lay off workers in response to shifts in the demand curve for their product. Thus there is a possibility that firms can cheat on the contracts that they form and get away with it. As a consequence, firms must compensate workers for the expected loss in lifetime earnings from potential cheating. Regardless of the exact structure of the compensation, bonding is not costless.

In the simplest form of his model, Hutchens showed that a component of the bonding cost is fixed if workers perceive that the probability of a firm reneging on a delayed payment contract is positive and firms perceive that the probability of worker shirking is positive. This fixed hiring cost is not unlike those discussed by Oi (1962). Because of costly bonding, a firm prefers to hire those workers with the longest expected tenure so as to minimize the number of times it hires and incurs the cost. As an empirical test of the model, Hutchens constructs an index of the propensity of firms to hire older workers, which is the proportion of recently-hired workers over age 55 among total employees over age 55 in industry–occupation cells of the 1970 census. Then, using the NLSOM, he looks at whether workers in jobs with a higher index are less likely to report that their firms engaged in practices consistent with the use of delayed payment contracts (for example, pension offerings and mandatory retirement). Hutchens finds evidence consistent with the predictions of his model.[30]

As with hiring, delayed payment contracts may affect a firm's promotion decisions. In Lazear's model, payments to workers are delayed to provide incentives for good performance early in their work life. If such performance is also rewarded with promotions that are associated with pay increases as well, then under these contracts promotions among older workers may be somewhat less common and wage growth somewhat lower; in other words, under delayed payment contracts, workers may 'climb the corporate ladder' faster. Factors that coincide with delayed payment contracts, such as pensions, may also induce early retirement (Burkhauser and Quinn, 1983; Kotlikoff and Wise, 1989). Thus the two outcomes that Adams (2002) finds to be correlated with being passed over for promotion – lower wage growth at older ages and early retirement – may be explained by the relationship between promotion practices and implicit delayed payment arrangements. Indeed, Adams (2002) also finds that employees with greater tenure and those enrolled in a pension plan at work are more likely to report that their firm passes over older workers for promotion. Moreover, the negative effects on older workers become smaller and non-significant when Adams controls for worker tenure and pensions, suggesting that his effects have much to do with the presence of delayed payment contracts, rather than blatant discrimination.

For the most part, the work of Johnson and Neumark (1997) stands as the only evidence to date showing that age discrimination, apart from the confounding influences of disgruntled workers or the presence of delayed payment contacts, negatively affects older workers. Their findings that age discrimination increases job separations hold up after controls are added for employee tenure and enrollment in pension plans, as well as after correcting for some problems associated with the use of self-reported data.

VI   Conclusions

Despite many conflicting results and alternative interpretations of those results, we are able to draw several conclusions about age discrimination in the United States:

- The industrial gerontology literature and the industrial psychology literature have produced more than a handful of studies showing that age is considered when making decisions about the relative worth of job applicants. Attitudes about older workers are considered in promotion decisions as well.
- The thousands of ADEA cases that are resolved and deemed worthy of merit by the EEOC indicate that age discrimination (at least as defined and recognized by the law) is a continuing phenomenon in US labor markets.
- While older workers perform relatively well in the labor market in terms of wages and employment, they perform poorly in terms of unemployment duration, the probability of getting hired, their incidence of displacement and the consequences of displacement in terms of re-employment earnings.
- Studies that estimate the link between age discrimination and adverse outcomes tend to find evidence of such a link. However, some of these studies have difficulty ruling out alternative explanations.

An additional point is worth noting as well. No study that has attempted to explain the disadvantageous position of older workers (in some respects) has analyzed empirically the motivation for the firm policies that may have caused the harm. If one can narrow the effect down to employer discrimination, there still remains the question of whether the discrimination arises out of a dislike of older workers or the application of a decision criterion based on age owing to the lack of enough credible information.

Thus future research will likely focus on whether age discrimination on the part of employers is due to animus, statistical discrimination or other economic considerations. And future policy debates are likely to wrestle with the appropriate public policy response to employers' use of age as a criterion in managerial decision making.

Notes

1. See, for example, Gustman and Steinmeier (1986), Kotlikoff and Wise (1989), Burkhauser and Quinn (1983) and Hurd (1990).
2. In focusing on the issue of evidence of labor market discrimination, this work is different from but complementary to some recent, broader surveys on age discrimination (Posner, 1999; Neumark, 2003). Both focus more on age discrimination legislation, with a great deal of information on the act, its legal interpretation and the meaning of age discrimination generally. Neumark (2003) also reviews evidence on how the legislation operates in light of existing theories on age and compensation in labor markets.
3. The studies that have looked at whether applicants are viewed differently because of their age suffer from the fact that it is impossible to present older and younger applicants equally. If the older worker is presented as having more experience, he may be treated better, even if there exist inclinations to discriminate on the basis of age. On the other hand, if applicants are given equal experience, the older worker may appear peculiar because he should have much more experience. Thus the results of these studies need to be interpreted with caution.
4. A substantial portion of material in this section is based on Neumark (2003).
5. Title VII, on the other hand, only allows exceptions with respect to race and sex in very special cases, in particular when race or sex is a bona fide occupational qualification (for example, as with actors or locker room attendants).
6. Much of the information presented in this section was calculated using EEOC enforcement data, which are available at www.eeoc.gov.
7. Hiring cases do make up a larger percentage of ADEA charges than of Title VII charges.
8. In a somewhat related recent study, Manning *et al.* (2004) note that even the decisions in court cases might be influenced by age biases among judges. They show that younger judges were less sympathetic in cases alleging age discrimination than older judges. In general, the decision patterns in age bias cases were more conservative than in race or sex cases. Epstein and Martin (2004) call their results into question, however, on the basis of a failure to stand up to alternative groupings of age categories in the data.
9. The state statutes are used because using federal legislation could attribute to the law other changes over time in factors influencing the relative employment of older workers. With the state statutes, the advent of the federal legislation can be separately identified by using states that already had an anti-discrimination statute to control for other aggregate changes in relative employment of older individuals, and using only the relative differences between these states and the other ('treatment') states to identify the effect of the policy change. In addition, because the state statutes are implemented at different times, their direct effects can be estimated to draw stronger inferences regarding the effects of age discrimination legislation.
10. They also study the effects of banning mandatory retirement but find no statistically significant effects.

11. Because the CPS surveys used do not have tenure data, Adams is forced to use transitions from non-employment (measured as of the prior calendar year) to employment (measured as of the current month). This measure is imperfect and may account for the finding of no significant effect.
12. For a skeptical perspective regarding the ability of the ADEA to address age discrimination, see Friedman (1985).
13. Shellenbarger (2001) and Weiner (2005) exemplify the articles that present such anecdotes. Common are stories about age discrimination against professionals in the field of information technology (IT). Evans (1999) painted a dire picture of the probability of IT professionals getting hired after the age of 40 during the late 1990s, citing not only the lack of necessary skills but discrimination by the younger managers making the hiring decision. Gaudin (2003) notes that this situation may be improving, as there is some evidence of more recent declines in job search times for older IT professionals. To our knowledge, however, rigorous study by economists of discrimination against older IT professionals has not occurred.
14. We also noted above that there are studies that do not find evidence of these attitudes.
15. A rigorous treatment of the properties of segregation curves is presented in Hutchens (1991).
16. On the other hand, Ruhm (1991a) offers evidence that the impact of displacement on older workers is not more severe once an adequate control group is used.
17. This calculation adjusts for tenure among employed workers and uses only those with three or more years of tenure.
18. See Neumark (2000) for a thorough review.
19. Fallick (1996) presents a thorough review of the literature on displacement.
20. Couch also shows that displaced older workers lose health insurance coverage, which may lead to more serious consequences for families of people who lose their jobs.
21. See Stanley and Jarrell (1998), Darity and Mason (1998) and Altonji and Blank (1999) for recent reviews of the literature on detecting sex and race discrimination.
22. The residual is measured either through the coefficient on a dummy variable for race or gender, or by a decomposition of race or sex differences into a component based on differences in observable characteristics and a component based on differences in coefficient estimates (for example, Oaxaca, 1973; Neumark, 1988).
23. Even with regard to sex and race, there are related problems; see, for example, Goldin and Polachek (1987).
24. There are several reasons for this. First, it may be due to the existence of efficient delayed payment contract schemes (Lazear, 1979), which were discussed in the introduction. Alternatively, it could be due to worker preferences for delaying earnings to later in life as a savings mechanism (Loewenstein and Sicherman, 1991; Neumark, 1995).
25. The Bureau of Labor Statistics provides tables in support of this point on their web page (www.bls.gov).
26. Age was not explicitly presented on the résumé but could be inferred from the year one's Bachelor's degree was received.
27. This is comparable to the polling results of Herz and Rones (1989).
28. Johnson and Neumark find that their attempts to control for heterogeneity in the reporting of age discrimination do not change their results substantially.
29. Firm opportunistic behavior in regard to delayed payment contracts has been observed by Gokhale *et al.* (1995), who showed that wage profiles flatten after hostile takeovers in firms with a more senior workforce. Orr (1998) also argues that firms use strategic bankruptcy to default on implicit contracts.
30. Although they do not test Hutchens' theory explicitly, recent findings by Hirsch *et al.* (2000) are consistent with the theory of delayed payment contracts influencing firm hiring decisions.

References

Adams, Scott J. (2002), 'Passed over for promotion because of age: an empirical analysis of the consequences.' *Journal of Labor Research*, **23**(3), 446–62.

Adams, Scott J. (2004), 'Age discrimination and the employment of older workers', *Labour Economics*, **11**(2), 219–41.

Altonji, Joseph G. and Rebecca M. Blank (1999), 'Race and gender in the labor market', in Orley Ashenfelter and David Card (eds), *Handbook of Labor Economics, Volume 3C*, New York: North-Holland, pp. 3143–3259.

Avolio, Bruce J. and Gerald V. Barrett (1987), 'Effects of age stereotyping in a simulated interview', *Psychology and Aging*, **2**(1), 56–63.

Bendick, Marc, Charles W. Jackson and Victor A. Reinoso (1994) 'Measuring employment discrimination through controlled experiments', *Review of Black Political Economy*, **23**(1), 25–48.

Bendick, Marc, Charles W. Jackson and J. Horacio Romero (1996), 'Employment discrimination against older workers: an experimental study of hiring practices', *Journal of Aging & Social Policy*, **8**(4), 25–46.

Bowman, Jan and Robert Eisenstadt (2000), 'Older workers and job displacement: what the last two decades tell us', *Southwest Journal on Aging*, **15**(2), 47–52.

Burkhauser, Richard V. and Joseph R. Quinn (1983), 'Is mandatory retirement overrated? Evidence from the 1970s', *Journal of Human Resources*, **18**(3): 337–58.

Cappelli, Peter (2000), 'Examining the incidence of downsizing and its effect on establishment performance', in David Neumark (ed.), *On the Job: Is Long-Term Employment a Thing of the Past?*, New York: Russell Sage Foundation, pp. 463–516.

Carrington, William J. and Asad Zaman (1994), 'Interindustry variation in the costs of job displacement', *Journal of Labor Economics*, **12**(2), 243–76.

Connor, Catherine L., Patricia Walsh, Debra K. Litzelman and Maria G. Alavarez (1978), 'Evaluation of job applicants: the effects of age versus success', *Journal of Gerontology*, **33**(2), 246–52.

Couch, Kenneth A. (1998), 'Late life job displacement', *The Gerontologist*, **38**(1), 7–17.

Darity, William A. and Patrick L. Mason (1998), 'Evidence on discrimination in employment: codes of color, codes of gender', *Journal of Economic Perspectives*, **12**(2), 63–90.

Epstein, Lee, and Andrew D. Martin (2004), 'Does age (really) matter? A response to Manning, Carroll, and Carp', *Social Science Quarterly*, **85**(1), 18–30.

Evans, Bob (1999), 'Age discrimination – are oldies still goodies?', *Information Week*, 5 April 1999.

Fallick, Bruce C. (1996), 'A review of the recent literature on displaced workers', *Industrial and Labor Relations Review*, **50**(1), 5–16.

Farber, Henry S. (1993), 'The incidence and costs of job loss, 1982–1991', *Brookings Papers: Microeconomics*, 73–132.

Finkelstein, Lisa M., Michael J. Burke and Nambury S. Raju (1995), 'Age discrimination in simulated employment contexts: an integrative analysis', *Journal of Applied Psychology*, **80**(6), 652–63.

Friedman, Lawrence (1985), *Your Time Will Come: The Law of Age Discrimination in Employment*, New York: Russell Sage Foundation.

Fusilier, Marcelline R. and Michael A. Hitt (1983), 'Effects of age, race, sex, and employment experience on students' perceptions of job applications', *Perceptual and Motor Skills*, **57**, 1127–34.

Gardner, Jennifer M. (1995), 'Worker displacement: a decade of change', *Monthly Labor Review*, **118**(4), 45–57.

Garstka, Teri A., Michael T. Schmitt, Nyla R. Branscombe and Mary Lee Hummert (2004), 'How young and older adults differ in their responses to perceived age discrimination', *Psychology and Aging*, **19**(2), 326–35.

Gaudin, Sharon (2003), 'Older workers becoming hot commodity', *Datamation* (obtained from www.itmanagement.earthweb.com; posted 16 October 2003).

Gokhale, Jagadeesh, Erica L. Groshen and David Neumark (1995), 'Do hostile takeovers reduce extramarginal wage payments?', *Review of Economics and Statistics*, **77**(3), 470–85.

Goldin, Claudia, and Solomon Polachek (1987), 'Residual differences by sex: perspectives on the gender gap in earnings', *American Economic Review*, **77**(2), 143–51.

Gordon, Randall A. and Richard D. Arvey (2004), 'Age bias in laboratory and field settings: a meta-analytic investigation', *Journal of Applied Social Psychology*, **34**(3), 468–92.

Gordon, Randall A., Richard M. Rozelle and James C. Baxter (1988), 'The effect of applicant age, job level, and accountability on the evaluation of job applicants', *Organizational Behavior and Human Decision Processes*, **41**, 20–33.

Gustman, Alan L. and Thomas L. Steinmeier (1986), 'A structural retirement model', *Econometrica*, **54**(3), 555–84.

Haefner, James E. (1977), 'Race, age, sex, and competence as factors in employer selection of the disadvantaged', *Journal of Applied Psychology*, **62**(2), 199–202.

Hellerstein, Judith K. and David Neumark (2004), 'Production function and wage equation estimation with heterogeneous labor: evidence from a new matched employer–employee data set', NBER working paper no. 10325.

Herz, Diane E. and Philip L. Rones (1989), 'Institutional barriers to employment of older workers', *Monthly Labor Review*, **112**(4), 14–21.

Hirsch, Barry T., David A. Macpherson and Melissa A. Hardy (2000), 'Occupational age structure and access for older workers', *Industrial and Labor Relations Review*, **53**(3), 401–18.

Hurd, Michael (1990), 'Research on the elderly: economic status, retirement, and consumption and saving', *Journal of Economic Literature*, **28**(2), 565–637.

Hutchens, Robert (1986), 'Delayed payment contracts and a firm's propensity to hire older workers', *Journal of Labor Economics*, **4**(4), 439–57.

Hutchens, Robert (1988), 'Do job opportunities decline with age?', *Industrial and Labor Relations Review*, **42**(1), 89–99.

Hutchens, Robert (1991), 'Segregation curves, Lorenz curves, and inequality in the distribution of people across occupations', *Mathematical Social Sciences*, **21**(1), 31–51.

Johnson, Richard W. and David Neumark (1997), 'Age discrimination, job separations, and employment status of older workers: evidence from self-reports', *Journal of Human Resources*, **32**(4), 779–811.

Kenney, Genevieve M. and Douglas A. Wissoker (1994), 'An analysis of the correlates of discrimination facing young Hispanic job-seekers', *American Economic Review*, **84**(3), 674–83.

Kotlikoff, Laurence J. and Jagadeesh Gokhale (1992), 'Estimating a firm's age-productivity profile using the present value of workers' earnings', *Quarterly Journal of Economics*, **107**(4), 1215–42.

Kotlikoff, Laurence J. and David A. Wise (1989), *The Wage Carrot and the Pension Stick*, Kalamazoo, MI: Upjohn Institute.

Lazear, Edward P. (1979), 'Why is there mandatory retirement?', *Journal of Political Economy*, **87**(6), 1261–84.

Lazear, Edward P. and Sherwin Rosen (1990), 'Male–female wage differences in job ladders', *Journal of Labor Economics*, **8**(1), S106-23.

Locke-Connor, Catherine and R. Patricia Walsh (1980), 'Attitudes toward the older job applicant: just as competent, but more likely to fail', *Journal of Gerontology*, **35**(6), 920–27.

Loewenstein, George and Nachum Sicherman (1991), 'Do workers prefer increasing wage profiles?', *Journal of Labor Economics*, **9**(1), 67–84.

Manning, Kenneth L., Bruce A. Carroll and Robert A. Carp (2004), 'Does age matter? Judicial decision making in age discrimination cases?', *Social Science Quarterly*, **85**(1), 1–18.

McCue, Kristin (1996), 'Promotions and wage growth', *Journal of Labor Economics*, **14**(2), 175–209.

McEvoy, Glenn M. and Wayne F. Cascio (1989), 'Cumulative evidence of the relationship between employee age and job performance', *Journal of Applied Psychology*, **74**(1), 11–17.

Medoff, James L. and Katharine A. Abraham (1980), 'Experience, performance, and earnings', *Quarterly Journal of Economics*, **95**(4), 703–36.

Neumark, David (1988), 'Employers' discriminatory behavior and the estimation of wage discrimination', *Journal of Human Resources*, **23**(3), 279–95.

Neumark, David (1995), 'Are rising earnings profiles a forced-saving mechanism?', *Economic Journal*, **105**(428), 95–106.

Neumark, David (1996), 'Sex discrimination in restaurant hiring: an audit study', *Quarterly Journal of Economics*, **111**(3), 915–41

Neumark, David (ed.) (2000), *On the Job: Is Long-Term Employment a Thing of the Past?*, New York: Russell Sage Foundation.

Neumark, David (2003), 'Age discrimination legislation in the United States', *Contemporary Economic Policy*, **21**(3), 297–317.

Neumark, David and Wendy A. Stock (1999), 'Age discrimination laws and labor market efficiency', *Journal of Political Economy*, **107**(5), 1081–125.

Oaxaca, Ronald (1973), 'Male–female wage differentials in urban labor markets', *International Economic Review*, **14**(3), 693–709.

Oi, Walter Y. (1962), 'Labor as a quasi-fixed factor', *Journal of Political Economy*, **70**(6), 538–55.

Ong, Paul M. and Don Mar (1992), 'Post-layoff earnings among semiconductor workers', *Industrial and Labor Relations Review*, **45**(2), 366–79.

Orr, Douglas V. (1998), 'Strategic bankruptcy and private pension default', *Journal of Economic Issues*, **32**(3), 669–87.

Pergamit, Michael R. and Jonathan R. Veum (1999), 'What is a promotion?', *Industrial and Labor Relations Review*, **52**(4), 581–601.

Perry, Elissa L., Carol T. Kulik and Anne C. Bourhis (1996), 'Moderating effects of personal and contextual factors in age discrimination', *Journal of Applied Psychology*, **81**(6), 628–47.

Polsky, Daniel (1999), 'Changing consequences of job separations in the United States', *Industrial and Labor Relations Review*, **52**(4), 565–80.

Posner, Richard A. (1995), *Aging and Old Age*, Chicago: University of Chicago Press.

Posner, Richard A. (1999), 'Employment discrimination: age discrimination and sexual harassment', *International Review of Law and Economics*, **19**(4), 421–46.

Richmond, Warren D. (1999), 'Retiring makes sense', *New York Times*, 22 August 1999; Sunday, Late Edition – Final, sec. 4, p. 12.

Rosen, Benson, and Thomas J. Jerdee (1977), 'Too old or not too old?', *Harvard Business Review*, **55**(6), 97–106.

Ruhm, Christopher J. (1991a), 'Displacement induced joblessness', *Review of Economics and Statistics*, **73**(3), 517–22.

Ruhm, Christopher J. (1991b), 'Are workers permanently scarred by job displacements?', *American Economic Review*, **81**(1), 319–24.

Salthouse, Timothy A., David Z. Hambrick, Kristen E. Lukas and T.C. Dell (1996), 'Determinants of adult age differences in synthetic work performance', *Journal of Experimental Psychology: Applied*, **2**(4), 305–29.

Shapiro, David and Steven H. Sandell (1985), 'Age discrimination in wages and displaced older men', *Southern Economic Journal*, **52**(1), 90–102.

Shellenbarger, Sue (2001), 'Baby boomers already getting agitated over age-bias issues', *Wall Street Journal*, 30 May 2001, p. B1.

Singer, M.S. and Christine Sewell (1989), 'Applicant age and selection interview decisions: effect of information exposure on age discrimination in personnel selection', *Personnel Psychology*, **42**: 135–54.

Stanley, T.D. and Stephen B. Jarrell (1998), 'Gender wage discrimination bias? A meta-regression analysis', *Journal of Human Resources*, **33**(4), 947–73.

Stone, Julia E. (1980), 'Age discrimination in Employment Act: a review of recent changes', *Monthly Labor Review*, **103**(3), 32–6.

Triandis, Harry C. (1963), 'Factors affecting employee selection in two cultures', *Journal of Applied Psychology*, **47**(2), 89–96.

US Bureau of Labor Statistics (2001), *Employment and Earnings*, Washington, DC: BLS.

Weiner, Steve (2005), 'Why that post-50 job is getting harder to find', *Career Journal.com* (available from www.wsj.com).

PART III

POLICY IMPACTS

PART III

POLICY IMPACTS

8 Discrimination in the credit and housing markets: findings and challenges

Gary A. Dymski

Economics all too seldom provides straightforward guidelines for designing and analyzing statistical materials on subjects of great social importance. Since the economic theory of discrimination does provide a simple approach, it is too bad that studies of whether banks discriminate in mortgage lending have not utilized these insights. (Gary Becker, 1993, p. 18)

Eventually, even the definition of discrimination comes to mean different things to blacks and whites. (Derrick Bell, 1980, p. 658)

1 Introduction

This chapter summarizes the main lines of research on discrimination in the housing and credit markets, and develops an explanation for the prevalence of the continuing controversies among analysts of these phenomena. There are sizable literatures on racial discrimination in the credit and housing markets.[1] However, this does not mean that academic researchers have agreed on a core set of findings and come to many definite conclusions. To the contrary, findings are contentious, and conclusions challenged. Studies often beget counter-studies. Taken as a whole, academic debate has reached no definitive conclusions about whether applicant race and gender and neighborhood racial composition per se affect housing and credit market outcomes. Residents of minority communities might regard this uncertainty as surprising, if not socially irresponsible. But this *is* the situation: premises that are common wisdom in lived communities are debated fiercely and inconclusively in think tanks and universities.

Consequently, this assessment must also investigate the persistence of academic controversy. This chapter attributes the inconclusiveness of the academic literature to several factors: the ambiguity of legal and theoretical definitions of discrimination; the inescapability of the point of view of the observer and observed in empirical studies of racial discrimination; and the way in which empirical methodologies require research questions to be framed. To achieve precise empirical results, academic researchers have focused on narrow portions of a broad conceptual and historical terrain. Only when this tension between the narrower terrain of empirical work and the broader terrain of the social dimensions of discrimination is acknowledged can analysts who have been talking past one another find ways to communicate.

This chapter touches almost exclusively on racial discrimination, with limited attention to gender discrimination and virtually none to sexual preference or other forms of discrimination. In addition, discussion centers on discrimination involving African Americans and Latinos.[2]

We proceed as follows. Section 2 describes the legal context of the economics of credit-market and housing-market discrimination. Section 3 sets out the theoretical behavioral models that have guided most empirical work in this area. Section 4 reviews empirical studies of racial 'redlining' and racial discrimination in the credit market. Section 5 considers the impact of the financial evolution on discrimination, with special attention to predatory lending. Section 6 then discusses empirical work on racial discrimination in housing markets. Section 7 considers work on gender discrimination in these two markets. Section 8 then explores the significance of cultural affinity, networks and wealth. Section 9 concludes.

2   The legal context of discrimination in credit and housing markets

The roots of the controversy over measuring racial discrimination in the credit and housing markets lie in the independent origins of empirical and theoretical work on these intertwined topics. Empirical work on housing and credit-market discrimination has its origins in Congressional action against racial and other forms of discrimination in the 1960s and 1970s. Theoretical models of discrimination evolved with virtually no reference to Civil Rights era legislation. The core models in this area of investigation suggest that racial discrimination may either be benign, in the sense that those who practice racial exclusion bear all costs of their discriminatory actions, or rational. So while the legal view of discrimination in these markets is prepared to find and punish perpetrators, theoretical models are predisposed to the conclusion that action against the racially biased is either unnecessary or inefficient.[3]

This section sets out the legal context. We begin with a definition.[4] At any point in time, discrimination occurs whenever agents who individually share some common characteristic can complete a market transaction only at a higher cost or more stringent terms than other agents; it also occurs when agents sharing this characteristic are less likely to succeed in an uncertain market transaction (such as applying for a loan), or have less access to resources. This discrimination can be based on one or more characteristics of agents: race, sexual preference, gender, age, national origin, and so on. Implicitly, the social (and legal) concern over prevalent discrimination arises insofar as it is consequential; that is, if it affects agents' relative well-being through time. John Roemer (1998) has suggested that equality of opportunity is compromised when two sets of agents have differential opportunities for success and achievement (and, we might add, for consumption) due to an ascriptive difference. Inequality of opportunity serves as a useful criterion for establishing whether discrimination is consequential.

Race is a protected category under the US Constitution's 'equal protection' doctrine; the 14th Amendment to the Constitution, passed in 1868 in response to various states' 'black codes', established that no state 'shall make or enforce any law which shall abridge the privileges or immunities of the citizens of the United States . . . [or] deprive any person of life, liberty, or property without due process of law, [or] deny to any person within its jurisdiction the equal protection of the laws'. Congress passed several statutes to implement this Amendment, including the Civil Rights Act of 1866, which guarantees the right 'to make and enforce contracts' (42 U.S.C. § 1981). However, over the years the Supreme Court restricted the applicability of the 14th Amendment to the action of states.

Federal housing policies to encourage home-ownership, until the 1970s, embodied overt racial bias against minorities and minority areas.[5] The rise of the Civil Rights movement in the 1950s created social pressure for change, especially with respect to racial injustice as it affected African Americans. In November 1962, Executive Order 11063 banned discrimination in all feder-ally assisted housing. Congress then used its powers to regulate inter-state commerce to pass the Civil Rights Act of 1964, which extended the 14th Amendment to the actions of individuals, universities and other entities. Subsequent statutes brought various substantive areas explicitly under the scope of this Act. The Fair Housing Act of 1968 makes it 'unlawful for any person or other entity whose business includes engaging in residential real estate-related transactions to discriminate against any person in making avail-able such a transaction, or in the terms or conditions of such a transaction' (42 U.S.C. §3601 *et seq.*).[6] This Act identifies seven classes protected by the law: race, color, national origin, religion, sex, familial status and disability. Similarly, the Equal Credit Opportunity Act (ECOA) of 1974 makes discrim-ination against loan applicants unlawful.

Numerous court cases and Congressional fine-tuning have clarified the legal meaning of discrimination and shaped federal policies. In March 1994, the federal agencies responsible for punishing credit-market discrimination issued a unified policy statement incorporating these clarifications. Three types of racial discrimination are identified (Marsden,1994):

- overt discrimination – refusing to initiate a transaction with a person of color;
- disparate treatment – screening minorities more harshly than whites in application processes, or subjecting minority applications to different application processes;

- disparate impact – conducting commercial practices that disproportionately harm a racial minority without being justified by a legitimate business need.

The first two elements of this list emphasize discrimination as intentional behavior. Both suggest that racial or other forms of discrimination can be traced back to racial 'perpetrators': in the first case, these perpetrators are engaging in willed and purposive behavior aimed at blocking minorities; in the second case, a behavior can be identified which may not be intentional, but which has non-neutral effects. There is observed evidence of discrimination, a 'smoking gun', for diligent investigators to unearth.

The third element of the above list is different. It refers to situations in which procedures that are racially neutral on their face lead to ex-post racial disparities unrelated to economic fundamentals. In effect, if no legitimate business-related reason for making racial distinctions can be identified, then racial divisions in market outcomes are presumed to be socially illegitimate. They inhibit all citizens' ability to 'make and enforce contracts'. No distinction is made about whether these racial divisions result from actions intended to produce these effects.

Many types of loan and housing markets could serve as vehicles for any of these types of discrimination. In the early 1970s, home-mortgage markets were brought to the fore in policy debates about discrimination in these markets, as a broad-based movement of community-based groups exposed the 'redlining' of inner-city neighborhoods. Redlining involves a decision by either lenders or realty agents to avoid or make fewer transactions in a given area, because of its 'riskiness'. Community groups, sometimes working with intrepid social scientists, collected data showing that systematically fewer home loans or insurance policies were being recorded in some areas than in others.[7] The areas being redlined typically had higher minority populations than other areas, so this behavior could be linked to lenders' or brokers' spatial racial biases. Ironically, until the mid-1960s, the federal government's principal home-mortgage underwriting program (the Federal Home Administration (FHA) program), which accounted for nearly half of all homes sold in the 1950s and 1960s, itself used explicitly racial (and racist) criteria about neighborhoods in making decisions about whether to approve FHA loans. So redlining was not a phantasm of overzealous activists: it had been official government policy. The relation between racial discrimination and redlining was then as follows: the former disadvantages an agent independent of her location; the latter disadvantages agents in a location independent of their individual characteristics.

To clarify the extent of this problem, Congress passed the Home Mortgage Disclosure Act (HMDA) in 1975; this legislation required lenders to report the number and dollar volume of residential loans by Census tract. The data collected under the HMDA, together with continued grassroots pressure, were sufficient to convince Congress to pass the Community Reinvestment Act of 1977 (CRA), which requires banks to meet credit needs in their entire market area.[8] This affirmative obligation to meet credit needs evenly was interpreted by community-based groups as a mandate to end redlining.

The existence of HMDA and the CRA mandate generated considerable controversy in localities throughout the nation. Local groups alleged bias; bankers and brokers responded that the allegedly redlined areas also had worse economic fundamentals than other areas, as well as a systematically lower demand for credit and home ownership. If the presence of racial bias as an important element in redlining (keeping in mind the legacy of the FHA program) could not be proved, its possibility could not be dismissed. When the thrift bail-out bill passed in 1989, activists and Congress members used the horse-trading possibilities this act afforded to require more detailed reporting under HMDA. As of 1990, banks and other mortgage lenders over a specific asset-size threshold have been required to report data on every mortgage loan application, including the applicant's race and income and the disposition of the application. These reporting requirements have been fine-tuned almost continuously since then; this fine-tuning takes the form of amendments to Regulation C, which implements HMDA. Most of this fine-tuning has been incremental, but, in 2002, changes to Regulation C required that, as of 1 January 2004, institutions report information about the loan rate charged and also more detailed borrower race/ethnic information.[9]

3   Theoretical models of discrimination and redlining in credit and housing markets

The politically charged rise of civil rights legislation concerning processes and outcomes in housing and credit markets (among other markets) found little initial support in the realm of economic theory. The one existing text that explicitly examined the behavioral foundations of racial discrimination from a theoretical viewpoint was Becker's (1957) volume, which he expanded in a 1971 second edition. This model traces race effects in housing and labor markets to individual agents' racial bigotry. It presupposes that some whites so dislike minorities that they will pay a premium or accept lower wages or profits to avoid dealing with minorities in home or business settings. Becker goes on to argue that discriminators themselves bear the costs of discrimination, given free entry into these markets. So discrimination will die a natural death as discriminators tire of its price; no policy intervention is needed to overcome it, just free entry into markets. This theory, in short, links discrimination to perpetrators, and perpetrators' behavior to racial preferences; and it concludes that little or no interference in the market is needed to address this evidently 'social' problem.

This story is deceptively simple: its conclusion follows only given a particular specification of preferences and market structure. The effects of racial preferences depend on the relative numbers of minority and white agents, on how many are bigoted, on the freedom of market entry, and on whether market participants face transaction and/or information costs.[10] Consider the housing market. If only *some* real-estate agents in a given area are bigoted, minority homeseekers should be able to turn to unbigoted agents for assistance, paying no penalty apart from shoe-leather costs. But if *all* real-estate agents are equally bigoted and entry into their business is costly, minorities may pay a premium for lower-quality homes. If white residents alone are bigoted, whites may pay a premium to live in areas with few minorities (Becker's case); but if racial covenants or other means of legal exclusion force all minority residents into restricted housing quarters, rents in minority areas will command a premium.

Several authors have extended Becker's model to the credit market. Dymski (1995) shows that racially neutral bankers might offer stricter credit terms to borrowers in white communities than in minority communities if enough whites are bigoted; but if some minorities prefer white communities, 'rational' (racially neutral) bankers might protect their profits by practicing personal discrimination against *these* prospective borrowers. Han (2001, 2004) develops a taste-based model more complete than Becker's in that it derives loan terms endogenously. He finds that whether loans to minority borrowers have higher expected profit rates (the mirror image of the 'perpetrator pays' view) depends crucially on how profitability is measured.

Some theoretical models of housing-market discrimination developed in the 1970s, which extend a Becker-type framework to the housing market, continue to inform contemporary audit tests.[11] These models examine what happens when housing search is costly and white agents or residents may be racial bigots; see Masson (1973), Lee and Warren (1977), Courant (1978) and Cronin (1982). These models uniformly suggest that Becker's perpetrator-pays property does not hold in the housing market. In particular, white prejudice makes housing search costlier for minority homeseekers than for white homeseekers; thus minorities will search less, pay more, and be less satisfied, *ceteris paribus*. Yinger's model of the rental market (1975) shows that racially neutral landlords with bigoted white residents might discriminate against minority tenants in choosing tenants – again, passing discrimination costs along to minorities.[12]

Overall, these results suggest that, when market entry is not free, when minorities as well as whites have racial preferences, or when information costs exist, discrimination costs may not be borne by bigots, and hence racial differences may not lessen over time. These results all are motivated by situations in which one or another set of agents have preferences about dealing with certain classes of agents. Agents in these models are taken one-by-one. Richer outcomes can emerge however, when agents' spatial locations are identified, and when agents in the same discriminatory category (such as race) live in concentrated areas. In this case, spillover effects among agents may emerge; and generalizations (for example, on the basis of the racial characteristics of an area) can be made. For example, Zenou and Boccard (2000) develop a model in which spatial mismatch exists (with jobs located disproportionately in the suburban fringe, not the urban core), in which black workers are subject to racial discrimination in the job market, and in which employers discriminate against urban-core workers. In this case, as the authors put it, 'both race and space are responsible for the high unemployment rate among blacks' (p. 260); spatial spillovers amplify racial biases and generate cumulative segregation and unemployment impacts.

Informational problems can lead to racial redlining even when no agents are Becker-type bigots. Shifting attention to the credit market, Stiglitz and Weiss (1991) show that the asymmetric distribution of information about creditworthiness between banks and potential borrowers in white and minority communities can lead to redlining. If banks cannot distinguish good from bad individual borrowers, but know that projects in the minority community are riskier than those in the white community, they may redline the minority community to avoid excess exposure to risk.[13]

Why will loans in the minority community be riskier? Two theoretical explanations have been proposed. The first argument, originally suggested by Guttentag and Wachter (1980), and then refined by Lang and Nakamura (1993), explains redlining as due to neighborhood externalities and information costs. The argument goes that in any community, the return on (or variability of) lending depends on the total volume of lending there. Given this, lenders concentrate their lending where other lenders are making loans. The second argument, made by the same authors, asserts that, if it is costly to gather information on individual borrowers, and if borrowers' race and economic fundamentals are correlated, lenders can 'rationally' use neighborhood racial composition as a low-cost substitute for costly information gathering.[14]

Neighborhood spillovers may also cause coordination failures among lenders: refurbishment effects, wherein home sales lead to refurbishment by their new owners, enhancing the value of all homes in the neighborhood; liquidity effects, wherein home sales enhance all neighborhood homes' values by increasing these homes' liquidity; and branch spillover effects, wherein bank branches function as pure public goods in their local neighborhoods (Dymski, 1995).[15] Further, intermarket linkages can also be pivotal in credit-market outcomes: given racial discrimination in the labor market (see Austin

Turner, Fix and Struyk, 1991), banks might 'rationally' discriminate against minority loan applicants who are as qualified as whites, owing to minority applicants' lower or more variable future earned-income levels. Discrimination could take the form of either disparate treatment of individual minority applicants or the redlining of minority neighborhoods. Feedback effects from the credit market to the markets for earned income, of course, are also possible, though these are not explored in this chapter.

Summary
Theoretical models have suggested three roots of discriminatory market processes – that is, market outcomes that widen racial differences in access to or control of economic resources:[16]

1. Personal discrimination (bigotry): racially differential outcomes that are due to racial preferences unrelated to economic factors.
2. Rational discrimination: racially differential outcomes which arise when agents use race or characteristics correlated with race to make valid statistical inferences about the distinct market prospects of different racial groups.
3. Structural discrimination: racially differential outcomes that arise because of identifiable economic factors associated with the agents or property involved.

Category (2) refers to outcomes based on anticipated disparities, and category (3) to those based on existing disparities. An example may clarify the difference. Suppose whites and minorities are members of a loan pool for a limited number of loans; and suppose credit will be allocated on the basis of their current levels of wealth and their prospective levels of earned income. Minorities are subject to structural discrimination if they have lower average wealth levels than whites and are chosen less often for loans on this basis; if minority and white wealth levels are the same, minorities are subject to rational discrimination if loans are based on prospective income and minorities' average prospective incomes are lower than whites.

Ideally, the theoretical framework that underlies any given literature should provide unambiguous basic behavioral categories that can be used to anchor applied analyses. This framework, however, does not generate clear and unambiguous linkages between motivations and outcomes, or between market processes and legal prohibitions against discrimination. Becker's model attempted to tell a simple and reassuring story: that racist agents in markets were not only economically irrational, but also self-liquidating. However, subsequent work on his framework has shown that even the meaning of discrimination becomes very murky in the presence of inter-market linkages, complex patterns of preference, or search costs. Racial perpetrators may not pay the costs of their discrimination, so Becker's conclusion that discrimination is unsustainable seems unwarranted. Worse, Han (2001) shows that, if taste-based discrimination exists, then outcomes that might be regarded as evidence of statistical discrimination (such as stricter terms and conditions, higher denial rates, and so on) may instead result from taste-based discrimination. Under at least some circumstances, then, taste-based and statistical discrimination may be observationally equivalent.[17]

Subsequent theoretical models, based on lender/borrower asymmetric information, showed that these phenomena can arise even without non-neutral racial preferences. 'Rational' discrimination can arise for several reasons, taking the form either of discrimination against individuals or redlining. So there can be racial bias without racial intent: there can be, so to speak, 'benign' racial perpetrators, motivated not by blind hatred but by profit. Indeed, Scalera and Zazzaro (2001) show that, with incomplete information, statistical discrimination based on misinformation or other prejudices about members of a group can generate worsened performance over time, justifying the initial perceived group effect.

Do these conceptual ideas about discrimination provide justifications for legal action against it? The mapping from the three categories of discriminatory market process to the three types of prohibited behavior is not exact. For certain, personal discrimination based on bigotry is identical with overt discrimination. And while the 'market' may in some cases 'punish' personal discriminators, as Becker envisioned, in other cases the discriminatees will pay the cost, justifying the existence of legal remedies on the basis of discrimination.

The last two items in the above list have a more uncertain link to civil rights law. Clearly, rational discrimination can both justify disparate treatment and generate disparate impact. This can be due to screening processes either at the level of individual applicants in a given market or at the level of residents of a given neighborhood; that is, either discrimination or redlining can be 'justified' on the basis of cost. This sets up at least a tradeoff between profitability and equal protection against unfair discrimination. The key question then becomes, what is the required level of effort by those controlling resource flows in the credit and housing markets? Suppose the standard is that equal protection considerations are relevant only if they do not impose *any* costs; then the disparate treatment and disparate impact criteria will apply only if evidence of bigotry in the application of these criteria is also found. But this reduces to the first legal criterion, against overt discrimination. Similarly, structural discrimination, insofar as it reflects the historical legacy of earlier market outcomes, can be the basis of a legal disparate impact claim only if overt discrimination can be identified in the markets in question.

Economists who have addressed the legality of rational discrimination (Guttentag and Wachter, 1980; Calomiris *et al.*, 1994) have argued for it. This reflects a judgment that lenders' (brokers') required level of effort in the profitability/equal protection tradeoff should be zero: that economic efficiency should absolutely dominate any other social criterion. But, in a contest between due process and economic rationality, should it be protection against disparate treatment that gives way? This is inescapably a political question, not *just* an economic one.

4   Empirical studies of redlining and discrimination in the credit market

Section 3 has shown that economic theories of discrimination have been developed independently of the legal benchmarks set out in section 2, with the result that the fit between theory and legal framework is inexact. Tensions exist about what constitutes discriminatory behavior, and consequently about what behaviors are illegal under civil rights law and what behaviors are unresponsive to the broader aims of housing and credit-market policy. Similarly, the theoretical models describing housing and credit-market discrimination use diverse methods and assumption sets. It is hardly surprising, then, that a wide range of empirical models have been used to depict discriminatory outcomes in housing and credit markets; nor is it surprising that the value of these empirical results has been a topic of continuing debate and controversy.

Data limitations have precluded the statistical study of racial inequality and discrimination in most credit markets. On occasion, researchers have been able to exploit data sets encompassing particular markets and historical periods. For example, Olney (1998) shows how racial discrimination by lenders and racial differences in household collateral interacted in complex ways in the markets for merchant and installment credit in the inter-war period. Olney's results suggest substantial discrimination in merchant credit markets, leading to racially differential liquidity constraints.[18] Martin and Hill (2000), in turn, find evidence consistent with the presence of statistical racial discrimination in the auto credit market; however, in contrast to Olney, they suggest that this discrimination may be 'rational' for lenders.

The exception to this rule is the case of housing credit markets. As noted in section 2, Congress passed into law in 1975 an act requiring lenders to report annual data on home mortgage flows. This has focused researchers' attention on redlining and/or racial discrimination in home mortgage markets. In effect, this federal legislation, as amended over time, has both provided data for innumerable studies and has called forth studies of home mortgage markets using other data and other approaches. Austin Turner and Skidmore (1999b) provide an excellent introduction to this vast body of work. They view discrimination in the context of a loan approval process they divide into four stages: advertising and outreach; pre-application inquiries; loan approval/denial and/or terms and conditions; and loan administration. Their volume reports on studies and industry trends involving each step of this process, documenting that the pattern and practice of discrimination involves interlinked multi-phase processes. Some trends that appear on the surface to be independent of racial discrimination are not: for example, these authors show that bank branch closures in minority neighborhoods have a discriminatory effect.

The next two subsections provide a more detailed summary of empirical studies of racial redlining and discrimination in the credit and housing markets that have relied on home mortgage loan data. The discussion then turns to audit studies of credit market behavior, studies of small-business credit markets, and finally, studies of subprime and predatory credit markets.[19]

The redlining model

For years, community activists have argued that banks have violated the CRA and ECOA and contributed to inner-city decline by leaving good credit risks there unfunded. Banks' defenders have responded that banks cannot afford uneconomic loans in the competitive post-deregulation era; and anyway, the market abhors a vaccuum, so non-bank lenders attuned to neglected neighborhoods will keep financial markets efficient by meeting any financial needs banks no longer serve.

HMDA data have served both sides in this debate, which has had two phases, corresponding to the two levels of bank reporting since HMDA became law in 1975. Initially, community-based organizations would simply amass counts of loans and dollar flows in different subareas of US cities. Once academic researchers were engaged, they could use HMDA data to construct redlining models of the following form:

Detrended mortgage flows in a given area $= f$ (Area economic
variables, area social variables [including area race]). $\qquad$ (8.1)

Prior to 1990, lenders covered by HMDA reported annually only on the number and dollar value of mortgages made by census tract; so dependent (left-hand-side) variables could be no more specific than that shown in equation (8.1). The logic of equation (8.1) is this: area economic variables might legitimately affect housing value and hence mortgage flows; but if mortgage decisions are based solely on economic fundamentals, then area social variables, including neighborhood racial composition, should be insignificant. Redlining arises when area racial composition affects loan flows, even after controlling for economic fundamentals.[20]

Three approaches have been used to establish redlining. One approach is to estimate equation (8.1) by census tract; redlining is inferred if loan flows fall as minority population increases. The first published studies of redlining using HMDA data (Ahlbrandt, 1977; Hutchinson *et al.*, 1977; Schafer (1978) took this approach. This is a flawed test if redlining occurs by *neighborhood*: Census tracts are too small to qualify as distinct 'neighborhoods' and larger communities are ignored.[21]

A second approach corrects this problem by separating data into geographic subsets corresponding to community boundaries. Bradbury, Case and Dunham (1989) grouped Boston's census tracts into 60 'neighborhoods'; Shlay (1989) divided Chicago into suburban, gentrified and 'neighborhood' areas. These studies (and others) have found that loan flows vary negatively with minority population, so minority and inner-city neighborhoods are not receiving what Shlay terms their 'fair share' of mortgage credit. This approach is subject to pre-selection bias.[22]

A third approach to redlining remedies the pre-selection bias problem by using a neutral method for sorting Census tracts. The well-known Atlanta study (Dedman, 1988) divided tracts into five tiers based on median income, and three distinct tiers based on minority population. A subsequent study of Los Angeles (Dymski and Veitch, 1994) divided that city's Census tracts into quintiles based on median income and on minority population. Both studies evaluated the sensitivity of loan flows to racial composition for each income tier separately. Both studies found dramatically lower loan flows in high-minority tracts.[23] This third method has the same flaw as the first: its tier groupings map spatially contiguous communities only imperfectly.

Numerous criticisms of all these models of redlining have been made. These studies do not control for whether lower loan flows in minority areas are due to lower loan demand there (Benston, 1981). Further, areas that are apparently redlined may have greater lending risks (Holmes and Horvitz, 1994), due to greater residential turnover and a higher proportion of renters (Canner, 1981) or to market failure (Guttentag and Wachter, 1980).[24] In effect, skeptics have viewed redlining as a spurious statistical result, and argued that only more complete data could determine whether what appears to be bank redlining behavior is dictated by economic factors. As Canner puts it:

> Far from being arbitrary or irrational lender behavior, redlining is the competitive market outcome of utility-maximizing households and profit-maximizing mortgage lenders. Conventional mortgage redlining is only slightly different in form from the more traditional price rationing that characterizes all competitive free markets. (Canner, 1981, p. 68)

This argument shifts the burden of proof from the presumption that fair market outcomes *should be* racially neutral to the presumption that efficient market outcomes *may be* racially non-neutral. If evidence of racial and other forms of redlining cannot prove racial or other biases in lending markets, neither is it true that all evidence of racial redlining signifies nothing. Given the US's legacy of residential segregation and the vast disparities in market and non-market resources among urban neighborhoods (Massey and Denton, 1993), evidence of racial redlining constitutes at least a warning beacon, an indicator that credit flows are contributing to or subtracting from the balance sheet of American racial inequality.[25]

Mortgage discrimination models

Several studies in the 1970s and 1980s, including the Atlanta study cited above, obtained non-HMDA data about individual mortgage applicants and found stronger evidence of discrimination. And as of 1990, HMDA reporting requirements have required lenders to collect data on applicants. These data allow researchers to estimate reduced-form discrimination equations that incorporate more elements of demand and supply, of the following form:

Probability of loan denial for a given applicant pool $= f$ (Individual economic variables, individual social variables [including individual's race], area economic variables, area social variables [including area race]).   (8.2)

The first study of the 1990 HMDA data (Canner and Smith, 1991) found that the denial rate for black applicants for conventional mortgage loans was 26.3 per cent, the Latino rate 18.4 per cent and the white rate 12.1 per cent. High-income blacks were approved less frequently than low-income whites. This result was consistent with, but did not conclusively prove, discrimination against minority loan applicants. Subsequently, the status of equation (8.2) as an investigative tool has come under intense scrutiny. Some researchers have interpreted it as a sufficient test of whether discrimination exists in housing credit markets; others have pointed out that the process of obtaining housing credit consists of many individual subprocesses, only one of which ends up as an observation in a HMDA data set. Evidence of minority disadvantage in equation (8.2) is consistent with the existence of discrimination in the residential credit decision, but does not prove it; on the other hand, evidence of no minority disadvantage in equation (8.2), while it suggests the absence of discrimination in the residential credit decision, says nothing about whether overall housing-credit market processes are race-neutral. Benston (1995), for example, argues that equation (8.2) studies are biased toward the finding of 'invidious' discrimination, while omitting data such as credit and employment history that may affect decision making.

A study by the Federal Reserve Bank of Boston (Munnell *et al.*, 1992) set new standards of rigor in implementing equation (8.2) models. Boston bank lenders provided researchers with complete access to their case files on 1990

home mortgage applicants, allowing a full accounting of applicant creditworthiness based on the information available to banks.

Probability of loan denial for a given applicant pool = f (Individual
economic variables considered by banks, individual social variables
considered by banks, individual's race, area economic variables
considered by banks, area social variables [including area race]).   (8.2a)

Equation (8.2a) differs from equation (8.2) in that the researchers have some
confidence that they are using precisely the variables considered by the banks
whose lending data they are evaluating. These authors found that African
American applicants had a 60 per cent greater chance of loan denial than
equally creditworthy whites.

For many analysts, this result was the statistical 'smoking gun' showing
that banks do discriminate by race. Nonetheless, critics have subsequently
challenged this study's result, following two lines of attack. Some have
pointed up methodological flaws such as coding errors, sensitivity to outlying
data points and the exclusion of factors important in bank decision making.
Others have challenged the adequacy of equation (8.2a) itself. Bostic (1996)
argues that race effects may operate through other variables, not independently; so he 'interacts' the borrower–race variable with variables linked to
borrower creditworthiness. The borrower–race variable per se loses significance; some race/creditworthiness variables are statistically significant and
suggest minority disadvantage. For Bostic, this suggests that only 'marginal'
borrowers are subject to racial disadvantage; he is not willing to term this
'discrimination'.

Rachlis and Yezer (1993) and LaCour-Little (1999), following Maddala
and Trost (1982), argue that a single reduced-form equation misspecifies
mortgage market behavior. Several decisions are made in a chronological
sequence by applicants and lenders: the applicant selects a lender; the applicant or lender selects a specific mortgage product, the lender approves or
denies the application, and then an approved applicant decides whether to
accept; and after funding occurs, the borrower decides over the life of the
mortgage whether to repay or default. In these authors' view, only a simultaneous equation approach can accurately depict this process. One-equation
models are likely to overestimate the significance of discrimination due to
partial observability bias. No single-equation model such as (8.2) is
adequately identified if the market processes in which it is embedded might
differentially affect the comparison groups (minorities and whites).[26] Further,
discrimination may occur at any of the distinct stages of the mortgage process,
not only at the application processing stage highlighted in equation (8.2).

Courchane and Golan (1999) have a different critique of equation (8.2).

They point out that, while this equation implicitly assumes that banks evaluate every borrower independently, on his or her own merits, in reality banks operate differently. They establish benchmark criteria for creditworthiness and then evaluate applicants in terms of those criteria. Racial discrimination then exists if banks evaluate minority applicants more strictly than they do other applicants. In terms of econometric methodology, then, the unordered discrete-choice model that is commonly used is inappropriate; the authors suggest a generalized maximum likelihood estimator that relies on information theory.

Some critics (for example, Brimelow and Spenser, 1993) have argued that equation (8.2) is irrelevant, because rational banks make loan decisions based on expected default rates. The empirical evidence on mortgage default rates and race is ambiguous; some studies find no significant differences, while others find minority default rates to be higher.[27] If lenders practice personal discrimination in mortgage markets, they must be forgoing good risks, and minority mortgagees should have lower default rates than white mortgagees. Since the empirical evidence does not support this conclusion, it follows, lenders are not discriminating.[28]

Both lines of criticism have been answered. Ross (2000) synthesizes the ideas that a simultaneous-equation approach is preferred in modeling credit-market outcomes and that racially differential default rates can be used to evaluate the presence or absence of preference-based discrimination. He argues, following Heckman (1976), that a 'two step' process incorporating (in this case) both the loan application and the loan-default step would best capture the presence or absence of personal discrimination by lenders. Ross attempts to overlay data collected separately for home-loan applications (using 1990 Boston) and for defaults (FHA data for Boston drawn from 1992) to estimate a two-step model of underwriting and default.[29] Unfortunately, no clear empirical results regarding the lending decision are obtained in this chapter.

Carr and Megbolugbe (1993) and Browne and Tootell (1995) take a different approach. These authors counter the methodological criticisms of the Boston study point-by-point, and demonstrate that this study's central conclusion is robust.[30] Galster (1993) counters the default rate critique; he argues that, if lenders do not discriminate, and if at the same time minorities face discrimination in markets other than the credit market, then minorities' ex post default rate on mortgages *should* be higher than whites'.[31] Galster assumes that 'rational discrimination' is illegal; as noted above, this assumption is not universally shared. Ross and Yinger (1999a) do a complete review of the Boston study and the criticisms thereof; these authors examine these criticisms, and sometimes re-estimate equations. They find first that the large racial gap in loan denial cannot be attributed to misspecification or data problems; and they find, second, that no study has demonstrated either the presence or the absence of disparate treatment discrimination or disparate impact discrimination in loan approval. These same authors undertake a thorough critical review of this discrimination literature (1999b). Their review encompasses the new literature on the use of default rates to detect discrimination; they agree with Galster that this approach is fundamentally flawed.

The advent of the Boston Fed study by no means put an end to research on access to housing credit using equation (8.2). HMDA data, when supplemented by data pertaining to applicant creditworthiness, even if it falls short of the Boston study's standard, does identify patterns of racial inequality in residential credit markets.[32] These patterns indicate that structural or personal discrimination, or both, may be present. Myers and Chan (1995) have experimented with instrumental-variable techniques as a way of identifying the presence of discriminatory credit standards. Dymski (1999) has used equation (8.2) to conduct comparative analyses of out-of-state banks, large banks, small banks and non-banks in various credit markets. Dymski (2001) and Dymski and Mohanty (1999) used an equation (8.2) model to compare the degree of racial disadvantage of Asian American, Latino and African American applicants in several metropolitan credit markets, over a multi-year time-span; Reibel (1997, 2000) uses equation (8.1) and equation (8.2) models to explore the problem of neighborhood disinvestment. Many such studies have been done, and are being done, for local markets by academics and activists. Such studies do not attempt to establish which lenders are behaving with explicit racial bias; they are efforts to unearth the broad patterns of inequality in credit flows. They establish benchmarks that can inform policy interventions.

Audit studies
The Boston Fed study sets a high standard for empirical models based on equation (8.2); researchers without that study's access to bank files will be hard-put to avoid the charge of omitted-variable bias. And, for some economists, even well-designed regression studies showing that race affects loan decisions cannot *prove* that lenders use applicants' race in their decision making.

Audit studies of bank behavior, by contrast, *can* demonstrate bankers' racial bias to these skeptics' satisfaction.[33] Audit studies are suited to detecting personal discrimination because they provide direct evidence and thus avoid the objection that observed racial differences are due to unobserved, unmeasured causes. This is not to suggest that audit studies are beyond criticism; as Calem and Longhofer (2002) point out, audit methodologies (like regression analyses of the determinants of credit flows or of the probability of loan denial) also have interpretive limitations.

The Federal Reserve and the Office of the Comptroller of the Currency have conducted numerous audit studies of banks' loan files in the course of making fair lending determinations. These studies have sometimes found evidence of racial bias. Pilot studies conducted by these agencies in Louisville, Chicago and New York have examined the pre-application stage and found subtle differences in the treatment of black and white testers. Lending officers were more likely to steer, switch or discourage minority applicants. Minorities were not given 'helpful hints', as were whites; and their financial ratios, when marginal, were interpreted negatively (unlike whites').[34]

The federal Department of Housing and Urban Development (HUD) recently conducted its own exploratory audit study of racial/ethnic bias in the Los Angeles and Chicago mortgage loan markets (Austin Turner, Freiberg *et al.*, 2002). This study, conducted in 2000, examines various steps that lending institutions and their representatives normally take in the multi-phase process of applying for and procuring a loan. It finds that most minority home loan seekers receive the same treatment as whites. However, a significant minority of black and brown applicants were subject to various kinds of disparate treatment: less coaching and more encouragement to consider an FHA loan (blacks in Los Angeles); less information about loan amount and house price, less product information, less follow-up (Latinos in Los Angeles, blacks in Chicago); lower loan amounts, less product information, less coaching (Latinos in Chicago).

Small-business credit markets and discrimination
Nothing like HMDA exists for small-business loans. Data on loan levels have been submitted by some lenders under the new CRA rules since 1996 and 1997. Initial studies of these data, conducted for a Federal Reserve Bank of Chicago conference in 1999 (Canner, 1999; Squires and O'Connor, 1999; Immergluck, 1999) find evidence suggesting that loans for small businesses are substantially less in lower-income and high-minority areas. However, limitations in data collection make it impossible to reach a definite conclusion about what forms of discrimination may be present.

Fortunately, various federal agencies also conduct periodic surveys of business owners. The samples collected are large enough to permit some comparisons on the basis of race. A few studies have used these data to explore the links between racial discrimination and small business activity. Grown and Bates (1992), using the Census Bureau's Characteristics of Business Owner survey for 1987, find that African American-owned construction firms are less well capitalized than other firms, and less likely to survive; banks make smaller loans to African American-owned construction firms, even taking firm characteristics into consideration. Bates's subsequent studies (1994, 1997) show that minority-owned businesses generally receive less credit than other businesses; African American businesses, in particular, have substantially less financial resources and access to banking services than do other firms.

Three recent studies have conducted formal econometric tests for racial discrimination in credit markets used by small businesses. Cavalluzzo and Cavalluzzo (1998) use data from the 1988–9 National Survey of Small Business Finances to analyze the presence of discrimination in the credit markets serving small businesses. These authors find that African American-owned firms are two-and-a-half times as likely to be denied loans, and approximately 13 per cent less likely to hold loans. Logit analysis of the probability of denial for those who applied for credit finds that denial rates for African American and Latino-owned firms are 35 per cent higher than for other firms, all else equal. They find little evidence that such businesses pay higher interest rates.

Blanchflower *et al.* (2003), in turn, use data from the 1993 and 1998 versions of the same survey to analyze the existence of credit-market discrimination against African American-owned small businesses. These authors use regression analysis to show that, even after controlling for differences in creditworthiness, African Americans are twice as likely as whites to be denied credit for their small businesses. Further, in contrast to the previous study, African Americans pay higher interest rates. These results for 1988–9 and for 1993 and 1998 are broadly consistent with the existence of discrimination. Cavalluzzo, Cavalluzzo and Wolken (2002), in turn, augment the 1993 data for the National Survey of Small Business Finances with data on local bank market structure and on firm credit-risk scores (drawn from Dun and Bradstreet data). This 2002 paper augments the results obtained in the other two papers by taking into consideration selection bias (per Heckman, 1979), differential firm risk and bank market structure. The racial disparities in access to credit and in interest rates paid remain even after controlling for these effects. Indeed, the more competitive the market, the less are the observed racial disparities.

5 Discrimination, predatory lending and financial evolution

Some research has begun to suggest that industrial organization aspects of banking and lending-market behavior may significantly affect credit-market processes and outcomes, and thus may significantly affect empirical results obtained from investigations of discrimination and/or redlining. The banking industry is in the midst of a fundamental reorganization of banking structures and practices. This reorganization, needless to say, has affected the extent and character of loan-market discrimination.

A merger and consolidation wave has currently seized the industry: failing savings and loan associations have merged or been bought out by banks, and smaller banks have been swallowed by larger competitors. This trend has been driven by intensified competition, which has also led banks to segment their customer markets: instead of offering uniform services to all depositors, banks are increasingly catering to 'upmarket' deposit and loan customers, while either shedding lower-balance customers or forcing them to pay high marginal rates.[35] Further, banks are systematically closing branches, especially in lower-income neighborhoods. Since minority communities and individuals are disproportionately found in the markets that banks are shedding, these shifts increase structural discrimination.

Another shift involves the increasing prominence of secondary markets; some lenders will only originate mortgage loans they can sell off. Secondary-market criteria may have a systematically disparate racial impact, since the wealth ratios and cash-flow measures they stress are lower for minorities than for whites.

In an equation (8.2) case study, Kim and Squires (1995) find that the approval rate for black applicants increases with the lender's percentage of minority employees, *ceteris paribus*. These authors suggest adding other lender characteristics as explanatory variables, including branch locations, counseling availability and bank marketing practices.

A few studies have scratched the surface of these issues. In a study of an Indiana county, Nesiba (1995) has found that mergers significantly affected credit flows and the extent of redlining in the 1985–93 period. In two studies of Los Angeles, Pollard (1995) and Dymski and Veitch (1996) find that the reorganization of bank functions and bank mergers have significantly affected credit flows and bank branch locations. And Dymski and Veitch (1994) find that area and individual race coefficients are larger (that is, indicate a higher probability of discrimination) for loans sold off to the secondary market than for other loans, in a study of 1990–92 data for Los Angeles. Dymski (1999, ch. 10) finds that the probability of loan approval varies inversely with the degree of banking-market concentration, in an equation (8.2)-type model that controls for applicant race and gender.

The emergence of predatory lending

In the past four years, a new form of discriminatory credit has come into focus: the subprime or 'predatory' lending market. This market appears to be a relatively new phenomenon in American credit markets. It refers to loans made on the basis of household or business collateral, under terms and conditions that are exculpatory.[36] These loans often lead to excessive rates of household and firm non-payment, and thus to foreclosures and personal financial distress. Certainly, usury has been a fine art in credit markets since the dawn of modern commerce. But a new term seems warranted for this form of lending, for several reasons. First, it involves two distinctive sets of practices. One is the aggressive telemarketing and sale of second mortgages based on demographic targeting – especially, the targeting of minority households that have traditionally been denied access to credit.[37] The second is the payday loan, the practice of advancing workers a portion of the money they stand to earn from their paychecks. Payday loans have become common in check-cashing stores. In both cases, financing is often provided by large bank holding companies.

Both these practices have had a heavy impact on the elderly, people of color and minority neighborhoods. Hence the question of discriminatory intent or impact arises. Many low-income and minority borrowers are obtaining loans at high interest rates and with very unfavorable terms from housing-related and payday lenders (Williams, 1999). For example, Canner *et al.* (1999, p. 709) found that, in 1998, subprime and manufactured housing lenders accounted for 34 per cent of all home purchase mortgage applications and 14 per cent of originations (new loans). These lenders' impact on low-income and minority individuals is even more pronounced. According to Canner *et al.*, in 1998, subprime and manufactured housing lenders made a fifth of all mortgages extended to lower-income and Latino borrowers, and a third of all those made to African American borrowers. According to ACORN (2000), subprime lending grew 900 per cent in the period 1993–9, even while other mortgage lending activity actually declined. A nationwide study of 2000 HMDA data by Bradford (2002) found that African Americans were, on average, more than twice as likely as whites to receive subprime loans, and Latinos almost one-half to over two times more likely.[38] This evidence suggests that lower-income and minority borrowers are being made targets by these specialized (and often predatory) lenders.

Industrial organization considerations, which are increasingly important in understanding discrimination in the mortgage market, also come into play in investigating predatory lending. Mergers and changing practices in consumer finance have led to ever more interpenetration between major banking corporations, finance companies and predatory lenders.[39] This may be linked to the shift in consumer finance toward a new revenue model: higher fees, paid upfront, for loans made on the basis of attachable assets. Since homes are most households' primary asset, especially later in life when mortgage loans have been paid down, the growth of the subprime mortgage lending market is readily grasped. The logic of the payday loan industry is very similar: next month's paycheck is sufficiently certain to serve as a collateral anchor for this new form of lending.

The subprime lending industry has exploded into prominence in the past several years because of the development of new technologies of securitization and risk pooling. Henriques and Bergman (2000) report that many of the largest investment banks on Wall Street have been channeling an increasing amount of funds to subprime lenders (an average of $80 billion annually in 1998 and 1999); further, some of the most prestigious Wall Street insurers have backed the mortgage-backed securities that subprime lenders have sold off into the markets. The business has grown quickly: one of the worst offenders, First Alliance of Irvine, California, conducted an initial public offering (IPO) in 1996. Further, some bank holding companies have purchased subprime lenders. Citicorp acquired Associates First Capital Corporation, which was then under investigation by the Federal Trade Commission and the Justice Department. Associates First represented a step toward Citi's goal of establishing its Citifinancial subsidiary as the nation's largest consumer finance company (Oppel and McGeehan, 2000). This drew an immediate response from fair-lending advocates. For example, Martin Eakes, founder of the non-profit Self-Help Credit Union in Durham, NC, commented, 'Those of us who have worked on the community level have seen the abuses outlined in the F.T.C. complaint, and many of us believe that Associates is a rogue company and may alone account for 20 per cent of all abusive home loans in the nation' (Oppel, 2001). In any event, this consumer-lending subsidiary helped to stabilize Citi's cash-flow during a period in which most megabanks' earnings slumped (Sapsford *et al.*, 2001; *Businessweek*, 2002).

These emergent practices have already drawn state and federal responses. Congress passed the Home Ownership and Equity Protection Act in 1994; amendments to federal Regulation Z in 2002, and a variety of state laws (notably those of North Carolina and Pennsylvania) have sought to rein in lenders' abusive treatment of borrowers. A variety of methods are used: heightened disclosure requirements, closer monitoring, limits on interest-rate margin, and/or limitations on the conditions under which these loans can be offloaded or resold, among others.

Academic studies of predatory lending
Most contemporary writing about subprime and predatory lending remains anecdotal. Academic research on predatory lending has only recently begun to emerge. Most of the initial empirical academic studies are collected in two journals' special issues. In both cases, these studies' central focus is on understanding the size and scope of predatory and subprime lending markets, and on the effects of policy interventions into these markets. One of these is volume 29, number 4 of the *Journal of Real Estate Finance and Economics*, published in 2004; the guest editors' introductory essay is Staten and Yezer (2004). Courchane, Surette and Zorn (2004) report statistics from a Freddie Mac survey of 8000 individuals who originated prime and subprime mortgages in 1999 and 2000. The response rate for this survey was disappointing (14 per cent). This survey (like the community-based surveys mentioned above) found that African Americans and Latinos are far more likely to receive subprime loans than are whites. These authors also find that a significant minority of borrowers with subprime loans may have been assigned to this risk pool inappropriately (based in particular on FICA scores). The authors present no statistical evidence about race and inappropriate classification. In turn, Calem, Gillen and

Wachter (2004) find in a study of Chicago and Philadelphia that subprime loans are far more likely to be made in minority neighborhoods than elsewhere.

The essays in volume 15, number 3 of *Housing Policy Debate* also focus substantial attention on the parameters of these emerging markets (McCoy and Wyly, 2004). Two articles (White, 2004; Lax *et al.*, 2004) present empirical results proposing that subprime lending rates are higher than adjustment for differential borrower risk might justify, suggesting that these markets are inefficient and that many borrowers in these markets are being exploited. Calem, Hershaff and Wachter (2004) expand greatly on Calem, Gillen and Wachter (2004): seven cities' data are covered; and the distribution of subprime loans is analyzed in the context of controls for neighborhood price risk, individuals' credit risk and the average educational attainment of neighborhood residents. After all these adjustments are made, there is a positive association between the percentage of African American residents in a neighborhood and the probability that residential loans in that neighborhood will be subprime. This is analogous to redlining, with the difference that previously loans would not be made, but now many more loans will be made, for a price. Terms and conditions on such loans are likely to be more onerous for borrowers than similar loans made elsewhere (Eggert, 2004). Wyly, Atia and Hammel (2004) show that African American and Latino borrowers have strongly elevated odds of loan rejection in lower-income areas undergoing gentrification, and much higher odds than elsewhere of receiving subprime loans when they are funded.

None of these academic studies has yet established directly that specific minority borrowers are significantly more likely to be sold a subprime or predatory loan than are non-minority borrowers with similar risk profiles. The post-2003 HMDA data should make it possible to conduct such tests. In the meantime, these preliminary studies strongly suggest that such results will be found; at the same time, experience with other models of lending discrimination suggests that results strongly suggesting racial discrimination in the subprime market will hardly put an end to empirical controversy.

6   Studies of racial discrimination in housing

As section 4 illustrates, leading credit-market discrimination studies have been conducted by many researchers inside and outside of government. By contrast, the definitive housing-market discrimination studies have been sponsored largely by HUD, with substantial continuity in core research team membership. These contrasts can be traced to two factors: first, the absence of anything like an HMDA for housing-market transactions; and second, the reliance of housing-market discrimination research on paired-testing (audit) studies. As Fishbein (1992) notes, audit studies are effective means of testing for overt discrimination and disparate treatment.

The Department of Housing and Urban Development has sponsored three audit studies of housing market practices, the Housing Market Practices Survey (HMPS) of 1977, the Housing Discrimination Study of 1989 (1989 HDS), and the Housing Discrimination Study of 2000 (2000 HDS). The HMPS used paired black and white testers in 40 cities, and established audit studies as a viable research methodology. The 1989 HDS, which encompassed 3800 audits in 25 cities, and the 2000 HDS, with 4600 audits in 23 cities, have provided information of unprecedented depth. Further, the latter two studies' methodology was designed in such a way as to permit comparisons of the extent of discrimination over time. Austin Turner, Struyk and Yinger (1991) provide a synthesis of the multi-volume 1989 HDS; the key results for the 2000 HDS are presented in Austin Turner, Ross, Galster and Yinger (2002).[40]

The 1989 HDS can be used as a benchmark for discussion here. It concluded that 53 per cent of black renters and 59 per cent of black home-buyers (as well as 46 per cent of Latino renters and 56 per cent of Latino homebuyers) experience discrimination by rental and sales agents: they are not shown available units, are shown fewer units, or are provided with less information and assistance. Further, just over 20 per cent of both blacks and Latinos are 'steered' away from white areas, higher-income areas and higher home-value areas. Rental and sales agents were disproportionately located in white neighborhoods, and are much more likely to recommend units in neighborhoods with higher concentrations of minority residents than the metropolitan average. Further, black- and Latino-owned units are less likely to be advertised or to be offered for open house than are white units. Page (1995) uses HDS data to estimate that on average, real-estate agents show African American and Latino housing seekers 80–90 per cent of the units they show to white customers.[41]

The 2000 HDS results differ somewhat from those obtained 11 years earlier. Overall, discrimination against blacks and Latinos remains significant at all stages of the housing search process, but the extent of discrimination is less. In rental markets, the overall incidence of consistent white-favored treatment relative to African Americans dropped from 26 per cent in 1989 to 22 per cent in 2000; Latinos' disadvantage increased slightly in these markets, from 25 per cent to 26 per cent. In home-sales markets, the overall incidence of white advantage relative to blacks dropped from 29 per cent in 1989 to 17 per cent in 2000; relative to Latinos, the overall incidence of white advantage dropped from 27 per cent to 20 per cent. This pattern, wherein discrimination against black and brown homebuyers and renters remains significant, but is less in 2000 than 11 years before, holds across all phases of the search process, except for one. That exception is racial steering, which increased substantially in the time period between the 1989 HDS and the 2000 HDS. The 2000 HDS included pilot investigations of Asian and Native American discrimination which were conducted in Phase 1 of 2000 HDS for three test cities: Los Angeles (Southeast Asians), Minneapolis (Koreans and Chinese) and Phoenix (Native Americans). These investigations found evidence that both groups' members are subject to housing-market discrimination.

In both the 1989 and 2000 HDS, the attention to survey methodology, comprehensive character of the investigation, and large sample sizes used make these audit studies' findings authoritative. Clearly, many real-estate agents are racially biased both in shunning minority clients and in treating the absence of black or brown residents as a locational advantage. The HDS findings do not necessarily suggest that there is a hard core of white real-estate agents who overtly dislike or hate minorities, or who are consciously promulgating racial inequities or segregation. More subtle biases could generate the HDS results; for example, a real-estate agent's perception of 'good' versus 'bad' neighborhoods may be racially coded, regardless of whether that agent intends to disadvantage minorities. In any event, real-estate agents might counter charges they are racially biased by noting that whites have very low tolerance for integration in neighborhoods (Massey and Denton, 1993, pp. 92–6).

Some indirect evidence from two different data sources on trends over time confirms the basic insights about trends in housing discrimination suggested by comparisons of the 1989 and 2000 HDS. Yinger (1997) applies a search model to data from the Panel Study of Income Dynamics, and finds that, because of discrimination, African Americans and Latinos pay a premium of approximately $4000 every time they look for a house to buy. Leigh (1992) reviews housing trend data from 1940 to the present. She finds that blacks' relative overexposure to unsafe or overcrowded housing conditions has fallen, and racial disparities in rent levels and in the probability of home ownership have been steadily reduced. Nonetheless, serious racial gaps in housing persist. The percentage of black homeowners has risen substantially; at the same time, the gap between the proportion of white and black homeowners has remained constant at approximately 20 per cent since 1940. As Leigh notes, blacks caught up with whites' 1940 homeownership rate only in 1987. Supplementing these results, Stone (1991) finds that blacks are more likely than whites to be in unaffordable or crowded housing.

One immediate consequence of discrimination in housing markets is deepening racial segregation. Austin Turner and Weink (1991) show that US residential segregation is higher than affordability considerations or individual preferences alone would predict; they suggest this 'extra' segregation is due to discrimination in housing allocation processes.

However, what sort of discrimination may be at work is difficult to establish. For one thing, the effects of behavioral and structural factors overlap. The disparate treatment of minorities documented in the HDS reduces minority demand for housing in white areas, and decreases the minority-owned housing supply offered to whites. Overt discrimination by real-estate agents and residents increases white demand in white areas, and reduces it in mixed areas. At the same time, structural discrimination leads to fewer minorities being able to afford homes. The correlation of minority status with lower incomes, and of minority neighborhoods with lower levels of public investment (what Keeney, 1988, calls the 'nexus of urban racial phenomena') encourages housing-market bias against minority areas.

Leigh (1992) documents the persistence and even growth of racial segregation and isolation: despite black gains in suburbanization, the elimination of racial covenants and the presence of fair-housing laws, racial segregation and isolation has remained stable or even deepened over time.[42] Massey and Denton (1993) argue that racial segregation, in turn, deepens structural discrimination independent of any other economic dynamics:

> With or without class segregation, residential segregation between blacks and whites builds concentrated poverty into the residential structure of the black community and guarantees that poor blacks experience a markedly less advantaged social environment than do poor whites. (1993, p. 125)

7 Gender discrimination in the credit and housing markets

Discussion in sections 2–6 has focused on racial inequality in credit and housing markets. The other protected categories under antidiscrimination laws, including gender and sexual preference, have not yet become a central focus of controversy among academics and policy makers. This is not to say that housing- and credit-market discrimination is not a problem for those in these other protected categories. However, no mechanism for the systematic collection of information exists; most of what is known is at the level of complaints registered at community-based and advocacy organizations. This section discusses gender discrimination in the credit market. No academic work exists on gender discrimination in the housing market, or on sexual preference discrimination in either the credit or housing markets.[43]

As with racial discrimination, the first empirical investigations of gender discrimination in the credit market were undertaken in the mid-1970s.[44] Edelstein (1977) and Schafer and Ladd (1980) examined gender discrimination in the mortgage credit market. These investigators found sizable gaps in credit approval for female applicants, but no clear pattern of gender-based discrimination. Little subsequent empirical work on women's access to credit has been done.

Gender-based research has been inhibited by the lack of an analogue to the HMDA; no systematic collection of credit-market data for gender effects has been required under law until 1990.[45] While the data collected under HMDA through 1989 permitted indirect examinations of race effects, they could not be used to undertake even indirect examinations of gender effects. HMDA data collected since 1990 do include gender data for both applicants and co-applicants.

The empirical work that has been done on the impact of gender on outcomes in residential credit markets has generated ambiguous empirical results.[46] Avery, Beeson and Sniderman (1996) conducted a study using 1990–91 HMDA data across several geographic markets. They found that, when women are the primary applicant for home purchase loans, the coefficient is insignificant irrespective of co-applicant status. Moreover, they found that male-only applications are 2–3 per cent more likely to be rejected than female-only applications. Hunter and Walker (1995) similarly found gender insignificant in determining loan approval in Boston. Dymski (1999) includes race and gender dummy variables in a study of 1992–6 home-purchase loan decisions in 23 states' metropolitan areas. He finds that, while most of the race variables consistently are statistically significant and negative, the coefficient for a female applicant is often insignificant; and when it is significant, it takes on both positive and negative signs.

Sanders and Scanlon (2000) used 1992 HMDA data for St. Louis to test whether women are more likely to be denied home mortgage loans. Their logistic regressions found that gender was significant; however, men were slightly more likely than women to be denied loans. Women who were primary applicants with co-applicants were more likely denied loans than women who applied independently. Mohanty (2001) generated more consistent results for applicant gender by 'racializing' the gender variable. Using 1992–8 HMDA data from a variety of California cities, she tested for the impact of being female and African American, female and Latino, and so on, on the likelihood of application approval (with race entered separately for male applications). In her logistic regression results, she finds for most cities that minority women are more likely to be denied loans than other applicants.

The modeling literature of gender effects in credit markets is even less developed than the slim empirical literature. Read (1998) reviews the asymmetric-information literature on borrower–lender relations, and finds it an inadequate vehicle for discussing gender effects because it does not take into account the gender-typed personality or the context – that is, history and other circumstances – that differentiate many female business-loan applicants from males. In effect, she identifies factors that might lead to personal or structural discrimination against women who apply for business loans. Dymski (2000) explores the theoretical basis for gender discrimination in credit markets by identifying key structural differences between gender and racial disadvantage. One key difference is that adult females share households with males far more frequently than minority adults; and female-headed households, while they do tend to cluster spatially, are far less segregated than are minority-headed households. When women head households and seek credit, the question of access to credit can be posed as it is for minority-headed households. When they share households with male adults, any link between gender disadvantage and the credit market operates at the level of social relations *within* the household. In such households, gender inequality may lead to unfair outcomes, but it is difficult to link these in any simple way to gender-based discrimination in the credit market.

8 Social and spatial embeddedness and housing and credit-market outcomes

The studies discussed thus far implicitly make two profound simplifications. First, they treat credit market and housing market dynamics as isolated topics, whereas in fact these markets' trajectories are tightly interconnected. Second, they assume that any individual's characteristics can be defined independently of the characteristics of any other individual and of the characteristics of any neighborhood; and similarly for neighborhoods' characteristics. This independence permits a simple portrayal of the housing choice and loan decision process: individuals seek to move to neighborhoods; and banks have more or less accurate information about individuals and/or neighborhoods; so individuals and neighborhoods may prosper more or less, depending on how lenders process creditworthiness signals.

These simplifications are encouraged implicitly by the literatures on these two markets. For example, once applicant-by-applicant tests of the probability of loan denial became possible, in the eyes of some analysts, credit-flow differentials by neighborhood are redundant or simply irrelevant. Several studies have tried to show that the correlation between area racial composition and lending flows disappears when more variables accounting for risk and economic fundamentals are included. Perle, Lynch and Horner (1993) use 1982 Detroit data to show that while lending flows appear sensitive to area racial composition in an equation (8.1) model with four variables, they no longer are in a more fully specified (11 variable) model. Schill and Wachter (1993) take this approach one step further; they use an equation (8.2) model with 1990 (application-level) HMDA data to study race effects in Philadelphia and Boston. They find that individual race is a consistently significant determinant of loan denial; but while neighborhood racial composition significantly determines loan denial rates in the absence of neighborhood 'quality' variables, it becomes insignificant when seven neighborhood 'quality' variables (including the percentage of residents on welfare) are added.[47]

Some researchers have questioned these simplifications and pointed the way toward richer models. These models promise to explore deeper consequences of the location of households and businesses in social and physical space, and of the intertwining of their housing and credit commitments.

The family home is the principal means of saving for most American households; and the mortgage loan on that home is most households' largest single liability. The ability of most households to accumulate wealth depends on whether the home they buy will gain in value, and on what terms and conditions they receive on their mortgage loans. Households' efforts to accumulate wealth on their journeys through space–time are not neutral in race and gender terms. Minorities and women tend to earn less income, all else equal. And these households' homes do not exist in cyberspace, but in real neighborhoods; to own a home is to make a commitment that is irreversible in the very short run, and which exposes the purchasing unit to substantial risk of loss. That is, to own a home is to take on financial fragility, and this financial fragility is inseparable from, and embedded in, the household's geographic locus (and similarly for business owners). The unique influence of place in the dynamic trajectory of agents locked into specific communities has been recognized by social scientists, especially sociologists and geographers.

A huge literature explores the links between discrimination and housing segregation; see, for example, Wilson (1987), Massey and Denton (1993) and Kain (1992). This literature investigates how racial segregation and isolation per se reproduce and deepen economic and social inequality.[48] The options any individual has depends not just on his initiative but on the resources with which he has to work, on the activities and resources of those around him, on the presence or absence of firms, and on these firms' resources and strategies.

These writings point toward a more general phenomenon: the significance of spillovers in social and economic outcomes. What is meant here is not just the informational spillovers that occur when lenders make rational-discrimination characterizations of places within their market areas, but spillovers of knowledge, resources, risk, and so on. 'Connections' with relatives or co-ethnics on the basis of shared blood or nationality are forms of spillover, ties that convert apparently autarchic masses of human beings into clusters of interlinked social honeycombs.

Models that emphasize the importance of inter-agent ties, of networks and of spatial spillover effects on economic outcomes are now emerging, some with the potential to demonstrate the impact of race effects on individual and community welfare. For example, the growing economic geography literature on financial exclusion (for example, Leyshon and Thrift, 1997) emphasizes the interactions among financial intermediary market strategies, credit flows and race in patterns of uneven urban development.

Some economists have used models with inter-agent spillovers to explain racial discrimination. Calomiris *et al.* (1994) and Hunter and Walker (1995) argue that, if lenders have 'cultural affinity' with white borrower applicants, but not with minority borrower applicants, their information costs for whites will be much less than with minorities, and they will make many more loans to whites than to equally creditworthy minorities.[49] Scalera and Zazzaro (2001) construct a model in which cultural affinity generates consistently inefficient outcomes. They show that persistent and inefficient group discrimination results under these conditions: if the development of any group's entrepreneurial skills is hampered by binding credit constraints, and/or if good firms can migrate elsewhere; if any group's quality changes over time; and if banks estimate group quality on the basis of past observed default rates. There can be permanent losses in an economy with these characteristics.

As with the literature on rational discrimination, it is not clear whether the 'cultural affinity' model is being proposed to criticize or to justify racial inequality in market outcomes. And in any event, pushed too far on its own, this model breaks down. For example, Black *et al.* (1997) show that, when the lending patterns of African American-owned and other banks are compared on a consistent basis, African American banks are no less likely to discriminate on the basis of race than are other lenders. These authors argue that this result constitutes yet another demonstration that racial discrimination is less important than some think. This interpretation is debatable on its own terms.[50] In turn, Ross and Yinger (1999b) interpret these banks' failure to lend more to African Americans as representing a failure of cultural affinity on the part of African American banks. This might be true, if all differences between racial credit-market applicants were eliminated. But this is hardly the case. African American-owned banks often have far weaker balance sheets than do other banks, making them relatively more cautious about loan-making, *ceteris paribus*.

Arrow (1998) himself recently suggested the importance of inter-agent networks and spillovers in understanding racial discrimination, but he also insisted on the importance of history and institutional context. To have the former without the latter is inappropriate, he writes. Unfortunately, this inappropriate path is precisely the one that has been followed thus far.[51] This same blind spot is evident in writing on informal financial networks among ethnic minorities. For example, Sowell (1981), among others, celebrates the success of various ethnic groups in using informal financial mechanisms to mobilize their savings, and wonders why African Americans cannot do the same – without taking into account the very special historical circumstances of every group's assimilation/segregation experience in America. Other empirical and theoretical work shows that ethnic network relationships are not the sole determinant of any group's success; instead, structural factors mediate the impact of networks on outcomes.[52] And, for some economists, cultural affinity should not be taken as exogenous, but instead regarded as an endogenous variable about which agents make decisions based on their positional power and their resources (Darity, Mason and Stewart, forthcoming); culture, in effect, is an illusory variable (Darity, 2002) which masks the effects of financial and social power.

One measure of this power is racial wealth differentials. Recent evidence (Chiteji and Stafford, 2000; Wolff, 2001; Barsky *et al.*, 2002) suggests that these differentials remain profound: some two-thirds are not attributable to income differentials. In other words, these differentials are both the legacy of history and a key binding constraint on agents' future economic activities. For example, racial wealth differentials have a great impact on the availability of credit and the likelihood of success of small business (Avery *et al.*, 1998). Elmelech and Lu (2004) show that these gaps are even more profound for minority women.

9   Conclusion

The literatures on discrimination in the credit and housing markets are compelling, incomplete, contradictory and controversial. They are compelling because the questions raised are central both in American experience and also in debates over the significance of racial inequality for social policy and social theory. Studies of credit markets in numerous countries now explore logics of discrimination.[53]

They are incomplete, first, because they cover only a portion of the legal ground protected under the Constitution and the Civil Rights Act. There are virtually no studies of credit-market and housing-market discrimination on the basis of sexual preference; there are few on gender. These literatures are also incomplete because the models developed thus far raise more questions than they answer. Consider the theoretical literature on redlining, for example: why is so little known about redlined neighborhoods, and why is the cost of collecting information there so high? What neighborhood spillovers does lending volume generate? Where do the poorer economic fundamentals of redlined neighborhoods come from? To the extent that theories leave these questions unanswered, they fail to confront fully the historical legacy of racial inequality. These theories offer circular explanations instead: because redlining existed before, less is known about redlined areas and returns there are more variable, so redlining exists today.

These studies are also – necessarily – contradictory. For one thing, the complementary but not identical legal principles of fairness for individuals (Civil Rights legislation) and fair access for communities (the Community Reinvestment Act) do not jointly identify a clear set of behaviors that infringe on the rights of a well-identified set of protected classes. Some regard an empirical study as successful when it depicts a clear pattern of racial difference in housing and credit flows; others define a study as successful only when it isolates predatory racial behavior which can only be attributed to racial animus. In one reading, then, a huge literature successfully documents many facets of racial inequality in housing and credit markets; in another reading, a huge literature has been unable to show conclusively that a problem exists to be addressed through extra-market means.

Finally, empirical tests for credit and housing discrimination are controversial. This controversy stems in part from honest disagreements among practitioners over the design and interpretation of statistical tests for discrimination. However, the skepticism of some commentators about econometric design is linked to their deeper skepticism about federal legislation in this area. These skeptics have both challenged the efficacy of civil rights laws and confused the mandates of the ECOA and the CRA. For example, Rachlis and Yezer write: 'the inability to use HMDA or other mortgage flow data in single-equation reduced-form models to test for discrimination in mortgage models are well known. Unfortunately, time and effort are still devoted to such seriously flawed analysis' (1993, p. 324). Reading further shows that, for these authors, these 'flaws' consist not just in econometric problems, but in the legal context of discrimination law. They go on to write that 'current definitions of discrimination in law and regulation are far too simplistic and vague to deal with the complex econometric issues that would be encountered should serious litigation . . . be focused on the problem of . . . testing for differential treatment' (ibid., p. 332).

Ronald Weink, formerly President Reagan's special assistant for fair lending at the Comptroller of the Currency, agrees; he argues that regulators should use audit studies of bank procedures and bankers to detect discrimination in credit markets, because assessments based on HMDA data will have them 'looking [for discrimination] in the wrong places' (1992, p. 227). In this same paper, Weink admits he 'could never quite define "fair lending" or "equal credit opportunity"' while in office. Lacker (1995), another critic of econometric tests of credit markets, is similarly confused about the law. He cites a federal prohibition of 'discrimination against neighborhoods', thus confusing the legal injunction against discrimination in credit markets (embodied in the 1974 ECOA) with the Congressional mandate that depositories reinvest in neighborhoods.

This pairing of a critique of civil rights law and econometric methodology is relatively rare. Most economists who worry about the econometric design of tests for discrimination accept the need to police racial perpetrators. Nonetheless, this leads, not to a profession-wide agreement on the need to conduct econometric studies that might identify discriminatory trouble spots, but instead to the sort of ambivalence that has been evident throughout our discussion. Most analysts would accept the view that overt discrimination and disparate treatment are illegal in that they reflect abuses by racial perpetrators. Some who hold this view then insist that econometric techniques are sufficient only if they serve to identify perpetrators in deed and in intention; others suggest a lower threshhold for econometric evidence should be used.

For example, Galster (1992) praises the (1992) Boston study as thorough, and argues that it uncovers disparate-treatment discrimination. But Galster tempers his praise, warning that equation (8.2) studies conducted without access to bank loan files cannot detect discrimination. Omitted variable bias is a 'fatal shortcoming', since 'crucial control variables such as credit and employment histories, indebtedness, and assets and characteristics of the property' (1992, p. 650) are missing. Glennon and Stengel (1994) argue that, since the controversial Boston study 'represents only one study, in one city, at one point in time', it should be replicated elsewhere. But this qualified call for more Boston-type studies is itself problematic. As these authors observe, 'the intense publicity and controversy generated by the release of the Boston Fed study' make it 'virtually certain that such a follow-up effort will never take place' (ibid., p. 36). Lenders are unlikely to cooperate as they did in Boston. Does this make innocent bystanders of all the economists who claim to be interested in discrimination in these markets, but who lack the ability to do the intensely detailed analysis of credit-market decisions that was possible on a one-time basis in one city?

What about HMDA-based studies that lack the comprehensive character of the Boston study? Stengel and Glennon (1995) cautiously affirm equation (8.2) studies. These authors used four anonymous banks' loan files to construct 'Boston-style' equations; they then compared this indirect evidence of disparate treatment discrimination with confidential case-file audits conducted by the Comptroller of the Currency. They find that, while differences in bank structure make it impossible to draw precise conclusions from regressions, regression evidence is a useful diagnostic tool for deciding when to conduct deeper inquiries into discriminatory practices.[54]

So there is no critique-proof methodology for assessing the presence or absence of discrimination. More refined or detailed empirical tests with improved HMDA data are unlikely to put all criticism to rest. As we have seen, audit studies too, as tools for identifying racial perpetrators, have their advocates and their critics. What about the legal injunction against disparate impact? This injunction, which is embodied in Civil Rights law, goes beyond the boundaries of what many economists consider acceptable – that is, to inherited, socially determined economic imbalances in wealth and resources. The empirical research cited in the previous section proves that these inheritances, these social divides, are profound and extensive. They are not remediable by shifts on the margin in market outcomes, though these might help.

And this leaves many economists, insofar as they want to consider issues of racial and gender inequality and social justice, with a dilemma. The focus of professional interest has increasingly centered on whether racial perpetrators can be caught in the act. But while racial perpetrators certainly worsen the extent of racial and gender difference in credit- and housing-market outcomes at the margin, existing structural divides in resources and wealth do most of the damage. That is, the professional focus is on one portion of a multidimensional, through-time process – that portion which is hardest to identify precisely – while the remainder of the process remains outside the view-range of the analytical binoculars.

So the problem of discrimination is seen through a glass darkly. Why should not economic debate begin, not by presupposing a state of nature in which ex ante structural racial/gender inequality do not exist, but instead by acknowledging analytically the historical legacy of racial and gender inequality. The latter is, after all, inherited from America's history. Is economics afraid of history? If not, why not develop a theory more appropriate for the legal context and historical basis of the nation's laws against discrimination? So much work has been done on the economics of discrimination in credit and housing markets. But so much work, and so many challenges, remain.

Notes

1. Literature reviews on credit and housing market discrimination include Austin Turner, Fix and Struyk (1991), Cloud and Galster (1993), Dymski (1997), Ladd (1998), and Austin Turner and Skidmore (1999a). Schmitt's original synthesis (2000) emphasizes credit scoring.
2. The terms 'black' and 'brown', respectively, are sometimes used to refer to these two racial/ethnic categories. The term 'Latino' only imperfectly captures the set of all individuals whose cultural and residential roots are in former colonies of Spain and Portugal; the term 'Hispanic', which is not used here, is perhaps more problematic. Since the term 'Hispanic' is often used in empirical investigations, this implies that the problematic classification of this population is built into many of the studies discussed here. There is virtually no attention herein to the credit-market and housing discrimination problems faced by Asian Americans, Pacific Islanders and Native Americans; this reflects the orientation of the studies reviewed here. Dymski (1999) does discuss these populations' experience with home-mortgage discrimination. His study, which encompasses 18 states and 120 metropolitan areas, incorporates areas where these populations' share of the borrower base permits meaningful empirical results.
3. Freeman (1978) first used the term 'perpetrators' in this context. In the 'perpetrator' perspective, all racial inequalities stem from biased perpetrators; so if perpetrators are deterred, discrimination will disappear.
4. An apology is also in order. There is a large, robust and adventurous legal literature on the topics of housing and credit-market discrimination. It is largely ignored here; the economics-based literature absorbs our attention. Those interested in legal perspectives on credit-market discrimination might begin with Schwemm (1995) and Swire (1995); those interested in housing discrimination, with Calmore (1998) and Wiggins (2002).
5. See Squires (1992); this author also provides an overview of the US community reinvestment movement. Stuart (2003) provides a remarkably thorough institutional analysis of the historical development of the home-mortgage industry in the US, with special attention to the problem of racial discrimination.
6. Dubovsky (1969) provides a blow-by-blow legislative history of the passage of the Fair Housing Act of 1968.
7. Early redlining studies are discussed Bradford *et al.* (1977, Part II). Redlining sometimes took the form of higher transaction costs or worse contractual terms and conditions.
8. The language of the act states that lenders 'have a continuing and affirmative obligation to help meet the credit needs of the local communities in which they are chartered' (para. 802(*a*)(3), 12 USC 1901; Title VII of Public Law 95-128, 91 Stat. 1147, Oct. 12, 1977). Fishbein (1992) discusses CRA's purposes and documents the evolution of HMDA reporting requirements.

9. For information on HMDA regulations, see http://www.ffiec.gov/hmda/about.htm. The loan rate information to be collected is rate-spread data: specifically, the difference between the loan rate and the rate on Federal government securities of comparable maturity.

10. Arrow's (1971) general equilibrium model of discrimination is much clearer than Becker's original model in exposing Becker's fundamental logic. Mason (1992) demonstrates that Becker's conclusions depend on his model's assumptions.

11. An audit study of discrimination, also referred to as a paired-testing study, probes for the presence or absence of behavioral bias by comparing the real-time responses of agents involved in the home-buying and/or loan-making process to white and to minority home and/or loan seekers. The idea is to train pairs of testers who play the role of home and/or loan seekers; in their roles as testers, these 'applicants' have identical economic character-istics (income, wealth, housing demand, debt, and so on); they differ only in their racial/ethnic (or gender, or age, or any other binary) characteristic. Then the treatment of 'applicants' with different profiles (racial/ethnic or other, as noted) is compared. This permits a direct behavioral 'audit' of the impact of the characteristic of interest on market outcomes. Audit studies of credit- and housing-market behavior, respectively, are reviewed in sections 4 and 6 below.

12. We also mention in this context Schelling's game-theoretic model of racial tipping (1971), which shows how static equilibria of the sort Becker theorizes can be dynamically unsta-ble.

13. Note that the authors set out this finding to explain this practice (not to condemn it). That is, given that missing information makes first-best equilibria (the most qualified applicants are readily identified and provided with loans) impossible, and given that some methods of achieving second-best equilibria are more costly than others, the use of neighborhood race may emerge as the most cost-efficient method of identifying a borrower pool with less risk than a randomly chosen pool.

14. This last idea is an application of the 'statistical' theory of discrimination, which Arrow (1971) and others developed to explain racial screening in the labor market.

15. The term 'coordination failure' refers to any occasion on which market processes fail to achieve outcomes that yield the highest achievable level of social welfare.

16. While the literature reviewed here has implications for all forms of discrimination in credit and housing markets, it has focused almost exclusively on race.

17. Arrow (1998) makes the same point in a more general discussion of racial discrimination.

18. Two recent papers, Hawley and Fujii (1990) and Crook (1999), use responses from the 1983 and 1995 Surveys of Consumer Finance to demonstrate in both cases that minority households are more likely than whites to refrain from applying for credit because they think they will be turned down, *ceteris paribus*. The implications of this finding for econo-metric studies of discrimination are noted below.

19. Implicitly, most advocacy regarding home mortgage credit, and most studies, have centered attention on the access of inner-city and minority neighborhoods and households to 'mainstream' markets (that is, markets serving customers with standard levels of income and earnings risk). This is not to ignore non-standard markets and practices, which histor-ically have been located in minority areas far more frequently than in non-minority neigh-borhoods. For example, Caplovitz (1967) documents the existence of many exculpatory financial practices in the 1960s; Barr (2004) and Caskey (1994) document the omnipres-ence of such practices, dubbed 'fringe banking', in the current period. Insofar as race, income and wealth levels are correlated, minorities are more likely to be victimized by such arrangements – or, to view things differently, to be recurrent 'cash and carry' in fringe banking arrangements.

20. Mortgage flows must be detrended to remove scale effects. This is normally done by divid-ing raw loan flows by the single-family housing stock in each census tract. The logarithms of loan flows can be used if the list of regressors includes single-family structures.

21. LaCour-Little and Green (1998) published a variant of this Census tract-based approach. Using the 1990 Boston data set (discussed in the next subsection of this chapter), they found that high-minority areas were likely to have systematically lower appraisals, a factor that would lead to lower mortgage flows, *ceteris paribus*. Offsetting this indirect evidence

of redlining by race was the fact that neighborhood quality and racial composition were correlated across census tracts, suggesting that the apparent impact of 'racial composition' on assessed-value levels might be due to 'neighborhood quality' factors.

22. Pre-selection bias arises because the suspicion that a certain geographic area is subject to redlining is not independent of the statistical test for whether it is. For example, a researcher could accuse a bank of unfairly treating neighborhood X, on the basis of data concerning loan-flow gaps in X. A variety of bank policies could generate gaps of the sort observed; finding X gaps is not sufficient to demonstrate the bank uses X as an operational variable in its decision-making process.

23. Both studies also supplemented HMDA data with transactions data to examine the impact of the non-bank mortgage lenders, especially mortgage companies, not covered under HMDA. In both cases, non-bank lenders did not close the lending disparity gaps left by HMDA reporting lenders.

24. Galster (1992) provides a comprehensive survey of studies that criticize the redlining model. Market failure occurs when markets fail to give the right resources to the right agents at the right prices as a result of one or more impediments. For example, market-failure redlining could occur if lenders fail to make loans in an area because they believe other lenders may avoid it too.

25. Contemporary redlining analyses are being used and interpreted in just this way. For example, informative annual assessments of mortgage lending in Boston are conducted for the Massachusetts Community and Banking Council. The MCBC has an equal number of community and bank members; and these annual assessments provide benchmarks that inform discussions about trends in community reinvestment. See Campen (1998).

26. LaCour-Little (1999) argues that misestimated coefficients can also arise when heterogeneous lender types and borrower types are not segregated in advance by modelers. He advocates not only pre-sorting data into such homogeneous categories, but also constructing a panel data set to evaluate dynamic borrower behavior through time.

27. Quercia and Stegman (1992) and Goering (1996) review this literature. Berkovec *et al.* (1994), an especially influential study which uses a random sample of FHA loans originated in 1987 and 1988, finds higher minority default rates. Han (2004) uses the Berkovec *et al.* data set and comes to the same empirical conclusion regarding minority default rates.

28. Offsetting any incidence of higher default rates is the fact that minority borrowers generate significantly lower levels of prepayment risk than do white borrowers. Kelly (1995) finds, however, significant racial and ethnic differences in mortgage prepayment rates on the basis of VA loans made in the 1971–89 period. After controlling for differences in mobility and in other borrower characteristics, African American homeowners still have a significantly lower rate of prepayments.

29. The mention of Heckman's work on specification problems brings up another point. It is by no means clear what the multiple equations that should be modeled are, in the case of racial differentials in the mortgage credit market. It may be that lenders are choosing different terms and conditions based on anticipated default rates that differ systematically by race. But the two articles summarized in note 18 suggest that minorities are much less likely to apply for credit than are whites, because of a fear of being turned down. This suggests another sort of specification problem: the failure to model separately the borrower's decision to apply as well as the lender's decision to accept. Controlling for a lender's view of a mortgage applicant's potential default further complicates the estimation process.

30. Similarly, Glennon and Stengel (1994) experiment with different regression specifications, and find that this study's empirical conclusions are robust.

31. Berkovec *et al.* also test for differences in default rates by neighborhood racial composition, and find no evidence that mortgages in minority neighborhoods have higher default rates. These authors, like Galster, regard the use of higher minority default rates, when unsupported by observable borrower economic characteristics, as illegal. Also see Ross and Yinger (1999c). Ferguson and Peters (1995) use a simple model of bank lending to show that *if* minority applicants are less creditworthy on average than white applicants, then it cannot simultaneously be true that minorities both have higher default rates and higher loan

denial rates – that is, the conceptual arguments behind the two empirical attacks on the Boston study are inconsistent (given the premise of lower minority creditworthiness).

32. The advent of application-level HMDA data has, however, thrown into question the status of studies of redlining. Tootell (1996) found, for example, that 'redlining' effects largely dissipated once racial-discrimination effects against borrowers were accounted for in the Boston data set. In other words, any apparent discrimination against areas with many minority borrowers could be attributed in this case to discrimination against minority borrowers; there was no independent discrimination against areas per se. Other studies of other cities, however, have found statistically significant redlining effects even after borrower race is accounted for (see Dymski, 1999).

33. In an 'audit' study, white and minority subjects pose as housing- and/or credit-market applicants, and then carefully record their experiences. The testers' contacts must be randomized and their experiences standardized to allow data collection. Cloud and Galster (1993) review audit studies.

34. These studies' methodologies and substantive conclusions are discussed by Dietrich (2001).

35. For further discussion of shifting bank strategies and patterns in bank consolidation, see Dymski (1999).

36. Staten and Yezer (2004) point out, in a special issue of the *Journal of Real Estate Finance and Economics* on subprime lending, that there is no commonly accepted definition of predatory lending. Engel and McCoy (2002) suggest that three categories of mortgage loan be differentiated: prime, legitimate subprime and predatory. They define predatory mortgage loans as those involving any of five characteristics: '(1) loans structured to result in seriously disproportionate net harm to borrowers, (2) harmful rent seeking, (3) loans involving fraud or deceptive practices, (4) other forms of lack of transparency in loans that are not actionable as fraud, and (5) loans that require borrowers to waive meaningful legal redress' (p. 1260).

37. A November 2001 study of California cities by the California Reinvestment Committee (CRC), using a borrower survey instrument, found that a third of subprime borrowers were solicited by loan marketers, and that minorities and the elderly are the targets in these marketing efforts. These loans often have onerous terms and conditions; in the CRC study, three in five respondents have punitive repayment penalty provisions, while 70 per cent saw their terms worsen at closing. Other common abuses include high upfront fees and costly lump-sum credit insurance.

38. Also see United States HUD (2000) and the extensive statistics in ACORN (2000). The Department of Housing and Urban Development, together with the Treasury Department, published a study that both discusses the core issues raised by subprime lending and reports on the results of several public forums and task forces (Joint Task Force, 2000). A report by Pennington-Cross, Yezer and Nichols (2000) challenges the idea that subprime lending has indeed grown in recent years, and goes on to challenge the idea that these loans are exploitative. The points made in this report are rebutted by Immergluck (2000).

39. For example, First Union Bancorp bought the Money Store in June 1998. First Union subsequently closed this unit in mid-2000 in the wake of massive losses (Mollenkamp, 2000).

40. The 2000 HDS is Phase 1 of a broader investigation that will eventually encompass 60 metropolitan areas and more racial/ethnic categories.

41. Ondrich, Stricker and Yinger (1998) and Ondrich, Ross and Yinger (2000) develop econometric models of discrimination using audit data from the 1989 HDS; using fixed-effects logit techniques, these authors confirm the finding of statistically significant discrimination.

42. The shift of some minorities to suburbs has often led to segregated suburbs, not to integrated ones; indeed, by numerous measures, minorities' geographical isolation has increased (Abramson *et al.*, 1995).

43. Literature on the legal aspects of gender discrimination in housing does exist (for example, Smith, 2000), and social activists have begun to organize around these forms of discrimination in the credit and housing markets.

44. Congressional hearings signalled policymakers' interest in these questions; a 1974 hearing (US House of Representatives, 1974) focused on gender discrimination in credit markets.

45. Similarly, there is no gender analogue to the CRA. Note that, whereas civil rights law

prohibits discrimination on the basis of both gender and race in credit markets, the CRA goes further in that it requires lenders to make proactive efforts to identify and meet credit-market needs throughout their market areas. There is no explicitly racial content to the CRA's mandate but, given the close correlation between inner-city areas and minority residential areas, this mandate embodies an implicit commitment to identify and meet minority borrowers' needs.

46. A literature on gender aspects of small-business credit market has begun to emerge. This work, which consists of small-scale empirical studies (Buttner and Rosen, 1992; Read, 1998), finds that credit availability constitutes an important barrier for female business owners, and that a large proportion of female entrepreneurs have felt that gender discrimination has colored their relations with banks.

47. Since neighborhood characteristics data are collected every ten years, while applicant data vary yearly, econometric comparisons of applicant vs. neighborhood effects are biased toward finding neighborhood characteristics irrelevant.

48. Kasarda (1993) documents that inner-city neighborhoods' degree of poverty and segregation has deepened. Galster and Mincy (1993) show that racial composition significantly affected the 'changing fortunes' of urban neighborhoods.

49. Strictly speaking, these authors model cultural affinity between white lenders and white borrowers, not racial antipathy between whites and minorities. However, this comes to the same thing as Becker's racial preferences, especially because cultural affinity ties arise exogenously.

50. For example, African American-owned banks often have far weaker balance sheets than do other banks, making them relatively more cautious about loan-making, leading to the apparent empirical evidence that they discriminate against African American borrowers as much as do white-owned banks.

51. Perlmann (1998) writes about the lack of historical and conceptual specificity in discussions of phenomena emphasizing the 'cultural affinity' of ethnic minorities in the US.

52. Aaronson *et al.* (2004) examine the data from the National Survey of Small Business Finance that was discussed above, and find that African American-owned firms have fewer close ethnic ties and less geographic proximity, and hence less trade credit, than do other minority firms. Dymski and Mohanty (1999) show that Asian American and African American banks in Los Angeles County have virtually identical records in responding to the needs of their co-ethnic communities; the key difference is in these banks' relative numbers. In effect, the existence of an ethnic network is not the only factor governing a group's success; objective institutional factors also matter. At the level of theory, Leitner (2002) shows that financial networks can be optimal for groups of interlinked agents, as it helps them counter the potential for contagion; however, when these agents' resources are small, the entire network can be liable to collapse.

53. Simmons and Supri (1999), for example, analyze discrimination in Indian credit markets, and Fukuyama *et al.* (1999) discuss discrimination in Japan against Korean-owned firms.

54. But this is precisely what some participants in this debate deny. Yezer, for example, reacts to the new CRA-based studies of small-business finance as follows: 'all of the problems inherent in the use of HMDA data to test for mortgage lending discrimination also apply to business lending. . . . implied statistical analysis of the data on business lending under the new CRA data requirements cannot demonstrate the presence or absence of discrimination. Proposals to supplement the business lending data, including demographic characteristics of the owner(s) and adding information on applications, will produce a data set whose only use is to produce false positive indications of lending discrimination' (1999, p. 88). The idea that the 'only use' of these data is to draw inappropriate conclusions is far from a consensus among researchers.

References

Aaronson, Daniel, Raphael Bostic, Paul Huck and Robert Townsend (2004), 'Supplier relationships and small business use of trade credit', *Journal of Urban Economics*, **55**(1), January, 46–67.

Abramson, Alan J., Mitchell S. Tobin and Matthew R. VanderGoot (1995), 'The changing geography of metropolitan opportunity: the segregation of the poor in US metropolitan areas', *Housing Policy Debate*, **6**(1), 45–72.

Ahlbrandt, Roger S. (1977), 'Exploratory research on the redlining phenomenon', *Journal of the American Real Estate and Urban Economics Association*, Winter.

Arrow, Kenneth (1971), 'The theory of discrimination', in Orley Ashenfelter and Albert Rees (eds), *Discrimination in Labor Markets*, Princeton: Princeton University Press, pp. 3–33.

Arrow, Kenneth J. (1998), 'What has economics to say about racial discrimination?', *Journal of Economic Perspectives*, **12**(2) (Spring), 91–100.

Association of Community Organizations for Action Now (ACORN) (2000), *Separate and Unequal: Predatory Lending in America*, Sacramento, CA: California, 31 October.

Austin Turner, Margery and Felicity Skidmore (eds) (1999a), *Mortgage Lending Discrimination: A Review of Existing Evidence*. Washington, DC: Urban Institute, June.

Austin Turner, Margery and Felicity Skidmore (1999b), 'Introduction, summary and recommendations' in Austin Turner and Skidmore (1999a), 1–22.

Austin Turner, Margery and Ronald Weink (1991), 'The persistence of segregation: contributing causes', mimeo, Urban Institute, Washington, DC.

Austin Turner, Margery, Michael Fix and Raymond J. Struyk (1991), *Opportunities denied, opportunities diminished*, Urban Institute report 91–9, Washington, DC: Urban Institute Press.

Austin Turner, Margery, Raymond J. Struyk and John Yinger (1991), *Housing discrimination study: synthesis*, Washington, DC: US Department of Housing and Urban Development.

Austin Turner, Margery, Stephen L. Ross, George C. Galster and John Yinger (2002), *Discrimination in Metropolitan Housing Markets: National Results from Phase I HDS 2000 – Final Report*, Washington, DC: Urban Institute, November.

Austin Turner, Margery, Fred Freiberg, Erin Godfrey, Carla Herbig, Diane K. Levy and Robin R. Smith (2002), *All Other Things Being Equal: A Paired Testing Study of Mortgage Lending Institutions – Final Report*, Washington, DC: Urban Institute, April.

Avery, Robert B., Patricia E. Beeson and Mark S. Sniderman (1996), 'Accounting for racial differences in housing credit markets', in John Goering and Ron Weink (eds), *Mortgage Lending, Racial Discrimination, and Federal Policy*, Urban Institute Press.

Avery, Robert B., Raphael W. Bostic and Katherine A. Samolyk (1998), 'The role of personal wealth in small business finance', *Journal of Banking and Finance*, **22**, 1019–61.

Barr, Michael S. (2004), 'Banking the poor', *Yale Journal on Regulation*, **21**, 121–237.

Barsky, Robert, John Bound, Kerwin Charles and Joseph Lupton (2002), 'Accounting for the black–white wealth gap: a nonparametric approach', *Journal of the American Statistical Association*, **97**(459) (September), 663–73.

Bates, Timothy M. (1994), 'An analysis of Korean-immigrant-owned small-business start-ups with comparisons to African American and nonminority-owned firms', *Urban Affairs Quarterly*, **30**(2) (December), 227–48.

Bates, Timothy M. (1997), *Race, Self-Employment, and Upward Mobility: An Illusive American Dream*. Baltimore: Johns Hopkins University Press.

Becker, Gary S. (1957), *The Economics of Discrimination*, Chicago: University of Chicago Press.

Becker, Gary S. (1993), 'The evidence against banks doesn't prove bias', *Business Week*, 19 April, 18.

Bell, Derrick (1980), *Race, Racism, and American Law*, Boston: Little, Brown and Company.

Benston, George (1981), 'Mortgage redlining research: a review and critical analysis', *Journal of Bank Research*, **12**, 8–23.

Benston, George (1995), 'The history and value of HMDA data for studies of invidious discrimination', *Fair Lending Analysis: A Compendium of Essays on the Use of Statistics*, Washington, DC: American Bankers' Association.

Berkovec, James, Glenn Canner, Stuart Gabriel and Timothy Hannan (1994), 'Race, redlining, and residential mortgage loan performance', *Journal of Real Estate Finance and Economics*, **9**(3) (November), 263–94.

Black, Harold A., M.C. Collins and K.B. Cyree (1997), 'Do black-owned banks discriminate against black borrowers?', *Journal of Financial Services Research*, **11**(1–2) (February), 189–204.

Blanchflower, David G., Phillip B. Levine and David J. Zimmerman (2003), 'Discrimination in the small business credit market', *The Review of Economics and Statistics*, **85**(4) (November) 930–43.

Bostic, Raphael W. (1996), 'The role of race in mortgage lending: revisiting the Boston Fed study', Division of Research and Statistics working paper, Federal Reserve, Washington, DC, December.

Bradbury, Katherine L., Karl E. Case and Constance R. Dunham (1989), 'Geographic patterns of mortgage lending in Boston, 1982–87', *New England Economic Review*, (October), 3–30.

Bradford, Calvin (2002), *Risk or Race? Racial Disparities and the Subprime Refinance Market*, a report of the Center for Community Change, Washington, DC: Center for Community Change, May.

Bradford, Calvin, and the Urban–Suburban Investment Study Group (1977), 'Redlining and disinvestment as a discriminatory practice in residential mortgage loans', Center for Urban Studies, University of Illinois; Department of Housing and Urban Development, Office of the Assistant Secretary for Fair Housing and Equal Opportunity, Washington,DC.

Brimelow, Peter and Leslie Spenser (1993), 'The hidden clue', *Forbes*, 4 January.

Browne, Lynn E. and Geoffrey M.B. Tootell (1995), 'Mortgage lending in Boston – a response to the critics', *New England Economic Review*, September/October, pp. 53–78.

Businessweek (2002), 'The besieged banker', 21 April.

Buttner, E. H. and B. Rosen (1992), 'Rejection in the loan application process: male and female entrepreneurs' perceptions and subsequent intentions', *Journal of Small Business Management*, **30**(1), 58–65.

Calem, Paul S. and Stanley D. Longhofer (2002), 'Anatomy of a fair-lending exam: the uses and limitations of statistics', *Journal of Real Estate Finance and Economics*, **24**(3) (May), 207–37.

Calem, Paul S., Kevin Gillen and Susan Wachter (2001), 'The neighborhood distribution of subprime mortgage lending', *Journal of Real Estate Finance and Economics*, **29**(4), 393–410.

Calem, Paul S., Jonathan E. Hershaff and Susan Wachter (2004), 'Neighborhood patterns of subprime lending: evidence from disparate cities', *Housing Policy Debate*, **15**(3), 603–22.

Calmore, John O. (1998), 'Race/ism lost and found: the Fair Housing Act at thirty', *University of Miami Law Review*, **52**, July, 1067–1130.

Calomiris, Charles W., Charles M. Kahn and Stanley D. Longhofer (1994), 'Housing-finance intervention and private incentives: helping minorities and the poor', *Journal of Money, Credit, and Banking* **26**(3, Pt 2) (August), 634–74.

Campen, James (1998), *Changing Patterns V: Mortgage Lending to Traditionally Underserved Borrowers and Neighborhoods in Greater Boston, 1990–97*, Boston: Massachusetts Community and Banking Council.

Canner, Glenn (1981), 'Redlining and mortgage lending patterns', *Research in Urban Economics*, **1**, 67–101.

Canner, Glenn and D. Smith (1991), 'Home Mortgage Disclosure Act: expanded data on residential lending', *Federal Reserve Bulletin*, 77, 863–4.

Canner, Glenn B. (1999), 'Evaluation of CRA data on small business lending', *Business Access to Capital and Credit*, Chicago: Federal Reserve Bank of Chicago, 53–84.

Canner, Glenn B., Wayne Passmore and Elizabeth Laderman (1999), 'The role of specialized lenders in extending mortgages to lower-income and minority homebuyers', *Federal Reserve Bulletin*, November, 709–23.

Caplovitz, David (1967), *The Poor Pay More*, New York: The Free Press.

Carr, James H. and Isaac F. Megbolugbe (1993), 'The Federal Reserve Bank of Boston study on mortgage lending revisited', *Journal of Housing Research*, **4**(2), 277–313.

Caskey, John (1994), *Fringe Banking: Check-Cashing Outlets, Pawnshops, and the Poor*, New York, Sage.

Cavalluzzo, Ken S. and L.C. Cavalluzzo (1998), 'Market structure and discrimination: the case of small business', *Journal of Money, Credit, and Banking*, **30**(4), 771–92.

Cavalluzzo, Ken S., Linda C. Cavalluzzo and John D. Wolken (2002), 'Competition, small business financing, and discrimination: evidence from a new survey', *Journal of Business*, **75**(4), 641–80.

Chiteji, Ngina and Frank P. Stafford (2000), 'Asset ownership across generations', working paper no. 314, Jerome Levy Economics Institute of Bard College, 20 September, Annandale-on-Hudson, NY.

Cloud, Cathy and George Galster (1993), 'What do we know about racial discrimination in mortgage markets?', *Review of Black Political Economy*, **22**(1) (Summer), 101–120.

Courant, P. (1978), 'Racial prejudice in a model of the urban housing market', *Journal of Urban Economics*, **5**, 329–45.

Courchane, Marsha J. and Amos Golan (1999), 'Estimation and evaluation of loan discrimination – an informational approach', working paper, Department of Economics, American University, 25 January.

Courchane, Marsha J., Brian J. Surette and Peter M. Zorn (2004), 'Subprime borrowers: mortgage transitions and outcomes', *Journal of Real Estate Finance and Economics*, **29**(4), 365–92.

Cronin, Francis J. (1982), 'Racial differences in the search for housing', in William A.V. Clark (ed.), *Modeling Housing Market Search*, New York: St. Martin's Press, pp. 81–105.

Crook, Jonathan (1999), 'Who is discouraged from applying for credit?' *Economics Letters*, **65**, 165–72.

Darity, William (2002), 'Intergroup disparity: why culture is irrelevant', mimeo, Department of Economics, University of North Carolina, Chapel Hill, April.

Darity, William A., Patrick L. Mason and James B. Stewart (forthcoming), 'The economics of identity: the origin and persistence of racial norms', *Journal of Economic Behavior and Organizations*.

Dedman, B. (1988), 'The color of money', *Atlanta Constitution*, 1–4 May .

Dietrich, Jason (2001), 'The effects of choice-based sampling and small-sample bias on past fair lending exams', Economic and Policy Analysis working paper 2001–2, Office of the Comptroller of the Currency, Washington, DC, June.

Dubovsky, Jean Eberhart (1969), 'Fair housing: a legislative history and a perspective', *Washburn Law Journal*, **8**, 149–58.

Dymski, Gary A. (2001), 'Is discrimination disappearing? Racial differentials in access to credit, 1992–1998', *International Journal of Social Economics*.

Dymski, Gary A. (2000), 'Racial and gender disadvantage in the credit market: social injustice and outcome equality', in Robert Pollin (ed.), *Capitalism, Socialism and Radical Political Economy: Essays In Honor Of Howard J. Sherman*, Cheltenham, UK and Northampton, MA, USA: Edward Elgar, pp. 227–46.

Dymski, Gary A. (1999), *The Bank Merger Wave: The Economic Causes and Social Consequences of Financial Consolidation*, Armonk, NY: M.E. Sharpe.

Dymski, Gary A. (1995), 'The theory of credit-market redlining and discrimination: an exploration', *Review of Black Political Economy*, **23**(3) (Winter), 37–74.

Dymski, Gary A. (1997), 'Why does race matter in housing and credit markets?' in Patrick L. Mason and Rhonda Williams (eds), *Race, Markets, and Social Outcomes*, Boston: Kluwer Academic Press.

Dymski, Gary A. and Lisa Mohanty (1999), 'Credit and banking structure: Asian and African American experience in Los Angeles', *American Economic Review Papers and Proceedings*, May.

Dymski, Gary A. and John M. Veitch (1996), 'Financial transformation and the metropolis: booms, busts, and banking in Los Angeles', *Environment and Planning A*.

Dymski, Gary A. and John M. Veitch (1994), 'Taking it to the bank: credit, race, and income in Los Angeles', Robert D. Bullard, Charles Lee and J. Eugene Grigsby (eds), *Residential Segregation: The American Legacy*, Los Angeles: Center for Afro-American Studies, 1994, pp. 150–79.

Edelstein, Dana Lenore Gilbert (1977), 'Women and credit discrimination', PhD dissertation, University of California, Davis.

Eggert, Kurt (2004), 'Limiting abuse and opportunism by mortgage services', *Housing Policy Debate*, **15**(3), 753–84.

Elmelech, Yuval and Hsien-Hen Lu (2004), 'Race, ethnicity, and the gender-poverty gap', *Social Science Research*, **33**(1), March 2004, 158–82.

Engel, Kathleen C. and Patricia A. McCoy (2002), 'A tale of three markets: the law and economics of predatory lending', *Texas Law Review*, **80**(6), 1255–1382.

Ferguson, Michael F. and Stephen R. Peters (1995), 'What constitutes evidence of discrimination in lending?', *Journal of Finance*, **50**(2) (June), 739–48.

Figlio, David N. and Joseph W. Genshlea (1999), 'Bank consolidations and minority neighborhoods', *Journal of Urban Economics*, **45**, 474–89.

Fishbein, Allen J. (1992), 'The ongoing experiment with "regulation from below": expanded reporting requirements for HMDA and CRA', *Housing Policy Debate*, **3**(2), 601–36.

Freeman, Alan (1978), 'Legitimating racial discrimination through antidiscrimination law: a critical review of Supreme Court doctrine', *Minnesota Law Review*, **62**.

Fukuyama, Hirofumi, Ramon Guerra and William L. Weber (1999), 'Efficiency and ownership: evidence from Japanese credit cooperatives', *Journal of Economics and Business*, **51**, 473–87.

Galster, George C. (1992), 'Research on discrimination in housing and mortgage markets: assessment and future directions', *Housing Policy Debate*, **3**(2), 637–83.

Galster, George C. (1993), 'The facts of lending discrimination cannot be argued away by examining default rates', *Housing Policy Debate,* **4**(1), 141–6.

Galster, George C. and Ronald B. Mincy (1993), 'Understanding the changing fortunes of metropolitan neighborhoods: 1980 to 1990', *Housing Policy Debate*, **4**(3), 303–52.

Glennon, Dennis and Mitchell Stengel (1994), 'An evaluation of the Federal Reserve Bank of Boston's study of racial discrimination in mortgage lending', Economic and Policy Analysis working paper 94–2, Comptroller of the Currency, Washington, DC, April.

Goering, J.M. (ed.) (1996), 'Race and default in mortgage markets: a colloquy', *Cityscape: A Journal of Policy Development and Research*, **2**.

Grown, Caren and Timothy Bates (1992), 'Commercial bank lending practices and the development of black owned construction companies', *Journal of Urban Affairs*, **14**(1), 25–41.

Guttentag, Jack M. and Susan L. Wachter (1980), 'Redlining and public policy', *Monograph Series on Finance and Economics*, no. 1, New York: Solomon Brothers Center for the Study of Financial Institutions.

Han, Song (2004), 'Discrimination in lending: theory and evidence', *Journal of Real Estate Finance and Economics*, **29**(1), 5–46.

Han, Song (2001), 'On the economics of discrimination in credit markets', Working Paper 2002–02, Division of Research and Statistics, Federal Reserve Board, Washington DC, October.

Hawley, C.A. and E. T. Fujii (1990), 'Discouraged applicants for consumer credit', *Economics Letters*, **33**, 83–6.

Heckman, James (1976), 'The common structure of statistical models of truncation, sample selection, and limited dependent variables and a sample estimator for such models', *Annals of Economic and Social Measurement*, **5**, 475–92.

Heckman, James. J. (1979), 'Sample bias as a specification error', *Econometrica*, **47**, January, 153–61.

Henriques, Diana B. and Lowell Bergman (2000), 'Profiting from fine print with Wall Street's help', *Wall Street Journal*, 15 March.

Holmes, Andrew and Paul Horvitz (1994), 'Mortgage redlining: race, risk, and demand', *Journal of Finance,* **49**(1), March, 81–99.

Hunter, William C. and Mary Beth Walker (1995), 'The cultural affinity hypothesis and mortgage lending decisions', working papers series: Issues in Financial Regulation, Research Department, Federal Reserve Bank of Chicago, July.

Hutchinson, Peter M., James R. Ostas and J. David Reed (1977), 'A survey and comparison of redlining influences in urban mortgage lending markets', *Journal of the American Real Estate and Urban Economics Association*, Winter.

Immergluck, Daniel (2000), 'A comment on "credit risk and mortgage lending: who uses subprime and why? By Anthony Pennington Cross, Anthony Yezer, and Joseph Nichols"', Woodstock Institute, Chicago, November.

Immergluck, Daniel (1999), 'Intraurban patterns of small business lending: findings from the New Community Reinvestment Act data', *Business Access to Capital and Credit*, Chicago: Federal Reserve Bank of Chicago, pp. 123–38.

Joint Task Force (2000), *HUD-Treasury Curbing Predatory Home Mortgage Lending*, a joint report of the Department of the Treasury and the Department of Housing and Urban Development, Washington, DC: Department of the Treasury and the Department of Housing and Urban Development, June.

Kain, John F. (1992), 'The spatial mismatch hypothesis: three decades later', *Housing Policy Debate*, **3**(2), 333–70.

Kasarda, John D. (1993), 'Inner-city concentrated poverty and neighborhood distress: 1970 to 1990', *Housing Policy Debate*, **4**(3), 253–302.

Keeney, M. (1988), 'Race, residence, discrimination, and economic opportunity', *Urban Affairs Quarterly*, **24**, September, 87–117.

Kelly, Austin (1995), 'Racial and ethnic disparities in mortgage prepayment', *Journal of Housing Economics*, **4**, 350–72.

Kim, Sunwoong and Gregory D. Squires (1995), 'Lender characteristics and racial disparities in mortgage lending', *Journal of Housing Research*, **6**(1).

Lacker, Jeffrey (1995), 'Neighborhoods and banking', *Federal Reserve Bank of Richmond Economic Quarterly*, **81**(2) (Spring), 13–38.

LaCour-Little, Michael (1999), 'Discrimination in mortgage lending: a critical review of the literature', *Journal of Real Estate Literature*, **7**, 15–49.

LaCour-Little, Michael and Richard K. Green (1998), 'Are minorities or minority neighborhoods more likely to get low appraisals?', *Journal of Real Estate Finance and Economics*, **16**(3), 301–15.

Ladd, Helen F. (1998), 'Evidence on discrimination in mortgage lending', *Journal of Economic Perspectives*, **12**(2), 41–62.

Lang, William W. and Leonard I. Nakamura (1993), 'A model of redlining', *Journal of Urban Economics*, **33**, 223–34.

Lax, Howard, Michael Manti, Paul Raca and Peter Zorn (2004), 'Subprime lending: an investigation of economic efficiency', *Housing Policy Debate*, **15**(3), 533–71.

Lee, C.H. and E.H. Warren (1977), 'Rationing by seller's preference and racial price discrimination', *Economic Inquiry*, **14**, 36–44.

Leigh, Wilhelmina A. (1992), 'Civil rights legislation and the housing status of black Americans: an overview', in Wilhelmina A. Leigh and James B. Stewart (eds), *The Housing Status of Black Americans*, New Brunswick, NJ: Transaction Publishers, pp. 5–28.

Leitner, Yaron (2002), 'Fragile financial networks – a preliminary analysis', Working Paper 02-9. Federal Reserve Bank of Philadelphia, June.

Leyshon, Andrew, Thrift, Nigel (1997), 'Geographies of financial exclusion: financial abandonment in Britain and the United States', in Andrew Leyshon and Nigel Thrift (eds), *Money/Space: Geographies of Monetary Transformation*, London: Routledge, pp. 225–59.

Maddala, G.S. and Robert P. Trost (1982), 'On measuring discrimination in loan markets', *Housing Finance Review*, **1**(3), 245–66.

Marsden, Madeline (1994), 'Board issues fair lending policy statement', *Financial Update*, Federal Reserve Bank of Atlanta, **7**(1–2), January–June, 1–3.

Martin, Robert E. and R. Carter Hill (2000), 'Loan performance and race', *Economic Inquiry*, **38**(1) (January), 136–50.

Mason, Patrick L. (1992), 'The divide-and-conquer and employer/employee models of discrimination: neoclassical competition as a familial effect', *Review of Black Political Economy*, **20**(4) (Spring), 73–89.

Massey, Douglas S. and Nancy A. Denton (1993), *American Apartheid: Segregation and the Making of the Underclass*, Cambridge: Harvard University Press.

Masson, R (1973). 'Costs of search and racial price discrimination', *Economic Inquiry*, 167–86.

McCoy, Patricia A. and Elvin K. Wyly (2004), *Housing Policy Debate*, **15**(3), 453–67.

Mohanty, Lisa (2001), 'Access to credit: a study of minority women in California', paper presented at the Western Social Science Association meetings, Reno, mimeo, University of California, Riverside, June.

Mollenkamp, Carrick (2000), 'Conceding failure, First Union plans to close money store unit', *Wall Street Journal*, 26 June.

Munnell, Alicia H., Lynn E. Browne, James McEneaney and Geoffrey Tootell (1992), 'Mortgage lending in Boston: interpreting HMDA data', working paper no. 92-7, Federal Reserve Bank of Boston.

Myers, Samuel L. and T. Chan (1995), 'Racial discrimination in housing markets – accounting for credit risk', *Social Science Quarterly*, **76**(3) (September), 543–61.

Nesiba, Reynold F. (1995), 'Deregulation and discrimination: an evaluation of the impact of bank mergers on residential mortgage lending patterns in St. Joseph County, Indiana, 1985–93', PhD dissertation, Department of Economics, University of Notre Dame.

Oliver, Melvin L. and Thomas M. Shapiro (1995), *Black Wealth/White Wealth: A New Perspective on Racial Inequality*. New York: Routledge.

Olney, Martha (1998), 'When your word is not enough: race, collateral, and household credit', *Journal of Economic History*, **58**(2), June, 408–31.

Ondrich, Jan, Stephen L. Ross and John Yinger (2000), 'How common is housing discrimination? Improving on traditional measures', *Journal of Urban Economics*, 47, 470–500.

Ondrich, Jan, Alex Stricker and John Yinger (1998), 'Do real estate brokers choose to discriminate? Evidence from the 1989 Housing Discrimination Study', *Southern Economic Journal* **64**(4) (April), 880–901.

Oppel, Richard A. (2001), 'U.S. suit cites Citigroup unit on loan deceit', *New York Times*, 7 March.

Oppel, Richard A. and Patrick McGeehan (2000), 'Citigroup announces changes to guard against abusive loan practices', *New York Times*, 8 November.

Page, Marianne (1995), 'Racial and ethnic discrimination in urban housing markets: evidence from a recent audit study', *Journal of Urban Economics*, **38**, 183–206.

Pennington-Cross, Anthony, Anthony Yezer and Joseph Nichols (2000), 'Credit risk and mortgage lending: who uses subprime and why?', working paper no. 00-03, Research Institute for Housing America, Washington, DC.

Perle, Eugene D., Kathryn Lynch and Jeffrey Horner (1993), 'Model specification and local mortgage market behavior', *Journal of Housing Research*, **4**(2), 225–44.

Perlmann, Joel (1998), 'The place of cultural explanations and historical specificity in discussions of modes of incorporation and segmented assimilation', working paper no. 240, Jerome Levy Economics Institute of Bard College, Annandale-on-Hudson, NY, July.

Pollard, Jane (1995), 'Financial exclusion in Los Angeles', *Environment and Planning A*.

Quercia, Roberto G. and Michael A. Stegman (1992), 'Residential mortgage default: a review of the literature', *Journal of Housing Research*, **3**(2), 341–70.

Rachlis, Mitchell B. and Anthony M.J. Yezer (1993), 'Serious flaws in statistical tests for discrimination in mortgage markets', *Journal of Housing Research*, **4**(2), 315–36.

Read, Lauren (1998), *The Financing of Small Business: A Comparative Study of Male and Female Business Owners*, London: Routledge.

Reibel, Michael (1997), 'Fair lending and neighborhood disinvestment in Los Angeles'. PhD dissertation, Geography, University of California, Los Angeles.

Reibel, Michael (2000), 'Geographic variation in mortgage discrimination: evidence from Los Angeles', *Urban Geography*, **21**(1) (January–February), 45–60

Roemer, John (1998), *Equality of Opportunity*. Cambridge: Harvard University Press.

Ross, Stephen L. (2000), 'Mortgage lending, sample selection, and default', *Real Estate Economics*, **28**(4), 581–621.

Ross, Stephen L. and John Yinger (1999a), 'Does discrimination in mortgage lending exist? The Boston Fed study and its critics', in Austin Turner and Skidmore (eds), pp. 45–83.

Ross, Stephen L. and John Yinger (1999b), 'Other evidence of discrimination: recent studies of redlining and of discrimination in loan approval and loan terms', in Austin Turner and Skidmore (eds), pp. 85–106.

Ross, Stephen L., and John Yinger (1999c), 'The default approach to studying mortgage discrimination: a rebuttal', in Austin Turner and Skidmore (eds). pp. 107–27.

Sanders, Cynthia K. and Edward Scanlon (2000), 'Mortgage lending and gender.' *Affilia*, **15**(1), 9–30.

Sapsford, Jathon, Paul Beckett and John Hechinger (2001), 'Citigroup, J.P. Morgan take earnings hits from bad loans, lower banking revenue', *Wall Street Journal*, 18 October.

Scalera, Domenico and Alberto Zazzaro (2001), 'Group reputation and persistent (or permanent) discrimination in credit markets', *Journal of Multinational Financial Management*, **11**(4–5) (December), 483–96.

Schafer, Robert (1978), *Mortgage lending decisions, criteria and constraints.* Cambridge: Joint Center for Urban Studies, MIT and Harvard, December.

Schafer, Robert and Helen F. Ladd (1980), *Equal Credit Opportunity: Accessibility to Mortgage Funds by Women and by Minorities: Final Technical Report*, US Department of Housing and Urban Development, Office of Policy Development and Research, Washington, DC: USGPO.

Schelling, Thomas (1971), 'Dynamic models of segregation', *Journal of Mathematical Sociology*, **1**, 143–86.

Schill, Michael H. and Susan M. Wachter (1993), 'A tale of two cities: racial and ethnic geographic disparities in home mortgage lending in Boston and Philadelphia', *Journal of Housing Research*, **4**(2), 245–76.

Schmitt, Brian T. (2000), 'From redlining to creditlining: the ways of white folks', mimeo, Department of Planning and Public Policy, Rutgers University, New Brunswick, NJ, May.

Schwem, Robert G. (1995), 'Introduction to mortgage lending discrimination law', *The John Marshall Law Review*, **28**, Winter, 317–32.

Shlay, Anne (1989), 'Financing community: methods for assessing residential credit disparities, market barriers, and institutional reinvestment performance in the metropolis', *Journal of Urban Affairs*, **11**(3), 201–23.

Simmons, Colin and Salinder Supri (1999), 'Failing financial and training institutions: the marginalization of rural household enterprises in the Indian Punjab', *Journal of Economic Issues*, **33**(4) (December), 953–74.

Smith, Shanna (2000), 'Women and housing discrimination', McAuley Institute, September.

Sowell, Thomas (1981). *Ethnic America: A History*, New York: Basic Books.

Squires, Gregory (1992), 'Community reinvestment: an emerging social movement', in Gregory Squires (ed.), *From Redlining to Reinvestment*, Philadelphia: Temple University Press, pp. 1–37.

Squires, Gregory D. and Sally O'Connor (1999), 'Access to capital: Milwaukee's small business lending gaps', in *Business Access to Capital and Credit*, Chicago: Federal Reserve Bank of Chicago, pp. 85–122.

Staten, Michael E. and Anthony M. Yezer (2004), 'Introduction to the Special Issue', 'Special Issue: "Subprime lending: empirical studies",' *Journal of Real Estate Finance and Economics* **29**(4), 359–63.

Stengel, Mitchell *et al.* (1995), 'Using statistical models to identify unfair lending behavior', in Anthony M. Yezer (ed.), *Fair Lending Analysis: A Compendium of Essays on the Use of Statistics,* foreword by Lawrence B. Lindsey, epilogue by William M. Isaac, Washington, DC: American Bankers Association, pp. 57–64.

Stiglitz, Joseph E. and Andrew Weiss (1991), 'Credit rationing in markets with imperfect information', in Gregory Mankiw and David Romer (eds), *New Keynesian Economics*, vol. II, Cambridge: MIT Press, 247–76.

Stone, Michael (1991), *One Third of the Nation*, Washington, DC: Economic Policy Institute.

Struyk, Raymond J. and Margery A. Turner (1986), 'Exploring the effects of racial preferences on urban housing markets', *Journal of Urban Economics*, **19**, 131–47.

Stuart, Guy (2003), *Discriminating Risk: The US Mortgage Lending Industry in the Twentieth Century*. Ithaca, NY: Cornell University Press.

Swire, Peter P. (1995), 'The persistent problem of lending discrimination: a law and economics analysis', *Texas Law Review*, **73**, March, 787–869.

Tootell, Geoffrey (1996), 'Redlining in Boston: do mortgage lenders discriminate against neighborhoods?', *Quarterly Journal of Economics*, **111**(4) (November), 1049–79.

United States House of Representatives (1974), *Credit Discrimination*; hearings before the Subcommittee on Consumer Affairs of the Committee on Banking and Currency, House of Representatives, Ninety-third Congress, second session. Washington, DC: USGPO.

US Department of Housing and Urban Development (HUD) (2000), *Unequal Burden in Los Angeles: Income and Racial Disparities in Subprime Lending*, Washington, DC: US Department of Housing and Urban Development, April.

Weink, Ron (1992), 'Discrimination in urban credit markets: what we don't know and why we don't know it', *Housing Policy Debate,* **3**(2), 217–40.

White, Alan M. (2004), 'Risk-based mortgage pricing: present and future research', *Housing Policy Debate*, **15**(3), 503–31.

Wiggins, Mary Jo (2002), 'Race, class, and suburbia: the modern black suburb as a "race-making situation",' *University of Michigan Journal of Law Reform*, **35**, Summer, 749–808.

Williams, Richard (1999), 'The effect of GSEs, CRA, and institutional characteristics on home mortgage lending to underserved markets', HUD final report, December.

Wilson, William Julius (1987), *The Truly Disadvantaged: The Inner City, the Underclass, and Public Policy*, Chicago: University of Chicago Press.

Wolff, Edward N. (2001), 'Racial wealth disparities: is the gap closing?', public policy brief no. 66, Jerome Levy Economics Institute of Bard College, Annandale-on-Hudson, NY.

Wyly, Elvin, Mona Atia and Daniel J. Hammel (2001), 'Has mortgage capital found an inner-city spatial fix?', *Housing Policy Debate*, **15**(3), 623–85.

Yezer, Anthony M.J. (1999), 'Studies of CRA lending on small business lending', *Business Access to Capital and Credit*, Chicago: Federal Reserve Bank of Chicago, pp. 139–45.

Yinger, John (1975), 'A model of discrimination by landlords', working paper 259–75, Institute for Research on Poverty, University of Wisconsin – Madison, February.

Yinger, John (1997), 'Cash in your face: the cost of racial and ethnic discrimination in housing', *Journal of Urban Economics*, **42**, 339–65.

Zenou, Yves, and Nicolas Boccard (2000), 'Racial discrimination and redlining in cities', *Journal of Urban Economics*, **48**, 260–85.

9 Equal employment opportunity and affirmative action

Harry J. Holzer and David Neumark

I Introduction

Public policies to combat discrimination against minorities and women in the United States – and to help narrow the gaps in labor market outcomes and socioeconomic status more generally – have a long and controversial history. The most important components of federal anti-discrimination policy are Equal Employment Opportunity (EEO) legislation and affirmative action. EEO legislation began with Title VII of the Civil Rights Act of 1964, which made it illegal to discriminate in hiring, discharge, compensation, and so on, on the basis of race, color, religion, sex or national origin, and evolved further with the Equal Employment Opportunity Act (EEOA) of 1972. Affirmative action was put in place with a set of Executive Orders.[1]

The accumulated body of research on anti-discrimination policy is literally immense. Broadly speaking, it can be divided into three areas. The first concerns the necessity of anti-discrimination policies. While non-economists generally take it as given that there is discrimination against minorities and women in labor markets and elsewhere, economists have worked hard to develop credible tests of this hypothesis, and more generally to estimate the relative roles of discriminatory and other explanations. This research is covered in other chapters of this *Handbook*, and hence is not covered here. Rather, this chapter emphasizes the more specific policy focus of the other two areas of research on anti-discrimination policy.

The second area of research concerns the empirical effects of EEO legislation and affirmative action, questions that focus in large part on whether these policies shift hiring or other behaviors so as to reduce the relative disadvantage of minorities and women. This research is, in a sense, pure policy analysis, in that it attempts simply to estimate the empirical impacts of anti-discrimination policies. While this type of analysis is not uniquely suited to economics, in that it does not have explicit economic content, economists have been at the forefront of such research.

Finally, adopting a more distinctly economic perspective, economists have begun more recently to try to assess more difficult questions concerning anti-discrimination policies. These have focused in large part on the efficiency or performance effects of these policies, motivated by arguments concerning whether EEO legislation or affirmative action increase efficiency and performance by discouraging costly discriminatory behavior, or instead whether these policies decrease efficiency and performance by forcing employers and other agents to pay attention to race and sex rather than merit in making their decisions. These questions have come to the fore particularly in the recent controversial debate over affirmative action, which continues to be played out in legislatures, the courts, and public debate.[2]

II Overview of equal employment opportunity legislation and affirmative action

Legislation and executive orders regarding employment discrimination

The basis of EEO legislation is Title VII of the Civil Rights Act, which prohibits sex and race discrimination. Actions defined as illegal under Title VII include using an individual's race, sex, ethnicity, and so on, as a basis for refusal to hire an applicant, discharge of an employee, or the setting of other conditions of employment (compensation, or terms, conditions or privileges of employment). The Act also regulates the behavior of employment agencies and labor unions. Among other things, these agents are prohibited from using any advertisement relating to employment indicating preferences or limitations based on race, sex or other group characteristics specified by the Act. The Equal Employment Opportunity Act (EEOA) of 1972, which expanded coverage and increased enforcement powers of the Equal Employment Opportunity Commission (EEOC), is widely viewed as having ushered in more strenuous application of Title VII.

Affirmative action cannot be traced so explicitly to any particular piece of legislation. Rather, its roots lie in a series of Executive Orders issued by US Presidents. Executive Order 10925 (issued in 1961) introduced the phrase 'affirmative action', encouraging employers to take action to ensure nondiscrimination (as opposed, presumably, to passively ceasing to discriminate). Executive Order 11246 (1965) required federal contractors and subcontractors (currently, with contracts of $50 000 or more) to identify underutilized minorities, assess availability of minorities, and if available to set goals and timetables for reducing the underutilization. Executive Order 11375 (1967) extended this to women.[3] The practical advent of affirmative action is often traced to Executive Order 11246, because in its initial implementation the Department of Labor developed what is referred to as the 'Philadelphia Plan'. This plan aimed to increase minority representation in construction, and is viewed as the 'precursor of the numerical "goals and timetables" obligations of federal contractors' (Bloch, 1994, p. 70). Contractors may be sued and barred from federal contracts if they are judged to be discriminating or not pursuing affirmative action, although this outcome is rare (Stephanopoulos and Edley, 1995).

As is typically the case with legislation, the law expresses the intent of Congress and provides some specifics, but the details of how the law is to be applied are fleshed out by the enforcing agency (subject, of course, to later court review) in the Code of Federal Regulations. Regulations promulgated by the EEOC lay out some important additional features of EEO legislation. For example, only very limited exceptions in which sex or race can play a role in labor markets are allowed (for example, in occupations such as locker room attendants and actors); otherwise race and sex are factors to be ignored. In the case of anti-discrimination policy, these regulations reflect concerns that arise out of specific economic hypotheses regarding discrimination. For example, they rule out statistical discrimination, such as 'refusal to hire a woman because of her sex based on assumptions of the comparative employment characteristics of women in general. For example, the assumption that the turnover rate among women is higher than among men' or the 'refusal to hire an individual based on stereotyped characterizations of the sexes'. In addition, the regulations clarify that Title VII does not address only employer discrimination (Becker, 1971), as they also specify as illegal refusal to hire an individual because of 'the preferences of coworkers, the employer, clients or customers'.[4]

In addition to regulations issued by the EEOC refining the meaning of anti-discrimination legislation (in particular EEO), another profound influence on the actual impact of legislation is the case law that evolves. This case law effectively defines how the law works in practice, helping to establish, among other things, the types of charges that will be found in violation of the law, the types of cases (or nature of evidence) that may be brought, and the burden of proof. In Title VII cases, the plaintiff's ultimate burden is to prove that the action of the employer (typically) was taken on the basis of race or sex; it does not require that these were the only factors, but were the determining ones. This can be proved in one of two ways. The first is to prove 'disparate treatment', established in *International Board of Teamsters* v. *United States* (1977) and other cases, which requires proof that an employer intentionally treated someone less favorably because of their race or sex. Such cases are distinguished by requiring proof of discriminatory intent. Other examples of proof of discriminatory intent may involve evidence that defendants made disparaging comments based on a worker's (or applicant's) race or sex.

In disparate treatment cases, plaintiffs first try to establish direct evidence of intent to discriminate, such as discriminatory statements. In the absence of such evidence, the precedents established in *McDonnell Douglas* v. *Green* (1973), and *Texas Department of Community Affairs* v. *Burdine* (1981) are used to determine whether intentional discrimination has occurred. First, the plaintiff tries to establish a prima facie case for discriminatory intent (which may rely in part on statistical evidence, ruling out the most likely nondiscriminatory explanations of the action). The burden of proof then shifts to the employer to offer a legitimate nondiscriminatory explanation. Finally, the plaintiff can then rebut the employer's explanation, most commonly by trying to prove that the nondiscriminatory explanation is false.

The second route is to prove 'disparate impact', established in *Griggs* v. *Duke Power Co.* (1971). Such cases do not rest on proving discriminatory intent, but require two things: first, that an employer's policy that may appear neutral in fact affects minorities or females more adversely; and second, that the practice cannot be justified by 'business necessity'. An instructive example is provided by the case referenced above, in which Duke Power required a test score that was equivalent to the education of an average high school graduate. While appearing neutral, at the time this disproportionately foreclosed employment for blacks. The Supreme Court eventually ruled in favor of the plaintiff because Duke Power could not establish that this level of education (or the test score) was related to success on the job (Bloch, 1994). A later decision (*Wards Cove Packing Co.* v. *Atonio*, 1989) imposed stiffer standards on plaintiffs, requiring them not only to present evidence of statistical disparities but also to identify specific discriminatory employer practices, and – if the defendant offers a business necessity defense – to 'persuade the court that alternative feasible practices were equally effective for the employer' (Bloch, 1994, p. 49). However, the Civil Rights Act in 1991 largely restored the pre-*Wards Cove* standards of evidence and burden of proof.

Education and contracting

Although the primary focus of research (and of this chapter) is on policies intended to combat labor market discrimination, there are also policies in place that cover education and government contracting. Title IX of the Civil Rights Act bars sex discrimination in any educational programs or activities receiving federal funding, while Title VI more generally bars discrimination on the grounds of race, color, or national origin in any program or activity that receives federal funding. These parts of the Civil Rights Act have spurred some controversy. For example, Title IX is the legal basis for efforts to achieve gender equity in sports at colleges and universities, and Title VI has been the basis of legal challenges to segregation of higher education and underfunding of historically black colleges and universities.

However, even more so than with respect to the labor market, affirmative action in education is far more prominent and controversial. Interestingly, although there are no explicit federal policies regarding affirmative action in university admissions, universities have implemented affirmative action admissions policies that are widely regarded as giving preferential treatment to women and minority candidates. Since that time, court decisions have shaped (and continue to shape) what universities can and cannot do. Preferential admissions policies initially came under attack in the *Bakke* case (*Bakke* v. *University of California Regents*, 1978), in which the Supreme Court declared that policies that set aside a specific number of places for minority students violated the 14th Amendment of the US Constitution, which bars states from depriving citizens of equal protection of the laws. As a consequence, the courts have ruled that the 14th Amendment applies to affirmative action programs at state and local levels of government. However, while this decision is viewed as declaring strict quotas illegal, it is also interpreted as ruling that race can be used as a 'flexible factor' in university admissions (Edley, 1996, p. 58).[5] Affirmative action in university admissions suffered serious setbacks as a result of Proposition 209 in California, and a court ruling against the University of Texas Law School in *Hopwood* v. *State of Texas*. The latter addresses an admissions program that granted preferential treatment to minorities in the evaluation of grade point averages and test scores. Proposition 209 addressed preferential treatment in any program, although most of the attention has focused on its impact on university admissions.[6]

Most recently, the Supreme Court in 2003 struck down the undergraduate admissions practices at the University of Michigan in the case of *Gratz* v. *Bollinger et al.*, finding that the point system used by the university in its consideration of race (and other criteria) was too rigid. At the same time, in *Grutter* v. *Bollinger et al.* it upheld the university's law school admissions procedures, finding that the more flexible treatment of race in this case did not violate equal protection, because it relied upon a narrowly-tailored use of race to further a compelling interest in expanding the diversity of the student body at this prestigious school.[7]

The third major component of affirmative action is contracting and procurement programs. At the federal level, these have principally taken the form of preferential treatment in bidding for small/disadvantaged businesses (SDBs), and small business administration programs of technical assistance.[8] These contracting and procurement programs focus more on minorities than women (Stephanopoulos and Edley, 1995, section 9). In addition to the federal level, numerous states and localities have used programs aimed at increasing the share of contracts awarded to minority-owned businesses.

As with affirmative action in education, court rulings in the last decade or so have challenged the legal standing of such programs. *City of Richmond* v. *J.A. Croson Co.* established strict criteria ('strict scrutiny') that must be met for state programs to be legal. However, because the 14th Amendment applies to state and local government policies, court rulings restricting federal programs (*Fullilove* v. *Klutznick* and *Metro Broadcasting, Inc.* v. *FCC*) initially applied less strict standards ('intermediate scrutiny'). However, in *Adarand Constructors, Inc.* v. *Pena*, the Supreme Court ruled that strict scrutiny could also apply to federal programs. The Court ruled that federal race-conscious programs will be evaluated on the basis of the 5th Amendment (which guarantees that citizens shall not 'be deprived of life, liberty, or property, without due process of law'), with much the same interpretation as that with which the Court had applied the 14th Amendment to non-federal programs. These various rulings do not prohibit race-based programs at any level of government, although they do raise the standards for their legal justification. It is too early to be able to characterize how local, state and federal programs will ultimately be shaped in response to these rulings.

EEO vs. affirmative action in the labor market
While it is possible to identify the specific laws, orders, rulings, and so on, which form the basis of EEO legislation and affirmative action affecting the labor market, in practice the distinction is not so sharp. First, what has ostensibly addressed discrimination in the workplace has also led to affirmative action in practice. Title VII of the Civil Rights Act of 1964, which established Equal Employment Opportunity (EEO) as law, allows for affirmative action as a means of remediation for past discrimination. While the main focus of this legislation is the prohibition of discrimination in employment, the Act also allows the courts, when finding that an employer is engaging in an unlawful employment practice, to 'order such Affirmative Action as may be appropriate, which may include reinstatement or hiring of employees'.[9]

More generally, in practice the difference is muddied further. Many employment discrimination cases concern hiring and are based on evidence of 'disparate impact', according to which underrepresentation of women or minorities (relative to some suitably-defined pool of job candidates) is sufficiently large to support an inference of discrimination. Much of the argument in such cases concerns the definition of the appropriate candidate pool (Epstein, 1992, ch. 18). But regardless of how this issue is settled, employers concerned with a possible disparate impact discrimination claim might seek to ensure that women and minorities are adequately represented among their hires. Indeed, EEOC guidelines for defining disparate impact essentially establish a system of numerical yardsticks, embodied in the '80 per cent' or 'four-fifths' rule, which states that 'A selection rate for any race, sex, or ethnic group which is less than four-fifths . . . of the rate for the group with the highest rate will generally be regarded by the Federal enforcement agencies as evidence of adverse impact.'[10] This is easily monitored for many companies, as employers with 100 or more employees are required to file EEO-1 reports indicating the percentages of female and minority workers in broad occupational categories.

As a consequence, we believe that, when analyzing affirmative action in the labor market, attention should not be limited solely to the effects associated with contractor status, but ought to focus as well on policies or actions that might encourage anything other than race- or sex-blind behavior. We can certainly examine the effects of a particular policy, as some of the research described in this chapter does. But we do not think that the two policies can always be separated, or that one necessarily obtains a sharper picture from an exclusive focus on either EEO or affirmative action.

Another point that this emphasizes is the difficulty of interpreting suggestions of some critics of affirmative action that we can do away with affirmative action but maintain vigorous enforcement of anti-discrimination laws (or 'color blindness').[11] Laws barring race- or sex-conscious behavior in hiring, promotions and discharges are likely to undermine not only explicit forms of affirmative action, but also any prohibitions of discrimination that rely on disparate impact analyses for their enforcement.

III   EEO policy

Evidence on the effects of EEO policy[12]
Most of the earlier research on the impact of EEO legislation on race and sex differences in labor market outcomes consists of time-series studies asking whether, concurrent with the passage of EEO laws, there was a jump or acceleration in the relative economic status of the groups protected by these laws. The primary focus is on examining evidence regarding alternative explanations of black economic progress in the late 1960s. Summarizing the empirical facts, Cain (1986) roughly characterizes black–white earnings ratios for all working men as stable 1948 to 1965, growing from 1966 to 1974 and stable again from 1975 to 1982. Heckman (1990) paints a slightly different picture, noting that relative improvements for blacks were concentrated in the period 1965–75, but began before 1964.

The primary question addressed in the time-series studies is, as Heckman (1990) puts it, 'Does continuous or discontinuous change characterize the recent economic history of black Americans?' (p. 242). That is, is there a discontinuity in the relative progress of blacks that is most consistent with an important role for federal EEO efforts, or does black economic progress simply reflect longer-term trends, perhaps obscured in some periods (and hence giving the impression of more rapid change in the 1960s and early 1970s) because of other changes? The latter view is put forth most forcefully by Smith and Welch (1989), who conclude that 'slowly evolving historical forces . . . education and migration – were the primary determinants of long-term black economic improvement. At best Affirmative Action has marginally altered black wage gains around this long-term trend' (p. 519).[13]

The empirical studies on this question are reviewed by Brown (1982), Heckman and Payner (1989) and others. These studies have a common goal of sorting out the question of continuous versus discontinuous change, asking whether the relative progress of blacks in this period could or could not be explained by changes in migration rates, changes in the relative educational attainment of blacks, and other supply shifts (leading the lowest-wage blacks to leave the labor force), business cycle fluctuations, other observable factors or other trends that may be difficult to relate to observables but that pre-dated federal legislation (see Butler and Heckman, 1977; Donohue and Heckman, 1991; Freeman, 1973, 1981; Culp, 1986; Vroman, 1974; Brown, 1984; Fosu, 1992; Smith and Welch, 1977). [14]

Many, but not all, of these studies reach conclusions consistent with the view that federal EEO efforts did have a positive effect on black economic progress. For example, Heckman (1990) takes a strong stand regarding the positive impact of federal policy (based on evidence in Donohue and Heckman, 1991, and a review of the earlier evidence), arguing that 'there is ample evidence of discontinuous change in the improvement of black status during the crucial period 1965–1975' (p. 242). Nonetheless, some ambiguities remain in the interpretation of this earlier time-series literature, stemming from difficulties of identifying the effects of EEO laws from time-series data.

There are far fewer studies of the impact of federal anti-discrimination policy on sex differences in labor market outcomes. Eberts and Stone (1985) use panel data to examine relative rates of promotion of males and females in public schools before and after the EEOA. They find declining evidence of discrimination in promotions of teachers in two states in the latter part of the 1970s, and conclude that the EEOA contributed to that decline. Beller (1979) estimates models for earnings of men and women using Current Population Survey data for 1967, 1971 and 1974, incorporating measures of Title VII investigations and settlements by region (large states and state groups), but not including a time trend or year dummy variables. She finds relatively weak evidence that these measures reduced the sex wage gap prior to the EEOA, but stronger evidence of this effect after the passage of the EEOA.

The core problem with time-series analyses of the impact of federal EEO legislation is that these laws have nearly universal applicability, which prevents identification of an appropriate comparison group that can be used to control for changes in the outcomes under study unrelated to the policy innovation. For example, if the black–white wage gap was narrowing prior to the passage of Title VII of the Civil Rights Act, and more so if other factors influenced the wage gap after Title VII passed, then testing whether Title VII narrowed the gap requires a comparison of changes in the black–white gap for workers covered by Title VII and workers not covered, in the same period.[15]

To attempt to address the fundamental problem with the time-series analyses, newer research on the effects of anti-discrimination legislation has sought to exploit other sources of identifying information. Donohue and Heckman's (1991) study can be interpreted in this light. They argue that black economic progress over the 1965–75 period was generated mainly in the South, at the same time that federal policy was directed toward the South. This can be interpreted as testing for the effectiveness of federal efforts by comparing changes in relative black economic status in two regions: the South, where enforcement was more vigorous, and the rest of the country, which because it experienced less vigorous enforcement serves as a crude control group. As long as underlying trends did not differ between the South and elsewhere, this may more reliably identify at least the qualitative effect of federal anti-discrimination laws.[16]

Although federal anti-discrimination laws expanded relatively quickly to near-universal coverage, Title VII coverage was initially extended only to firms with at least 100 employees, with the minimum workforce size falling to 25 by 1968. The 1972 EEOA extended coverage to employers with as few as 15 employees. Chay (1998), Carrington et al. (2000) and Hahn et al. (1999) have exploited these coverage differences to develop tests of the effectiveness of federal anti-discrimination laws based on black–white differences in employment and earnings across firms or establishments of different sizes. For example, Chay (1998) exploits the extension of coverage to smaller establishments with the EEOA, as well as the existence of state laws that in some cases had already extended coverage beyond that mandated by the EEOA, to obtain treatment and control groups. In particular, he uses Current Population Survey (CPS) data on establishment size, coupled with information on state laws, to identify those industries and regions that should have been most affected by the EEOA, and finds that in these industry–region cells black men had the largest gains relative to white men in terms of employment, earnings ratios and occupational status. Chay concludes that the EEOA had positive effects on the labor market status of blacks.[17]

While Chay's (1998) study utilizes one of the more compelling research designs in the literature on the effects of federal anti-discrimination laws (complemented nicely by the richer, more historical studies by Heckman and his co-authors), it does lead to some large estimated policy effects.[18] Furthermore, it is somewhat limited in restricting attention to policy effects in firms or establishments in a particular size range, and to black versus white males. Indeed, we would argue that many of the newer studies (Chay, 1998; Carrington et al., 2000; Hahn et al., 1999; and Heckman and Payner, 1989), in providing more compelling evidence of the positive impact of federal anti-discrimination policies on relative labor market outcomes for blacks, have also, as a result of their research designs, generated more narrowly-tailored evidence, and hence evidence that does not necessarily justify inferences regarding overall effects of these policies. However, this is a common feature of research designs that focus on a unique (and generally more compelling) source of identifying information.

An alternative approach that is closer in spirit to the earlier time-series studies in providing estimates of overall policy effects, but also builds on the empirical strategy of constructing statistical experiments that solve the identification problem inherent in the time-series analyses, is to exploit state-level variation in anti-discrimination policy. In particular, prior to the enactment of the federal legislation, many states enacted similar laws or practices (called Fair Employment Practices Acts, or FEPAs) barring discrimination in wages and employment. Because these laws or practices were passed at different times in different states, a more natural control group is provided. Specifically, the experimental design afforded by the variation across time and over states allows us to assess the impact of state anti-discrimination statutes while using for comparison data for the same time span from states that did not enact such statutes.

The earliest study of this type was done by Landes (1968).[19] Neumark and Stock (forthcoming) present a more recent analysis using this same strategy, which differs in a few important ways, most notably looking at state sex discrimination laws as well, and using richer specifications that permit the effects of antidiscrimination laws to evolve over time. Like past research, the evidence points to positive impacts of race discrimination laws on the relative earnings of black men.

The analysis of sex discrimination laws differs because states passed equal pay laws, rather than EEO-type laws governing hiring and employment more generally. It would be expected that sex discrimination laws focusing on equal pay would boost the relative earnings of females. Interestingly, though, sex discrimination/equal pay laws appear to have reduced the relative employment of black women and white women, a result that is consistent with theory but has received relatively little attention previously. While this does not imply that laws prohibiting wage discrimination based on sex do not on net help women, it emphasizes that such laws may impose tradeoffs between higher wages and lower employment. Such considerations may become increasingly important if there is some retrenchment of affirmative action in the US, which would likely weaken policies combating employment discrimination.

Thus, while some differences in specific results clearly remain, most of the research on the effects of EEO policy over the past 30 years finds evidence consistent with reductions in labor market discrimination against blacks and women.

Limitations of EEO policy
Despite the evidence that EEO laws reduce labor market discrimination, it is

also clear that race and sex gaps in employment and earnings persist over time, and it is our view that discrimination against minorities and women persists as well in the labor market.[20] Why have EEO laws not rooted out discriminatory behavior more completely? Are there ways of making them more effective?

One possible explanation of the persistence of discrimination is that it is particularly difficult to monitor employer behavior in certain contexts. For instance, the evidence suggests that discrimination against blacks is greatest in small establishments (Holzer, 1998),[21] or those with predominantly white customers in suburban areas (Holzer and Ihlanfeldt, 1998; Holzer and Reaser, 2000). Given the diseconomies of scale in monitoring small establishments or those with relatively few minority applicants or workers, it is probably sensible that the scarce resources of litigants and various agencies be allocated primarily to larger establishments or those with more minorities.[22]

Another problem, however, may lie in how resources are allocated across different kinds of potential discrimination cases. For instance, Donohue and Siegelman (1991) note that the vast majority of employment discrimination cases involve charges of wrongful discharge or promotion rather than hiring. Furthermore, unexplained gaps between whites and minorities, especially blacks, are now concentrated in employment rather than wages (Neal and Johnson, 1998); and much of the discrimination that persists against them appears to occur at the hiring stage rather than later.[23] There are a few potential reasons why hiring cases are more rare. First, damages in hiring cases are likely to be small, as the applicant is an active jobseeker, and hence is more likely to be employed in the near future than a worker who has been terminated and entered unemployment. (This is likely to be exacerbated if, as seems likely, the terminated worker is older and more-tenured.) Second, in the case of terminations or lack of promotions, current (or former) workers can compare their situations, which may make more clear patterns of discrimination and may also lead to a class action suit. In contrast, the typical job applicant acts alone, and has no simple way to compare experiences to those of other applicants to the same employer (see Bloch, 1994). Whatever the explanation, it is quite possible that the strong focus of anti-discrimination activity on post-hiring issues not only ignores discrimination at the hiring stage but might even encourage it, if employers feel that the costs and risks of conflict or litigation afterwards can be minimized by avoiding minorities in the first place, at the hiring stage.[24]

These findings imply that the effectiveness of anti-discrimination policy might be enhanced by making available more resources targeting small and/or suburban establishments more effectively. Alternatively, we might consider ways to focus more effort on discrimination in hiring as well as in promotions or discharges. One possibility is a greater reliance on various non-traditional means of monitoring practices at certain establishments, such as the use of job applicant 'auditors' or 'testers' in selected areas or sectors.[25]

Of course, to the extent that persistent hiring discrimination may be *statistical* in nature (that is, based on the inability of employers accurately to assess individual skills and productivity) rather than being based on preferences for whites or males, a purely regulatory strategy may not be optimal. In that case, enabling employers to have access to greater information might enable them to make more informed and therefore less discriminatory judgments in hiring. For instance, some recent evidence suggests that employers who administer tests to their applicants or who do background checks actually hire more blacks (Moss and Tilly, 2001; Holzer *et al.*, 2002; Autor and Scarborough, 2004), presumably because the improved information enables them to better assess the skills or work-readiness of individual applicants.[26]

If so, then providing employers with greater information may be part of a strategy of reducing discrimination in hiring. For instance, encouraging the use of various labor market intermediaries to help link workers to employers and to provide greater information about the former to the latter might actually improve hiring outcomes for certain members of disadvantaged minorities, such as young and less-educated black men. These intermediaries could include private/for-profit 'temp' agencies, various nonprofit agencies, or even government efforts such as the Employment Service and America's Job Bank/Talent Bank.[27] The greater ease with which criminal background or educational checks can be done over the Internet might also enhance the accuracy of employer information on skills and legal backgrounds over time (Holzer *et al.*, 2003).

Finally, we note that persistent wage or employment gaps between whites and minorities or between men and women reflect a range of other factors besides discrimination, including skill gaps (in the case of race), issues related to childbearing or childrearing (in the case of sex) and a variety of other problems.[28] Clearly, anti-discrimination policy alone is unlikely to reduce the socioeconomic gaps that are attributable to these other sources.

IV   Affirmative action

As we noted above, affirmative action remains vastly more controversial than anti-discrimination activity, even though, in the labor market, at least, the distinctions between them are clearer in theory than in practice. The critics of affirmative action argue that it transfers jobs, university admissions and business contracts to minorities and women, at the expense of white males who might be more qualified and therefore more deserving. If so, it might constitute a form of 'reverse discrimination' against white males, which could be inefficient and also unfair. In contrast, the supporters of affirmative action claim that extra efforts beyond just the removal of explicit discrimination are necessary to overcome the many inherent disadvantages that minorities and women face in universities, the labor market and the business sector. In this view, affirmative action is necessary for equal opportunity (or 'fairness') and would not necessarily reduce efficiency. Indeed, it might even raise overall efficiency by making available a wider pool of talent on which businesses and universities could draw, or because diversity itself has positive impacts.

While notions of fairness are inherently subjective, it is crucial that this debate be informed by empirical evidence on (1) the actual magnitude of the *redistribution* in jobs, university admissions or business contracts from white males to minorities or women, attributable to affirmative action; and (2) any deleterious effects on *efficiency* that are created, as measured (for example) by the credentials or performance of those who receive these preferences relative to those who do not.

The redistributive effects of affirmative action

At this point, there seems to be little doubt that racial or gender preferences redistribute certain jobs or university admissions away from white men and towards minorities and women. The question, instead, involves the magnitudes of these shifts. In terms of the labor market, a wide range of studies have demonstrated that affirmative action has shifted employment within the contractor sector from white males to minorities and women. But the magnitudes of these shifts are not necessarily large. For instance, Leonard (1990) found that employment of black males grew about 5 per cent faster in the critical period of 1974–80 (when affirmative action requirements on contractors were rigorously enforced for the first time) than did employment of white males, while for white females and black females somewhat more modest effects appeared. Others, such as Smith and Welch (1984), suggested additional and perhaps even larger effects in the late 1960s and early 1970s (though, as we noted above, they also believe that the long-run effects of affirmative action were not large). Looking at cross-sectional differences across establishments that did and did not use affirmative action in hiring (rather than using actual contractor status), Holzer and Neumark (1999) found that the share of total employment accounted for by white males was about 15–20 per cent lower in establishments using affirmative action than in those that do not, which is broadly consistent with the findings of Leonard and others.[29]

Of course, this does not necessarily imply that employment of white males overall is reduced by affirmative action, but only that it is redistributed to the non-affirmative action sector. Since wages and other benefits of employment are likely higher in the contractor than the non-contractor sector, this redistribution might reduce the relative wages of white males somewhat, which could in turn affect their labor force participation rates (Juhn, 1992); but again, the overall magnitudes of any such effects are likely to be modest, given the fairly small shifts involved and the very small elasticities of labor supply that have generally been estimated for prime-age men (Ehrenberg and Smith, 2000).

As for university admissions, some uncertainty remains about the magnitude of the redistribution from white males to minorities or women generated by affirmative action. On the one hand, test scores of those admitted are considerably higher among whites than minorities across the full spectrum of colleges and institutions (Datcher Loury and Garman, 1995). But at least part of these differences could be generated even with a common test score cutoff, given the racial gaps in test scores that exist in the population. And, if test scores are worse predictors of subsequent performance among blacks than whites, it might be perfectly rational for schools to put less weight on them in the admissions process for blacks (Dickens and Kane, 1999).

Furthermore, analyses of micro-level data on applications and admissions by Kane (1998) and by Long (2004) suggest somewhat modest effects of affirmative action on overall admissions of minorities, but both studies suggest that the magnitudes rise with the selectivity of universities.[30] In fact, Bowen and Bok (1998) find quite large effects at a set of the most elite colleges and universities. Indeed, their work suggests that admissions among minorities at these schools could be severely curtailed if affirmative action were abolished, a view consistent with the initial effects of Proposition 209 in California on admissions at Berkeley.[31] The magnitudes of racial preferences in admissions in a variety of graduate programs are also fairly large, while gender preferences are much more modest.[32]

Overall, the elimination of affirmative action in admissions to elite schools or graduate programs would likely generate large reductions in minority student enrollments, but only modest improvements in overall grades and test scores at these institutions, as the whites who would be admitted in place of them appear to perform only marginally better in terms of these measures (Bowen and Bok, 1998). Implementing the reforms that have been recently used in Texas, Florida, and elsewhere, which are based on class rank rather than minority status, would likely generate major reductions as well in the presence of minorities on campus (Long, 2004).[33] And using preferences based on family income instead of race or gender in admissions would also result in large declines in minority representation at universities, unless the income-based preferences were implemented in addition to those based on race and gender (Carnevale and Rose, 2003).

As for the redistribution of contracts from white-owned to minority- or female-owned businesses, we know of no study that has attempted to measure carefully the magnitude of this shift, though some summary studies suggest that these effects might be substantial.[34]

The efficiency and performance effects of affirmative action
Before reviewing the empirical literature on efficiency and performance effects of affirmative action, it is useful to review what we can learn from various theoretical considerations concerning the labor market or university admissions in this regard.

With respect to labor markets, it is fairly clear that affirmative action could reduce efficiency in well-functioning labor markets in the short run, if minorities or women are assigned to jobs for which they are not fully qualified (Welch, 1976); while it could increase efficiency if it opens up to minorities or women jobs from which they have been excluded, especially if less qualified white males are used instead. On the other hand, affirmative action might also lead minorities and women to invest in more education and training, as the rewards to their doing so would be increased; under some circumstances, these higher investments would be efficiency-increasing (Lundberg and Startz, 1983; Coate and Loury, 1993). The positive benefits on skill development across generations might be important as well (Loury, 1977). Finally, diversity per se may bring benefits, such as in fostering mentoring relationships (Athey *et al.*, 2000). In general, the more important the imperfection in the labor market associated with the lower relative status of minorities – such as negative externalities generated for other members of the community, or imperfect information driving the outcome – the greater the chance that affirmative action will not reduce efficiency, and might instead raise it.

A similar point can be made regarding university admissions. Significant market imperfections are likely to impede university admissions for some groups, such as imperfect information among university officials about individual candidates (or vice versa), and capital market problems that limit the access of lower-income groups to financing. Furthermore, important externalities might exist in the education process, at least along certain dimensions. For instance, students might learn more from one another in more diverse settings; indeed, the value of being able to interact with those of other ethnicities or nationalities might be growing over time, as product and labor markets become more diverse and more international. Alternatively, race-specific or gender-specific role models might be important for some individuals in the learning process.

More broadly, it is simply erroneous to believe that university admissions have ever operated as simple meritocracies, in which slots have been rationed according to grades and test scores alone. The preferences of university officials across types of students are complex and multidimensional, as are the preferences of student applicants across colleges and universities. Many elite schools have long favored a diverse student body in terms of geographic backgrounds and student talents. Preferences for certain groups of students, such as children of alumni, have long been part of the admissions process in some places. Thus, the 'efficiency' of the matching process at universities cannot be simply measured by any gaps in grades or test scores that might be attributable to affirmative action policy.

Given this view, what does the empirical evidence on the efficiency of affirmative action and the performance of affirmative action beneficiaries show? In labor markets, a variety of methods have been used to answer this question, differing on the critical issue of how to measure quality of output or performance. For instance, some studies have used actual data on production, costs or stock values across companies or industries as measures of performance, and tried to relate them statistically to demographics in the workforce or a company's use of affirmative action. But these studies either are too aggregate to find any effect or are flawed along a variety of dimensions.[35]

An alternative to this approach is to look at measures of individual employee credentials or performance, by race and/or sex, and to see whether or not affirmative action generates major gaps in performance between white males and other groups. In an earlier paper (Holzer and Neumark, 1999), we compare a variety of measures of employee credentials and performance, where the former include educational attainment (absolute levels and relative to job requirements), and the latter include wage/promotion outcomes as well as a subjective performance measure on a scale from 0 to 100, across these groups.[36] In particular, we evaluate whether or not observed gaps in credentials and performance between white males and females or minorities are larger among establishments that practice affirmative action in hiring than among those that do not.

The results indicated virtually no evidence of weaker credentials or performance among females in the affirmative action sector, relative to those of males within the same racial groups. When comparing minorities to whites, the picture is somewhat more complicated. We found quite clear evidence of weaker educational credentials among the former group, but relatively little evidence of weaker performance. Our results were quite consistent with a study of performance ratings by race and sex in federal personnel records (Lewis, 1997).

But our results generate the following puzzle: how could it be that affirmative action results in minorities with weaker credentials but not weaker performance, if educational credentials generally are meaningful predictors of performance?[37] In a separate paper (Holzer and Neumark, 2000b), we consider the various mechanisms by which firms engaging in affirmative action might offset productivity shortfalls among those hired from 'protected groups' that would otherwise be expected. We found, among other things, that firms engaging in affirmative action (1) recruit more extensively, (2) screen more intensively, and pay less attention to characteristics such as welfare recipiency or limited work experience that usually stigmatize candidates,

(3) provide more training after hiring, and (4) evaluate worker performance more carefully.

Thus, these firms tend to cast a wider net with regard to job applicants, gather more information that might help uncover candidates whose productivity is not fully predicted by their educational credentials, and then invest more heavily in the productivity of those whom they have hired. This view is consistent with a variety of case studies (Hyer, 1985; Vernon-Gerstenfeld and Burke, 1985; Badgett, 1995) and other work in the literature on employee selection (Silva and Jacobs, 1993; Campbell, 1996), which suggest that affirmative action works best if employers use a broad range of recruitment techniques and predictors of performance when hiring, and when they make a variety of efforts to enhance performance of those hired. In these studies, affirmative action need not just 'lower the bar' on expected performance of employees hired, and generally does not appear to do so (though some exceptions clearly exist).

A variety of other studies have been done within specific sectors of the workforce, where it is easier to define employee performance in a meaningful fashion. Among the sectors that have been so studied are police forces, physicians and university faculties. The results of these studies again show no evidence of weaker performance among women, and generally limited evidence of weaker performance among minorities.[38] In contrast, the evidence of potential social benefits from affirmative action in the medical sector is quite strong, as minority doctors appear more likely to locate in poor neighborhoods and treat minority/low-income patients.[39]

Thus the existing research finds evidence of weaker credentials but only limited evidence of weaker labor market performance among the beneficiaries of affirmative action, and some fairly clear evidence (at least in one important sector) consistent with positive externalities.

Can a similar story be told about university admissions? As noted earlier, there are gaps in high school grades and test scores between white and minority students admitted to universities, and the college grades of minorities lag behind as well. Black students fail to complete their college degrees in significantly larger numbers, especially at institutions with higher average test scores (Datcher Loury and Garman, 1995), although the evidence for law schools indicates the opposite.[40] The former findings appear consistent with the notion that affirmative action may actually hurt minority students by generating a poor 'fit' between them and the colleges or universities that they attend.[41]

On the other hand, there is some evidence that the lower college completion rates among blacks at more selective institutions disappear once one controls for the effects of attending the historically black colleges and universities (Kane, 1998). Earnings are generally higher among blacks (as well as whites) that attend more prestigious and highly-ranked schools, despite their higher rates of failure there. Also, dropout rates of minorities at the most elite institutions are generally lower than elsewhere (Bowen and Bok, 1998), which is inconsistent with the notion that they would be better served if they attended weaker schools.

Along some other dimensions, the benefits of affirmative action in generating greater understanding and positive interactions across racial groups has been documented as well at these schools (Bowen and Bok, 1998), although direct educational benefits of diversity are harder to establish. On the other hand, the evidence of positive 'mentoring' and 'role model' effects of having female/minority faculty members for similar students is decidedly mixed.[42]

Finally, the evidence on the performance of female- or minority-owned businesses that obtain more contracts as a result of affirmative action rules is somewhat inconclusive as well. Amendments to Section 8(a) rules on federal contracting do not allow companies to receive contracts under these provisions for longer than nine years, and apparently those who 'graduate' from the program seem to perform (at least in terms of staying in business) as well as firms more generally (Stephanopoulos and Edley, 1995). On the other hand, there is some evidence of higher failure rates among firms that currently receive a high percentage of their revenues from sales to local government (Bates and Williams, 1995). The higher failure rates may be attributable to the fact that a significant fraction of the latter are 'front' companies that have formed or reorganized in an attempt to gain Section 8(*a*) contracts. There was also evidence that failure rates can be limited with the right kinds of certification and technical assistance, especially if the reliance of the companies on governmental revenues is limited as well.

In any event, this evidence suggests that failing companies are not being 'propped up' by government contracts, as is commonly alleged. But stronger data and analysis are needed in this area before conclusions can be made with a greater degree of confidence on the issue of the efficiency of minority contracting programs.

V Conclusions

This paper presents an overview of EEO laws designed to outlaw employment discrimination, as well as affirmative action efforts actively to raise the status of minorities and women in employment, university admissions and government procurement. We review the laws, court decisions and practices, as well as the empirical evidence on their effects.

The evidence is generally most consistent with the conclusion that EEO laws have contributed to the improvement in relative economic status of blacks that occurred during the mid-1960s. These effects were particularly strong in the South, where discrimination against blacks historically was greatest. On the other hand, although equal pay laws should raise women's wages, consistent with economic theory they also tend to reduce their relative employment.

Nonetheless, it is also clear to us that discrimination persists in some parts of the labor market, and contributes to (but does not fully account for) persisting wage/employment gaps between white males and other groups. The inability of EEO laws to eliminate labor market discrimination completely may lie in the difficulty of monitoring employment activities in certain kinds of establishments (that is, those that are small or have few minority applicants and workers), or in imbalances in how and where EEO lawsuits are pursued (with much less emphasis placed on discrimination in hiring than promotion or discharges) or in the nature of discrimination itself (since statistical discrimination may require greater dissemination of information rather than just regulation and litigation).

Accordingly, some of these gaps might be remedied with more resources for EEO employment monitoring, a different allocation of resources between hiring and other cases, or a different set of enforcement practices, such as a greater reliance on applicant 'audits' in hiring. The use of labor market intermediaries to provide more information to employers in hiring disadvantaged groups might help as well. But, to the extent that persistent wage and employment gaps reflect a wide range of other problems (such as skill gaps, family time allocation issues and the like), a much wider range of efforts is required if the goal is to generate greater parity in labor market outcomes across demographic groups.

Turning to affirmative action, the evidence clearly shows that these programs tend to redistribute employment, university admissions and government procurement away from white males and towards minorities and females, as expected. On the other hand, the magnitudes of these shifts in employment and in most universities are not large, though there are some exceptions (such as admissions to elite colleges and universities as well as some graduate programs). Thus the replacement of race- and sex-based affirmative action policies in admissions with a different set of practices, such as those based on income or class rank within schools, would likely reduce the presence of minorities on campuses, in some cases quite substantially.

On the more controversial issue of whether the beneficiaries of affirmative action are less qualified than white males, our review of the evidence paints a more complex picture. There is virtually no evidence that the qualifications or performance of females lag behind those of males within any racial group. In contrast, the credentials of minorities often lag behind those of their white counterparts, in part because they lag behind in the population, and in part because of the preferential admission and hiring policies generated by affirmative action. But evidence of weaker performance in the labor market on the part of minorities who benefit from affirmative action is much more limited.

Apparently, companies can offset any expected performance shortfalls of those whom they hire through a variety of practices that include improved recruitment and screening, greater training efforts and better evaluation activity on the job.

While the classroom performance of minorities in colleges and universities lags behind that of whites, and their noncompletion rates are substantially higher, minority students still seem to benefit overall from their higher rates of admission to better schools. The evidence of positive effects from mentoring and role models in universities is mixed. But there is also evidence of social benefits from affirmative action in certain sectors, such as medical care, in which minority physicians are more likely to provide care to minorities and the poor than are white physicians.

Finally, there was some evidence of weaker performance of minority-led companies that receive government procurement contracts, but also evidence that these difficulties can be avoided with the proper credentialing and technical assistance. Overall, the evidence on this aspect of affirmative action policy was thinnest.

While EEO laws and activity are widely accepted in the US, affirmative action programs (particularly in college and university admissions) remain under challenge. The University of Michigan affirmative action cases appear to have protected certain types of admissions programs for a while, but popular referenda at the state level will likely continue for years to come, and other court challenges may well arise. In the end, whether or in what form affirmative action survives will depend on whether Americans think it is *fair* to give preference to minorities or women in some contexts, to overcome the barriers they continue to face from current discrimination, past discrimination and a variety of other causes. Views on fairness are very subjective, and sometimes impervious to empirical evidence. Political forces and the relative political power of different groups will no doubt play a large role in how these controversies are resolved as well.

Nevertheless, we believe that the empirical evidence on the effects of EEO policies and affirmative action should inform this debate and should be considered in the formulation of any alternative approaches to problems or minorities and women. At the same time, we emphasize that our evidence to date is quite limited, particularly on the relative performance of affirmative action beneficiaries, and most notably in the debate on government procurement activities. Thus research on the effects of EEO and especially affirmative action should continue to be high on the agendas of social scientists.

Notes
1. Pay discrimination within jobs was addressed by the Equal Pay Act of 1963, which requires equal pay for equal work, while noting some exceptions.

2. See Holzer and Neumark (2000a) for a summary of recent policy initiatives and legal cases concerning affirmative action.
3. For detailed discussions of these legislative and executive policies, see Epstein (1992) and Bloch (1994). There were some earlier Executive Orders issued by President Roosevelt in 1941 prohibiting racial discrimination in the defense industry and in training for defense production.
4. See *Code of Federal Regulations*, Title 29, Volume 4, Part 1604 (2001).
5. Specifically, the decision allowed admissions officers to 'take race into account' as a means to secure the educational benefits of a student body with diverse backgrounds and experience (William Bowen and Derek Bok, 1998, p. 8).
6. In addition to admissions procedures, financial assistance programs may give preferential treatment to particular minority groups, and other programs also seek to increase representation of women or minorities through incentives for higher education (see Holzer and Neumark, 2000a, for more discussion).
7. See also Gurin *et al.* (2004).
8. Bid price preferences allow contracting officers to add a specified amount to non-SDB bids (typically 10 per cent at the federal level) and then to award the contract based on the adjusted bids. Another mechanism is rule-of-two set-asides, which allow contracting officers to 'limit bidding on a particular contract to . . . SDB's if two or more such firms are potential bidders and the officer determines the prevailing bid will likely be within 10 per cent of the fair market price' (Stephanopoulos and Edley, 1995, section 9).
9. This occurred, for example, in *Firefighters Local Union No. 1784* v. *Stotts*.
10. See *Code of Federal Regulations*, Title 28, Volume 2, Section 50.14 (2001).
11. For example, Steele (1990) writes, 'I would . . . like to see Affirmative Action go back to its original purpose of enforcing equal opportunity – a purpose that in itself disallows racial preferences' (p. 123). See also Stephen Carter (1991).
12. Much of the material in this subsection is taken from Neumark and Stock (forthcoming).
13. While this quote refers to affirmative action, it is clear from the context of their article that Smith and Welch are referring to prospective EEO effects as well. While their views have evolved on the topic, they generally conclude that anti-discrimination policies may have had significant short-run effects that were dissipated over the longer run by a leveling off of affirmative action pressures on the demand side of the labor market and a strong positive supply response to the higher relative earnings of young black college graduates. See, in particular, Smith (2000).
14. For a more recent look at the evolution of relative earnings by race (focused to some extent on issues other than anti-discrimination policies), see Bound and Freeman (1992). Their paper also points to a jump in economic outcomes for blacks after 1965, and helps establish that the apparent stagnation or decline in black relative progress beginning in the mid-1970s is attributable to a decrease in the price of less-skilled relative to more-skilled labor, as blacks were overrepresented among the less skilled.
15. These concerns are echoed by Chay (1998), who points out that 'the timing of the legislation (in the mid-1960s) corresponds with the timing of many other significant changes in the US labor market. In addition, the nature of these laws, and in particular their nearly universal coverage, makes it difficult to control for changes that would have occurred even in the absence of the legislation' (pp. 608–9). Similarly, Hahn *et al.* (1999) note that the lack of consensus over the impact of Title VII and related laws 'probably stems in part from the difficulty of assessing the impact of laws that have near universal coverage' (p. 14).
16. Heckman and Payner (1989) take this type of analysis to an even finer level, looking at changes in relative black employment and wages in one Southern state (South Carolina), and noting that the sharpest improvements came in the textile industry, which was the target of the EEOC. Their study also does a thorough job of exploiting data across counties in South Carolina to demonstrate that it is difficult to explain relative improvements for blacks in textiles without relying on a role for government anti-discrimination efforts.
17. Carrington *et al.* (2000) instead look at the overall effect of federal anti-discrimination efforts by asking whether black and female representation at large firms increased during the period in which these efforts were introduced. Much of the time-series evidence appears

consistent with this. However, while acknowledging the existence of state fair employment practices that would have made the impact of federal efforts (by race) vary across states, they conduct no analysis of potential treatment and control states other than a South/non-South breakdown (as these practices were not implemented in Southern states).

18. Chay's employment estimates indicate that black employment shares grew by 0.5 to 1.1 percentage points more per year at newly-covered than previously-covered employers. These effects are larger by a factor of about 10 than those found in the affirmative action literature (Leonard, 1990; Donohue and Heckman, 1991). They are not large relative to evidence regarding the federal role in increasing access of blacks to manufacturing employment in South Carolina (Heckman and Payner, 1989), although this latter evidence pertains to an isolated industry in one state that was particularly strongly targeted by the EEOC. Chay's earnings estimates indicate that the black–white earnings gap narrowed by 0.11 to 0.18 log points more at newly-covered than previously-covered employers. These estimates are roughly in line with those obtained in a time-series analysis of the effect of the Civil Rights Act (with the possible flaws discussed earlier) by Freeman (1973, p. 101).

19. Collins (2003a) carries out a similar analysis, and Collins (2003b) studies the determination of the timing of adoption of state laws prohibiting race discrimination, focusing on factors related to demographics, politics and labor organization.

20. See the discussion of this issue in our earlier paper (Holzer and Neumark, 2000a).

21. Of course, establishments with fewer than 15 workers are not even covered by federal EEO law, which could imply that smaller employers are not more discriminatory per se, but rather that discrimination persists among these employers because the law does not prohibit it.

22. See Leonard (1984) for evidence that the Office of Federal Contract Compliance Programs targets larger contractors and those with relatively more minorities for compliance reviews.

23. Some of the strongest evidence of discrimination comes from 'audit' (or 'tester') studies of hiring (for example, Fix and Struyk, 1994; Neumark, 1996), in which matched pairs of applicants for jobs (or housing) differ by race or sex but otherwise have identical credentials in terms of education, experience and the like. However, the interpretation of these results continues to be debated (for example, Heckman, 1998 versus Darity and Mason, 1998). Other evidence of discrimination can be found in various studies of employer hiring behavior (Holzer, 1996; Moss and Tilly, 2001). Ethnographic evidence (for example, Kirschenman and Neckerman, 1991) also suggests discrimination primarily in hiring.

24. Though we have no direct empirical evidence to bear out this claim, it is consistent with some of the ethnographic evidence cited above (Kirschenman and Neckerman, 1991; Moss and Tilly, 2001) and with anecdotes from employers (Moss and Tilly, 2001, pp. 238–9).

25. The EEOC has issued a policy statement in which it upholds the use of evidence from tester studies to enforce EEO statutes. The Supreme Court has also upheld the use of tester evidence in a case involving housing discrimination (*Havens* v. *Coleman*). See Boggs *et al.* (1994) for more discussion of this issue.

26. On the other hand, the findings of Altonji and Pierret (2001) raise questions about the extent to which statistical discrimination accounts for wage differences between whites and blacks. Neumark (1999) provides an empirical analysis of the reliability of labor market information about various groups, and finds that employers have worse information about female new hires than male new hires, although not about minority relative to non-minority new hires.

27. The role of 'temp' agencies in providing information to employers is stressed in Autor (2001). Nonprofit agencies that seek to play similar roles include 'America Works' and many others, which are often service providers for local workforce boards. The potential role of these intermediaries in reducing employer discrimination and racial conflict has been emphasized in the Annie E. Casey Foundation's 'Jobs Initiatives' in several US cities.

28. The issues of skill gaps, spatial/informational problems and other factors in the persistence of black/white employment gaps are reviewed in Holzer (2000). For evidence on the growing importance of childbearing as a factor in perpetuating sex gaps among younger workers, see Waldfogel (1998).

29. The employment share of white males was 30 per cent in establishments not using affirmative action in hiring and 24 per cent in those that did use affirmative action. This categorization is based on self-reported activities of those responsible for hiring in these

establishments, and was based on a sample of establishments in four large metropolitan areas in the period 1992–4. The net effect of affirmative action in hiring was reduced somewhat in regression equations that control for a variety of establishment characteristics.

30. Using data from the High School and Beyond Survey, Kane found significant racial differences in admissions (conditional on test scores and many other personal characteristics) only in the top quintile of colleges and universities by test scores. Long, using data from the National Educational Longitudinal Study (NELS), found significant effects on admissions in all quintiles. But the magnitudes of these differences were not large in absolute terms: the probability that minorities are accepted at their top choice would decline by less than two percentage points (14.7 per cent v. 16.4 per cent) in the aggregate and about 2.5 percentage points in the top quintile in the absence of affirmative action.

31. In their study of 30 very elite institutions, Bok and Bowen estimate that acceptance probabilities for black applicants would fall from 42 per cent to 13 per cent in the absence of affirmative action. The declines in admission rates for blacks at Berkeley right after the implementation of Proposition 209 in 1997 were of similar magnitudes: from 48.5 per cent to 15.6 per cent (Bowen and Bok, 1998).

32. See Attiyeh and Attiyeh (1997) for a study of PhD programs, Dugan *et al.* (1996) for graduate business programs, and Davidson and Lewis (1997) for medical schools.

33. On the other hand, Card and Krueger (2004) argue that minority applicants with high SAT scores have continued to apply to elite schools in California and Texas at the same rate as before these changes in admissions policies were implemented.

34. See, for instance, Stephanopoulos and Edley (1995), Bates and Williams (1995), Bates (1993), and Chay and Fairlie (1998).

35. See the review of this work in our earlier paper (Holzer and Neumark, 2000a). The studies reviewed include papers by Leonard (1984), Griffin (1992) and Wright *et al.* (1995).

36. Since the wage and promotion measures might themselves be functions of affirmative action, we also included a private supervisory evaluation of performance that should not have been affected by company policy. Specifically, the subjective measure was also gauged for typical workers in the same job, and measures of performance were analyzed both absolutely and relative to this other measure. The latter approach enables us to 'difference' away fixed effects of the supervisor in evaluating workers.

37. Even if we do not believe that education directly augments productivity, virtually no economists dispute that education should be correlated with some measure of personal skill and productivity. The rise in the economic returns to skill over the past two decades implies, if anything, that the correlation between education and workplace productivity has risen over time. On the other hand, the importance of a variety of non-cognitive skills or attributes (Bowles *et al.*, 2001) should not be understated.

38. See Lovrich and Steel (1983) or Carter and Sapp (1991) for credible evidence on police departments, and Elmore and Blackburn (1983), Barbezat (1989) and Kolpin and Singell (1996) on academic publication records. One study of police departments (Lott, 2000) claimed to show evidence of higher homicide rates because of affirmative action in police hiring, but we found the study to be seriously flawed (see our review paper, 2000a). One of the three studies of academics found evidence of weaker publication records among minority faculty members, especially controlling for salaries. The medical studies showed that minority physicians had greater difficulty passing board exams and were less likely to specialize, but showed little evidence of weaker actual performance within their chosen fields and after certification.

39. The medical evidence is presented in Penn *et al.* (1986), Keith *et al.* (1987), Cantor *et al.* (1996) and Davidson and Lewis (1997).

40. Sander (2004) argues that affirmative action in law schools leads to higher drop-out rates and higher failure rates on bar exams among black law school graduates. But this does not necessarily follow from his evidence. For example, the drop-out rate is lower the higher quality the law school, and the race difference in drop-out rates is smaller at the better law schools.

41. This theme is emphasized, among others, in Thernstrom and Thernstrom (1997). Others, such as Carter (1991) and Steele (1990), emphasize that affirmative action reduces the expectations or standards for performance to which minorities are held, though this claim is

very hard to test empirically. Recent work by Besharov and Brown (2001) stresses the important role of financial factors in generating higher college drop-out rates among blacks.
42. See Dynan and Rouse (1997), Canes and Rosen (1995), Rothstein (1995) and Neumark and Gardecki (1998).

References

Altonji, Joseph and Charles Pierret (2001), 'Employer learning and statistical discrimination', *Quarterly Journal of Economics*, **116**(1), 313–50.

Athey, Susan, Chris Avery and Peter Zemsky (2000), 'Mentoring and diversity', *American Economic Review*, **90**(4), September, 765–86.

Attiyeh, Gregory and Richard Attiyeh (1997), 'Testing for bias in graduate school admissions', *Journal of Human Resources*, **32**(3), 524–48.

Autor, David (2001), 'Why do temporary help firms provide free general skills training?', *Quarterly Journal of Economics*, **116**(4), 1409–48.

Autor, David and David Scarborough (2004), 'Will job testing hurt minority workers?', NBER working paper no. 10763

Badgett, Lee (1995), 'Affirmative action in a changing legal and economic environment', *Industrial Relations*, **34**(4), 489–506.

Barbezat, Debra (1989), 'Affirmative action in higher education', *Research in Labor Economics*, **10**, 107–56.

Bates, Timothy (1993), *Banking on Black Enterprise*, Washington, DC: Joint Center for Political and Economic Studies.

Bates, Timothy and Darrell Williams (1995), 'Preferential procurement programs and minority-owned businesses', *Journal of Urban Affairs*, **17**(1), 1–17.

Becker, Gary S. (1971), *The Economics of Discrimination*, 2nd edn, Chicago: University of Chicago Press.

Beller, Andrea H. (1979), 'The impact of equal employment opportunity laws on the male–female earnings differential', in Cynthia Lloyd, Emily Andrews and Curtis Gilroy (eds), *Women in the Labor Market*, New York: Columbia University Press, pp. 203–30.

Besharov, Douglas and Christopher Brown (2001), 'An exploration of the African-American middle class', discussion draft, presented at the Joint Center for Political and Economic Studies, Washington, DC, 18 July.

Bloch, Farrell (1994), *Antidiscrimination Law and Minority Employment*, Chicago: University of Chicago Press.

Boggs, Roderick, Joseph Sellers and Marc Bendick (1994), 'The use of testing in civil rights enforcement', in Michael Fix and Raymond Struyk (eds), *Clear and Convincing Evidence*, Washington, DC: Urban Institute Press, pp. 345–75.

Bound, John and Richard B. Freeman (1992), 'What went wrong? The erosion of relative earnings and employment among young black men in the 1980s', *The Quarterly Journal of Economics*, **107**(1) (February), 201–32.

Bowen, William G. and Derek Bok (1998), *The Shape of the River*, Princeton, NJ: Princeton University Press.

Bowles, Samuel, Herbert Gintis and Melissa Osborne (2001), 'The determinants of earnings: a behavioral approach', *Journal of Economic Literature*, **39**(4), 1137–76.

Brown, Charles (1982), 'The federal attack on labor market discrimination: the mouse that roared?', *Research in Labor Economics*, **5**, 33–68.

Brown, Charles (1984), 'Black–white earnings ratios since the Civil Rights Act of 1964: the importance of labor market dropouts', *Quarterly Journal of Economics*, **99**(1), 31–44.

Butler, Richard and James J. Heckman (1977), 'The government's impact on the labor market status of black Americans: a critical review', in Leonard J. Hausman (ed.), *Equal Rights and Industrial Relations*, Madison, WI: Industrial Relations Research Association, 235–81.

Cain, Glen C. (1986), 'The economic analysis of labor market discrimination: a survey', in Orley Ashenfelter and Richard Layard (eds), *Handbook of Labor Economics, Vol. 1*, Amsterdam: North-Holland, pp. 693–785.

284 Handbook on the economics of discrimination

Campbell, John (1996), 'Group differences and personnel decisions: validity, fairness and affirmative action', *Journal of Vocational Behavior*, **49**(2), 122–58.
Canes, Brandice and Harvey Rosen (1995), 'Following in her footsteps? Faculty gender composition and women's choices of college majors', *Industrial and Labor Relations Review*, **48**(3), 486–504.
Cantor, Joel, Erika Miles, Laurence Baker and Dianne Baker (1996), 'Physician service to the underserved: implications of affirmative action in medical education', *Inquiry*, **33**(2), 167–80.
Card, David and Alan Krueger (2004), 'Would the elimination of affirmative action affect highly qualified minority applicants?' NBER working paper no. 10366.
Carnevale, Anthony and Stephen Rose (2003), *Socioeconomic Status, Race/Ethnicity and Selective College Admissions*, Washington DC: The Century Foundation.
Carrington, William J., Kristen McCue and Brooks Pierce (2000), 'Using establishment size to measure the impact of Title VII and affirmative action', *Journal of Human Resources*, **35**(3), 503–23.
Carter, David and Allan Sapp (1991), 'Police education and minority recruitment: the impact of a college requirement', discussion paper, Police Executives Research Forum.
Carter, Stephen (1991), *Reflections of an Affirmative Action Baby*, New York: Basic Books.
Chay, Kenneth Y. (1998), 'The impact of federal civil rights policy on black economic progress: evidence from the Equal Employment Opportunity Act of 1972', *Industrial and Labor Relations Review*, **51**(4), 608–32.
Chay, Kenneth and Robert Fairlie (1998), 'Minority business set-asides and black self-employment', unpublished paper, University of California at Berkeley.
Coate, Stephen and Glenn Loury (1993), 'Will affirmative action policies eliminate negative stereotypes?', *American Economic Review*, **83**(5), 1220–40.
Collins, William J. (2003a), 'The labor market impact of state-level anti-discrimination laws, 1940–1960', *Industrial and Labor Relations Review*, **56**(2), 244–72.
Collins, William J. (2003b), 'The political economy of state-level fair employment laws, 1940–1964', *Explorations in Economic History*, **40**(1), 24–51.
Culp, Jerome McCristal (1986), 'Federal courts and the enforcement of Title VII', *American Economic Review*, **76**(2), 355–8.
Darity, William A, Jr and Patrick L. Mason (1998), 'Evidence on discrimination in employment: codes of color, codes of gender,' *Journal of Economic Perspectives*, **12**(2) (Spring), 63–90.
Datcher Loury, Linda and Kenneth Garman (1995), 'College selectivity and earnings', *Journal of Labor Economics*, **13**(2), 289–308.
Davidson, Robert and Ernest Lewis (1997), 'Affirmative action and other special considerations admissions at the University of California, Davis School of Medicine', *Journal of the American Medical Association*, **278**(14), 1153–8.
Dickens, William and Thomas Kane (1999), 'Racial test score differences as evidence of reverse discrimination: less than meets the eye', *Industrial Relations*, **28**(3), 331–63.
Donohue, John and James Heckman (1991), 'Continuous versus episodic change: the impact of civil rights policy on the economic status of blacks', *Journal of Economic Literature*, **29**(4), 1603–43.
Donohue, John and Peter Siegelman (1991), 'The changing nature of employment discrimination litigation', *Stanford Law Review*, **43**, 983–1033.
Dugan, Mary Kay, Nazli Baydar, William Grady and Terry Johnson (1996), 'Affirmative action: does it exist in graduate business schools?', *Selections*, **12**(2), 11–18.
Dynan, Karen and Cecilia Rouse (1997), 'The underrepresentation of women in economics: a study of undergraduate economics students', *Journal of Economic Education*, **28**(45), 350–68.
Eberts, Randall W. and Joe A. Stone (1985), 'Male–female differences in promotions: EEO in public education', *Journal of Human Resources*, **20**(4), 504–21.
Edley, Christopher (1996), *Not All Black and White*, New York: Hill and Wang.
Ehrenberg, Ronald and Robert Smith (2000), *Modern Labor Economics: Theory and Public Policy*. New York: Addison Wesley Longman.
Elmore, Charles and Robert Blackburn (1983), 'Black and white faculty in white research universities', *Journal of Higher Education*, **54**(1), 1–15.
Epstein, Richard (1992), *Forbidden Grounds: The Case Against Employment Discrimination Laws*, Cambridge, MA: Harvard University Press.

Fix, Michael and Raymond Struyk (1994), *Clear and Convincing Evidence*, Washington, DC: The Urban Institute.

Fosu, Augustin Kwasi (1992), 'Occupational mobility of black women, 1958–1981: the impact of post-1964 anti-discrimination measures', *Industrial and Labor Relations Review*, **45**(2), 281–94.

Freeman, Richard B. (1973), 'Changes in the labor market for black Americans, 1948–72', *Brookings Papers on Economic Activity*, **1**, 67–120.

Freeman, Richard B. (1981), 'Black economic progress after 1964: who has gained and why?', in Sherwin Rosen, (ed.), *Studies in Labor Markets*, Chicago: University of Chicago Press, pp. 247–94.

Griffin, Peter (1992), 'The impact of affirmative action on labor demand: a test of some implications of the LeChatelier principle', *Review of Economics and Statistics*, **74**(2), 251–60.

Gurin, Patricia, Jeffrey Lehman and Earl Lewis (2004), *Defending Diversity: Affirmative Action at the University of Michigan*, Ann Arbor, MI: University of Michigan Press.

Hahn, Jinyong, Petra Todd and Wilbert Van der Klaauw (1999), 'Evaluating the effect of an anti-discrimination law using a regression-discontinuity design', NBER working paper no. 7131.

Heckman, James J. (1990), 'The central role of the South in accounting for the economic progress of black Americans', *American Economic Review*, **80**(2), 242–6.

Heckman, James J. (1998), 'Detecting discrimination', *Journal of Economic Perspectives*, **12**(2), 101–16.

Heckman, James J. and Brook S. Payner (1989), 'Determining the impact of federal anti-discrimination policy on the economic status of blacks', *American Economic Review*, **79**(1), 138–77.

Holzer, Harry (1996), *What Employers Want: Job Prospects for Less-Educated Workers*, New York: Russell Sage Foundation.

Holzer, Harry (1998), 'Why do small establishments hire fewer blacks than larger ones?', *Journal of Human Resources*, **33**(4), 896–914.

Holzer, Harry (2000), 'Racial differences in labor market outcomes among men', in Neil J. Smelser, William J. Wilson and Faith Mitchell (eds), *America Becoming: Racial Trends and their Consequences, Vol. II*, Washington, DC: National Research Council, pp. 98–123.

Holzer, Harry and Keith Ihlanfeldt (1998), 'Customer discrimination and employment outcomes of minority workers', *Quarterly Journal of Economics*, **113**(3), 835–68.

Holzer, Harry and David Neumark (1999) 'Are affirmative action hires less qualified?', *Journal of Labor Economics*, **17**(3), 534–69.

Holzer, Harry and David Neumark (2000a), 'Assessing affirmative action', *Journal of Economic Literature*, **38**(3), 483–568.

Holzer, Harry and David Neumark (2000b), 'What does affirmative action do?', *Industrial and Labor Relations Review*, **53**(2), 240–71.

Holzer, Harry and Jess Reaser (2000), 'Black applicants, black employees, and urban labor market policy', *Journal of Urban Economics*, **48**(4), 365–87.

Holzer, Harry, Steven Raphael and Michael Stoll (2002), 'Perceived criminality, criminal background checks and the racial hiring practices of employers', discussion paper, Institute for Research on Poverty, University of Wisconsin at Madison.

Holzer, Harry, Steven Raphael and Michael Stoll (2003), 'Employer demand for ex-offenders: recent evidence from Los Angeles', discussion paper, Institute for Research on Poverty, University of Wisconsin at Madison.

Hyer, Patricia (1985), 'Affirmative action for women faculty: case studies of three successful institutions', *Journal of Higher Education*, **56**(3), 282–99.

Juhn, Chinhui (1992), 'Decline of male labor force participation: the role of declining market opportunities', *Quarterly Journal of Economics*, **107**(1), 79–122.

Kane, Thomas (1998), 'Racial preferences and higher education', in Christopher Jencks and Meredith Phillips (eds), *The Black–White Test Score Gap*, Washington, DC: The Brookings Institution, pp. 431–56.

Keith, Steven, Robert Bell and Albert Williams (1987), *Assessing the Outcome of Affirmative Action in Medical Schools*, Los Angeles, CA: Rand.

Kirschenman, Joleen and Kathryn Neckerman (1991), 'We'd love to hire them but . . .', in Christopher Jencks and Paul Peterson (eds), *The Urban Underclass*, Washington, DC: The Brookings Institution, pp. 203–34.

Kolpin, Van and Larry Singell (1996), 'The gender composition and scholarly performance of economics departments: a test for employment discrimination', *Industrial and Labor Relations Review*, **49**(3), 408–23.

Landes, William M. (1968), 'The economics of fair employment laws', *Journal of Political Economy*, **76**(4), 507–52.

Leonard, Jonathan (1984), 'Anti-discrimination or reverse discrimination? The impact of changing demographics, Title VII and affirmative action on productivity', *Journal of Human Resources*, **19**(2), 145–74.

Leonard, Jonathan (1990), 'The impact of affirmative action regulation and equal opportunity law on employment', *Journal of Economic Perspectives*, **4**(4), 47–63.

Lewis, Gregory (1997), 'Race, sex and performance ratings in the federal service', *Public Administration Review*, **57**(6), 479–89.

Long, Mark (2004), 'Race and college admissions: an alternative to affirmative action?' *The Review of Economics and Statistics*, **86**(4), 1020–33.

Lott, John (2000), 'Does a helping hand put others at risk? Affirmative action, police departments, and crime', *Economic Inquiry*, **38**(2), 239–77.

Loury, Glenn (1977), 'A dynamic theory of racial income differences', in Phyllis A. Wallace and Annette A. LaMond (eds), *Women, Minorities, and Employment Discrimination*, Lexington, MA: DC Heath, pp. 153–88.

Lovrich, Nicholas and Brent Steel (1983), 'Affirmative action and productivity in law enforcement agencies', *Review of Public Personnel Administration*, **4**(1), 55–66.

Lundberg, Shelley and Richard Startz (1983), 'Private discrimination and social intervention in competitive labor markets', *American Economic Review*, **73**(3), 340–47.

Moss, Philip and Chris Tilly (2001), *Stories Employers Tell*, New York: Russell Sage Foundation.

Neal, Derek and William Johnson (1998), 'Basic skills and the black–white earnings gap', in Christopher Jencks and Meredith Phillips (eds), *The Black–White Test Score Gap*, Washington, DC: The Brookings Institution, pp. 480–97.

Neumark, David (1996), 'Sex discrimination in restaurant hiring: an audit study', *Quarterly Journal of Economics*, **111**(446), pp. 915–42.

Neumark, David (1999), 'Wage differentials by race and sex: the roles of taste discrimination and labor market information', *Industrial Relations*, **38**(3), pp. 414–45.

Neumark, David and Rosella Gardecki (1998), 'Women helping women? Role model and mentoring effects on female PhD students in economics', *Journal of Human Resources*, **33**(1), 220–46.

Neumark, David and Wendy A. Stock (forthcoming), 'The labor market effects of sex and race discrimination laws', *Economic Enquiry*.

Penn, Nolan, Percy Russell, Harold Simon, Teresa Jacob, Claire Stafford, Eddie Castro, Jeannette Cisneros and Mary Bush (1986), 'Affirmative action at work: a survey of graduates of the University of California, San Diego Medical School', *American Journal of Public Health*, **76**(9), 1144–6.

Rothstein, Donna (1995), 'Do female faculty influence female students' education and labor market attainments?', *Industrial and Labor Relations Review*, **48**(3), 515–30.

Sander, Richard (2004), 'A systematic analysis of affirmative action in American law schools', *Stanford Law Review*, **57**(4), 368–483.

Silva, Jay and Rick Jacobs (1993), 'Performance as a function of increased minority hiring', *Journal of Applied Psychology*, **78**(4), 591–601.

Smith, James P. (2000), 'Race and ethnicity in the labor market: trends over the short and long run', in Neil J. Smelser, William J. Wilson and Faith Mitchell (eds), *America Becoming: Racial Trends and their Consequences, Vol. II*, Washington DC: National Academy Press, pp. 52–97.

Smith, James P. and Finis Welch (1977), 'Black–white wage ratios: 1960–70', *American Economic Review*, **67**(3), 232–8.

Smith, James P. and Finis Welch (1984), 'Affirmative action and labor markets', *Journal of Labor Economics*, **2**(2), 269–301.

Smith, James P. and Finis Welch (1989), 'Black economic progress after Myrdal', *Journal of Economic Literature*, **27**(2), 519–64.

Steele, Shelby (1990), *The Content of Our Character*, New York: St. Martin's Press.

Stephanopoulos, George and Christopher Edley (1995), 'Review of federal affirmative action programs', unpublished White House document.

Thernstrom, Stephen and Abigail Thernstrom (1997), *America in Black and White: One Nation, Indivisible*. New York: Simon and Schuster.

Vernon-Gerstenfeld, Susan and Edmund Burke (1985), 'Affirmative action in nine large companies: a field study', *Personnel*, **62**(4), 54–60.

Vroman, Wayne (1974), 'Changes in black workers' relative earnings: evidence from the 1960s', in George Von Furstenberg (ed.), *Patterns of Racial Discrimination, Vol. II*, Lexington, MA: DC Heath, pp. 167–96.

Waldfogel, Jane (1998), 'Understanding the "family gap" in pay for women with children', *Journal of Economic Perspectives*, **12**(1), 137–56.

Welch, Finis (1976), 'Employment quotas for minorities', *Journal of Political Economy*, **4**(4), pt. 2, S105–39.

Wright, Peter, Stephen Ferris, Janine Hiller and Mark Kroll (1995), 'Competitiveness through management of diversity: effects on stock market valuation', *Academy of Management Journal*, **38**(1), 272–87.

Concluding thoughts
William M. Rodgers III

The chapters in this *Handbook* provide a wealth of new tools, information and insights. The following is a summary of the key lessons that I have learned from my colleagues. I am certain that, as I use the chapters with my students, many more lessons and insights will emerge.

All of the researchers agree that discrimination continues to be a significant feature of American markets, yet our ability to measure its magnitude continues to challenge us. Although obvious, the following still needs to be stated. No single theory, method, data source or study should be relied upon to assess the magnitude, causes and remedies for discrimination. Each theory, method, data source and study has its advantages and limitations.

New econometric methods have helped to provide richer descriptions of inequality. Experimental methods offer the ability to control for supply and demand factors that researchers have difficulty accounting for in traditional regression and decomposition methods. Experimental methods provide useful information on how preferences to discriminate and statistical discrimination can emerge. Matched employer–employee data sets provide an excellent response to the omitted variable and weighting problems inherent with regression-based tools. We learn a great deal about employer attitudes from well-structured qualitative employer suveys.

The Baldwin and Johnson, Adams and Neumark and Badgett chapters remind us that discrimination is not limited to African Americans, Hispanics and women. There are many other groups in American society that experience adverse treatment in a variety of markets. Although discrimination in hiring, compensation and dismissal among people with disabilities, older workers and gay, lesbians and bisexuals is not a new phenomenon, economists are beginning to pay greater attention to these demographic groups. A key task for researchers, practitioners, policymakers and funders of social science research will be to improve data availability and quality.

What does the future hold for the economics of discrimination? As my colleagues have demonstrated, we know a great deal about discrimination, but there remain many unanswered questions. Discrimination has and will continue to be a dynamic process. Demographic shifts in the composition of the US population, globalization, technological change, changes in the structure of US social policy, and even unexpected geopolitical events, such as

9–11 can change attitudes and perceptions about particular demographic groups (for example, attitudes toward Arabs and immigrants). To keep up with and anticipate change, economists must continually rethink existing theories, develop new econometric methods and create new data sets. The profession must also demonstrate greater diversity in its empirical studies and aggressively, but objectively, continue with efforts to identify the effects of policies that seek to remedy discrimination.

Index

observed traits 97
occupational decomposition 22–5
occupational dimension, wage gap
    decomposition 12
occupational qualification, age as 191
occupational segregation 48–9
occupations by sexual orientation 173
offer wage 122–3, 127–8, 141, 145
Office of the Comptroller of the
    Currency 230–31
Ohio State University 100
older workers
    attitudes towards 188–91
    disadvantageous position of 195–200
    employment rates 194–5
    perceptions of 187, 189–90
Ordinary Least Squares (OLS)
    regressions 16
organization
    characteristics 66–7
    policy versus workplace reality
        70–71
    variables 62, 64
overt discrimination 217–18, 223, 236,
    239

Panel Study of Income Dynamics (PSID)
    135, 238
part-time work, same-sex couples
    174–5, 179
payday loans 233–4
pensions 198
perfect competition, wages/productivity
    under 37–44
performance
    incentives 205–6
    measurement of 275–6
    race and gender differences 80–84
perpetrator pays principle 220
personal discrimination 222, 223, 230,
    240
Philadelphia 67–8, 236, 241
Philadelphia Plan 261
Phoenix 238
physical distance 133
physical impairments 125, 129, 134,
    138, 140, 149
physicians 276
piece-rate work 35
police forces 276

policies, disabled employment 152–3
policy context, sexual orientation-based
    discrimination 161–3
political barriers, disability
    discrimination 119–20, 150–51
pooled wage regressions 132, 148
populations, relative size of 105–6
pre-application stage, bank loans 231
pre-labor market discrimination, controls
    for 130
pre-screeners 77
pre-selection bias problem, housing
    markets 226
predatory lending 232–3
    academic studies of 235–6
    emergence of 233–5
prejudice ranking, disability 133–4, 138,
    148
    see also customer prejudice;
        employer prejudice
price-preference auctions 109–10
PriceWaterhouse 180
prior experience, observation of 106
privately undertaken surveys 63
product market field experiments 111
production function-based tests, wage
    discrimination 37–50
productivity 106–7
    age effects 200–201
    disabled workers 124–5, 128–30
    health-related losses 145–6
productivity data 34–7
productivity differentials 20–30, 32, 33
productivity measures 33–4
productivity-adjusted wage/employment
    differentials 136, 141
productivity-related wage differentials
    130
promotion
    age effects on 190, 197, 203–4,
        205–6
    discrimination claims 194
    gender effects on 64–5
    racial effects on 65–6, 86
Proposition 209, California 264, 273
protected workers, employment rates
    194–5
psychology experiments 3–4, 97–101
public service agencies, recruitment
    procedures 71–2